THROUGH A LAND OF EXTREMES

THE LITTLEDALES OF CENTRAL ASIA

ELIZABETH & NICHOLAS CLINCH
Foreword by Sir Chris Bonington

To Ellen Lapham, who has had a few adventures of her own. With all good wishes from her friends,

Nick & Betsy

SUTTON PUBLISHING

First published in the United Kingdom in 2008 by
Sutton Publishing, an imprint of The History Press
Cirencester Road · Chalford · Stroud · Gloucestershire · GL6 8PE

British Library Cataloguing in Publication Data
A catalogue record for this book is available from the British Library.

Hardback ISBN 978-0-7509-4782-4

Typeset in Sabon.
Typesetting and origination by
The History Press.
Printed and bound in England.

To the memory of
Willie, Olive, and Audrey Fletcher,
whose enthusiasm and trusting generosity
inspired us to 'last the course'

Contents

Foreword

I am seated in front of a computer terminal in a cyber cafe in Manali, which was once a quiet mountain village and is now a vibrant tourist resort in the Kullu range of the Indian Himalaya. We are just 48 hours out of the United Kingdom.

What a difference to what it was like 100 years ago, when it would have taken six months just to reach this spot. I can't help envying those pioneers who ventured into Central Asia in the nineteenth century and found travelling 'Through a Land of Extremes' especially enthralling. The story of the research and writing of this book is a fascinating detective story in itself.

Nick Clinch is America's most outstanding expedition leader, with successful and happy expeditions making major first ascents in the Karakoram, Central Asia and Antarctica. But he is much more than that. An assiduous student of mountain history, he has one of the finest collections of mountaineering books in the world, and he is a superb ambassador for his sport worldwide.

Betsy is a former researcher for the *National Geographic* magazine. She stumbled across the Littledales while looking for any information on remote Ulugh Muztagh, where Nick wanted to go. It was possibly the highest mountain outside the Himalaya. The Littledales had gone past the mountain in 1895 but there was little more than that tantalising mention. In the 1980s Nick led an expedition to Ulugh Muztagh, and upon his return he and Betsy started their search for more information.

Their ingenuity, perseverance and considerable charm enabled them to put together the intricate jigsaw that made this fascinating account possible. It encompasses not only adventure but also a vivid picture of the terrain, the people and the politics of Central Asia.

Through a Land of Extremes is particularly appropriate today when the ruthless pace of modernisation is penetrating the most distant valleys of this vast, once untamed, area.

Sir Chris Bonington, 2007

Expedition Chronology*

* Does not include many other trips to far-flung destinations and to the Continent.

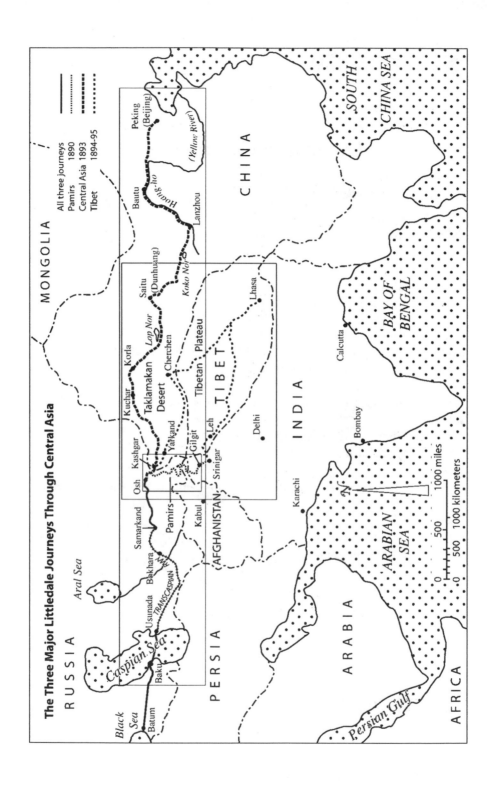

The Three Major Littledale Journeys Through Central Asia

All three journeys
Pamirs 1890
Central Asia 1893
Tibet 1894-95

RUSSIA

MONGOLIA

Black Sea
Batum
Baku
Caspian Sea
Usunada
TRANSCASPIAN
Aral Sea
Bokhara
Samarkand
Osh
Kashgar
Pamirs
Kabul
AFGHANISTAN
PERSIA
Persian Gulf
ARABIA
AFRICA
ARABIAN SEA
Karachi
Bombay
Delhi
Srinigar
Gilgit
Leh
Yarkand
Kuchar
Korla
Taklamakan Desert
Lop Nor
Cherchen
Saitu (Dunhuang)
Koko Nor
Tibetan Plateau
T I B E T
Lhasa
I N D I A
Calcutta
BAY OF BENGAL
Hoang-ho (Yellow River)
Lanzhou
Bautu
Peking (Beijing)
C H I N A
SOUTH CHINA SEA

0   500   1000 miles
0   500   1000 kilometers

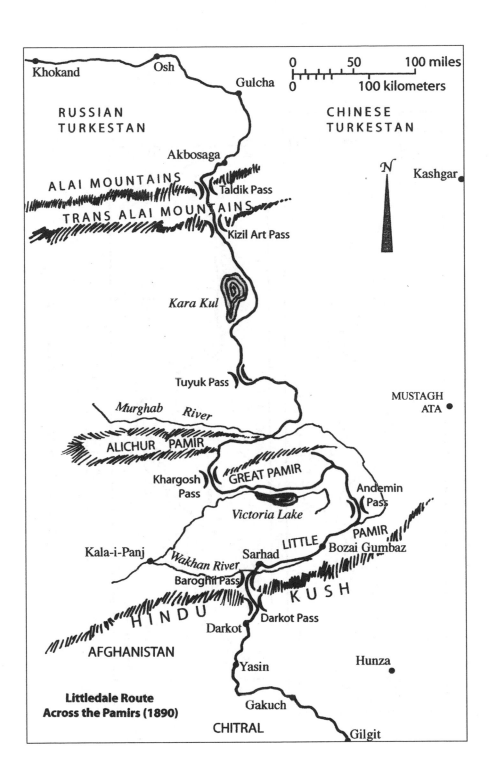

Littledale Route
Across the Pamirs (1890)

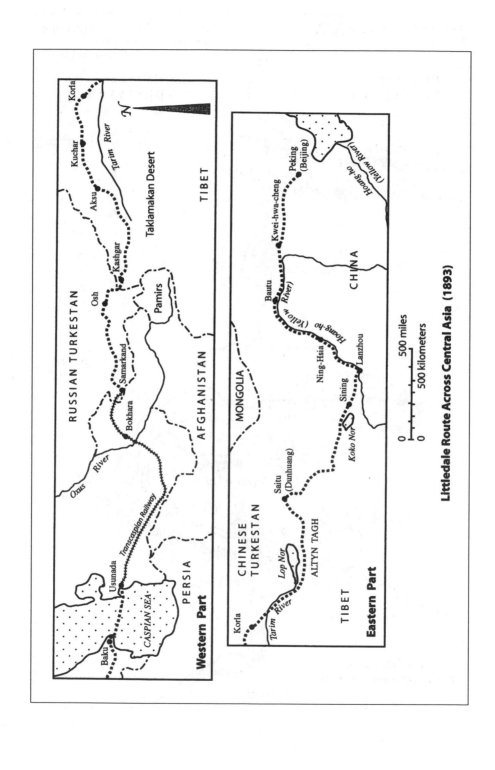

Littledale Route Across Central Asia (1893)

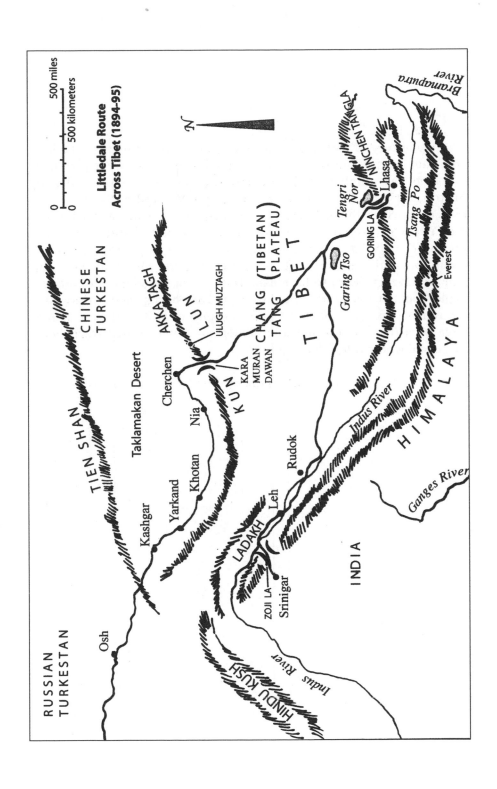

500 miles

500 kilometers

**Littledale Route
Across Tibet (1894-95)**

N

RUSSIAN
TURKESTAN

Osh

TIEN SHAN

CHINESE
TURKESTAN

Taklamakan Desert

Kashgar

Yarkand

Khotan

Nia

Cherchen

AKKA TAGH

ULUGH MUZTAGH

K U N L U N

KARA
MURAN
DAWAN

CHANG TANG (TIBETAN PLATEAU)

T I B E T

Garing Tso

Tengri
Nor

GORING LA

NINCHEN TANGLA

Lhasa

Tsang Po

Rudok

Indus River

Leh

LADAKH

ZOJI LA

Srinigar

HINDU KUSH

Indus River

INDIA

Ganges River

H I M A L A Y A

Everest

Brahmaputra
River

'. . . the history of British adventure can shew several pairs of the kind who rank as enthusiastic explorers of the highest type. We might single out from the number of these a few such as Sir Richard and Lady Burton, Mr. and Mrs. Theodore Bent, and Mr. and Mrs. St. George Littledale, where the wife has been entitled equally with the husband to the fame which is won by an arduous journey in barbarous lands. . . . Of these remarkable yoke-fellows in adventure perhaps the most ubiquitous and most successful have been Mr. and Mrs. Littledale. This pair of travellers seem to have exhausted all the possibilities of modern exploration, at least with regard to Asia. They have penetrated together the remotest recesses of that Continent, and in two or three instances have been the first Europeans to enter some unexplored tract, being successful where others have failed.'

Graham Sandberg, *The Exploration of Tibet*, 1904

INTRODUCTION

On the Trail of the Littledales

Where *is* the stuff?
The authors

On 4 August 1895, on the north side of the Goring La in Tibet only 50 miles from Lhasa, a 43-year-old Englishman, his 55-year-old wife, his 25-year-old nephew, 7 Ladakhi servants, 3 Pathan sepoys, and a fox terrier confronted over 150 Tibetans armed with primitive matchlocks. The Englishman was St. George Littledale, a modest man with a self-deprecating sense of humour, whom King Edward VII was later to call 'my greatest traveller'. His wife Teresa, despite almost constant ill health, had shared in all of his adventures although to her this expedition seemed like one trip too many. His nephew, W.A.L. Fletcher, one of Oxford's greatest oarsmen, had been brought along for additional support. The fox terrier, Tanny, provided love, distraction, and an occasional warning bark at night.

It must have been an incongruous scene, yet it was a fitting climax to the Littledales' adventurous lives, calling forth all the qualities of character that had made them so successful in their prior travels and explorations: courage, intelligence, sensitivity to other people and decisiveness. Victorian England was not lacking in eminent travellers. It was the height of the British Empire, and the Royal Geographical Society was at its zenith in promoting and recording discovery. Just who was this couple, now lost in the mists of time and in the obscurity of footnotes? St. George and Teresa Littledale had come closer to the Forbidden City of Lhasa than anyone else, including even Nikolai Prejevalsky and Sven Hedin, until 1904 when Sir Francis Younghusband marched in with the British Army. The Littledales were incredibly competent. They were known in their day but they have been almost totally forgotten. They never wrote a book. A book would at least have put their names permanently in bibliographies and they would have become known to scholars and collectors. Why had they never written one?

Our involvement with the Littledales began indirectly over thirty years ago as a result of a visit from Eric Shipton, one of the great mountain explorers. He had made numerous expeditions to the Himalaya including five to Everest. In the 1940s he was the British Consul-General in Kashgar, the crossroads of Central Asia. In his sixties he had travelled across the icecaps of Patagonia and was president of the Alpine Club.

Nick asked him the obvious question. 'Eric, you have been everywhere and done everything. If you could go anywhere in the world, where would you go?' First he mentioned Namcha Barwa, a mountain in eastern Tibet. His second choice was Ulugh Muztagh, an 'unknown' mountain over 25,000ft high in the Kun Lun range of northern Tibet. It was extremely remote but he wished he had tried to get there instead of spending so many years on Mount Everest. We pulled out a National Geographic atlas and there it was, Ulugh Muztagh, 25,340ft high. If that height was correct, it was the highest mountain on earth outside the Himalaya.

Eric Shipton died in 1977, but lingering on were the intriguing words '25,340 feet' and 'unknown'. The more Nick thought about it, the more he wanted to go there. However, getting permission from the Chinese seemed hopeless. The whole area was rigidly closed to foreigners. Nick contacted Bob Bates, a veteran of many Alaskan and Himalayan expeditions, including two attempts on K2 in the Karakoram. Bob had run the Peace Corps in Nepal and was respected throughout the mountaineering world. If anyone could get permission, he could. Eric Shipton had also mentioned Ulugh Muztagh to Bob. Nick and Bob agreed to work together to reach the mountain.

They did not have any useful information.[1] They obtained satellite photographs that showed a peak surrounded by large glaciers in the middle of a wasteland, yet in the literature they could find only a few scattered references. Someone must have known something. What was the source of the 25,340-ft elevation shown in the National Geographic atlas?

Finally Betsy, a former editorial researcher for *National Geographic*, decided to help. She found a reference to Ulugh Muztagh buried in Sven Hedin's nine-volume *Southern Tibet* and a footnote a few pages away citing an article by a St. George Littledale in the May 1896 *Geographical Journal*. In the article Littledale described a journey he had taken to Tibet with his wife, nephew, and fox terrier. During the expedition they had gone right past Ulugh Muztagh. It was Littledale who had determined the height of the mountain. His description of the trip contained sufficient detail about the terrain to plan an expedition from it, while a sketch map accompanying the article was so good that Nick could follow the Littledale route on satellite photographs.

We found two other articles by Littledale in the *Geographical Journal*. One described a journey across the Pamirs from Russia to

India in 1890, and the other an expedition in 1893 across Russian and Chinese Central Asia all the way to Peking. Each one of their trips was remarkable. To have done all three was extraordinary. Why had we never heard of them? Embarrassed inquiries to our more scholarly friends revealed they had never heard of them either. How could people that good disappear so completely?

There was no time to answer those questions. Nick's attention was focused on getting to Ulugh Muztagh. It took eight years to get the permission. In September 1985 eight Americans and forty-three Chinese drove to the mountain in French army trucks. They had to go off-road for the final 300 miles. Ulugh Muztagh was not technically difficult but it was cold, there were storms, and the constant wind penetrated everything. Five Chinese climbers reached the summit. Meanwhile, back in California Betsy was waiting – and waiting. She had met Nick at a National Geographic reception for the 1963 American Mount Everest Expedition. She had been assigned to the Everest articles and was working with Tom Hornbein, who had just made the first traverse of Everest with Willi Unsoeld. Nick was not a member of that expedition but had gone to base camp to see his friends. Hornbein and Unsoeld had stripped him of his new Kelty pack and carried it over the mountain. It was Tom who introduced Nick to Betsy at the reception.

After we were married, Betsy found herself vicariously immersed in the affairs of the American Alpine Club. There was a steady stream of mountaineers, domestic and foreign, passing through the house. The Alpine Club of Pakistan was started in the living room.

Betsy's understanding of Central Asia expeditions came from more than books and houseguests. The Baltoro region in the Karakoram range of northern Pakistan had been closed to foreigners for years until 1974, when Nick, Tom Hornbein, and another friend talked the Pakistanis into reopening the area for climbers. What resulted was a 'family' expedition to Paiyu, a granite citadel guarding the entrance to the Baltoro Glacier. Nick had climbed on five continents: the Alps, the stormy Coast Range of British Columbia, the Peruvian Andes, and had organised two successful expeditions to the Himalaya and one to Antarctica. The Paiyu trip was his worst expedition.

Unfortunately Betsy was along. She got the full Karakoram experience – rubble-filled gullies, swaying rope bridges, and cantilevered trails suspended out high over roaring glacial torrents. Even worse, after watching a traditional polo match, she was chased by a mob across Skardu. Later during the expedition a Pakistani climber fell to his death, and Betsy flew back out to Skardu in a high-altitude Pakistan Army helicopter that had come to retrieve the body. She underwent a lengthy interrogation about the accident and then was stranded in Skardu for a week because all flights were cancelled. It was monsoon season in Rawalpindi and the planes could not get up the Indus River gorge. Betsy was now an unescorted western woman in a Muslim area that had become unaccustomed to foreigners. By the time she flew home, she had taken part in two expeditions at the same time, her first and last.

In 1985 while Nick was on Ulugh Muztagh, Betsy had to manage everything at home while enduring weeks of silence from Central Asia. Upon Nick's return she said, 'We never do anything together.' Nick then uttered the fateful words, 'I know what we can do together. We can write a book on the Littledales. You found them.' Thus began what we would later refer to as our 'joint blame venture'.

At first all we knew about them came from the three articles in the *Geographical Journal*. We did not even know Teresa Littledale's first name. She was known simply as Mrs Littledale, even in her obituary. We learned the name of her dog before we learned her first name.

In May 1986 we made a preliminary trip to England to locate the Littledale papers. Our first stop was the Royal Geographical Society in London. We were confident the RGS would have everything. To our surprise the Society produced only a few letters from the Littledales. The librarian suggested we try the Natural History Museum because St. George was a big game hunter and had contributed many specimens to the museum. The papers were not there.

At this point any reasonably sane person would have abandoned the project. Instead we looked at each other and said simultaneously, 'Where *is* the stuff?' It never occurred to us there might not be any 'stuff' or we would not be able to locate it. There had to be 'stuff' somewhere. All we had to do was find it. We went back to the RGS and examined the few letters they had. One was written in a big bold hand thanking the Society for a silver dog collar given to Tanny. The middle name of the signature was illegible but the first name was not. It was Teresa. We were making progress.

The librarian at the Natural History Museum had shown us part of St. George's will and a bequest letter regarding a nephew, Lionel Fletcher. He suggested we visit the British Newspaper Library at Colindale to look for funeral notices in the hope of finding the names of other relatives and descendants. The Littledales had no children but there were many Fletchers descended from St. George's sister Edith. At Colindale we found accounts of a funeral in 1935. One obituary Nick was reading listed not only the people who had attended the service but also their relationship to the deceased. Then he spotted a *Who's Who* on the shelf behind him. Although fifty years had passed, he started looking up the names in case someone was still alive and noteworthy enough to be listed. He went through the entire funeral list with no success until he reached the last name. There it was. Christopher York. That evening we reached him by telephone from our hotel. We described our mission, our American accents adding credibility to our story, and he confirmed it was his wife, a Fletcher, whom we were seeking. He handed her the phone. She said, 'You should call my cousin Willie. He has all the family papers.' She gave us his telephone number.

The next morning we reached Willie Fletcher. Nick began speaking rapidly like a salesman on amphetamines. '. . . a Fellow of the Royal Geographical Society and a member of the Alpine Club. . . .' Fletcher interrupted, 'Alpine Club? My wife's uncle was Frederick Gardiner.' Nick responded frantically, 'Yes, W.A.B. Coolidge once wrote a book, *The Alpine Climbs of Frederick Gardiner*.' (Only fifty copies were published). 'That's right,' said Fletcher. 'Why don't you visit us sometime?' Our flight home was leaving in a few days so Nick said, 'How about tomorrow?'

The Fletchers lived on the Wirral Peninsula between Chester and Liverpool. Although we were total strangers, Fletcher, his wife Olive, and his sister Audrey welcomed us enthusiastically. Within an hour we were on a first-name basis. Our host produced a 42-ft genealogy chart and an old leather-bound diary he had inherited from his uncle, W.A.L. Fletcher. He had not read it.

While Nick talked with Willie and immersed himself in the genealogy chart, Betsy began to examine the diary. A needle and thread were inserted on the inside of the front cover. Opposite the needle was a wallet-sized calendar for 1894/5. Betsy looked at the first entry. It was dated 10 November, the date the Littledales had embarked on their great journey to Tibet. She was holding Fletcher's private diary of the Tibet expedition. She looked at the last entry. Nick was busy writing down the names of Teresa's relatives.

Betsy quietly nudged him and whispered, 'When did the Tibet trip end?' Nick whispered back, 'They didn't cross the Zoji La until November.' Betsy continued, 'This diary stops at the end of June and they are slipping past Tibetans in the dark. There must be another volume.'

In a voice best described as deliberately casual, Nick said, 'Willie, do you happen to have another diary?'

'Well, there is something else upstairs. I don't know what it is.'

Back he came with another book. It was volume two of the Tibet diary. Nick asked about arranging to have the books copied. Willie's reply amazed us. 'Oh, just take them home with you. Bring them back when you are through.'

The Fletchers served us a delicious roast beef dinner. Afterwards we placed the diary carefully in Nick's briefcase, and when we left, he felt as if he was carrying the plans for D-Day. All the way back to California the briefcase never left his side.

Back at home we concentrated on Teresa's family. We had learned from the genealogy chart that she was a Harris from Canada but the question was where in Canada? Now armed with names, Betsy visited our local public library in the unlikely event someone was mentioned in a biographical dictionary. She did not expect to find anything. Perusing the reference shelves, she was distracted by something bright yellow. She looked up and saw the *Dictionary of Canadian Biography*. She checked for the names of Teresa's parents just to confirm they were not listed. To her surprise there was a lengthy entry on Teresa's mother, Amelia Harris. She was described as a diarist and author who had twelve children and lived in the oldest house in London, Ontario, now a museum. We telephoned the author of the article, a Robin Harris, and learned he had in his possession some of the Harris family papers and the rest were at the University of Western Ontario.

Locating the Harris papers so quickly was another stroke of luck but we still could not find the Littledale papers. Several trips to England proved fruitless. During one brief visit to London, Betsy spent a week tracking down relatives. On her last day she made thirty-three telephone calls to the various leads she had developed. Her calls got through. It was the wedding day of Prince Andrew and Sarah Ferguson, and everyone was at home watching the ceremony on television. Betsy managed to interrupt them all, but with no results.

Meanwhile, Nick was transcribing the Fletcher diary. His knowledge of Central Asia was useful but the combination of handwriting, geographical terms and foreign words made it slow going. However, the frustration was more than compensated by the excitement of watching the Tibet expedition unfold and by the knowledge that we were the first people to read the diary. Fletcher had written nothing in hindsight. The entries had been made daily. When we saw that his private account matched the published description in the *Geographical Journal*, we knew we had a hidden window into history. The published article, dramatic as it was, was tame compared to what we were reading.

By now we were getting desperate for the Littledale papers. Every time we had a new lead, we were convinced it would take us to the mother lode, but one disappointment followed another. Dozens of carefully wrought letters produced nothing.

In the summer of 1987 we took the family to England, rented a small house in London, and gave ourselves six weeks to find the missing papers. St. George Littledale had five siblings and we tracked all of them down to the present. After reaching a dead end on four of them, Betsy 'knew' the papers had to be in the possession of the only child of the only child of St. George's older brother. The grandchild in question was living at an unknown address under an assumed name and had an unlisted telephone number. Betsy found her anyway. She did not have them.

After exhausting further avenues of research, we were reduced to looking for a dog collar. Tanny's silver collar from the Royal Geographical Society would not have been thrown away. We hoped that whoever had the collar would know what had happened to the papers. Three days before the flight home, we found the collar in Canterbury. The owner had sold the Littledale diaries, letters, official documents, photographs, personal library, hunting trophies, even instruments, to a big game hunter living in Needles, California. Now we were looking for Elgin T. Gates.

With two more days in England, Betsy concentrated on the Littledales' servants. On the last day she located the nephew of their chauffeur, though a meeting with him would have to wait. It was time to fly home. At last we were hot on the trail of the Littledales. We were as high as our plane.

Nick knew the mountain world, but for both of us big game hunting was another universe. Before we contacted Elgin Gates, we needed to learn something about him. Nick telephoned Ellen Enzler-Herring of Trophy Room Books. She knew Mr Gates. All big game hunters knew him. In 1963 an international jury had voted him one of the world's six greatest living hunters. We learned that Gates had a hunting museum in Needles. Then came the shocker. In 1977 his house and museum burned to the ground together with everything he owned. We were stunned. After all our work the papers were gone.

We wanted confirmation that the Littledale collection had indeed been destroyed. With Ellen's assistance, we located Elgin Gates in Idaho Falls. Nick spoke to him on the phone. Gates became excited when he heard about our book. He told us that in his opinion Littledale was the greatest big game hunter of all time. Later he sent us his book, *Trophy Hunter in Asia*. He had written an inscription: 'Thank God there are at least two more genuine admirers of St. George Littledale!! For 35 years I've felt I was the only one in the world who fully admired his outstanding exploits of exploration and big game hunting – all of which were greatly underrated and underrecognised.'

During our conversation, Gates said he had intended to write a book about Littledale but the fire was such a personal catastrophe that he gave up the idea. However, the papers had been in the basement and were merely flooded, not burned. He had not touched them since the fire. We suggested he send us one diary so that we could see the condition for ourselves. We requested Teresa's Tibet diary because we could compare it to the Fletcher account.

In a few days a box arrived in the mail. We placed it on the kitchen table and eagerly began to open it. It was beautifully packaged but when we unwrapped the diary, charcoal flew across the room. The diary had been both burned and flooded. The pages were stuck together and could not be opened. Worse, the diary was covered with mould and mildew, and green and black growths oozed across the paper. It was not an encouraging sight.

We took the diary to a book conservator at nearby Stanford University who named several restorers in the Bay Area. His top recommendation was Linda Ogden in Berkeley but he warned us she was in great demand and would probably turn us away. A freelance conservator, she restored illuminated manuscripts for the Getty Museum in Los Angeles.

Betsy phoned her anyway and the next day she met Betsy and saw Teresa Littledale's diary. Linda was intrigued by our project. Most of her work involved restoring beautiful or historic pages for display under glass. We were the first people who wanted a document restored in order to access the information it contained. She became almost as excited as we were about our subject. While working her magic on Teresa's diary, she would call us from time to time to fill us in on the Littledales in Tibet.

After the diary was restored, we sent a transcription to Elgin Gates. He promptly gave us the rest of the damaged papers. Some documents were charred beyond repair and the photographic albums were utterly destroyed. However, there were great black chunks of letters and diaries with material buried inside that might be salvageable with treatment. We began taking a few sections at a time to Linda. When they were done, we would collect them and give her more. It was a long process.

In September 1988 we visited Elgin Gates in Idaho and experienced first-hand his passion for the Littledales. Before the fire he had read nearly everything in his Littledale collection, and we knew that what knowledge he had would be invaluable. We planned to see him again soon. Shortly after our visit, Nick was reading the paper at breakfast and saw a short notice that Gates had died suddenly of a heart attack. We had boxes of burned and flooded papers, and now the only person who had read them was gone.

It became apparent that if we continued, years of work still lay ahead. We had each been sacrificing our own personal interests for the book. On the other hand, the Littledale story needed to be told and we were the only people who could tell it. Besides, we had already invested so much time and effort in the project that we were loath to quit. Above all, many trusting people in England, Canada, and the United States had gone out of their way to help us, had become our friends, and were looking forward to the finished product. Time was passing and we were afraid some of them would not live to see it completed. So we made another fateful decision. We would see the book through.

The amount of research left to do was intimidating. The more we learned, the more questions were raised. We had a jigsaw puzzle on our hands with too many pieces missing. Still, we were tantalised by an array of unanswered questions. How did the Littledales meet? Where is King Edward's ibex? Was St. George working for British intelligence? The loss of what friend hastened his death? Who was the Reverend H.W. Moss? How did the wapiti (elk) get to New Zealand? At a meeting of the Royal Geographical Society, Littledale was praised for managing to rescue dried plants from 'the shipwreck'. *What* shipwreck?

In 1996 we visited China as guests of Chinese friends. They flew us all the way to Kashgar, where we saw Chini Bagh, the home of George Macartney, the British agent (representative) with whom the Littledales stayed during two expeditions. A few years later we went in opposite directions. Nick joined a small group that travelled along the southern branch of the Silk Road. The route covered two sections through which the Littledales had passed. Meanwhile, Betsy flew to England and immersed herself in the Foreign Office papers at the Public Record Office (National Archives) at Kew.

She returned to England again the following year. The weather was terrible and it was hard to get anywhere, which made travelling difficult. It was even more difficult to find useful material. Then she had an unexpected breakthrough. St. George Littledale left the bulk of his estate to the son of his younger brother. He was a bachelor according to distant relatives, but Betsy had learned he had married at the age of 60. It was his widow who possessed Tanny's silver collar.

Her first husband had been a British Army officer in India, and he had died in a plane crash on the Northwest Frontier in 1945, leaving her with two children. One of the children was Christopher Inward, a flight engineer for British Airways. We had visited him in 1987 just before we saw the dog collar at his mother's house. He had shown us two stacks of small white envelopes. The few we opened were invitations to events at Windsor Castle. We had ignored the rest because we had other priorities. Now the invitations would help us fill out the social life of the Littledales in England. Betsy asked to see the stacks of invitations but Chris said he did not remember having any. He added that he did have two stacks of letters and he was quite sure she would find them of interest. Betsy could not get to his house because the tracks were flooded and the trains were not running so he mailed the letters to her hotel in London.

When Betsy opened the package she could not believe what she was seeing. Elgin Gates did not get everything. These were not invitations.

These were original letters from Lord Curzon, Lord Roberts, Prince Christian, and other prominent people. Best of all was a series of private letters from Sir Robert Morier, the British Ambassador to Russia. He had written them at the height of the Great Game, and he was coaching St. George Littledale on exactly what to do to obtain permission from Russia to travel across Russian Central Asia. It was a tremendous reward for leaving no stone unturned.

After pursuing the Littledales for so long, we finally knew who they were and what they had accomplished. During our journey of discovery we had turned up unknown information about the Great Game and Central Asia and we had gained fascinating new insights into known historical figures. But even after all this time, we found it hard to believe the magnitude of what we had uncovered. The Littledales deserved the years of effort. Here is their story.

Elizabeth and Nicholas Clinch
Palo Alto, California

1

Central Asia, Land of Extremes

They have no fields or ploughlands,
But only wastes where white bones lie
Among yellow sands.
Li Po (eighth century)[1]

In the latter half of the nineteenth century, the vast and barren heart of the Eurasian land mass known as Central Asia was a major objective of world exploration. It was a land of extremes both geographically and historically: sand, snow, silk, and slaughter. The terrain was extreme, the climate was extreme, and the inhabitants were extreme. Out of it came trade and war, mostly war.

Scholars have argued over a definition of Central Asia almost as vigorously as warriors have fought over its land. An appropriate description is the following: 'The vast area which lies between Siberia to the north, China to the east, India to the south and the Caspian Sea on the west. . . . It is divided today into three main regions: Sinkiang or Chinese Turkestan, lying south of Siberia; Tibet, north of India; and what is now Russian Central Asia. . . .'[2] The Littledales travelled through all three regions.

In 1870 George Hayward, an explorer who had reached Kashgar the previous year, his four servants and his munshi (native clerk), were brutally murdered in a valley below the Darkot Pass while trying to cross the Hindu Kush. The crime reverberated throughout British India. This was no ordinary robbery and killing. Hayward had published an article in an Indian paper describing the atrocities committed by Kashmiri troops suppressing a revolt. Rumours abounded as to who was responsible for the murders. Suspects included the Maharaja of Kashmir, in whose territory Hayward was travelling.

The Maharaja sent Frederick Drew, an Englishman who worked for him, to investigate the killing.[3] Drew described Hayward:

A keen sportsman, and a hardy, energetic, and courageous traveller, he had many of the qualities that make a good explorer. But he was more fitted to do the part of an explorer of a continent like Australia than in Asia, where nearly every habitable nook is filled up, and where knowledge of human nature and skill in dealing with various races of men are at least as much wanted as ability to overcome physical obstacles.[4]

It was an apt summary. It took more than determination and courage to be a successful traveller in Central Asia. It required the sensitivity to handle a people with a long history of violence and conquest, a people formed by their land.

The Littledales would have to contend with even more than the land, the climate and the people. The rivalry between Russia and Britain in Central Asia, a cold war known as the 'Great Game', was coming to a climax just as Teresa and St. George entered the scene in 1888, and it was a major obstacle they had to overcome.

Central Asia has the highest mountains on earth and one of the lowest regions, the Turfan Depression, almost 1,000ft below sea level.[5] In the north a grassy steppe stretching from Manchuria westwards to the Caspian Sea provided an unbroken military highway for tribal horsemen. South of the steppe are the world's greatest mountains, some of its bleakest deserts and the uninhabited Chang Tang or Tibetan Plateau.

The mountains radiate out from the high Pamir like a giant pinwheel frozen in stone and ice: the Hindu Kush to the south-west, the Trans Alai to the north-west, the Tien Shan to the north-east, the Kun Lun to the east, and the Karakoram and Himalaya to the south-east. Except for the major rivers that rise in Tibet, the waters from these ranges flow inland and not into the ocean. The two largest rivers, the Amu Darya (Oxus) and the Syr Darya, rise in the Tien Shan and the Pamir and flow into the Aral Sea. This region includes the deserts of Kara Kum south of the Oxus River and the Kyzyl Kum south-east of the Aral Sea. In the Tarim Basin of Chinese Turkestan is the Taklamakan Desert. The name means 'He who goes in will not come out.' To its east lies the Gobi Desert.[6]

The interior of Central Asia is almost 2,000 miles from any ocean. A little moisture manages to penetrate from the Baltic and Black Seas to Lake Baikal almost 4,000 miles away, but the mountains of the Karakoram and the Himalaya block the monsoon winds from the Indian Ocean. As a result the climate is dry with extremes of hot and cold.[7] The temperature can vary as much as 54°F (30°C) in a few hours.

The inhabitants of Central Asia reflect their harsh environment with a history that is ancient, complex and violent. For millenniums a bewildering number of tribes were at each other's throats and at the throats of their more sedentary neighbours in the settled lands around them. Although there was agriculture and trade, the people were mostly nomadic, living and fighting on horseback and following their herds. Where the grass went, they could go. They could change from peace to war almost as fast as they could change horses.

There were certain constants in the history of the steppe people. They were militarily superior to their neighbours, the tide of conquest flowed from east to west, and their tribal organisation was unstable.[8] With the compound bow and mastery of the horse due to centuries of a hunting and nomadic existence, the people of the steppe maintained military dominance over their agriculturally-based neighbours for over 2,000 years.[9] This relationship did not change until the coming of gunpowder and artillery.

The fierce hordes of Huns who overran Europe from the fourth century were forced westward by even tougher warriors to their east. Perhaps this was because the farther east, the harsher the terrain. The nomads of the eastern steppe were hardened by their implacable land, giving them a margin of superiority over their western neighbours. Tribe after tribe pushed west and south, displacing their nomad rivals or establishing themselves as rulers of the settled civilisations, coming to a climax with Genghis Khan and the Mongol conquest in the thirteenth century, and not ending until the eighteenth century.[10]

A mitigating factor was the tribal organisation of the nomads. Every group including small tribes and large confederations depended upon the ability and personality of its leader. A nomad empire was the personal property of the man who created it and he could leave it to anyone he wanted. Frequently a nation was divided among the chief's sons. Thus steppe political organisations were inherently unstable.[11]

Where there was sufficient water, there were settlements and agriculture. These oases made possible the trade routes of Central Asia, later called the Silk Road. It was not a road in the modern sense. At its best it might be a narrow trail, and at its worst just a direction across a trackless waste.

The Silk Road began at Changan (Xian), the capital of China, and went west through the Kansu Corridor to Dunhuang, where it split. The northern route followed the flank of the Tien Shan (Heavenly Mountains) through the Tarim Basin along the northern side of the Taklamakan, past the oases of Hami, Korla and Kucha to Kashgar. The southern route skirted the southern edge of the Taklamakan through Cherchen, Khotan and Yarkand before reaching Kashgar. At Kashgar, the trade routes divided again. One route went over the Terek Pass through the Tien Shan to Samarkand, Bukhara and then to Merv. Another route crossed the Pamir and went down the Wakhan Corridor of Afghanistan to Merv. From there various routes led to the eastern shores of the Mediterranean. There were also several routes to India. Everything travelled along these routes, not only trade goods but also peoples, cultures and religions, especially Buddhism, which brought art and monasteries to the oases of eastern Central Asia.[12]

During the seventh century, Islam erupted out of the Arabian Peninsula followed by the Arab conquests of North Africa and the Middle East.[13] In 751 the major forces in Central Asia met at the Talas River, a tributary of the Syr Darya, and fought one of the most important battles in history. The Turks, Arabs and Tibetans routed a Chinese army and drove it back across the Tien Shan.[14] The long gradual conversion of Central Asia to Islam began. It did not move with the speed of a whirlwind but with the slowness and irresistibility of a glacier burying everything as it moves.

At its height in the thirteenth century, the Mongol Empire stretched from the Pacific Ocean to the Black Sea. A journey from the Black Sea to what is modern Beijing might take as long as 300 days but it could be done.[15] Central Asia had become the centre of a single Eurasian system.

The most famous traveller along the trade routes was Marco Polo. With his father and uncle he set out in 1269 to visit the Great Khan in Cathay, as they called China. It took years. They passed over the Pamirs to Kashgar, then along the southern branch of the Silk Road to Dunhuang and on to China.[16] *A Description of the World or the Travels of Marco Polo* was one of the most influential books ever written. It was read by generations of statesmen, bankers, geographers and explorers, stimulating their interest in China and the Far East. Christopher Columbus had a copy in which he made annotations in the margins. In the late 1800s the Littledales tried to match their observations with those of Marco Polo.[17]

When Genghis Khan died, his empire was divided into khanates ruled by his surviving sons. Inevitably the various khanates began to split apart. For the next few centuries after Marco Polo, Central Asia reverted into a number of Turkic and Mongol states that constantly squabbled, fought, combined with, seceded from, collided, and bounced off each other like molecules in a heated test tube. It was only when China and Russia began to use gunpowder that the balance of power gradually shifted away from the steppe people.[18]

The Ming Dynasty, which followed Mongol rule, turned China inward, became corrupt, and was racked by insurrection that in turn led to the Manchu conquest of China in the seventeenth century.[19] Finally a Chinese army defeated the Mongols by using artillery. By the mid-eighteenth century the Chinese had recaptured what is now

Xinjiang and were back on the border of the Pamir and the Tien Shan.[20] The tide of war had permanently changed.

The Russians were the last sedentary people to escape the Mongol yoke. The khans levied their tribute through local Russian princes whose administration reflected the ruthlessness of their masters. By 1450 the Russians began to manufacture muskets and started on a road that eventually led to a clash of empires in the late 1800s in a remote region in Central Asia through which the Littledales would be travelling.[21]

While the Russians were advancing by land, the British were coming by sea. The East India Company began to establish trading posts in India, including what were to become Bombay, Madras and Calcutta. By 1804 the British held Bengal and southern India and had political agents in nearly every native state.[22] Now they began to think about a threat from Russia, the traditional invasion route from the west and their exposed frontiers. The storms of Britain and Russia were moving toward each other but the clouds were still small and far apart.[23] Even so, British officials were afraid of the inflammatory effect Russian agents might have on the Indian population.[24] The British army was too small to be controlling a country of over two hundred million people. Moreover, everything was wrapped in a fog of geographical ignorance that magnified their concerns.

Russia and Britain had been sending agents into Central Asia since the early 1800s. William Moorcroft of the East India Company went to Bukhara in 1825 with two companions. All of them died on the return journey. In 1830 Lieutenant Arthur Conolly travelled overland to India through Persia and Afghanistan. It was he who first used the term 'Great Game' to describe the increasing rivalry between Britain and Russia in Central Asia.[25]

In 1841 the British suffered an unmitigated disaster in Afghanistan. Dost Muhammad, the ruler, was displeased with the British and began negotiations with the Russians. The Viceroy of India ignored the advice of his representative in Kabul and decided to remove Dost Muhammad and replace him with Shah Shuja, a poor choice. The British army marched to Kabul and placed Shah Shuja on the throne. The presence of foreign troops unified the quarrelling Afghans and the tribes rose. The British army was defeated and then destroyed during its retreat in winter. Out of 16,500 British and Indian troops who left Kabul, only one man, a doctor, rode into Jalalabad. The rest had been killed or taken prisoner. It was one of the worst defeats in the history of British arms.[26]

The British returned to Kabul, installed Shah Shuja's son as ruler, and then withdrew. Within three months the son had been overthrown and

Dost Muhammad was restored to power. Everything was back where it was before. Among the repercussions from this fiasco, the vicious slave-trading Emir of Bukhara, unafraid of retribution, executed two British prisoners including Arthur Conolly.[27]

The Indian Mutiny of 1857 occurred fifteen years later. Problems had been festering for a long time in the British Indian Army. The sepoys (native soldiers) increasingly distrusted their British officers. Finally, troops rebelled, shot their officers, marched on Delhi, and had their old king proclaimed Emperor of India. Lucknow was besieged. After ferocious fighting and atrocities on both sides, Delhi was recaptured, the siege at Lucknow lifted, and the uprising was suppressed.

The Indian Mutiny confirmed that British dominance was largely an illusion. They were ruling by bluff. Lord Roberts, Commander-in-Chief of the Indian Army, later wrote, 'The whole secret of our successful rule in the East is that our supremacy has never yet been doubted, either by our own subjects or by our neighbours. . . .'[28] The British would always be scattered pieces of seaweed floating on an ocean of Indians. However, there were measures they could take. The British government ended the rule of the East India Company and took direct control of the country. They gave the Indian soldiers better treatment and training, and they increased the ratio of British soldiers to Indian soldiers. Even this force was spread too thin to handle a full-scale uprising, so the British adopted a policy of responding quickly and forcefully to even the smallest incidents.[29]

It was inevitable that Russian expansion would spread through Central Asia like spilled ink across a map. At the highest levels of the Russian government, especially in the War Ministry, there was loose talk about invading India, but there remained a reluctance to do anything that would bring about a confrontation with Britain. At the same time, Russian military officers in the field were inspired to take action against the khanates with their slave-raiding and constant wars. Russian soldiers would conquer an irritating khanate while the Foreign Ministry was assuring British officials that no such action was planned. After the khanate was taken, the Russians would state that there were no plans to annex the new territory permanently, which of course they did. This ambiguity was symbolised by the simultaneous dismissal and decoration of one officer who had made the latest seizure.[30]

In 1878 history repeated itself in Afghanistan. During a crisis between Russia and Britain in Turkey, the Afghan ruler welcomed a Russian mission while rejecting a British one. A British envoy went into Kabul with an army escort, the ruler fled and peace was made with his son, who agreed to the presence of a British representative. Three months later Afghan soldiers attacked the British residency and killed the British envoy and his escort. A British army under General Sir Frederick Roberts marched to Kabul and sent the son into exile in India. This time the British were smarter than in 1841. They reached an agreement with Abdur Rahman, who was neither pro-Russian nor pro-British but pro-Afghan and was the only man who could control the Afghan people. Rahman agreed to have no relations with any country except Britain, and in return Britain agreed not to interfere in his territory. For a while Afghanistan became relatively stable, at least for Afghanistan.[31]

Meanwhile, the Russians were having their own difficulties. In September 1879 they attacked the Turcoman fortress of Geok-Tepe, roughly halfway between the Caspian Sea and Merv, but were soundly defeated by the Turcomans. Two years later the Russians stormed Geok-Tepe successfully. They massacred the defenders and the population. Then they annexed Merv.[32]

The centre of the rival storm fronts now moved east to the wild country of indefinite borders and unknown rugged terrain of eastern Afghanistan, the Pamir, and western Chinese Turkestan. The empires of Russia, Britain, and China were beginning to meet – and not very gracefully.

The British knew almost nothing about Tibet, which bordered on India and was becoming increasingly important as the Russians moved east. In the seventh century Tibet had converted to Buddhism and expanded throughout Central Asia. At the height of its empire, Tibet's rule extended throughout the Tarim Basin from Kashgar to Dunhuang. Then the empire fell apart and centuries of chaos ensued. By the nineteenth century Tibet was a theocracy under the control of the Yellow Hat sect, a reformed Buddhist group, and was ruled by a Dalai Lama, one of a series of reincarnated rulers. After the death of the Seventh Dalai Lama in 1751, Tibet was governed by a series of regents for a period of 120 years because, peculiarly, no Dalai Lama ever reached maturity.

Chinese influence on Tibet waxed and waned according to Tibetan politics and external threats. The Tibetans acknowledged a formal link with China but the regents ran the country as they pleased. Then in 1792 Tibet was attacked by the Gurkhas of Nepal. An Imperial Chinese army arrived and, with the Tibetans, they drove the Gurkhas out. Until this time Tibet had been relatively open, but after the war Tibet closed its frontiers to travellers because of Chinese influence and the concern of the ruling Lamas that foreigners were a threat to the Buddhist religion. The last visitors were the French Lazarist priests Evariste Huc and Joseph Gabet, who reached Lhasa from Peking (Beijing) in 1846.[33]

The phrase 'blank on the map' may warm the heart of an explorer but it does not reassure statesmen and military planners. The British needed to evaluate the Russian threat accurately. However, they had limited information concerning Russia's capability and intentions, and even less knowledge regarding the geography of the terrain. Something might be hidden behind the ranges. As the Russians approached India, the British grew even more concerned about their topographical ignorance. They sent out Lieutenant John Wood of the Indian Navy to explore the source of the Oxus. In 1838 he reached Victoria Lake in the Pamirs, but for almost forty years he was the only Englishman to reach the area.[34]

In 1846 the British gave possession of Jammu, Kashmir and Ladakh to Gulab Singh, the Hindu ruler of Jammu. Gulab Singh acknowledged the supremacy of the British Government, which in turn agreed to help him protect his territories from external enemies. The British had placed a Hindu ruler over a Muslim population in a country with boundaries extending into Central Asia, and over whose foreign relations the British had only indirect control. Moreover, the boundaries extended far into the mountains and their exact locations were indistinct, leaving considerable room for expansion and confusion.[35] It was a formula for trouble.

The following year the British tried to delineate the boundary between Ladakh and Tibet in order to stabilise the border. A British surveyor reached the Karakoram Pass. In 1857 Adolphe Schlagintweit crossed the pass and reached Kashgar, where he stumbled into a civil war and was killed.[36] The British were caught in a dilemma. As the fate of Schlagintweit demonstrated, it was dangerous for Europeans to travel in lands where the British government had little influence, and they did not want any incidents to occur for which they could not effectively retaliate because their actual weakness would be revealed. Yet the regions to the north of India were a mystery to them. Something had to be done.

A dramatic attempt to solve this problem was the creation of a corps of native explorers recruited and trained by the Great Trigonometrical Survey of India. Using concealed instruments such as compasses in the heads of walking sticks and notes hidden in Buddhist prayer wheels, they crossed the frontiers disguised as pilgrims or traders. They later became known as the 'Pundits'. The results were extraordinary. For over twenty years they travelled throughout Central Asia from the frozen valleys of the Pamirs to the jungle gorges of south-eastern Tibet. They even reached Lhasa in an era when no westerners got in and only rumours came out.[37]

By the mid-eighteenth century the Chinese had recaptured Xinjiang including Kashgaria, but had left the administration of the district to local Muslim chiefs. Religious opposition to the Chinese resulted in a series of uprisings. By 1864 the Chinese had lost control of much of the country, and Yakub Beg, a Kokandi adventurer, seized power. By 1873 he ruled all of the country south of the Tien Shan.[38] The Chinese retook Kashgaria in 1877 but China was weak, Peking was far away, and Russia was near. In 1881 the Treaty of St Petersburg confirmed the right of the Russians to have a consulate in Kashgar, and its strong Consul-General, Nikolai Petrovsky, exerted an overwhelming influence over the Chinese governor.[39]

Meanwhile, despite the risks, Russian and British explorers became increasingly active. Russian map-makers were approaching the Hindu Kush, which bordered India. In 1884 the British and Russians agreed to a Joint Afghan Boundary Commission to delineate the northern frontier of Afghanistan, but the Commission left the Pamirs as a no-man's-land inhabited only by wolves and a few Kirghiz nomads. Through this frozen vacuum the Russians were moving south toward the passes leading to Hunza, Chitral and India.[40]

British intelligence knew by 1890 that the Russian army could not pour through the Hindu Kush. However, this did not lessen their concern.[41] The passes could still be used as a pathway for subversion. Through and beyond the inhospitable mountains of the Hindu Kush and the Karakoram, the number of travellers greatly increased. They included scientists, army officers, and hunters with sharp eyes and retentive minds. In 1888 Captain B.L. Gromchevsky, whom Lord Curzon described as the 'stormy petrel' of Russian expansion, paid a visit to Safdar Ali, the Mir of Hunza. Gromchevsky's activities in and near Hunza inspired the theme for Kipling's *Kim*, in which Russian agents posing as hunters try to infiltrate India from the north.[42]

The Great Game, or 'Tournament of Shadows' as the Russians called their rivalry with Britain, was approaching its climax when into this remote land of extremes came an innocuous-looking English couple, Teresa and St. George Littledale. What were they doing there?

2

Teresa Harris

I believe I have a little of the 'Bedouin Arab' in me.
Teresa Harris Scott

Eldon House is the oldest existing house in London, Ontario, a two-storey Georgian-style home overlooking the Forks of the Thames. Today it is a museum in the centre of a city of 360,000 people, but in 1834 when John Harris, Teresa's father, built Eldon House for his growing family, the city had a population of only 500 and was known as London-in-the-Bush.[1]

Very little is known about the early life of John Harris. He was born in 1782 at Dartington in Devon, England. Church records refer to him as 'the son and base child of Mary'. When he was twelve, he ran away to sea. Harris became an apprentice in the Merchant Marine, and later was impressed into the Royal Navy. He showed intelligence and ability and quickly rose through the ranks. In 1811 Harris was appointed Master of the HMS *Zephyr*, and when the war of 1812 broke out, he was sent to Canada, where he was severely wounded in an attack on Fort Erie. After the war he remained in Canada and became a hydrographer.[2]

In 1815 the British began an extensive survey of the Great Lakes. That spring Harris was sent out from Kingston to determine the best site for a harbour and ship-building facility on the north shore of Lake Erie. He travelled in a large canoe manned by half-a-dozen men. As the canoe pulled into the little dock at the tiny settlement of Port Ryerse, the entire community, about twenty people, was waiting for them. Among them was a girl of 17. According to family legend she saw John Harris standing in the approaching boat and said to a friend, 'There's the man I shall marry.' Whether or not the story is true, Amelia Ryerse married John Harris two months later.[3] At 33 he was almost twice her age, but their marriage was probably the best thing that ever happened to them.

Amelia was the only daughter of Colonel Samuel Ryerse and his second wife Sarah Underhill, a widow. Colonel Ryerse was born and raised in New Jersey. During the American Revolution he fought with the British as a captain in the 3rd New Jersey Volunteers.[4] After the war the Ryerses moved from New Jersey to New Brunswick. As a Loyalist refugee from the United States, Ryerse received a grant of 3,000 acres near Long Point on Lake Erie, and it was there that his family settled. Port Ryerse was named after him.

As the daughter of a Loyalist, Amelia was also entitled to a land grant. She selected property at Port Ryerse, where she and John Harris built a house and took up farming. Amelia had four uncles with land grants in the area, so the family was firmly established as leaders in the developing region, a situation that would greatly influence her husband's future.[5] With the support of Amelia's relatives, John Harris was appointed treasurer of the district. The job was powerful and paid well, and he was to hold it for the rest of his life.[6] He was now a member of the political, social and financial elite of Upper Canada.

The Harris family grew rapidly, with a new baby arriving every two years. All but two lived to adulthood. The first eight surviving children were born at Port Ryerse: Sarah, Amelia, twins Mary and Eliza, Charlotte, John Fitzjohn, Edward and Helen.

When the district headquarters was shifted to London, the Harris family moved there and occupied Eldon House. Then an event occurred that was to affect the Harris family. The financial crisis of 1837 and the actions of an unusually inept lieutenant governor triggered the 'Mackenzie Rebellion'.[7] At Eldon House there was a rumour that the rebels were going to kill John Harris and burn down the house. When the wife of the Anglican minister visited Eldon, she found Amelia and the children making bullets for the militia. Shortly thereafter, John Harris helped precipitate an international incident. William Mackenzie, the Canadian politician who was leading the rebellion, had fled to the United States and set up an outpost on the Canadian side of the Niagara river at Navy Island, where he prepared to invade Canada. His rebels were being supplied from the New York shore by a small American paddle steamer, the *Caroline*. Harris observed the activity and suggested an attack. On the night of 29 December 1837, he was in a party of forty volunteers who rowed across the Niagara river, captured the steamer at a wharf on the American side, and sank the *Caroline*. The Canadian authorities were embarrassed retroactively and the commander of the expedition was court-martialled, but John Harris became a local hero.[8]

The rebellion was followed by cross-border raids and threats, compelling the British to reinforce their troops in western Ontario. London became a garrison town. By the 1840s it was the most important military station west of Toronto, transforming it financially, culturally and socially. Best of all, as far as Amelia Harris was concerned, the rotating regiments provided an endless supply of wealthy, upper class, single officers, aptly described as 'bored out of their minds with life in a provincial backwater'.[9]

At Eldon House Amelia gave birth to another son, George, and on 12 August 1839 she had her twelfth and last child, a girl. They named her Theresa Newcomen Julia Eveleigh Harris.* The name Julia came from the baby's godfather, Julius Airey, but Newcomen and Eveleigh were two army lieutenants stationed in London, Arthur Newcomen in the Royal Artillery and Henry Eveleigh in the 32nd Regiment.[10]

There were now ten children living in Eldon House and it was crowded. The three boys shared a back bedroom on the second floor and six girls filled three other bedrooms. The largest bedroom was reserved for guests. Teresa slept downstairs with her parents. The details of her early years are few but the life of the Harris family is well documented. Everyone wrote letters and many were saved. In 1857 Amelia Harris began a diary that she continued for twenty-five years. Once she started it, there was little privacy left in the family. She covered all the gossip, threw in her strong opinions, and left the diary out on the parlour table for everyone to read.[11]

The prominence of the Harris family, the talents of Amelia as a hostess, the presence of many daughters, and the location and size of Eldon House meant there was a constant flow of visitors, and Eldon House became the social centre of London. Distinguished guests, including Governors General and British aristocrats stayed at Eldon and enjoyed the Harris hospitality. There were dinners, parties, dances and outdoor activities such as croquet in summer and sleigh rides in winter. On New Year's Day as many as fifty people would call at Eldon House.[12]

The first daughter to get married was Sarah, who married Captain Robert Dalzell of the 81st Regiment in 1846. He was English and the fourth son of the Marquis of Carnwath. In August 1850 Mary married Lieutenant Shuldham Peard of the 20th Regiment at Eldon House.

John Harris had been in poor health and was so ill on Mary's wedding day that he could not leave his room to attend the ceremony. Two days later he died. Upon his death both his Navy pension and his salary as Treasurer of the District ceased, precipitating a financial crisis in the family. Furthermore, the District Council was pursuing a claim against him for £2,000, a substantial amount. Amelia had an annual income of about £260, a large sum for that time but not enough to

---

*   Theresa was the spelling used by the family until about 1856 when the 'h' was dropped.

maintain the Eldon House lifestyle. Nevertheless she was determined to ensure that her sons were successful and her daughters found suitable husbands. The District Council accepted another house owned by the Harrises in payment for the £2,000 and Amelia's application for a Royal Navy pension was approved. She also received rental income from other property she owned. Even so, her finances were precarious.[13]

Amelia was a strong, domineering woman, and taking full advantage of her position and associations, she made sure that for the sake of her children the social life at Eldon House continued as before. Her efforts were successful and her daughters continued to marry well. Eliza, Mary's twin sister, married Lieutenant-Colonel Charles Crutchley of the 23rd Royal Welsh Fusiliers, and Helen married Maurice Portman, the wealthy son of a British peer.[14] Four of the sisters settled in England. Meanwhile, John Fitzjohn completed his legal training and by 1855 he was prospering. Much of his income came from managing the investments of his British brothers-in-law. His brother Edward joined him in a partnership. With financial stability restored, Amelia's remaining challenge was the future of her youngest daughter.[15]

Teresa was always the baby and slept in her mother's bed until the day of her marriage, a practice that was not uncommon in Canada. She was tutored in the usual subjects for young women including music, drawing and French. However, because of the family's financial difficulties, she did not receive as much formal education as her older sisters, and it was mostly her sisters who taught her.[16] Her minimal education is apparent in her diaries, in which she demonstrates a limited vocabulary and speaks in absolutes, although her repeated hyperboles such as 'the most beautiful' and 'the most wretched' could have reflected a strong personality.

In the mid-nineteenth century illness was a constant presence. Medicine was primitive and death was never far away. There were also frequent accidents. Teresa's sister Charlotte and her two small children drowned in a shipwreck in the Mediterranean. John, the eldest son and mainstay of the fatherless family, was constantly ill. Amelia complained about her own health throughout her life, just as Teresa would do. There is no question that Teresa was a sickly child. In 1854 Amelia commented that Teresa was 'very delicate'. Three years later she wrote that Teresa had not been out of the house for months. 'You know her throat was ulcerated all winter and now her ears are diseased. She had to have leeches behind them last night. . . . Doctor Robertson says it arises from poorness of the blood and if the strictest attention is not paid to her the first thing we know she will be in a decline. It is a long time since she has been well.'[17]

Amelia was also concerned that Teresa might be thought homely. Edward even voiced the opinion that his mother would be 'clever' if she could marry Teresa off.[18] Then, in November 1858, William John Scott wandered into the matrimonial spider web that was Eldon House. Scott was from Roxburghshire, Scotland. Born in 1827 in Melrose, he was the son of Dr James Scott of Darnlee and his wife Agnes. His father died when he was eleven but his mother had money and she bought an estate called Teviot Bank from a nephew for £17,000. It was a large turreted house on 240 acres, and in 1851 there were five servants in residence and nine farm labourers. Six years later Agnes died and William John Scott inherited the property.[19]

Scott had come to Canada to visit friends, probably including Maurice Portman, Helen's husband. After several visits to Eldon House, he left with Portman for Mississippi, where Portman had bought a plantation. From there Scott travelled on to Havana. In February 1859 Scott revisited Eldon House and distributed presents from Havana including cigars for Edward and a carved ivory card case for Teresa as well as a gold half dollar. He looked rather pale and said the climate in the South did not agree with him. He made several more visits to Eldon, had dinner with the three Harris brothers, and then later that month sent a letter to Teresa's brother John, acting head of the family, and in a 'very gentlemanlike manner' stated that Teresa was the great attraction, and with the family's approval he wished to marry her. Amelia recorded the family's reaction:

> We thought it best not to tell Teresa at present as it would make her feel very awkward when Mr. Scott called. . . . Mr. Portman wrote to Teresa that if Mr. Scott proposed for her not to take him. What his reasons & objections are we do not know. As far as we can judge Mr. Scott is an excellent match. He has upwards of £2,000 a year and his conduct appears to be very correct. In personal appearance he is certainly the reverse of handsome but I do not consider beauty an essential in a matrimonial connection.

Later that day Scott came to tea. His ordeal was just beginning. He came to dinner a few days later and played cribbage with Teresa, George and Amelia. Amelia wrote, 'Mr. Scott I think improves very much upon acquaintance.' He called again the next day but Teresa refused to see him. 'When we were going to bed she told me she would not marry Mr. Scott, that she did not like him well enough. Oh Great God enable me to put my whole trust in Thee and to believe Thou will over rule all things for good.'

It grew more complicated. Amelia told John what Teresa had said, but her son remarked that he considered Scott to be an honourable and upright man. Teresa however noticed that her brother seemed out of sorts and asked her mother if she had passed on her remarks about Scott. Amelia replied that she had and that Scott had made a proposal. 'I then stated his worldly advantages, and that I believed that he was a worthy man and would make a good husband. Against this is that he is excessively plain and not at all a taking man with ladies but that I considered him superior, far superior, in all that pertains to a gentleman to anyone here.'

Teresa replied that she did not know if she could learn to like him better. Her mother told her she might not have such an offer again. 'If we could only see clearly what is right, but we are so apt to be influenced by our own wishes or prejudices and likes and dislikes, too often formed without cause or foundation and which would not bear the test of common sense for a moment.'

Several days later Scott had lunch at Eldon House and the following day he joined Teresa at church. Amelia commented, 'Teresa flutters like a young bird when she sees Mr. Scott. She cannot help feeling nervous although he does not know that she is aware of his matrimonial wishes.' When Scott came to dinner again he was in a bad mood but later he apologised, saying he was not feeling well. He also mentioned he had received letters from England informing him of the death of an old aunt who had left him £4,000 with a chance at £50,000 more. He was rapidly learning the game.

Maurice Portman believed Scott was a drunkard. Edward disagreed. John agreed with Edward. 'Teresa,' Amelia wrote, '. . . felt herself now at liberty to refuse Mr. Scott without having a feeling that she might be doing wrong in refusing a worthy man (though not a very attractive one).' A few days later she wrote, 'The property which Mr. Scott most probably will become heir to has been registered at £60,000. . . .' Things were looking slightly better for Scott again.

Teresa could not decide what to do, but was 'quite sure' she would accept his proposal if she could be certain he did not drink.[20] So the family stalled Scott for two months in order to check him out. Amelia wrote to Shuldham Peard in England, Mary's husband, and asked him to go to Scotland to make inquiries.

The tide continued to turn in Scott's favour. On 5 April Amelia wrote, 'Mr. Scott gave Teresa a small diamond ring very pretty but not very good and a bracelet of the new metal called almoninam [aluminum]. It is very pretty.' Letters started coming from Teresa's sisters in England. Mary and Eliza both wrote that Teresa would be a great fool if she refused Scott. In the meantime the visits from Scott continued. He presented Teresa with books and bouquets of flowers. He even offered her three more rings. Amelia advised him to keep them for two or three weeks until Teresa's decision was known or, as she confided in her diary, 'in other words until we heard from Shuldham'.[21]

Peard reported that he had gone to Roxburghshire and everything he found confirmed what Scott had said. Now that the family no longer objected, Teresa would have to decide for herself. To add to the drama at Eldon House, John, the older brother, was awkwardly courting a Miss Elizabeth Loring from Toronto. He was doing only slightly better than Scott. The young lady's mother thought the Harrises were 'all incorrigible matchmakers'. Then Scott and Teresa had a minor falling out. Amelia summed up the situation: 'We have a fine household. Mr. Scott is in love with Teresa (I wish she was in love with him). John is in love with Miss Loring, this is mutual I believe. Ned [Edward] and Miss Widder are very much in love with each other for the time being and George looks on with supreme disgust and thinks they ought all to put on cap and bells.'[22]

On 25 May Teresa finally accepted Scott's proposal. Amelia was impressed when Scott wrote her a letter inviting her to stay with him and Teresa. She seemed more impressed when Scott settled £10,000 on Teresa that she would inherit if she survived him. If there were no children, he left Teresa the entire income from all his property during her lifetime. The marriage document was signed the day before the wedding. It named Maurice Portman and John and Edward Harris as trustees to manage the money. The nuptials could begin.[23]

The wedding took place at Eldon House on 18 August 1859. Teresa was twenty and Willie, as Scott was known, was thirty-two. Amelia wrote:

> How wretched I felt this morning. . . . The guests punctual in their attendance at one o'clock but the ceremony did not take place until two. Teresa's spirits gave way altogether towards the last and it was some time before they could get her sufficiently composed to come downstairs. . . . Teresa and Mr. Scott pronounced their vows very feebly. . . . There was a good deal of speechifying. Mr. Scott returned thanks when the bride's health was drank and made a very good speech. A carriage took them to the station for a train to Niagara Falls. Mrs. Harris, the cook, threw an old shoe after them for luck and Teresa was gone. . . . Sophia came and took Teresa's place in my bed.

At Niagara the honeymooners invited members of the Harris family to join them and watch Blondin making his spectacular tightrope walks across the Niagara Gorge. Maurice Portman accepted and reported that Willie and Teresa were 'very spoony'.[24]

From there the spoony couple leisurely made their way to Toronto, Montreal and Quebec, visiting friends along the way. Finally they sailed to New York, where they went shopping for two weeks. Willie wrote to Amelia that Teresa 'seems to stand travelling tolerably well. . . .'[25] It was an auspicious start to her future travels.

The Scotts returned to Eldon House in early October and promptly became immersed in family business problems. The brothers were squabbling over the handling of financial matters including the £10,000 Scott had given them to invest on Teresa's behalf. As a result, Willie decided he had to live in Canada to look after his investments.

They sailed for England later that month to introduce Willie to Teresa's sisters and to sell Teviot Bank, the Scottish estate that Willie had inherited. Teresa wrote, 'It was rough two days – we had the end of what had been a frightful storm. The Royal Charter was lost in it. What a horrible thing that was – there were 451 lives lost and only 90 feet from land.'[26] Having written this, she then described her own experience as a 'splendid voyage'. She had been seasick, but as Lord Chesterton used to say, 'Adventure is discomfort seen from the proper point of view.'

In London the Scotts visited the Crutchleys. Eliza had not seen her sister for years. 'We like her extremely and I am surprised at her having grown up with her wits so well about her, and with such good sense and judgment. Mr. Scott appears most devoted. He evidently knows what he is about but as you say is not polished.' Amelia Harris wrote:

> . . . Eliza and Mary . . . make a good many remarks about Mr. Scott and his want of manner. They are severe upon his lying upon the sofa in the drawing room and his coming to dinner with <u>a net string</u> around his neck in the place of a white tie, and also about coming to breakfast in slippers after two days acquaintance. Poor Mr. Scott has not passed muster very well. . . .

A few days later his 'mustering' improved. 'Mr. Scott expects to be able to send early in May £25,000 for Harris and Brothers to invest, which will be a great thing for them.'[27]

After a lengthy stay, the Scotts went to Edinburgh to sell Teviot Bank, but a medical crisis interrupted their plans. In early December Teresa wrote to her mother:

> The reason I have not written to you . . . is because I have been so ill. . . . You know what Dr. Robertson gave me medicine for but it never set me quite right and I never felt strong. . . . So I sent for Dr. Simpson

thinking he would give me a tonic or something to strengthen me, instead of which he examined me and found that the womb had never opened and said that it must be opened for me or I should never be well. The idea of an operation frightened me to death. . . . He gave me chloroform which I did not want to take but the Doctor said it would be so painful . . . that he could not do it without. He told Mr. Scott that he had to tear the flesh very much. . . . Dr. Simpson told me that if I ever had a baby that I never could bear the pain that I should have to endure if he did not perform what he did. He comes every day to use great balls of healing ointment. . . . Dr. Simpson is such a kind old man – he is so gentle just like an old woman.[28]

Teresa's doctor was the famous Scottish physician Sir James Young Simpson, one of the leading doctors of the time. He had discovered the anaesthetic powers of chloroform and used it to help deliver Queen Victoria's child, Prince Leopold, in 1853. His medical care was far ahead of the usual standards of the day but the kind doctor had every reason to worry about his patient. Teresa should have recovered from the procedure in a few days but infection must have set in, for she required a long period of treatment and recovery. The importance of antisepsis to prevent bacterial infection was unknown, and antibiotics would not be invented for a long time. Teresa was never able to bear children.[29]

She did not feel well enough to travel to Teviot Bank until early January 1860. Willie sold the property at auction and in early March they moved out. 'We were dreadfully sorry to leave. . . . We left all the servants in tears. They are all so fond of Mr. Scott.'[30] While visiting Edinburgh, they received the shocking news from Eldon House that Helen Portman had died from complications following childbirth, compounded by medical incompetence. Teresa was stunned, as she had loved Helen best of all her sisters. The Scotts sailed from Liverpool three months later, arriving at Eldon House in July with two hunting dogs and 'Tiny', a English Toy Terrier that fitted in Teresa's pocket. Amelia thought her daughter looked tired and thin.

The Scotts moved in, unpacked their silver and linens, arranged the books brought from Teviot Bank, many of them sermons, stored Willie's wine collection, and settled into their routines. There were now six people living at Eldon House besides the servants: Amelia Harris, her sons George and Edward, their cousin Sophia whom Edward had married, Teresa and Willie. As always, there was little privacy. Although the Scotts were wealthy enough to live wherever they wanted, their choosing to live at Eldon House is indicative of Amelia's strong hold on her youngest child.

It was not an easy time. The following February Amelia collapsed and remained ill for months. Members of the family took turns caring for her, especially Teresa. 'All my family are most kind but Teresa's attention never flags.' She had just begun to recover when her son John Fitzjohn Harris died in England, where he had gone for treatment.[31]

After two long years at Eldon House, the Scotts decided to move to England permanently. In June 1862 Willie broke the news to Amelia. It must have been difficult. Amelia wrote:

> . . . Mr. Scott is not very well. Teresa thinks and hopes that a winter in England may do him good, but I doubt whether either of them will be as happy away as they have been at Eldon. Here they have had many comforts and have been free from care and they have had the conscious feeling that they were adding to my comfort and perhaps lengthening my life.[32]

The Scotts did not leave for another three months. The real reason for their move is unknown, but life at Eldon House had not been quite as stress-free as Amelia indicated. However, Teresa had never lived anywhere else, not even after her marriage, and now she was leaving not only her home but her country. She wrote to her mother from New York, 'I wish we were going to sail for home instead of for England tomorrow. I dread it like nightmares but it cannot be helped.'[33]

They reached Liverpool in September and went on to London. Their plans were uncertain, but they finally decided to rent a house in Berkshire near the Peards because it would be less lonely for Teresa and they would get to know the neighbours more quickly.[34] By early November they had found a place, Coopers Hill in Bracknell, only a couple of miles from the Peards and not far from the Crutchleys in Ascot. It stood on top of a hill overlooking the railroad station. The Scotts intended to keep a cow and several pigs.

Willie was watching his finances. When John died, Edward had taken sole control of the family investments but he had been late in sending Scott his money from Canada. Willie had bought the City Hotel in London, Ontario. In October he wrote to Edward that he would consider selling it for £20,000, adding that he hoped Edward was sending him some money. Two months later Willie acknowledged receipt of a draft for £250 and in his response expressed the hope that he would soon have a long letter giving a good account of the City Hotel property. A few days later he wrote again, saying he needed more cash. 'The last supply was spent before your draft arrived. Send me another £500 as soon as you can.' A trend had begun.[35] Later the City Hotel was to burn to the ground under suspicious circumstances.

As usual, Edward Harris kept Willie in the dark. Even so, Willie tried to maintain good relations with his brother-in-law.[36]

Willie was interested in horses and fox hunting and considered himself a 'horsey man' but his hunting activities were sporadic. Shuldham Peard wrote, '. . . he is an idle fellow and does things by extremes. He hunts hard one day, does nothing for the two next and feeds enormously. Consequently he has frequent bilious attacks.'[37]

As for Teresa and horses, Mary Peard wrote, '[Shuldham] put Teresa on her pony and sent her up and down in the park. At first she was so pale, but she improved. Mr. Scott will never teach her to ride. Shuldham might.'[38] Initially Teresa did little riding, but at least she was gradually getting accustomed to horses. No one, least of all Teresa, could have anticipated that she would be riding horseback across Central Asia.

During this period, Teresa was busy adjusting to her new life. When reading about the activities of Victorian families such as the Harrises and the Scotts, it is easy to forget that their lives rested on an unseen foundation of servants. They were often talked about or complained about by their masters but rarely acknowledged. Wealthy Victorians supervised estates comparable to small hotels today, with family and friends as guests and the servants as staff, and Teresa found she had her hands full running the household. She had to hire maids or replace them and she was looking for a footman, but she was gradually learning how to handle people, a skill that would prove indispensable in the future.[39]

Willie was frequently absent and Teresa felt lonely when he was away. For recreation she studied French and took up drawing. She also saw her sisters. Eliza Crutchley wrote, 'She has a lovely figure and her manner gains on everyone.'[40]

Once again though she developed health problems. In 1863 after the Royal Ascot she complained of swollen glands, a sore throat and 'piles' that the doctor diagnosed as 'debility'. A German doctor in London told her a month in the waters at Bad Kissingen would strengthen her. Scott was not thrilled. 'Poor Willie feels as if he were being taken to execution.'[41] He would have felt even worse had he known how long they would stay.

They left England that June. After a month Willie wrote to Amelia, 'Day after day is the same thing over and over again, dinner is about the only event . . . I often wonder how Mr. Portman would stand this kind of life. I think he would go and drown himself in the wells before the week was over. It's the only clear place for the purpose here.' After a second month Teresa wrote, 'Here we are still. It seems to me that we shall never get away. . . . I am taking mud baths now. I sit up to my chin in them.' Willie added, 'I hope that all this washing and scrubbing and drinking may do Teresa good. At present she is a fright – yellow face and neck.'[42] Teresa probably had hepatitis. The Scotts endured a third month at Bad Kissingen and even added two more weeks at another spa.

During that time Amelia pleaded with the Scotts to return to Canada, even though she knew Teresa was ill. The reason she gave was that Amelia Griffin, one of Teresa's sisters, was expecting a child and needed someone to be with her during her confinement. Both Teresa and Willie felt so intimidated by Amelia Harris that they did not simply decline but felt obligated to reply with long letters from each of them setting out in great detail the financial and health problems the trip would entail.[43]

When the Scotts finally arrived home, one thing had not changed, Edward's failure to send money. At least the Scotts had resources.[44] The Peards and Dalzells were not so fortunate. By December the Peards' financial situation was so serious that they had to move to Taunton, where Maurice Portman's father, Lord Portman, had obtained an adjutancy for Shuldham in the militia that would provide more income. Teresa would miss them. The Crutchleys also moved away. Charles was promoted to general and given the command at Gibraltar. Then the Scotts received word that Amelia Griffin's child had been stillborn, greatly increasing the pressure on them to return to Canada. They decided to make the journey.

The Scotts arrived at Eldon House in May 1864 and stayed for five months. It was not a happy place. Teresa's sister Amelia and her husband Gilbert Griffin were not getting on with each other, Edward and George, who had joined the business partnership, quarrelled constantly over the business, and Edward and his wife Sophia had been estranged for over a year. Meanwhile, letters were coming in from unhappy family members in England trying to get their money out of Edward.

On 18 August Amelia Harris wrote, 'The anniversary of Teresa's wedding day and I am thankful to say that her marriage appears to be a very happy one.' Even so, the differences between Teresa and Willie were becoming more apparent. Scott always appeared to lack energy and enthusiasm. He did not like social activities and travel. He would have preferred a quiet isolated life at home. His main interest was his investments, and with Edward Harris mishandling much of his assets, he was kept busy. Perhaps he had a low-level malaise that sapped his strength. In later years he clearly had some kind of chronic illness.

Teresa, on the contrary, was outgoing and was coming into her own. She turned 25 at Eldon House. Despite her bouts of illness, she was filled with vitality. The world was opening before her. She had been the ugly duckling of the family, and while she may not have become a beautiful swan, she had turned into an attractive and lively woman, perhaps even too lively and a little naive. One day a Colonel Peacocke, a bachelor, visited Eldon House. Amelia Griffin wrote, 'Teresa amused him excessively. She was so impulsive & ridiculous at times. Mamma made them all laugh by saying one night she thought Scottie must feel sometimes as if he were tied to a kite.'[45] On 1 November the Scotts departed for England. With them were their servants and a mountain of baggage – as well as Colonel Peacocke. During the trip the Colonel spent considerable time with Teresa, telling her of his 'family problems' and expressing his regret that he had never married. Teresa thought he had a crush on a Miss Laird but it was obviously Teresa who interested him.[46]

Back at Coopers Hill there may have been a problem with the marriage. In July 1866 Teresa's mother wrote in her diary, 'I got a letter from Teresa. It is private so I burn it.'[47] As Amelia was not in the habit of throwing away anything, and considering what she did save for others to read no matter how personal, one has to wonder what Teresa wrote that shocked her mother into destroying the letter.

The Scotts kept returning to Canada for interminable stays at Eldon House. Teresa did not seem able to break her ties to home. However, she began to show signs of an increasing adventurous spirit. In 1868 her sister Eliza Crutchley invited her to Gibralter. Willie was opposed. 'Teresa has been far from well & I think it will half kill her.' However, in May 1868 Teresa went anyway, accompanied by her ever-indulgent husband.[48] They were still there in July and went on a trip to Spain. Willie wrote, 'Teresa worked night & day sightseeing (at least from 6:30 am to 11 pm). She is as strong as a horse. . . .'[49]

In Gibraltar Teresa took to horseback riding more enthusiastically. Willie underestimated her. 'I suppose she will have another try at riding again when she gets home but I am afraid I shall never be able to get a horse quiet enough for her at home. Here they are like old cows. . . .' But Teresa wrote, 'Carey [Crutchley] and I are going . . . to ride without stirrups. Yesterday we rode into Gib without stirrups and with both legs over the second pommel. If my horse had shied I should have shot off without a moments hesitation. I am so glad I have got over my cowardice. . . .'[50]

Just when Willie thought they would be living on Gibraltar forever, Teresa got sick, so sick that they sailed for England on 4 hours notice. She was still recovering two months later.[51]

Willie maintained his business correspondence with Edward but the news was never good and the stress was beginning to affect him both mentally and physically. In July 1870 Shuldham Peard visited and described him:

> He was very crusty & seedy whilst I was there for a week & as weak as a wafer. The wonder is that he does not become a confirmed invalid, but there is nothing the matter organically with him but laziness. . . . Teresa is a nice woman & we like her very much indeed, but I don't think he likes to see her enjoy herself – as he is always grumbling & growling.**[52]

That October the Scotts bought nearby Wick Hill House. Fixing it up became a project for Teresa, who wanted it to be as beautiful as other homes she had seen, but she was restless. She began pushing Willie to take a lengthy trip, and in 1872 he finally relented. 'We have I think quite decided to go up the "Nile". . . . I . . . did not think Willie would have gone, but it was his own suggestion in the end. . . . I have planned so many trips that I have been quite getting up on my geography. We shall bring back a live crocodile as a pet.'[53]

The Scotts sailed on 7 November on the *Pekin*. Willie dreaded ocean travel because it made him desperately seasick. 'The window at which we are writing looks out on the sea and every time I look out, I feel horrid qualms of what we are doomed to undergo in a few hours.' In contrast to Willie, Teresa was excited: 'We shall spend a fortnight at Cairo at any rate and see all that is to be seen.'[54]

Upon reaching Alexandria, the Scotts continued on through the Suez Canal. Teresa wrote from Cairo:

> It seemed so curious to be sailing through the desert with nothing but miles of sand as far as one could see . . . on either side and here and there a miserable low green shrub trying to grow. We saw one dog and one jackal and here and there a few Arabs with camels. . . . Suez is a wretched place, full of bugs, fleas, and bad smells. We slept there and came on here next morning. . . . The railway journey is long, nearly twelve hours but it was all so new that we did not feel it long. . . . Cairo is a most curious place but the fleas nearly eat me up.

She went on, 'The Capt. of the "Pekin" was very civil to me. He left the dinner to put me into the boat himself. They all chaffed about it for he did not take much notice of anybody.' She concluded, 'I have been so

---

** In Victorian England the words 'lazy' and 'indolent' were often used to describe people suffering from chronic illnesses that were not understood.

well since I came away and enjoy it all so much and like going about seeing everything, which, unfortunately, Willie does not, but there is a gentleman here who . . . I go about with a good deal and it is stupid not to see all one can and there is so much to see.'[55] Teresa was having the time of her life, with or without Willie.

In 1872 Egypt was becoming a vacation destination. A tourist could go by train from Alexandria to Cairo and take a small steamer up to Aswan, and Thomas Cook was starting tours. However, for the more adventurous the preferred means of transportation was the shallow, flat-bottomed, two-masted dahabeah that sailed up the Nile on the prevailing wind and then drifted back down the river. The Scotts hired a dahabeah for three months. They would make the trip with the Strutts, friends from Canada, and a Miss Balfour, Mrs Strutt's sister. 'Our boat belongs to the chief eunuch of the Viceroy's harem. We shall carry the Viceroy's flag, which they say will be an advantage as it will act as a passport. The Strutts have taken a boat called, "Nigma." We go together with only one dragoman [interpreter and factotum] named "Ali Nubia" but live each in our own boat.' The Scotts' boat had no name so they christened it the *Teresa*.[56]

The river trip would not begin for ten days, and in the meantime the Scotts took in the sights of Cairo. Teresa was fascinated by everything. She went to the 'Citadel' to see the illuminated Mosque and to watch the 'howling and dancing dervishes'. She also visited the Viceroy's harem, which she described in long letters to her family. One day they visited the pyramids.

Teresa was intrigued by more than the sights. 'The Arab and Egyptian men are the most wonderfully graceful people I ever saw and their dress adds to their grace. I went for a ride on a camel and had my photo taken dressed as an Arab sitting on the camel. . . . It is so nice to ride. . . .' She also enjoyed riding donkeys, though Willie did not. 'He says he would rather walk. I think it is such fun. . . . Mr. Strutt's donkey fell the other day and sent him straight over his head. He landed full length flat on his face.'[57]

At last they began the long, slow, 964-mile floating crawl up the Nile in their dahabeahs to the Second Cataract.[58] Teresa wrote to her niece, Julia Crutchley, 'I cannot fancy a more delightful trip than this for an invalid, everything to make it pleasant but it is very quiet. . . . I am picking up Arabic fast. I can ask for nearly everything on the dinner table. Our waiter takes a great interest in my Arabic and tells me what everything is when he brings it in.' She concluded, 'I think Willie enjoys the life very much but he is lazier than I am. I like a certain amount of excitement.'[59]

By the next time Teresa wrote to Julia, she had found her certain amount of excitement. Their dahabeah had reached Nubia and the Second Cataract and had turned around. 'We enjoyed coming up the

Cataract. How anybody can possibly be afraid is perfectly astonishing for there is nothing in the world to be afraid of unless the ropes broke. . . . I am looking forward to the going down. . . .' Later she described the return:

> The sensation was perfectly delightful. I should like to descend every day. . . . We shipped a good deal of water. . . . When we got down, the men belonging to the Cataract who take your boat down, in their excitement came and shook hands with me and said 'Salaamat'. . . . Today we have had a horrid day. It has blown a perfect gale and the dragoman cannot understand why when I was so frightened today, I was not frightened coming down the Cataract yesterday when he says everybody else was frightened. 'It is very curious,' he says.[60]

The Scotts returned to Cairo in March 1873. A week later Teresa wrote that they had just about made up their minds to go to Jerusalem. Then she added, as if matters were settled, which they undoubtedly were in her mind if not in Willie's, that they would take a steamer to Jaffa, then go to Jerusalem, Smyrna, Ephesus, Beirut, Damascus and on to Constantinople. At the start of the journey Teresa had been enthusiastic about the Strutts. Now she wrote, 'I do not care to see them again', a reminder of the wisdom of the Islamic saying, 'How do you know he is your friend? Is he your neighbour or have you gone on a long trip with him?'[61]

They remained in Cairo for another week. 'You would laugh if you could see me sitting down in the bazaars beside an Arab drinking coffee with him and spouting what Arabic I have picked up and haggling for what I want to buy. It amuses me immensely. After buying some silver bangles the other day, I made him give me some baksheesh so he gave me a silver ring. When I got home I caught fourteen fleas.' But not even the ubiquitous fleas dampened her enthusiasm. '. . . I should not at all mind spending the whole winter here.'[62]

The Scotts left for Jerusalem, where they spent three weeks. Teresa wrote a long, illuminating letter to her sister Mary describing their visit in great detail, especially the company she kept:

> I think I saw everything there was to be seen thanks to a Monsieur Murad, the interpreter to the German Consulate. He is an Armenian and such a nice young fellow, we became perfectly devoted to each other. He took me everywhere. . . . I went every night to all the Greek and Latin Easter ceremonies with him. . . . They are never over until twelve or one o'clk and one night we were there until three o'clk in the morning. . . . Willie never went. It bored him so much but I am

very glad to have seen them all and might go to Jerusalem a hundred times and never see [as much as] I did this time. I cannot think why he took so much trouble for an utter stranger. . . . There were five or six gentleman foreigners who sat at the dinner table besides us who regularly took me under their wing and one of them was the Spanish Consul something. . . . They used to puzzle their brains as to what I should go to see next.[63]

A letter to her mother from Constantinople provides additional intriguing detail:

We had a very pleasant trip through Palestine and Syria. I never enjoyed a trip more altho it is very hard work for one has to ride in a very hot sun for from six to eight hours a day. All the boxes and tents are carried on mules backs and one camps every night. The tent life is delightful. . . . We met Col. Clifton again at Damascus. [Apparently she first met him in Jerusalem]. He has taken the most absurd fancy to me and would hardly let me out of his sight and always calls me 'wifie' and the night we left Damascus he astounded some strangers at the dinner table by announcing that his wife had gone off with some fellow named 'Scott', these people not understanding all that had passed before. He is in very bad health and comes abroad every year. He is between fifty and sixty and enormously rich. He wanted us to go to Candia [in Crete] and Cyprus in his yacht. . . . I used to chaff him so much and he used to tell me sometimes that he hated me. I told him on the contrary he knew he was perfectly devoted to me and he certainly was. He gave me a beautiful Rufigeh, a sort of handkerchief the Arabs wear on their heads and offered me an Arab dress which I stupidly refused. A Mr. Elliot who was also at Damascus gave me a splendid Rufigeh all one mass of gold. It is the handsomest I ever saw.
    Since we left Beyrouth, we have been travelling with a Major Williamson and a Mr. Chichester. The latter will be Lord Templemore. He has been sent abroad as he was growing rather wild in England but he is very young and I think will turn out a nice fellow. I like the boy very much. He is 19 and it all depends upon what hands he falls into in the next two or three years. . . . Mr. Chichester has given me a very handsome silver dagger for my belt. . . .[64]

This is a change for Teresa. Ever since her marriage to Scott, her letters to Canada were filled with the names and detailed descriptions of the women she had met. Now her letters would describe men. It was as if she had just discovered them. She was lively and flirtatious and she obviously enjoyed their company. Moreover, the men perceived her as available. Although it was not considered proper for a married woman to accept expensive gifts from other men, Teresa delighted in writing to her family about receiving them, seemingly unaware that there might be anything wrong.

She continued, 'Constantinople is such a lovely place, quite the most beautiful I have ever seen. . . . One thing which has made me enjoy myself so much is that I have been so well. I think living so much in the air and such an active life does me good. I never was so strong.' Willie had a different view:

> Here we are still in foreign parts. I am beginning to think we shall never get home again. Teresa never, never tires of sight seeing and does not seem to know what it is to feel knocked up. We did all Syria and pretty hard work it was. We had about 30 days riding all together. It is a wretched country & never could have been anything else unless the people knew how to cultivate rocks. . . .'[65]

The Scotts finally returned to England in July 1873. Within the first week, many of the men Teresa had met abroad arrived on their doorstep, Lord Templemore, Major Williamson, and a Captain Brodijan whom they also met in Syria. 'Major Williamson has just been to see us and is coming again after luncheon and we are going to spend the evening with him. He is very nice. He is so gentlemanlike.' Then, 'Major Williamson came before lunch and stayed for an hour and a half and then came back directly after his lunch and remained all the afternoon.'[66]

The trip to the Middle East was a watershed in the Scotts' relationship. In Egypt Teresa discovered her fascination with strange lands and peoples, and she enjoyed an adventurous outdoor life, but Willie did not. He only wanted to make his young wife happy, but as his health worsened, it became harder and harder for him to keep up. It is clear he had been suffering from a serious chronic illness for years. He was not well even before their marriage. However, something else was hampering their relationship. The daughter that Amelia Harris was afraid might never get married was displaying a remarkable ability to attract men, and from Teresa's letters it is hard to tell that Willie was even there. Why did the men think she was available? Why did Willie appear indifferent to the attention his wife was getting? One is reminded of the private letter that Teresa wrote to her mother in 1866 that Amelia had destroyed. Could the subject have been so intimate that not even Amelia would preserve it?

By the time the Scotts went to the Middle East, Willie felt so sick he rarely left his room. He had done everything he could for Teresa despite his illness, but the trip turned out to be too much for him and he simply gave up. Meanwhile, men continued to flock around his wife. It is unlikely they got what they may have wanted. The fact that Teresa described to her sister and even to her mother her late nights and gifts would indicate she was engaged in no activities other than seeing the sights with her male companions. If anything else was going on, she would probably have remained silent.

Teresa continued to be restless. Eliza wrote to their mother, 'She has returned home very listless. Finds her house very dull and seems to be counting the days to be off again. She says they will let their house for two years and spend that time with you in going to San Francisco, Japan, India, etc. . . . Their house looks so very nice and their conservatory so pretty that I wonder at her discontent but she has no tribe of children to pull at her. . . .'[67]

In October Colonel Clifton invited himself to Wick Hill House for two days. 'We met him several times in Syria and he took a great fancy to me. He is in very bad health and his brain is softening or doing something. . . . I do not know what on earth we shall do with him. He is very rich . . . and if he were only in his right mind would be a most useful and charming acquaintance.' Later Teresa wrote, 'On the 15th Dec. we go to Lancashire to stay with Colonel Clifton. . . . We have never seen his wife . . . and I do not know what she will think of me. . . . Col. Clifton is devoted to us, me in particular. . . . He is an extraordinary gentleman. He told us he had £40,000 a year.'[68]

As 1873 ended, Teresa was dreaming of her next trip. 'I believe I have a little of the "Bedouin Arab" in me. I like wandering about the world so much. I am reading up on India and Japan violently. I think the latter country will be very amusing [interesting] and so thoroughly different from other countries.'[69]

On 2 May 1874 the Scotts sailed from Liverpool for New York. It is hard to understand why Willie undertook this trip. He must still have been determined to please Teresa. They reached Eldon House in mid-May and stayed for over three months.[70]

In late August they started west by train. In Omaha they changed trains and met another passenger, a Mr English, who lived in Calcutta and would be travelling with them as far as Japan. Teresa must have impressed the engineer with her lively enthusiasm for she spent a good part of the time looking at the scenery from the cab of the locomotive. Crossing the Rockies at 8,500ft, she was bothered by the altitude. 'The air is so rarified that it positively pained my chest.'[71] She could never have imagined that someday she would spend months at twice that elevation.

Teresa held strong opinions. At Ogden, Utah, they made a detour to Salt Lake City, where they visited the Mormon Tabernacle. 'Heard the most awful rubbish preached by one of the Mormon elders.' They also visited the Mormon leader. 'I thought Brigham Young odious.' They arrived in San Francisco on 2 September and she wrote, 'We have walked about the town and am much disappointed. It is a bad imitation of New York.'[72]

Two days later they sailed for Japan on the *China*. The steamer was slow and it took twenty-six days to cross the Pacific. Captain Phillips, who had been on their train, was captain of the ship and Teresa spent a lot of time in his cabin. Mr English was on board as well. There were not many passengers and most of them were British. One was Charles Davis, a young man who was to become an amusing companion to the Scotts in Japan. The Scotts disembarked at Yokohama and rode to the Grand Hotel in rickshaws.[73]

Teresa spent the first week shopping and resting. One afternoon she and Willie went to Tokyo with several new acquaintances including Charles Davis, who had 'attached himself to us'. A few days later they set out on an excursion to Mount Fuji (12,388ft). Besides the Scotts and a couple named Brent, the party included the now ubiquitous Charles Davis. They started in horse-drawn vehicles and then rode in kangos (chairs carried by porters) or walked. Two days later they reached the base of Fuji. Willie walked almost the entire way. The following morning Mr Brent and Charles Davis set out in the dark to climb Fuji, but at 11,000ft they had to turn back because the snow was hard and they had no way of cutting steps. The next day everyone left the mountain and returned to Yokohama.

Three days later Teresa wrote in her diary: 'Monday, 26th Oct. – Yokohama. Went out shopping with Mr. Littledale.'[74] It was the first time the name Littledale appeared in her diary. It would not be the last.

3

St. George Littledale

'Lazy'

Nickname at Shrewsbury School

St George's Hall is one of the most prominent buildings in Liverpool. In the early nineteenth century the city was growing rapidly and the triennial musical festivals had outgrown St Peter's Church. The city needed a larger and separate building. It also needed space for new law courts. The energetic citizens formed a committee, raised £23,000, and work began on a massive, neoclassic building in the centre of town. They named it after England's patron saint.[1]

The first stone was laid on 28 June 1838, the day of Queen Victoria's coronation. Thirteen years later the royal family visited Liverpool. It was a memorable occasion both because of the exuberance of the citizens and the drenching rain. After ceremonies in the Town Hall followed by lunch, the Queen went to St George's Hall. She later wrote in her diary, 'It is worthy of ancient Athens, the architecture is so simple and magnificent . . . the interior . . . quite unfinished but . . . the taste so good and pure.'[2]

On 8 December 1851, with the law authorities and the town council in full official costume, the building was ceremoniously dedicated for judicial use. The mayor was Thomas Littledale. He helped preside over the ceremony, and at his personal expense he gave a splendid lunch in the Town Hall for the judges, the Queen's counsel, aldermen, and councillors of the city and their wives.[3] His own wife could not attend. Julia Royds Littledale was at home giving birth to their fifth child and second son. The boy was named Clement St. George Royds Littledale after his maternal grandfather and the town monument. They called him St. George.

The Littledale family originated in the Lake District, where they became merchants in Whitehaven. For generations they traded there, shipping goods down to Liverpool and to ports on the continent. Thomas Littledale, St. George's grandfather, moved from Whitehaven to Liverpool and founded a brokerage firm with his cousin Isaac under the name T. and I. Littledale. The firm dealt primarily in cotton and was extremely successful.[4]

In 1815 Thomas Littledale married Ann Molyneux, eldest daughter of Thomas Molyneux of West Derby, Liverpool. For centuries the Molyneux family had been one of the most influential in the city. To house his family Littledale bought Highfield House in Old Swan, West Derby. Built in 1703, it was an enormous home with spacious grounds. Thomas and Ann Littledale had six children. As frequently happened in those times, two died in infancy. A boy named Thomas was born and died in 1817. The following year they had a second son to whom they gave the same name. He would become the father of St. George Littledale.

Thomas Littledale junior was sent to Rugby School. Afterwards he joined the Littledale firm as an apprentice and became a partner. The business was by now worldwide and included almost any article of commerce and produce: wool, silk, tea, coffee and sugar, as well as the all-important cotton. An example of the size and reputation of the Littledale firm came during the financial panic of 1847. Twenty-eight Liverpool mercantile and banking firms failed. When the Littledale firm lost its local bank, it applied to the Bank of England to open an account. Such was the firm's reputation that it was immediately granted credit in the enormous amount of £100,000 without any security.[5]

In 1842 Thomas Littledale married Julia Royds, who was from a prominent family in Rochdale, Lancashire. Her father, Clement Royds, was a banker. After their marriage, the younger Littledales probably lived at Oak Hill, adjacent to the grounds of Highfield House. When Thomas Littledale senior died, they moved into Highfield. Thomas and Julia Littledale had six children: Julia, Nora, Edith, Alfred, St. George, and Edmund. All of them grew to maturity, something that could not be taken for granted in those days.[6]

St. George's father had a great love of the sea. He was one of the early members of the Royal Mersey Yacht Club and became its second commodore.[7] He owned a yacht, *Queen of the Ocean*, and participated in many regattas. In 1848 he became involved in one of the most dramatic rescues in British maritime history.

Throughout the 1840s there was a surging transatlantic traffic in immigrants to the New World. Ships that had been making long voyages to the Orient were hastily converted for fast Atlantic trips with human cargo. In August 1848 the 1,300-ton *Ocean Monarch*, crammed with over 300 immigrants, sailed out of Liverpool for Boston. The ship was under full sail about 6 miles off the coast when it caught fire. Men and women clutching children jumped into the ocean and drowned. Burning masts crashed down on the deck. Finally the captain, surrounded on all sides by fire, leaped into the water.

Thomas Littledale was returning from a regatta when he spotted the *Ocean Monarch* in the distance hoisting a distress flag. Then he saw smoke and flames. He turned and sailed his yacht as fast as possible toward the stricken vessel. As he approached, a heavy swell prevented him from pulling alongside the flaming ship but the crew managed to launch the dinghy. Littledale and his guests handled the yacht while the crew rowed out and pulled thirty-two victims from the cold water, transferring them to the yacht. One of the men they rescued was the captain. Other ships joined in the rescue. Over 200 people were saved but 178 lives were lost. Bodies washed up on the beaches of North Wales for weeks.[8] The famous marine artist Samuel Walters made several dramatic paintings showing the progressive stages of the disaster, with the *Queen of the Ocean* and other rescue boats hovering around the stricken *Ocean Monarch*. Numerous other paintings and drawings featured Littledale's yacht.[9]

In the mid-nineteenth century Liverpool was booming. The Industrial Revolution had begun in England, and Liverpool was its port. By the mid-eighteenth century it was the central port of Britain.[10] Then the inventions of the late eighteenth century caused factories to proliferate. In 1830 the first railway in the world was opened between Liverpool and Manchester, linking the port with the great cotton manufacturing area.[11] The citizens of Liverpool constructed the finest docks ever built in England. Herman Melville compared them to the Great Wall of China. By the end of the Victorian Age, Liverpool was among the three or four greatest ports in the world. It had one-seventh of the world's total registered shipping. One in every ten ships sailing the oceans was from Liverpool.[12]

Thomas Littledale senior had served on the town council and was Mayor of Liverpool. Thomas Littledale junior followed his father's example. Chosen to represent the Exchange Ward on the town council, he was also put on the Dock Committee, which at that time ran the great port. After only three years he became chairman, and in 1851 his fellow councillors unanimously elected him mayor. At age thirty-three, the junior Thomas Littledale was the youngest Mayor of Liverpool in over a century. He did well. 'His administration of dock affairs, and his attention to the business of the mayoralty, took the town by surprise as he had generally been looked upon as a man of pleasure rather than of business habits. He showed, however, that he possessed great tact and prudence, and his speeches during his mayoralty displayed considerable ability.'[13]

It was a Liverpool custom that if a child was born to the mayor while he was in office, the leading citizens of the town would present a silver cradle to the mayor's wife. On 6 October 1853 a delegation of over twenty civic leaders gathered at Highfield House to present to Julia

Littledale an elaborate silver 'table ornament' 2ft high. The piece was so unique that a drawing of it appeared in the *Illustrated London News*.[14] Silver figures and a cradle rested on a base decorated with panels illustrating the history of Liverpool. According to the *Liverpool Mercury*, the silver figures represented 'the birth, cradle, and progress of maritime commerce'. Beneath the figures was a poem entitled 'Ye Spirit of Ye Legende':

> Gif Leverpooles good maior sd everre bee
> Made fatherre inne hys yerre off maioraltee
> Thenne sal bee giften bye ye townemenne free
> Ane silverre cradle too hys faire ladye.

The mayor made a short speech to Julia and she replied 'with much dignity and gracefulness of manner. . . .'[15]

The silver cradle presented to Julia Littledale to commemorate the birth of St. George was symbolic of the spirit of the merchant leaders of Liverpool in that dynamic era. The good burghers had the enthusiasm and confidence of miners in a California gold rush town. There was nothing they could not do. The Littledale family was immersed politically, economically and socially in the Liverpool scene. It was in the heady atmosphere of the ruling class of this confident and cosmopolitan city in the wealthiest country in the world that St. George spent his boyhood.

A description of St. George's father appeared in the *Liverpool Mercury* in 1857 when he was still on the Town Council:

> Mr. Littledale is tall in person, most gentlemanly in his manners, generous and kind hearted; indeed, his good tempered face is an index of his mind. . . . His general appearance and manner give the notion that he is a man of great modesty. In spite, however, of his retiring manner, he can display energy when it is requisite. . . . There are few members of the Council more generally popular. . . .[16]

A similar description would later be applied to St. George.

We do not have specific details of St. George's early life but it must not have been easy. In March 1861 Thomas Littledale went to London to see a doctor, and he died suddenly in the doctor's office of a heart ailment. He was 42 years old. A short time later, on a rainy April day, he was buried in a family vault that had just been built at St John's Church a short distance from Highfield House.[17] Despite the bad weather and the family's intention that the funeral be strictly private, a large number of influential but uninvited gentlemen attended and 'a considerable number of the working classes, most of whom resided in the neighbourhood, occupied part of the gallery of the church'. It is unlikely that the nine-year-old boy who rode with his older brother Alfred in the third coach of the funeral procession was aware of this demonstration of the high regard in which his father was held by his fellow citizens.

The year 1866 must have been difficult for St. George. In January he entered Rugby School, a family tradition. He was assigned to a house supervised by the Reverend Philip Bowden Smith, who taught modern languages. The boy had just turned 14. Although Rugby, with its emphasis on character building and its broad curriculum, would appear to have been a suitable school for him, he left after a short time. The reason is unknown.[18]

In August his mother put him back in school, entering him at Shrewsbury, and in October she remarried. Her new husband was Horace Turner, a widower with adult children. He was a retired administrator from Antigua in the British West Indies and had become a prominent Liverpool merchant.[19] Like his father before him, Horace Turner was a member of the powerful Merseyside Dock Board.

A number of Liverpool merchants sent their sons to Shrewsbury to acquire some polish, but it was an inappropriate school for St. George, who was not a good student. However, the relative proximity to his home may have had its advantages. More importantly, Horace Turner was an Old Salopian, as the alumni were called. This connection undoubtedly eased any difficulties St. George may have had in gaining admission.

Shrewsbury was famous for producing scholars. The main curriculum was classics. The other courses were mathematics and French, a concession to modern times and not taken seriously. In fact the sixth form took mathematics and French only on Saturday mornings. Although Old Salopians were found in all professions including the army, a large number of them became professors or clergymen. Shrewsbury students won a disproportionate number of the awards given by Cambridge and Oxford for such skills as writing original verse in Latin and Greek.[20]

St. George's arrival in August 1866 coincided with the arrival of a new headmaster, the Reverend H.W. Moss. Moss was a brilliant product of Shrewsbury's classical education. He was only 25 years old and was to serve as headmaster for forty-two years. When the term began, St. George was the first student to be entered in Moss's first school register. The date was 16 August 1866. His mother had brought him and he was to board with the headmaster.[21] So St. George Littledale, 14 years old, having already attended and left Rugby School, his father dead for five years and his mother about to remarry, entered into another life-shaping experience.

St. George's academic record was mediocre though he displayed some facility for modern languages, an ability that would prove advantageous to him in later years. However, his experiences at Shrewsbury outside the classroom were probably more significant for his development. Moss was cold and distant to the boys. His 19-year-old sister managed the house, and conditions were spartan to say the least. Today if criminals were housed under such conditions, there would be a demand for prison reform. There were four boys to a room, no indoor toilet facilities, no hot water and of course no indoor heating. Drinking water came from a conduit near the school. They bathed under a rain spout, a method not conducive to inspiring cleanliness. Breakfast consisted of bread and milk, lunch was bread and beer, and supper bread and cheese. There were two morning classes, a break until 3 o'clock, and an afternoon class. However the students were not confined to the school premises and could wander about town between roll-calls. Many of the boys had a little money and could supplement their boarding rations with more palatable food available in town.[22]

Unlike Rugby, the school lacked organised sports, but the students engaged in various unsupervised activities on their own. The most popular one was cross-country running done in the form of 'Hare and Hounds'. Every year a club called the Royal Shrewsbury School Hunt organised numerous runs, each with its own special name. The trail was laid out by the 'fox', who left pieces of paper to show the route.[23] A sixth-form boy was master of the hounds, other sixth formers were whippers-in, and the rest were hounds. From time to time the runners would stop to regroup and let the stragglers catch up. The winner was said to have 'killed' the fox. The runners carried sticks with a notch carved in them for each hunt in which they had participated, and if they had killed the fox, they put a cross on their stick. The club assigned each of the hounds an alliterative nickname using the first letter of his last name. St. George Littledale became 'Lazy'. The runs had begun in 1819 and were tolerated but not sanctioned by the school. In 1856 the headmaster tried to stop them unless the boys complied with certain restrictions, one being that at the 'Hounds' Slay', a dinner held at 'Mother Wade's' at the end of the season, 'bitter beer' was allowed but no hard liquor.[24]

On 18 November 1866 St. George earned a place in Shrewsbury School history. After finishing the 7-mile 'Long Run', he passed out and remained unconscious for 12 hours. Among those who witnessed the event was the Reverend G.W. Fisher, a Shrewsbury master who recalled it many years later:

I went with a new master to see the 'run in'. Hearing that there were some boys behind exhausted, I went to meet them and, after a bit came upon the boy in question, supported by two others, and, though with eyes open, evidently unconscious. I took him first into the nearest house and tried to rouse him in various ways till a Fly [carriage] could be procured. Then I brought him home to Jee's Hall and got him put to bed. All sorts of things were tried by the doctors, including mustard plasters on the soles of his feet. I remember one of them putting a feather to Littledale's eyeball without producing the slightest effect. It was about 8am next day before any signs of consciousness appeared.[25]

The episode was an early display of the tremendous determination St. George would exhibit all his life. It also gave the Reverend Moss a welcome excuse to issue regulations, and he eliminated the Long Run entirely because it was too arduous for young growing boys. He also required that the headmaster be informed in advance in writing of any run taking place. Many Old Salopians were dismayed by this affront to their freewheeling traditions but the young headmaster held firm. St. George seemed undeterred by the experience. He made three runs the next year and in one of them he placed second.[26]

St. George left Shrewsbury in 1869 before finishing. He had been there for three years. His ability to compose verse in Latin and Greek may have left something to be desired but his French was passable. It was probably a relief to both him and the headmaster that he did not return for a fourth year. However, his experience there had made him more independent and considerably tougher. If the ability to absorb discomfort is a measure of character, St. George Littledale had developed character.

In 1868 his sister Edith married Alfred Fletcher. Edith was St. George's favourite sibling and he was a groomsman at her wedding. The Fletcher family lived at Allerton, a large estate on the outskirts of the city. William Fletcher, Alfred's father, had married a shipping heiress and was the local agent for the Bank of England. The Fletchers and Littledales would become closely entwined.[27]

After Shrewsbury School, St. George may have found himself at a loose end. In 1870 he clerked in the office of a Mr Lummis, a barrister, and the following year he was a clerk in a mercantile office.[28] He did not remain long. That year he began to travel. He went to Norway, probably for shooting (hunting). We do not know when and where St. George took up either fox hunting or shooting. They were almost mandatory sports for the aristocracy and the wealthy merchant class, and he became extremely proficient at an early age. Apparently his stepfather had no interest in such activities, but it is possible he acquired his enthusiasm and skill from the family of his father's brother, John Bolton Littledale, an accomplished sportsman and hunter living in Tarporley, Cheshire.

At the end of 1872 St. George gained a considerable measure of financial independence when he turned 21 and came into the inheritance left to him by his father, which included a substantial income and the Oak Hill estate next to Highfield. In the nineteenth century it was the custom for the children of the British upper classes to finish off their education by going on a 'Grand Tour' of Europe. With the advent of the steamship and the steam locomotive, Europe began to seem limited, and it was a relatively small step to send the more adventurous ones around the world. Bolstered by the income from his recent inheritance, St. George decided on the world tour.

In January 1874 a young and confident St. George Littledale started around the world. His first stop was the British West Indies, where his stepfather had been stationed. He went to Barbados and then took an inter-island steamer to Antigua. He shot many birds, skinning them and sending them home from Havana or New Orleans. Horace Turner must have given him letters of introduction, for he dined with the bishop and the governor. He also rode an old horse that Turner had bought when he lived in Antigua. St. George may have been a little homesick. 'As far as I have seen there is not a good horse in the island, not one as handsome as Shoofly. . . . I think on a cool evening here you could quite well suppose you were in England in summer.'

From Antigua he went to St. Thomas, where he would catch a ship for Havana on 16 February. His plans were indefinite. 'I suppose I shall be in New Orleans in about 3 weeks or a month. . . . I have been inhaled into the mysteries of cane crushing and sugar boiling. Tell Mr. Turner he will . . . be able to account for the small crop this year by the number of canes I have eaten.'[29]

On 28 April St. George wrote to his mother from Chicago. He had visited New Orleans and gone to New York City, which he left before his clothes arrived. He had moved on to Canada, where he visited both houses of Parliament in Ottawa. He wrote:

Tell Alfred [his brother] that if [he] did not find the Severn sufficiently difficult that there is a small brook here called the Niagara River which would finish, if it did not satisfy, him. I was very much pleased with the falls. . . . It looked very grand to see huge blocks of ice come flying right over your head and drop down below the ice on which we were standing. I was almost glad to leave Niagara as I had quite an inclination to go and throw myself in. I saw a rock close to the edge where a man clung for two days. They let a boat down with a rope and he got in. They dragged him to shore but he jumped too soon, fell in, and went over. A week later they found a leg of his trousers.

In Chicago he visited General Philip Sheridan, the famous Union cavalry leader, to obtain letters granting him access to some military posts in the west. Sheridan was commanding the Department of the Missouri. St. George's plans remained flexible. 'I shall leave here for St. Louis tomorrow night and I shall only remain there one day so unless I get some shooting on the way, I shall soon be [in] San Fran. . . .' He added that he would not be in California after June, and suggested that letters be sent to a contact in Japan.[30]

St. George found the opportunity to shoot on the way. He spent two months hunting in Estes Park, Colorado, where Rocky Mountain National Park is today. He shot thirteen mountain sheep and three wapiti (elk) as well as deer. There was snow on the ground making it easy to track the animals.[31] We do not know when he reached San Francisco. When he wrote to his sister Nora in early August from Yokohama, he had already been in Japan for some time and had met up with a man from Hong Kong to climb Mount Fuji:

A Japanese cook who I had sent for from Yokohama joined me and we started up the hill. I found my man swindling me but not being able to speak the language, could not do much. At last we joined a young Dane who spoke Japanese and he told us that my man had done us more than I suspected but still we must have a cook of some sort so we went on. . . .

We came to a rest house on the mountain. The cook went in to make a bargain and came out with an extortionate price but offered to let the Dane in for nothing if he would not tell us so we did not stop there but went on. . . . While we were talking about the price, the cook would tell them to charge us double or treble. At last I had the pleasure of breaking my Alpenstock across his face but he still came with us swollen face and all. He had joined with two coolies at the bottom of the hill and they all twice followed into a hut where we were going to sleep. . . . The half of my Alpenstock made a very good weapon and our troubles did not last long.

They came within 200ft of the top but a powerful storm kept them from reaching the summit:

. . . if I had been the whole of Japan I could not have got any higher. . . . Going down . . . the wind behind you lifted you almost into the air.

We came down in 9 minutes, what took us the night before 2½ hours to go up. I found the cook waiting for me at the tea house at the bottom . . . but revenge made them send in a bill which to put in mild terms was at least 10 times what it ought to have been. We found they had charged for a table and the window shutters so we made out our own bill and paid our own price.[32]

What should have been a fairly routine climb turned out to be a miniature expedition and gave St. George a taste of what can happen. Mount Fuji is a pilgrimage for thousands of Japanese going from hut to hut with their special alpenstocks that are branded at each hut. They have a saying, 'May our five senses be pure and may the weather on the mountain be fair.' St. George learned what a difference weather can make on a mountain. He was also exposed to the perversity of human nature. The cook's behaviour was extremely provocative but the brash 22-year-old Englishman grossly overreacted. Giving vent to his anger in such a violent manner may have been impulsive and undisciplined youth, but he must have learned that his conduct was both outrageous and counterproductive. There is no evidence that St. George Littledale ever did that again. He handled future confrontations with calculated subtlety and self-control.

After his attempt on Mount Fuji, he travelled into the interior of Japan. 'It was not unmitigated pleasure as the fleas were simply fearful. I am prepared to bet that I have more than 1,000 bites on my body now. . . .'[33] Nonetheless, St. George longed for still more adventure. He had heard about the bears on Hokkaido, the northernmost island of Japan, known at that time as Yesso. It was the home of the Ainu, the original inhabitants of Japan to whom the bear was sacred. Even today, with its mountains, forests and lakes, it is Japan's last frontier.

St. George and a companion named Mitchell booked passage on a small steamer to Hakodate on the south-west tip of the island, and then travelled by pony and canoe. They reached Sapporo, the capital, and went up the Ishikari River. It was hard work in rough country and they never saw any bears. Riding on crude pack saddles, they were 'eaten alive' by mosquitoes and fleas while dealing with swamps, cane brakes and numerous rivers and streams. After a month they returned to Sapporo.

The trip back to Hakodate was unusually difficult. A typhoon had struck the island earlier, flooding the countryside, making rivers unfordable and destroying the roads. When Littledale and Mitchell reached the coast, tremendous breakers were crashing against the shore. They rode their ponies for 9 hours on the uncomfortable pack saddles to a little port only to learn there was no steamer going to Hakodate.

However, a 45-ft schooner was leaving so they climbed on board. Unfortunately, the crew had not sailed the boat before and was not very adept at doing so. St. George, an experienced sailor, stayed on deck to help. 'They did not know how to take in a reef without lowering the mainsail. If they had lowered it we would have broached to and had the deck swept.' Once he went out on the end of the boom and yelled to the crew to keep the sheet tight, 'when some idiot slacked it off & at the same time ran her right up into the wind & so the boom swung from side to side with me clinging to it . . . & down I fell. Luckily I was over the boat & landed on the top of the Japanese who I had given the helm to when I went out on the boom.'

When they finally returned to Hakodate, they learned there was no steamer to Yokohama and sometimes months went by before a ship came. Moreover, permits they had requested for travel overland had not arrived. Lady Parkes, wife of the British ambassador, and her children were in Hakodate to avoid the hot weather, and it had been arranged to send the HMS *Thalia* for them if there was no steamer. After another two weeks a ship arrived with the passes for overland travel. Mitchell decided to go overland but St. George waited still longer and took the steamer with Lady Parkes and her family. It was a rough voyage through the edge of another typhoon. By the time he arrived in Yokohama, a ship he was supposed to take to Shanghai had sailed. There would be no steamer for another week. He had missed his boat and it would change his life.[34]

4

Together

A man needs a companion for life.
Without one, the world truly is a desolate place.

Tibetan proverb[1]

It was 22 October 1874 when St. George Littledale arrived in
Yokohama to find that his ship had sailed. By coincidence he ran into
an old schoolmate from Shrewsbury, Charles Davis. He knew Davis
well because they had both boarded with the Reverend Moss. St.
George wrote, '. . . he and I have joined Mr. and Mrs. Scott who are
also globe trotting. They are <u>so very nice</u>.' Although St. George could
have met Teresa on his own, Davis was probably the link between
them.

Teresa and St. George wasted no time getting better acquainted. On
26 October they spent an entire day shopping together. Two days later
St. George joined Willie and Teresa on a sightseeing trip to Tokyo. The
next day the Scotts sailed for Shanghai on the *Costa Rica*. Also on
board were Charles Davis and St. George Littledale.[2]

On the second day out Teresa wrote, 'Very rough and I was very sick
in the morning but dressed and went on deck where Mr. Littledale took
care of me. Willie did not get up until dinner time.'[3] The following day
the weather was better and Teresa and St. George played cards. The
next day they reached Kobe, where a local English banker invited the
Scotts to lunch. They took St. George with them. For the next several
days they sailed through the Inland Sea to Nagasaki. The water was
filled with small Japanese junks. One night the ship ran over a junk and
had to rescue its crew. They reached Nagasaki late in the evening and
left for Shanghai the next afternoon.

They arrived on the morning of 7 November and the Scotts went
straight to the Astor House, where they were given a cottage on the
grounds. Littledale and Davis stayed with them. That afternoon they
enjoyed the races and a cricket match. For several days they wandered
around Shanghai while planning a trip on the Grand Canal. St. George
accompanied Teresa on her excursions. 'Mr. Littledale and I went to the
native walled town. It is frighteningly dirty and the stones so slippery

one can hardly walk. . . . We went to see a temple. The curio shops are pretty good but everything very dear.' The next night Teresa and St. George rode in a rickshaw. 'There is a seat on each side. Mr. Davis tried to wheel it and nearly upset us and then Mr. Littledale tried to wheel Mr. Davis and I. Mr. Davis suddenly jumped off and nearly sent me flying as I had nothing to balance [with]. We all had a good laugh.'[4]

The Grand Canal runs 650 miles between Hangzhou and Tientsin and connects the Yangtze with the Yellow River. Begun about AD300, it was second only to the Great Wall as the largest engineering project in the history of China.[5]

They spent fifteen leisurely days on the canal, with the Scotts in one boat and St. George and Charles in the other. They made frequent stops for shooting. When they reached Hangzhou, they stayed only briefly, visited a pagoda, and then resumed the journey. St. George seemed to prefer shooting to sightseeing. His talent for the sport was evident, although he was about to make a terrible mistake.

Teresa's diary gives a good picture of their routine: 'Friday, Nov. 13th. "China" Grand Canal. The usual life. We keep moving on. Mr. Littledale and Mr. Davis shoot in the morning, return to tiffin [lunch] and shoot again in the afternoon. Willie and I walk in the morning and again in the afternoon. We dined with them. The weather beautiful. Played whist.' The next day she wrote, 'We have been stationary today as the shooting is good here. Mr. Littledale shot a deer. Mr. Davis cannot shoot at all. Never hits anything. Willie and I walked. The Chinese people are very civil to us and very curious about me. They say my clothes are "not good warm." They dined with us and we tiffined with them.'

From the diary it would appear that the main activities were shooting, walking, and alternating meals on each other's boat. 'We dined with them. They tiffined with us.' 'Tiffined with them. They dined with us.' On 15 November life suddenly became more serious and exciting:

> Remained stationary in the same place as yesterday. Shot as usual in the morning but not in the afternoon. Mr. Littledale fired at a pheasant and shot a Chinaman!!!!! Consequently we moved on a few miles. The Chinaman howled terribly. He was shot in the leg. Mr. Littledale paid him $5. The usual price of shooting a man is $2. Mr. Littledale was in an awful fright. At first he did not know how much he had shot him. We dined with them. They tiffined with us. They skinned birds all the afternoon.

Evenings were spent at cards. 'We play whist every night. Mr. Littledale and I always win.' They also played little games during meals.

'They [St. George and Charles] took a great deal of trouble to write us out a menu in French. We had great fun over it for it was full of mistakes.' Yet Teresa could not ignore her human surroundings. 'A lot of Chinese men and women came down to the boat. One woman offered me her baby. I declined with thanks. One woman showed me her foot, which had been made small. It was a fearful deformity. The instep was pressed up in an arch. The bone must be almost broken.'

Upon their return to Shanghai, they took a small coastal steamer, the *Dragon*, to Fuzhou, where they had to change to a larger vessel. The ship was delayed and they spent 5 days in Fuzhou waiting for it. Teresa's diary continues to focus on St. George. 'Mr. Littledale and I went ashore and for a long walk over the hills. The views are lovely. We should be very dull without him.' They reached Hong Kong on 9 December. The next day Teresa wrote, 'Out with Mr. Littledale all the morning and in the afternoon we went to the top of the hill where one gets a splendid view.' They visited Canton for 5 days, returned to Hong Kong, and went on to Saigon and Singapore.[6]

Although St. George Littledale was only twenty-two, already he must have displayed his 'charming', even 'enchanting', personality, words used by many people to describe him in later years. He seems to have swept the 35-year-old Teresa off her feet. At the very least, she was infatuated with him. In her diary she mentions him more than the places they visited, and she refers to her husband of fifteen years so infrequently that one is barely aware of Willie's presence.

From Singapore they went to Java and visited Batavia (Jakarta). 'Mr. Littledale and I went for a walk but it was too hot.' They went up to Buitengong (Bogor) and stayed in a hotel with a 'lovely view over the valley with the "Salak" volcano beyond'. Willie was not well. He thought it was prickly heat but Teresa thought it was more serious than that. Despite Willie's incapacity, she still had an escort. 'Mr. Littledale and I drove out to the baths. . . . In the afternoon Mr. Littledale and I walked in the gardens.' 'Mr. Littledale and I went out for a very pretty drive this morning.' Several days later they returned to Batavia and sailed back to Singapore, arriving there on 6 January 1875.

St. George was to leave the Scotts for two months to go hunting in India. Teresa wrote, 'The French steamer in which Mr. Littledale goes on is not yet in. I am very glad. I shall miss him very much when he is gone. He is so good about taking me out. I felt very grateful to him for thinking of giving up his journey . . . to stay with us if Mr. Scott was going to be ill. . . . Mr. Littledale and I went out to see about steamers.' They also went shopping together. 'I bought such a pretty pair of fire screens from Canton made with blue feathers and embroidery on silk $12 a pair.' The next day St. George sailed for India. 'So sorry to see him go. I do not know what I shall do without him since Willie has been ill and unable to go out. I have been so dependant upon him and he has been so kind to me. We both like him very much. He meets us again in Calcutta in March if he does not change his mind, which is more than probable.'[7]

Three weeks later St. George was in the Nilgiri Hills of southern India. They rise abruptly on the western side of the subcontinent to a height of over 8,500ft with high rocky precipices and slopes covered with sholahs (thickets). The British built several hill stations there to escape from the heat of the plains. The most important was Ootacamund, commonly called Ooty. St. George arrived at Silk's Hotel, where there was only one other guest, Edmund Loder, another young Englishman. It was the beginning of a lifelong friendship. They both wanted to hunt the Nilgiri tahr (mountain goat) so they joined forces. Both men were expert shots, and St. George bagged the second largest Nilgiri tahr on record. He then made a quick trip down to Bandipur in an unsuccessful hunt for bison. By 1 March he was in Madras, where he caught the P&O steamer to Calcutta.[8]

Meanwhile, the Scotts remained in Singapore for a while. Willie was still not feeling well. 'I have been laid up for the last fortnight with prickly heat so bad that I can hardly bear the clothes on my back & I cannot go about at all.'[9] Eventually they left for Burma, spending several days at Moulmain. Teresa went ashore with the captain of the ship, visiting a Buddhist temple ruin and some caves with Buddhist images and ceilings black with bats. St. George was on her mind. 'I miss Mr. Littledale in the expedition ashore terribly. Willie was afraid to go.'

After a visit to Rangoon, the Scotts sailed for Calcutta where they stayed for nearly a month, apparently waiting for St. George to arrive. They spent their time socialising. Willie sent a letter of introduction to Government House, resulting in dinner with Lord Northbrook, the viceroy. There were about forty-five guests including the Maharaja of Travancore. One night they went to the opera and saw *Lucretia Borgia*. Teresa thought it 'very badly done and the very ugliest actors and actresses I ever saw'.[10] Willie was impressed with Calcutta, '. . . the most flourishing city we have been in. Everything seems to thrive & men make money fast.' Teresa had another view. 'I think the ladies of Calcutta look very Calcutta-ish, rather second-rate.'[11] Her judgment may have been clouded by a bad mood stemming from her enforced idleness and St. George's absence.

On 6 March St. George finally arrived. He met the Scotts just as they were returning from a walk. Four days later he wrote to his mother, 'We are going to start tonight for Benares, then on to Delhi, Lucknow,

Cawnpore, etc. They [the Scotts] have persuaded me to go up to Cashmere with them so there will be another delay before I return. . . . It is a very delightful place, splendid scenery and living very cheap.' He was being less than candid with his mother in extolling the virtues of Kashmir while suggesting the Scotts had talked him into it. He had long since decided to go there. In a letter dated 27 January, Edmund Loder wrote, 'He [St. George] proposes going into Cashmere in April – I expect he will get good shooting there at that season.' Teresa wanted to go with St. George, and when the time came for the expedition, Willie must have felt obliged to go along. He was not enthusiastic. 'I wish we were going to spend the summer at Eldon instead of in this beastly hot country.'[12] Twenty-four years older than St. George and in poor health, he was not suited for the rough adventure.

Kashmir was well known for its hunting, a principal recreation for the British in India, especially army officers. They took extended leave to shoot ibex and markhor (wild goats) in the remote mountains, where the nullahs (large gullies) teemed with game. April, May, and June were prime months for hunting in Kashmir.

The party left Calcutta on the evening of 10 March as planned and arrived in Benares the following evening. After several days in Benares, with its burning funeral pyres on the ghats beside the Ganges, the trio went on to Lucknow, where they visited the ruins of the Residency in which the British had been besieged during the Indian Mutiny. By 18 March they had reached Agra. Teresa wrote, 'Went in the afternoon . . . to see the Taj. It is perfectly lovely beyond all description. It is built entirely of white marble inlaid.' It was the last entry in her diary.[13]

It is almost two months before there is any further record of their activities. Both St. George and Willie wrote letters from Kashmir in mid-May at the end of a long trip. Most of their time had been spent hunting, and from that standpoint it was a successful expedition. St. George shot 9 bear, 6 ibex, 3 musk deer and 1 barasingh (Kashmir stag).[14] Willie, however, wrote that they were leaving early and returning to England, partly because of his bad leg:

We are quite out of the world here. I have not seen a paper for six weeks. We are 60 miles from a Post Office and it takes a Coolie a week to get there and back. We have had a rough time of it lately & the roads or rather tracks are so bad, that we can only get on by walking which I don't think suits me. I bought two nice ponys for myself & wife . . . but we were obliged to leave them behind in one of the passes of the Himalays a fortnight ago on account of the snow & I have not seen them since. We had to tramp for ten miles (7 hours work) through the snow & camp on the first bit of dry ground we could find. I don't think there is one woman in fifty could or would have done it for pleasure. . . . We have about 40 coolies, 60 with Mr. Littledale's, when we are on the march to carry our tents, luggage, etc. . . . The coolies have to carry about a maund each [80lb] on their backs 10 or 15 miles a day – for this they get the large sum of 3 pence.[15]

There is no exact record of where they went but they probably visited the Astor region near Nanga Parbat.

It had been a major excursion. When they returned to Srinagar, Willie had had enough but still there was no rest. They left early on 16 May, hoping to sail on the *Italia* out of Bombay on the 29th. It would not be easy. First they had to get to Rawalpindi, by boat and then on horseback with porters carrying their loads. From Rawalpindi they would take the train to Bombay. St. George wrote, 'I don't at all look forward to 3 days in the train for Bombay nor do I expect the Red Sea to be an especial pleasure.' As they left the Vale of Kashmir, their opinions differed. Teresa thought it was beautiful. Willie had a darker view as evidenced by the end of his letter to Edward: 'Teresa writes to your mother [by the] same post as takes this – she will say what she thinks of Cashmere no doubt. I think it is a humbug and going through a great deal to find out very little, as Mr. Weller said of matrimony.' He ended with a postscript: 'love to all at Eldon. The time we had there was the only enjoyable time to me we had this year.'[16] There had to have been more than ill health behind this comment. Scott had gone to extraordinary lengths to please Teresa, but her uncharacteristic silence after the visit to the Taj Mahal may well indicate she was having an affair with Littledale. Either way, the situation must have been terribly distressing for Willie.

Their efforts to reach Bombay in time were in vain. St. George wrote, 'We had a tremendous race all the way down from Srinagar to catch a steamer on the 29th but she never went. The "Macedonia" went instead on the 27th & we just missed her by one day having taken double marches all the way for about 170 or 80 miles.' He was also worried about their new transportation home, a dirty old rust bucket. 'I trust my precious body on board the "S.S. Palestine" which sails tomorrow.'[17]

Willie had serious qualms about the voyage itself. 'I can't say I look forward without dread to our long & hard journey home. Tropical heat & winter snow is all alike to my cork leg but these sudden changes don't suit me.'[18] However, he was reasonably well when the *Palestine* left Bombay on 30 May. Even so, things were not comfortable on the ship, and only two days out, whenever the Scotts wanted something they were told it was used up. Then three days out of port the ship's baker died of 'heat apoplexy'. He had been active at 10 o'clock but by noon he was dead.

The tragedy reinforced Scott's fears. He began saying that half of them would not get through the Red Sea alive. Several days later he complained of internal pains and he could not eat anything. He spent the days either lying down or resting in a lounge chair. His condition continued to deteriorate. Ten days after the onset of his illness, the ship's doctor concluded he had typhoid fever. When the *Palestine* arrived at Aden, St. George and Teresa went ashore and returned with Trilby's extract of meat, the only thing Willie would eat. They had also obtained 150lb of ice that the steward told them would last until Suez, but it melted in two days.

By now Willie was much worse. St. George described his final days. 'He was delirious most of the time for the last three days not knowing anybody. The night before he died he was conscious for a minute or two and said Teresa 3 times. He died about a quarter past one in the daytime. . . . I was so seedy myself that I could not nurse him. Mrs. Scott was dreadfully tired and in great grief.' It was 16 June 1875. They were one day out of Suez.[19]

St. George to the rescue. Littledale took charge immediately. He wrote to the family and took on the complex arrangements to return the body to England. A few hours after Scott's death, he wrote to Eliza Crutchley:

When he died I took [Teresa] down to her cabin & the Doctor brought her a sleeping draught but it was some time before she went off. She was much more composed when she awoke & she went to say the last goodbye & cut off some of his hair. Afterwards she gave me a lock of her hair & asked me for a photo she had given me & at her request I had them placed on his heart. She could not bear the idea of his being buried in the sea, so we are going to try & have a lead coffin made at Suez & have it sent home by the first steamer that will take it, but it is quite probable that they will refuse to let it be landed & if so it will have to be taken back again out to sea. . . . I expect the steamer will arrive in Liverpool between the 3rd and 6th of July. . . . I shall still try & make her take a rest at home for two or three days before she goes to Wick Hill. I will write to you again from Port Said. . . . I am so very sorry as it is such a blow to her, what an ending to such a pleasant 15 months.[20]

Getting Scott's body back to England would not be simple. First of all, it would be a long voyage. 'The old tub was never guilty of more than 8½ knots.' Because Scott had died of typhoid, the authorities would not let the body be unloaded at Suez. Worse, they would not even let the ship go though the canal. St. George quickly solved that problem. He could not alter the cause of death but he could alter the certification of it. 'I gave the health officer 5 pounds & he winked at it – gave a wrong certificate etc.'[21] The official Marine Register of Deaths lists the cause of death as 'enteritis'.

The next problem was the coffin. St. George managed to obtain enough lead at Suez to enable the ship's crew to make one. Even so, he doubted it would work because of the intense heat. He also orchestrated arrangements in England. He invited the Crutchleys to stay with his mother in Liverpool and he wrote to his mother asking her to invite them.

Finally there was the matter of moving the coffin. He instructed his mother, 'Will you . . . ask Alfred [his brother] to have some arrangement made with an undertaker about receiving a coffin weighing 19 or 20 cwt [about 2,000lb] but not to bind himself as it is possible it may not keep airtight & then overboard it will have to go.' St. George was thinking of everything. No point in wasting money on a binding contract when it might not be necessary. As for Teresa, he wrote to her brother Edward, 'Mrs. Scott seems to get more cheerful every hour. . . .'[22]

The *Palestine* arrived in Liverpool on 6 July and was met by Eliza Crutchley and Edward Harris, who was visiting England with his wife. Sophia wrote to Teresa's mother, 'What a great comfort Mr. Littledale has been to Teresa. His Mother [Mrs Turner] asked the whole party to her house at Liverpool. . . . Eliza and Teresa were there three days and received the greatest kindness. The family are very rich and have about the finest place in Liverpool 4 miles from town.'[23]

Teresa and Eliza returned to Bracknell three days later. The next morning, 10 July, they went to Easthampstead Parish Church to put flowers on the coffin in preparation for the funeral that afternoon. At the service the only mourners present besides Teresa were Edward and Sophia Harris, the Crutchleys, a few distant Scott relatives, and David Scott Moncrieff from Edinburgh, who handled some of Scott's investments. Mary Peard may have been there as well. After the service, Scott was buried in the churchyard. Sophia wrote, 'Teresa was much overcome and said she never realised Mr. Scott's death before, but after dinner she was cheerful again and today quite herself. Eliza says she is too sensible to make any demonstration but will of course do what is English and proper.'[24] Life would go on.

In fact life had long since been going on – for eight months. Why did St. George have a picture of Teresa that she took back to place on

Willie's body? They had been travelling together and he would not have needed it. She must have given it to him back in early January when he left for India. By that time he had already been with the Scotts for over two months.

It is difficult to assess William John Scott. One is inclined to think of him as a bland preliminary act that precedes the colourful main event. His marrying Teresa and then dying and leaving her his fortune was instrumental in making possible her subsequent remarkable life. However, his memory deserves better than that. When he first appears in the pages of Amelia Harris's diary one has the impression he was just a wealthy lightweight. He participated in the activities of the upper class such as hunting, shooting and the races, but he was not comfortable with the social life that Teresa craved. He did not feel a need to prove himself, and he even made fun of being admitted to an exclusive London club. He could be a fine host but there was a rough edge to him and he did not care. His later correspondence reveals a different side to his character. In his business letters he emerges as a decent and competent man. He was supervising investments, many in Canada, and his judgments were perceptive. Even more striking is the restraint he showed in dealing with the mishandling of his business affairs by Edward Harris. Scott treated the Harris family as if it was his own, or perhaps even better. Edward consistently mismanaged investments for all his brothers-in-law, losing their money and not bothering to send them statements or even their own money when it was due. In contrast to the Dalzells and Peards, Scott had financial resources, enabling him to display an unusually high level of tolerance towards Edward, just as he had done with other members of the family who were manipulating him even before he married Teresa. He invited his new mother-in-law to live with them in England, and he lived at Eldon House for two years. There must have been other reasons besides looking after his investments. Perhaps he needed a family because his own family in Scotland was so limited.

Scott's relationship with Teresa was unusual. She was considerably younger, and initially he treated her as his 'pet', indulging her every materialistic whim. However, she had the impression that his business activities and his horses took priority over her. Teresa complained many times to her sister Mary that Scott left her too much to herself. Yet he was willing to shape his life to her wants, as dramatically illustrated by his sitting in the mud baths of Bad Kissingen for three months. The journeys to the Middle East and around the world were for his wife. With his fragile health and his susceptibility to seasickness, he disliked travel. Teresa, however, was unhappy unless she was travelling, and so he paid for the trips and participated reluctantly. Furthermore, he apparently said nothing when she attracted men like a magnet. But Scott could not have been happy. There is a cryptic line in a letter from Eliza Crutchley to Sophia Harris: 'The heart is such an easy thing to know about and S. seems to have been going to the bad for the last two years.'[25] He and Teresa had not been suited for each other. Sickly and glum, he was not good company but he was a good man.

After the funeral Teresa stayed with the Crutchleys at Brooks Lodge, Sunninghill, where she received both emotional and practical support. Charles Crutchley, Eliza's husband, had made the arrangements for Scott's funeral and was named an executor of his estate, which was considerable. Scott's assets were divided between Canada and Scotland. They included £30,000 worth of real estate and mortgages in Canada, £19,000 in shares in various English railways and mines and £11,000 in shares in the National Bank of Scotland. Wick Hill House and its contents were estimated to be worth about £7,000. In 1875 that was a substantial amount of money. The widow would be all right financially.[26]

Teresa remained with the Crutchleys until mid-August while Wick Hill House was being refurbished. She planned to wear a widow's cap for six months and to stay in mourning for one full year. For the first few weeks she made occasional trips to Wick Hill and visited Willie's grave, but she remained at Brooks Lodge. After she returned to Wick Hill, the Dalzells visited. They had missed the funeral. Sarah wrote, 'She . . . so feels her husband's death & the loneliness of Wickhill very much . . . the Morning Room poor Scott used always to sit in . . . is full of sad memories.'[27] Teresa's life remained quiet. 'Sometimes for nearly a week I do not once speak to a creature excepting to give an order to a servant. . . .' Eliza wrote, 'She looks thin & ill and having to manage all her affairs worries her.'[28]

One thing Teresa had to worry about was managing her money. She asked Edward to send her £5,000 because she thought it unwise to keep everything in the Ontario Savings Bank, 'not that it was unsafe but I do think it a mistake to place all ones eggs in one basket'.[29] Others may have been handling her finances but Teresa kept a close and knowing eye on them.

As time went on she gradually became more active while adhering to a strict code. She exchanged visits with friends, yet refrained from attending dinners or parties. 'I never go anywhere. . . . A Mr. Davis came to see me on Tuesday. He crossed the Pacific with us, and we saw a good deal of him in Japan and China. I was very glad to see him again.'[30] Then there were the Kings. 'Mr. King is a queer mixture.

I believe he has taken a great fancy to me.' Sophia Harris wrote, 'He wants to ride down to Wick Hill by himself. It is funny what friends they have become.'[31]

Church played an important part in Teresa's life just as it had for her mother, and she attended Sunday services whenever possible. And she had not forgotten Willie. She went to London and met with the renowned artist Edward Coley Burne-Jones to arrange for two stained glass windows in Willie's memory for Easthampstead Parish Church. It may have been a combination of love and guilt, but Teresa wanted the best for her late husband. Burne-Jones's exquisite windows can be found in many English churches including Christ Church, Oxford, and Birmingham Cathedral.[32]

Among an increasing number of visitors to Wick Hill was St. George Littledale, and he must have visited frequently. In May 1876 Sophia wrote from Wick Hill, 'I wish you could see how Mr. Littledale hops about from morning till night. There is not a thing Teresa can do without his assistance and he generally does it all. By this time he ought to be intimately acquainted with the contents of every bureau and drawer she owns.' After he left, Sophia commented that Teresa seemed lost without him.[33]

Sometime in the late summer St. George went to Newfoundland for hunting. During his absence, his mother Julia Turner took Teresa to Llandudno, Wales, for a week or so. Teresa told her mother Amelia that she was going to Wales but did not mention that it was St. George's mother who had invited her. This was out of character for Teresa. Usually she described to Amelia the high social status of her hostesses, their wealth and their large estates. Why did she not mention the wealthy and prominent Julia Turner?

Upon her return, Teresa began making arrangements to rent out Wick Hill House for a long time. She told Amelia she was planning a trip to the Middle East. She wrote, 'There are a good many things in this world pleasanter in theory than reality. Solitude is one of them.' Yet a Middle East trip does not make sense. It would not have cured her loneliness, and with St. George in the picture, she would not have wanted to be away for so long. She and St. George must have already decided to marry and to rent out Wick Hill House during a long honeymoon. His mother knew about the plan, which would explain the invitation to Wales. Teresa knew that her own mother would strongly disapprove of the marriage, so she and St. George probably decided to keep the news to themselves as long as possible while arranging their elaborate honeymoon.

St. George returned from Newfoundland in early November.[34] On 6 December Teresa was in Taunton visiting the Peards. Mary wrote,

'I never saw Teresa looking better, younger or in better spirits. . . . Helen says she is not the same woman she was last winter & Shuldham sees a great difference in her since June, but she is so close about everything.'[35] Teresa went on to Sidmouth to visit the Dalzells, but that was as far as she got. In hot pursuit was St. George Littledale. For months he had been fluttering around her like a moth near a flame. Finally he flew into it and proposed. Teresa accepted. At least that is the sequence of events in Teresa's version to her mother: 'He followed me down here and it has all happened since I have been with Sarah.' No one was surprised and almost everyone in the Harris family disapproved.

Teresa wrote to Amelia, 'I know that you will regret the difference of age which of course is a pity and I am sorry for it, but we have learnt to like each other and I would never have married anybody else, caring for him as much as I do. . . . I am glad to say that both Colonel Dalzell and Sarah like him very much. He has nearly £3,000 a year and I do think I know him well enough to say that he has not a vice.'[36]

After Christmas Teresa went to Liverpool to visit St. George's sister, Edith Fletcher. Teresa liked the Fletchers but her interfering brother-in-law, Robert Dalzell, was there as well, and it did not take long for trouble to start over money. Teresa wrote, '. . . Colonel Dalzell has argued and squabbled with Mr. Littledale and Mr. Fletcher. It seems to me if a man offers to settle £20,000, Col. Dalzell immediately thinks if he offers that much, he must be able and ought to offer £40,000.'[37]

The twelve-year age difference was the focus of everyone's disapproval. Moreover, the generational age difference between St. George and Scott was striking. The overall impression of St. George was reasonably favourable, at least at first, but everyone in the large Harris family threw in their opinions, just like the old days at Eldon House. Mary Peard took the most positive position. 'It is very odd, that the Littledales all seem to like the marriage and I do not hear that his mother has complained of her age. It is a great pity as the marriage seems to be very good in every other way and Crutchley says his connections are very good.'[38] However, Sarah Dalzell wrote, 'The Littledales are a highly respectable people and family but in quite a different circle to any of us. He gains connections by his marriage.'[39] This reveals more about the Dalzells than about the wealthy and prominent Littledales. Robert Dalzell was the impoverished son of a Marquis. At that time it was still customary for the nobility to look down upon businessmen, even highly successful ones, for being engaged in trade. The Dalzells were hard-pressed for money so they clung to their status all the more.

Teresa kept trying to reassure her mother. 'I do not suppose I should have learnt to care for Mr. Littledale had we not been thrown together as we were, but having learnt to care for him it would be marrying him or nobody and young as he is I do not think I am wrong in trusting him. He is amiable, religious and well principled and I think I must know him pretty well. . . .' Later she wrote, 'I am sorry dearest Mother that you are so displeased with me for marrying as I am doing but I suppose there is always a risk in a marriage. . . . The danger for me is that my young husband may repent in a few years having married an older wife than himself. . . . I do think it is my one danger. He is very sensible and amiable, never drinks anything, and is perfectly steady.' St. George wrote, '. . . how sorry I am that you disapprove of my marriage with your daughter. . . . We were thrown together at a time when perhaps we learnt to know each other better than years of an ordinary acquaintance, and for her sake I hope to gain in time the affection of her family.'[40]

The similarity of thought and the identical phrase, 'thrown together', indicate that Teresa and St. George collaborated on their story to Amelia. It is unclear when the Harris family was made aware of St. George. Although he and Teresa had been travelling together for eight months before Scott died, their letters to Eldon House give the impression that somehow they were 'thrown together' as a result of Scott's death. Amelia did not change her mind.

What attracted Teresa and St. George to each other despite their diverse backgrounds and age difference? Money was not an issue. Both had it. Teresa must have been drawn to St. George by his great personal charm, masculinity, energy, and love of travel and adventure. She wanted to see and do everything and he was someone with whom she could do it. If she married him, the exciting life she craved was guaranteed. Teresa was not beautiful, but St. George would have been attracted by her lively, exuberant personality and her passion for everything new and foreign. She was willing to endure the arduous travel and rough camping required to experience remote wild areas. Not many women in that period would have enjoyed that kind of life. The couple were well suited. They made a good team. Essentially, two adventurous people had found each other.

The church that Teresa and St. George selected for their wedding was St George's Hanover Square in London. However, the bride-to-be was required to live in the parish for three weeks in order to be married there. Teresa went to London on 31 January and stayed with her friends, the Kings, on Albemarle Street. St. George was not idle. 'Mr. Littledale has been here most of the time and we have been sending a good many things out to India to meet us for we are going out to Cashmere.'[41]

They wanted a quiet wedding attended only by the immediate family. There would be no wedding breakfast. Besides the rector, the only non-family member invited was Teresa's hostess, Mrs King. Her husband did not want anything to do with the marriage. 'Mr. King has a good deal given me up. I suited him very well as a widow! but with a husband attached the fun disappears.'

Teresa had ordered a dark brown silk and velvet wedding dress from Paris. When it arrived, she found that quantities of pale blue fabric had been added as trimming and furthermore it did not fit. She was suffering from a bad cold so she turned the dress project over to Mary Peard only four days before the wedding. Her sister somehow managed to have a dress made in time for the ceremony. It was ivory satin with matching shoes and stockings. Mary thought the bride looked lovely. We do not know what Teresa thought.[42]

There was a more serious problem than the wedding dress. Thanks to meddling by well-meaning others, the marriage settlement was falling apart. The Harris family thought Teresa was being too liberal with her money. The situation became so deadlocked that it could be resolved only by arbitration. Teresa selected General Crutchley to represent her, St. George chose Alfred Fletcher, and at the last minute those two gentlemen worked it out. St. George settled £10,000 on Teresa, the equivalent of almost half a million pounds today. They signed the settlement on 26 February. The ceremony could proceed.

The next day, 27 February 1877, St. George Littledale married Teresa Scott at St George's. The service was conducted by Osborne Gordon, the old rector at Easthampstead Parish Church. Teresa's cold was at it peak. The Dalzells did not attend. 'We were too poor to go to London and take a lodging and no one offered to take us in, not even our Mary!' Even Mrs King did not attend. Her husband took her off to Brighton. However, St. George's mother and stepfather, Horace Turner, were there as well as the Fletchers, and on the bride's side the Crutchleys and Peards. General Crutchley gave the bride away. There were no bridesmaids, but it was customary for widows who were remarrying to have a married friend stand near them. At Teresa's request, Eliza Crutchley performed the role. St. George and Teresa left immediately after the ceremony for Paris, their first stop on the way to India.

More anguished letters crossed the Atlantic. Amelia Harris wrote, 'I got a letter from Eliza. She says everyone thinks that Teresa has thrown herself away.' Sarah could not understand why Teresa would go to Kashmir.[43] But Kashmir offered more to the bride and groom than fond memories and good hunting. It had terrible communications.

* * *

The Littledales reached Bombay on 22 March. They did not spend any time in that great city but left by train for Lahore the next day, a routine they were to follow for many years. Once the Littledales began a trip they kept moving, almost frantically so, until they reached their destination. If they stopped, it was to buy supplies. In Lahore they repacked their baggage into smaller loads that could be carried on a march. Then they were off to Rawalpindi and Murree.[44]

When St. George wrote to his mother on 8 April, they were doing double marches on their way to Srinagar. Two and a half weeks later they were in the mountains on their way to Astor. They had regrouped in Srinagar, rehired the same shikari (hunter) and gun bearer who had served them in 1875, recruited porters and started up the Gilgit road. Teresa wrote to her mother on 25 April from Gagnai, a hunting ground:

> Here we are far in the wilds of Kashmir. The marching up was rather hard work as there is so much snow. . . . I do not walk much as I have a dandy [sedan chair] and eight kahars [kuhars or bearers], so I can always be carried unless the road is too bad. I had to walk over most of the snow. . . . I am busy all day doing nothing. . . . We are very comfortable in our tents. We have a very good cook and bearer. . . . Eight other coolies who came at Bandipoor . . . said they had been with us before and wanted to be engaged again so we have a number of old faces around us.

She added, 'Georgie and I as far as we have gone are getting on very well together so I hope we always shall.'[45] They were off to a good start.

In England Teresa's relatives were still recovering from their shock. Mary Peard wrote, 'Teresa says "Georgy"! has lumbago. Fancy her calling him by such a babyish name.' The Harris sisters were unaware that he was known as 'Georgie' inside his own family. The men seemed less concerned about his nickname. Shuldham Peard wrote in a business letter, '. . . it is Mr. Barrow's opinion that according to English law, Scott's will did not leave Teresa an absolute right to her settlement money after her death. She appears only to have a life rent in it. What will poor Georgie say if such is the case?'[46]

If 'poor Georgie' had known, he probably would think it was less important than what was happening to him in Kashmir. The Littledales reached Astor but were turned back in sight of a markhor nullah that he had been looking forward to for a long time. There were tribal disturbances along the frontier from Chitral all the way to Baluchistan. The Maharaja of Kashmir was sending troops and needed all the porters available to support the army, so travellers were ordered to return to Srinagar. Instead the Littledales decided to head for 'Skardo,' with a stop at another nullah along the way.[47]

Two months later Teresa wrote that they had left Skardu and were heading up the Indus River toward Ladakh. Today the country remains the same as Teresa described it 130 years ago: 'We have been marching through the most barren country I ever was in. Nothing but mountains, the "Karakorum" range. They are very grand entirely composed of a black & white granite. Not a blade of grass on them, but one comes suddenly upon a village where there is water, and green is no name for it.'[48] There may be more elegant descriptions of Baltistan but none more accurate. The stark, rugged terrain inspires awe, not rapture. Even the Baltis, who for centuries have scratched out a living on their irrigated plots, seem like trespassers on the land.

One of the incongruous sights of that mountain land is a polo match.[49] Polo probably began in Persia. Somehow the sport migrated across Central Asia into Tibet and then into the hill states of the western Karakoram, where for centuries it has remained permanently embedded in the culture. As played in Baltistan it resembles a small wild cavalry skirmish using mallets instead of sabres. The players go at each other and occasionally the ball, while a band of flutes and drums plays on the sideline, its frenetic music augmenting the chaos on the field. Visitors are sometimes invited to join in the fray but most of them wisely decline. Not St. George. In Parkuta, a small village along the Indus River, the Lambardar (village headman) loaned his pony to St. George, who then joined the Nawab (provincial governor), two rajahs, and all their attendants in a traditional free-for-all polo match. Their guest enjoyed it thoroughly. Afterwards the Nawab 'presented him with three ibex horns for which he made pretty speeches'.

Most of the time Teresa continued to ride in the dandy, reducing her exertions but increasing her apprehension, especially when they had to thread their way through the narrow gorges of the Indus. 'I get frightened out of my wits sometimes when the kahars slip with me and . . . I am hanging over a precipice, perhaps three or four hundred feet or more. The places I thought dreadful when I came into Cashmere seem nothing now. We have been over some really awful places.'[50]

By the middle of July the Littledales had reached Gya, a small village about 50 miles beyond Leh, capital of Ladakh. It was good hunting country, perhaps too good. St. George wrote, 'We came here to slay some ovis ammon, a kind of sheep as big as a donkey with splendid horns. . . . A serious coolness has arisen between Teresa & myself, because instead of shooting she complacently looked at a large ovis ammon which came to interview the camp during my absence, although she had my big rifle & lots of cartridges.' He added:

> We are camped now within a few feet of the height of Mont Blanc & when I go out shooting some 2–3,000 feet higher there is not the slightest difficulty in getting out of breath. . . . We are going for a few days to the Tso Morari Lake to get Kyang, a wild horse, Goa, an antelope, & Ovis Ammon, then to Hanle & back to Leh by the Pangong Lakes and the Chang Chenmo. We have determined to postpone going to Yarkand as we hear the Chinese are fighting there and our journey home through Persia is put aside. . . .[51]

The Yarkand trip was an ambitious program to contemplate, much less do, but St. George's remarks show that even at this stage in their lives, there was little beyond the scope of their imagination.

As it turned out, even their short-term plans could not be accomplished because Teresa developed altitude sickness. They decided to return to Leh and then start back to Srinagar. It would require 17 marches and they would have to cross the Zoji La, the famous pass between Ladakh and the Vale of Kashmir, but they would take their time. St. George commented that they were both now very fit.[52]

Teresa enjoyed the life but had spells of loneliness. 'The days are sometimes very long when Georgy is out from four in the morning till six in the evening. I get very tired of my own society. . . .' But she kept busy. 'I have just made Georgy 6 prs of linen coolie drawers. He is so fascinated with them he won't part with them for a day.' So St. George should have been happy. He got new underwear as well as game. He shot bharal and Ovis ammon but was disappointed in not getting shappoo, the Ladakhi urial, a wary, wild sheep.[53] Teresa was not left entirely alone: 'I have a great big dog to take care of me now, a Tibetan mastiff. We bought him in Leh. He inspires respect for he looks so cross but is good temper itself.' Later on they picked up a second dog, a playful Ladakhi puppy. They called their dogs Lassa and Lama.

Teresa wrote, 'A great deal of our journey is <u>very</u> hard work. I had not anything like it the last time I was in Kashmir. But I am so glad to have seen it all. . . . & Georgy is very happy & enjoys it all immensely. . . . Many times there is not even a village, only a level spot just large enough for the tent. You do not know what a wild life we are leading.'[54]

The Littledales crossed the Zoji La and reached Srinagar on 4 September. They spent 10 days sightseeing, shopping, and socialising, even attending a dinner with the Maharaja of Kashmir.[55] Then they set off again for six weeks, this time to hunt bear near Bandipur.[56] It was getting late in the season and they were caught by snowstorms that came a month earlier than normal, collapsing their tents. A nearby hunter slipped on a snowy slope and fell to his death, a reminder of how dangerous their activity was. The accident made an impact on both Teresa and St. George.[57] The pass leading back to Kashmir was closed to ponies by the heavy snows, but several hundred soldiers arrived and reopened it.

The Littledales got through to Srinagar, returned to Rawalpindi, and then went shooting and shopping across India. They reached Calcutta about 10 December and settled down for a while to enjoy the social life there. Calcutta was a constant round of garden parties, dinners and balls, frequently with the Viceroy and Lady Lytton. Teresa described the scene:

> We have an invitation for every Sunday and also for two garden parties, and two dances on Monday. I went to see Lady Lytton . . . and on Wednesday we dined at Government House (and I had a dirty napkin) but the evening was very pleasant. . . . Lord Lytton is a most insignificant-looking man. . . . Tomorrow we go down to Barrackpore to a garden party. . . . We go in the Viceroy's yacht, and on the 4th Jan. there is the state ball.

They also took in the races and the opera.[58]

They intended to go to Ceylon, Madras, and the Nilgiri Hills, but the details of their next four months are unknown. Earlier Teresa had written, '. . . there is a great charm in the gypsy sort of life'.[59] She had become almost as inured to the hardships of an outdoor life as St. George. Their long honeymoon had established the pattern of their lives.

From the Rockies to the Caucasus

. . . the passion for shooting game did much
for what was best in our civilization.
                    G.M. Trevelyan[1]

The Littledales arrived back in England in June 1878. Even after their
long absence, St. George did not make a favourable impression on his
in-laws. Julia Crutchley wrote, 'Aunt Littledale looks very well and is
very lively. He, poor creature, is most uninteresting. I look at him and
wonder – Mama's Baby.'[2] Julia was close to St. George in age, which
may have influenced her. Even so, the rest of the Harris women shared
her opinion.

St. George was even less interested in English social life than Scott. Like
Scott he owned horses and enjoyed fox hunting, but unlike Scott he was
not indolent. For almost all of his life he would follow the hounds every
chance he had. However, the great passion for wealthy Englishmen was big
game hunting, and here St. George went far beyond his contemporaries. It
became the centre of his life, the foundation of his achievements, and the
driving force behind his travel adventures. It was not simply the bagging of
trophies that intrigued him. As he was later to explain in an interview, he
craved the challenge of hunting in mountains. He found it exhilarating. His
prey were horned game, the mountain sheep and goats that dwelled in their
fastness. They were 'the best sport'. He never hunted in Africa because,
despite the large and exotic game, mountains were 'scarce'. South America
had mountains but no respectable horned animals. He hunted in the
mountains of the northern hemisphere where the terrain was the challenge
as well as the game, where a trophy head was not only a prize but a symbol
of difficulty and danger faced and overcome.[3]

Teresa was not a hunter. She stayed in camp when St. George went
out to shoot. Yet she, too, loved the excitement of going to strange and
difficult countries, to wild lands inhabited by wild people and visited by
few foreigners. Frequently during the course of an especially difficult
trip, she would ask herself why she was doing it and swear she would
never do it again, but she always did. Wick Hill House would become
the base camp of their lives.

Although St. George was only twenty-six when he and Teresa returned to England, he had demonstrated both the skill that would make him one of the world's greatest hunters and an enthusiasm for collecting specimens to be studied by others. In the West Indies in 1874, the start of his first major trip, he was already stuffing birds for home. From then on, boxes of heads, skins and horns were constantly being shipped back, many for the Liverpool Museum. Collecting gave his hunting a purpose. He had also begun to obtain record heads such as the Nilgiri tahr.[4] It was the beginning of a symbiotic relationship. Museum officials would help him obtain the necessary permissions to travel and he would bring back new specimens for them to study.

After their honeymoon, a major event for Teresa was the installation of the two Burne-Jones windows she had commissioned for Easthampstead Parish Church in memory of Willie. The windows are stunning, especially the angels, a feature for which Burne-Jones was famous.[5] Viewing the windows, one can imagine the depth of Teresa's affection for her first husband and her appreciation of him. Despite their differences, Willie had taken care of her. He had earned those windows.

For a number of years the Littledales concentrated on hunting trips in North America, where they gained experience and honed their skills. In 1879 they went to the Big Horn Mountains of Wyoming. Teresa's mother, on a rare trip away from Eldon House, met them in New York. It was there that Amelia met St. George for the first time. She wrote, 'Mr. Littledale does not look as young as I expected to see him looking.' However, she did not rush to judgment. The next day she added, 'I rather like St. George but must know more of him before I can decide upon all his merits.'[6]

The Littledales spent the winter in England. St. George's standing with his in-laws still had not improved. Mary Peard wrote, 'With all Scott's ways people <u>did like</u> him. No one cares for St. George.'[7] However, despite his perceived faults, life with St. George was never dull. The Littledales were always on the move. In June 1880 they took a 3-month trip to Scandinavia, including the North Cape. Teresa wrote, 'Certainly the scenery in Norway is very beautiful, more like Cashmere than any scenery I have ever seen.' They climbed to the top of the North Cape at 3 o'clock in the morning, they rode across the Norwegian countryside in carioles, little horse-drawn carriages that held only one person, and they spent the night at simple rest stations along the way.[8] Even an 'ordinary' Littledale trip was not routine.

They returned to the Big Horns in the summer of 1881 with Captain Otho Shaw, whom they had run across in Kashmir during their honeymoon.[9] It was an eventful experience. The excitement began in Bismarck, Dakota Territory, where Teresa was suffering from a cold.

... last night the moment I arrived I had a mustard plaster, hot lemonade, & chlorodine & went to bed with every intention of remaining in bed a good part of today but Alas! it was not to be.*[10] Heavy rain & a thunder storm came up about 11 o'clk which continued on & off till about 2 o'clk, when it finished in a perfect cyclone. . . . I think without the least exaggeration there were hail stones as large as my fist. Every window in the house is smashed. . . . Our window was at the head of our bed. At last I could stand the thumping & crashing of glass no longer & begged St. George to take me out in the passage. . . . I had no time to find my slippers. In a few minutes every creature in the hotel appeared more or less in an awful fright. About five minutes after we left our room St. George went in for my dressing gown & found everything wet through including our bed & covered with glass. . . . The Pullman cars are knocked to pieces. . . . They say they have never had such a storm. . . . Mr. Shaw's Gillycock hat was hanging on a peg the opposite side of the room from the window & a hail stone has cut a hole in it. You could put your hand in.[11]

The next morning they took the train to Glendive, Montana, the end of the line for the Northern Pacific Railway, which was under construction:

[It was] . . . the roughest bit of living I have ever experienced. The hotel was a shed put up in a day with a canvas roof, some tents hung up at our desire to screen our bed from the men. . . . The food was simply uneatable. I lived upon bread & milk which was fortunately fresh but after three days I came to the conclusion that I had passed the time of life when milk was all I required.[12]

They travelled on by boat on the Yellowstone River to Miles City, Montana, and then by horse and wagon south through forest fires and past abandoned forts to the Big Horns. In the nineteenth-century American West, life was dangerous and raw. The isolation magnified the seriousness of any mishap. Away from a remote hunting camp

---

* Dr J. Collis Browne's Chlorodyne. An all-purpose concoction, it contained opium, chloroform, morphine, marijuana and other ingredients. It may not have cured anything but it certainly put the enthusiasm into the British Empire. Used by travellers everywhere, it reduced your pain, improved your mood and knocked you out. Throughout the 1890s the British Medical Association tried to get it banned.

St. George was skinning an elk, something he had done many times, but it was snowing and he was in a hurry to get back. His knife slipped off the skin of the animal and plunged into his thigh, cutting an artery. 'I remember distinctly seeing my knickerbocker pulsing out with each stroke of my heart as the blood gushed out, and then I fainted. I fainted five times from sheer loss of blood, but at last I reached home.'[13] Somehow he managed to survive. But he learned. In a long life of hunting and skinning animals, he never made that mistake again.

On the way out, they continued to hunt. One day, just as St. George shot an elk, the wagon train went off in the wrong direction and he raced after it, leaving Teresa and one of the men to finish killing the wounded animal. Teresa wrote, 'I stayed with Glen & cut the elk's throat. I was in an awful fright & felt as if the elk would get up and run at me.' Perhaps it was her pioneer background but Teresa was not squeamish. What bothered her was the risk, not the gore. It was an early display of her toughness.

Farther on, the Littledales visited the Custer battleground. It was only five years after the Battle of the Little Big Horn and Teresa picked up a jawbone on the field. From there they returned to Miles City, passing places with descriptive western names such as Froze to Death Ranch.[14]

On their way home they stopped at Eldon House. Because of financial difficulties with Edward Harris, their stay was unpleasant.[15] In mid-November the Littledales finally left for England. Amelia Harris wrote, 'The parting was sad as I never expect to see them again & their visit has been made very painful to us all, but it is over & has left me with a heartache.'[16]

Amelia died the following March at the age of eighty-four. Although Teresa knew her mother's death was imminent, it was a great blow. She wrote, 'I feel as if it was a month since I received that telegram. . . . It is very sad getting our letters each week telling us how she is when we know it is all over and that we have lost the dearest of Mothers. . . . There never was anybody so sweet and good and fit for a better world. . . . The feeling comes over me at times that it must be all a bad dream. . . .' Teresa summarised her mother's place in the Harris family: '. . . I cannot realize that we have really lost our mother, the magnet that has kept us all together. I do not know any other mother that could die & leave that feeling so strongly behind her.'[17]

Amelia Harris was a forceful, materialistic woman. She never gave up her efforts to influence or even dictate her children's lives. She poured guilt on them with a ladle while doing everything in her power to advance or protect her family's position in life and in society. One can see some of her character traits in Teresa, especially the blatant social climbing and love of material objects. Amelia's diary gives one the impression of an overbearing, frequently unpleasant woman. Yet, as is so frequently the case, her faults were those of her time and place and were the qualities she needed to cope with the circumstances into which she had been thrust. The death of John Harris could have been a disaster for the family. Instead, Amelia took advantage of her material and social assets. Her children often resented her interference but they knew she would do anything for them. Teresa's comments had summed up the feelings of all of them.

In 1882 the Littledales returned to Montana and Wyoming, this time to visit Yellowstone National Park. Although encounters with hostile Indians had recently diminished, the Littledales were given a cavalry escort for safety. When they arrived at the Upper Geyser Basin, they seemed unaware of any danger. Oblivious to the boiling water underneath their feet, they stood on the thin crust next to the hot pools. 'Our men put some clothes in Old Faithful to wash. They went in but did not come out!'[18] Fortunately the most famous geyser in the world survived this attempt to turn it into a laundry.

For years St. George had been making significant contributions to the Liverpool Museum. Already he had supplied the Ovis ammon, the bharal, and the Himalayan ibex from his Kashmir trips, and such animals as elk and pronghorn antelope from the western United States. He had also donated a large number of birds from his earliest travels. One animal was missing, the Rocky Mountain or white goat. Thomas Moore, the Director, wanted a specimen for study, so in 1884 the Littledales decided to return to the Rockies. However, on the train across the United States they met a missionary who persuaded them to change their plans and go to Alaska instead. It was an early display of confidence in their ability to cope with any situation.

They made their way to Vancouver, British Columbia, bought supplies, picked up an interpreter, and sailed to Juneau, which at that time was a small gold mining town only four years old. They obtained a 45-ft dugout canoe and hired a crew of Hoonah Indians to paddle it. Several days later the heavily laden canoe was lowered off a steamer into choppy seas. The passengers climbed aboard and paddled for a week into Glacier Bay. They were completely isolated in steep, dangerous mountain terrain. St. George shot a goat, and an Indian carrying it back to camp slipped on snow-covered ice and began to fall down a steep ravine to his death, but the goat on his back jammed in some rocks and stopped the fall. The party paddled for days back out into the ocean and was picked up by the steamer on a return trip to Juneau.[19]

Despite all odds, the Alaska trip had been successful. One of the goats that St. George obtained was listed in Rowland Ward's *Records of*

Big Game, and he donated two 'fine male specimens' to the Liverpool Museum and wrote a paper for Thomas Moore on obtaining them. Moore read the paper at a meeting of the Literary and Philosophical Society of Liverpool.[20] The Littledales were now ready to renew their travels at a greater level of difficulty and sophistication.

*   *   *

They could never remain in one place for long, and by March 1886 they were restless and anxious to be off again. St. George wrote to Thomas Moore at the Liverpool Museum, 'We are thinking of making a little tour somewhere this summer, British Columbia, Japan or Mount Ararat & the Caucasus. Have you any suggestions? With your habitual modesty you will doubtless find a want.'

Soon they decided upon Ararat and the Caucasus. It would not be easy to arrange. For a century Russia had been expanding south through the Caucasus, fighting wars against Turkey, Persia, and the Muslim and Christian tribesmen of the region. These local peoples waged a surprisingly effective guerrilla war for decades. The British were encouraging Persia to be a bulwark against Russian expansion. Then, in March 1885, the rivalry in Central Asia between Britain and Russia flared again. The Russians captured Pandjeh, a small oasis halfway between Merv and Herat, with great loss of life. This threatened Afghanistan, and the British mobilised for war against Russia. The crisis was averted diplomatically, largely through the efforts of Sir Robert Morier, the British Ambassador to Russia, and Nikolai de Giers, the Russian Foreign Minister.

The Caucasus was away from the action but the natives were restless and the region was sensitive. Foreigners were allowed but access was controlled and various permits were required. Being a British subject complicated matters and permissions had to come from military authorities concerned about security, not from a tourist bureau. The Littledales would have to do more than pack their bags.

St. George knew that the permits he sought would require the approval of the highest levels of the Russian government and that his application to the Russians would need the strong support of the Foreign Office. Furthermore, the British officials would not promote his request unless they were confident the proposal was reasonable, preferably useful, and there was minimal chance of embarrassment or trouble through misconduct or incompetence. In April he wrote to Moore:

We are thinking of going this autumn to Mount Ararat to get some Natural History specimens & I think you might be able to give us some valuable assistance. The part of the Ararat Range to which we wish to go is, I believe, in Russia but as it is probably in a rather unsettled condition it might not be very judicious going there without some kind of a guard. How[ever] as I am going there for Scientific purposes of which the Museum will probably largely benefit, I think if you would place the matter in a proper light before the Committee [of the Liverpool Museum] they might see their way to either write direct to the Russian Ambassador or through the minister of Foreign Affairs & ask if they would allow me an escort of three or four policemen or solders from either Tiflis or Evian for a couple of months from about the end of July. As I have never been in the Army & am only going for wild beasts the Russian Government need have no ground for suspicion. As we should have to start not later than the end of June there is not much time to spare. The Wapiti heads look very well indeed. We have them in the dining room.[21]

It is a classic letter: the low-key statement of his intentions, the modest request for assistance without assuming it will be granted, the emphasis on being just a simple hunter whose efforts will benefit science, a comment regarding urgency due to their travel deadline, and finally, a subtle expression of thanks for prior benefits rendered. St. George takes the opportunity to point out that some hunting trophies prepared by Moore's sons have a place of honour in his house.

The Liverpool Museum sent the requested letter to the Foreign Office. It established St. George's credentials and helped provide job protection for any official approving the application. He was also thinking of future trips: 'If the government will give an escort for Ararat, they might possibly be induced to give one in Siberia for Ovis Poli next summer. We will see how the cat jumps this time. Mrs. Littledale will, of course, accompany me & perhaps a friend.'[22]

While waiting for the permits, Littledale asked Moore to let him know if there was any particular rare bird, animal, or plant he wanted, and he also requested information on the goats, sheep, and deer in the area where he hoped to hunt.[23] Among the usual last minute crises, a friend who was to accompany the Littledales withdrew from the expedition. 'It was impossible to go on a trip of that kind alone so I wired my eldest brother. The ninth telegram to him got a favourable answer. . . .' Alfred Littledale was planning to get married in the fall but fortunately the wedding date had not yet been set. St. George was so persuasive that Alfred joined the expedition after promising his fiancée they would marry no later than 3 November.

Ambassador Morier asked the Russian officials in St Petersburg for the escort to Ararat but they did not think an escort would be needed.

St. George had his doubts. 'Did you see the account in the Times on Wednesday. I think of brigands in Armenia. We have to pass the very place where they committed those murders. It seems that an escort is not so unnecessary as the Russian authorities imagine.'[24]

Permission finally came, and the Littledales left Bracknell on 8 July 1886.[25] They made their way to Vienna, waited for Alfred to join them, and then started down the Danube. At Galati, Romania, they changed to a Russian steamer that continued down the Danube and onto the Black Sea. They arrived at Odessa on 24 July. It took sixteen men to examine their passports but they had surprisingly little trouble. At the British Consulate they met Patrick W. Stevens, deputy for the Consul, who was away. Stevens was posted in the region for years and would become an essential contact for the Littledales during many future expeditions. 'We asked Stevens to dine with us. Dinner first rate. The fish arrived with two enormous fins sticking out like a peacock tail. The waiter said its name was in Russian "Sea Cock" & that it was the best & rarest fish in the whole of the Black Sea. When we received the a/c we wished that he had been more rare.'

The Littledales could not find an interpreter in Odessa so they had to go south to Tiflis to get one. Tiflis was hot and they dosed themselves with quinine to prevent malaria. St. George hired an Armenian interpreter, Karabet Foidjan. They called him Charles. He did not speak English but he knew French. They still wanted an escort so they went to see Prince Shérématieff, second in command for the governor, Prince Dandukoff Korsakoff, who was away. He politely told them they could not go to Ararat because the Kurds were fighting and a bandit named Kareim, who had over a hundred followers, was on a rampage. It would not be safe no matter how large the escort. He recommended that they go instead to the north side of the Caucasus to the area west of Mount Elbruz, where most of the game could be found.

The Littledale party left Tiflis by phaeton, a light four-wheeled horse-drawn vehicle, to cross the Caucasus over the Dariel Pass to the north side. They were following a road known as the Georgian Military Highway, built in the late eighteenth century. They spent two uncomfortable nights on the road. Teresa wrote, 'It is most beautiful, the grandest pass I have ever seen . . . the fleas are awful. . . . No blankets. . . . I slept in my fur coat or rather tried to if the fleas had not been so hungry.' Then they travelled by train, changed to a tarantass, left the post road and the ride got worse. 'Cart entirely guiltless of springs.'[26]

They reached the Baksan valley and on 21 August arrived at their shooting ground at about 8,000ft on Mount Elbruz. They were joined by Sotaef Achia, a great hunter, whom they had picked up at the last village. In 1868 Achia had accompanied Douglas Freshfield, the famous English mountaineer, on his climb of 16,800ft Elbruz, the highest peak in Europe.[27]

After several days of effort, St. George managed to shoot what he thought was a male tur. To his chagrin, the tur was a female.[28] He spent the next day in camp cleaning the skin and skeleton for the Liverpool Museum, 'a tedious job'. The shooting of females was against his principles, the only exception being when one was requested by a museum for scientific study. He once said, '. . . it spoils the sport for future comers. The Americans have no such scruples, and that is why they are destroying the best game country they have left.'[29]

On 9 September they caught a train for Armavir to the north-west along the Kuban River. They arrived late that night and set up their camp beds in the ladies room at the train station. St. George's diary entry for the next day is succinct: 'Friday. Have arrived today somewhere.'

Three days later they bounced their way to Maikop (Maykop) and pitched camp. The region had a reputation for excellent hunting and there were a few auroch (European bison) near the headwaters of tributaries of the Kuban River.[30] Although the shooting of auroch was forbidden, St. George thought the local authorities might make an exception for the Liverpool Museum. The police chief mentioned to St. George that if he wanted auroch, nothing would be said, so he decided to take the chance. The next day the chief showed him on a map where to find them.[31]

It took the Littledales 5 days of difficult travel to get to their destination at the head of the Tscebai River. After a night in a monastery, they reached their first camp during a torrential rain and had trouble finding a site for their tent. '[It] is pitched on a great slope. No trouble emptying the bath.' From their permanent camp St. George shot a variety of animals but he never saw an aurochs. By now it was late September and time to leave. Alfred left for England and the Littledales returned to Tiflis, where St. George made several visits to Dr Gustav Raddé, Curator of the Tiflis Museum and an expert on the flora and fauna of the Caucasus.[32] He also sent to the Liverpool Museum some of the mammals he had obtained. They included a male and female ollen, a male and female chamois, a female bear, and a male and female West Caucasian tur. The tur were especially rare and few institutions had specimens, not even the Tiflis Museum.

The Littledales arrived back in England in early November. Shuldham Peard described Teresa: '. . . she does not look at all well & no wonder.' Six weeks later he wrote, 'I hear Teresa is mending but she should not attempt those expeditions which are not fit for women.'

Meanwhile, Alfred Littledale married Marian Harriet Atkinson at St Margaret's Westminster on 3 November. He had kept his promise to his fiancée.[33]

Moore was delighted with St. George's donations. 'The fatigues of a hard day's stalking are sufficient for most men, and even the superintendence only of skinning the quarry after, for Museum purposes, must be a heavy tax to pay into the cause of science. Mr. Littledale has always paid it most cheerfully, and without a previous failure.' Littledale's tur (Caucasian goats) are listed in Rowland Ward's *Records of Big Game*, where they are ranked near the top.[34]

In January 1887 the Littledales went to Cheshire for 6 weeks of fox hunting. St. George took his horses. Mary Peard wrote, 'If I were Teresa, I should like to enjoy my house for a few months in the year.' But Mary was not Teresa. Already the Littledales were preparing for a second trip to the Caucasus. St. George, disappointed that he was unable to obtain an aurochs on his prior trip, was determined to try again.[35]

Meanwhile, Thomas Moore was so impressed by the quality of the specimens from the Littledales over the years that in an act of great generosity, he wrote a letter introducing St. George to Dr Albert Gunther, Keeper of Zoology at the Natural History Museum in London. At Moore's request, St. George sent to Gunther a chamois skin and skull from the Caucasus and two bear skulls acquired in Kashmir ten years earlier during his honeymoon.[36] The introduction was a major milestone for the Littledales. St. George was now considered a professional collector, and both he and Teresa took it seriously. From now on the two of them, working as a team, would obtain flora and fauna for the distinguished national institution. It validated their expeditions and gave purpose to their lives.

In preparation for the Caucasus, St. George wrote to both Gunther and Moore for a list of what they wanted him to obtain. He told Gunther he needed a description and the scientific name of 'the bird beast plant or whatever else you may particularly require'. To Moore he also mentioned reptiles. The Littledales were willing to collect anything.[37]

They left London on 27 June 1887, going by way of Vienna and Odessa, where they dined again with Patrick Stevens, now the Consul. This time they did not have 'Sea Cock'. Continuing on by boat, train and cart, they reached Maikop about mid-July. There they hired local Circassian hunters and then travelled with pack animals for six days until they reached their former campground at the headwaters of the Tscebai River. They remained there until late September.[38]

The auroch were in the valleys below them. To hunt them, St. George had to descend 3,000ft into a valley, cross it, and climb 3,000ft up the opposite side, and then repeat the route to return to camp. He followed this routine for days but never encountered an aurochs.[39]

Unlike auroch, tur live high in the mountains. Moreover, they have to be hunted from above, preferably at dawn. St. George established a hunting camp high above the main camp as a base for stalking them. His shikaris stayed at the high camp but he did not. Local men were milling about the main camp down below and he was unwilling to leave Teresa alone there at night. St. George had to leave camp in the dark at 3 or 4 o'clock in the morning, follow a local guide up thousands of feet to the hunting bivouac, hunt all day, and return all the way back down at night, arriving after dark. He did this for weeks with few rest days. It demonstrated not only his tremendous energy and stamina but also his concern for Teresa. As always, she was the only woman in the party, but the situation in this camp was different and he was more cautious.

We have no description of Teresa's activities during her husband's absence but judging from records of their other expeditions, she baked bread, washed and sewed clothes, and mended tents. However, her most important job was to keep the camp running smoothly, and this was no small chore. The Littledales tended to have a number of men assisting them and base camp was often a large establishment. Nevertheless, Teresa enjoyed her camp life even though her specific tasks were similar to those handled in England by their servants.

The Littledales broke camp in late September and in wind and heavy rain made their way by cart to Armavir, where they shipped the horns and skins to England. Back in Tiflis they tried to get to Mount Ararat, but as it was still in bandit-infested turmoil, they had to settle for views of it from afar. On 23 October they left for England, arriving home in early November. It had been a 'highly successful' trip. St. George had obtained six ollen and seven tur, as well as chamois and bear. There was one exception. 'We have got some splendid heads but the wily Aurochs completely beat me. I never caught a glimpse of one the whole time. . . .'[40]

The Alai and the Altai

. . . the most innocent pair of English eyes . . .
Sir Robert Morier

Teresa had come back from the Caucasus in good spirits. Perhaps it was partly because she and St. George were already planning their next expedition and she was excited. By early December 1887, St. George had contacted Gunther at the Natural History Museum. He also wrote to Moore at the Liverpool Museum. 'We are discussing the pros & cons of a visit to the Altai Mountains in Siberia next summer. Dr Gunther has promised some valuable assistance but it is a more serious expedition & there are a great many points to be considered before embarking on it.'[1] St. George was now engaged in a balancing act in determining which institution should get what. The Liverpool Museum still had first choice but he wanted to satisfy Gunther as well.

Buoyed by the success of his prior trip, his next objective was the elusive Ovis poli, the grand prize for all sheep hunters. The Marco Polo sheep is large and has long, widespread spiral horns. It lives in the most remote regions of the Alai and the Pamir. Only a few specimens had been obtained but none by an Englishman. The Transcaspian Railway, begun by the Russians in 1880, was about to reach Samarkand, enabling easier access to the region. However, the political difficulties still remained formidable, especially for English travellers. The Great Game crises were moving east, and by the late 1880s they were hovering over the Pamir. The Littledales had several advantages. Hunting was a sport of the ruling classes in both Russia and Britian, and St. George was rapidly becoming known as one of the finest hunters in the world. Thus he was much admired by the authorities with whom he had to deal. In addition, the Littledales always went out of their way to ingratiate themselves with everyone. If anyone could get the permits, they could, but they could not rely upon it.

Once again St. George asked the Foreign Office to approach the Russians for the permits. His request was reinforced by a letter of recommendation from William H. Flower, Director of the Natural

History Museum, to Lord Salisbury, the Foreign Secretary. 'Mr. Littledale is well known as an energetic sportsman and successful collector of zoological specimens.' He then pointed out the contributions St. George had made to both the Liverpool Museum and the Natural History Museum. Lord Salisbury and Sir Robert Morier did not need further urging. The Littledales were known and trusted. Morier made an all-out effort to get approval from the Russians and he had the full support of de Giers, the Russian Foreign Minister. Although each faithfully represented the interests of his respective country, the two men had the highest regard for each other and together had managed to ameliorate many potential crises between Britain and Russia. However, both men could only influence events, not control them.[2]

One difficulty in dealing with Russia was that because all power was centered in the Czar, various ministries reporting directly to him worked independently and were frequently at cross purposes with each other. This was especially true with the Foreign Ministry and the War Ministry. The War Ministry pushed Russian expansion as fast as possible across Central Asia, while the Foreign Ministry tried to maintain decent relations with England and was kept busy apologising for each new expansion while promising there would be no future ones. The Littledale request illustrates the problem. In April 1888 Morier wrote to Salisbury:

> I have written two official notes requesting the permission asked for on behalf of Mr. and Mrs. Littledale, who wish to shoot big game in Fergana, and Monsieur de Giers is using his very best efforts to obtain this permission from the Minister of War. It is, however, unfortunately just one of those cases in which the chronic animosity between the two Departments blazes up and . . . M. de Giers . . . has already met with one refusal and has only gone to a fresh charge on the strength of a very strong private letter I have written to him, showing the ill effect which such a refusal would have in view of the supposed good relations established in that part of the world by the successful delimitation of the Afghan frontier.[3]

Fortunately for the Littledales, de Giers prevailed. On 26 April he sent a private letter to Morier informing him that Prince Dondoukoff Korsakoff, Governor General of the Caucasus, did not object and that he, de Giers, had received official approval for the trip. The permission, especially to travel on the Transcaspian Railway, was a significant coup on Morier's part.[4]

Things began to move rapidly. St. George wrote to Thomas Sanderson, the Assistant Under Secretary at the Foreign Office, 'We hope to get off the last days of May or 1st or 2nd of June & shall push on as fast as we can to the Pamir in case they change their minds.' Later he asked Gunther for a letter of introduction to Dr Strauch, the Director of the Academy of Sciences in St Petersburg. 'He might be able to give me some information as to the most likely place to look for that big baa lamb or Ovis Poli & the more I mix with those sort of people & keep clear of the military element the better chance we shall have in Central Asia.' A few days later he thanked Gunther for the letter to Dr Strauch. 'I am sure it will be <u>most useful</u>. . . . We start tomorrow & as usual on these occasions are not half ready. P.S. I had a letter from Dr. Lansdell at Tashkend.'*5

On 27 May 1888 a ceremony was held to open the Transcaspian Railway from the Caspian Sea to Samarkand. Three days later the Littledales left England. They reached St Petersburg on 2 June. At a station along the way 'Teresa put on her most winning manner and best Parisian accent & asked a French woman how soon the train started. She replied, 'Madame, je ne parle pas Anglais!'6

On 8 June St. George went to meet Morier for the first time. It was the beginning of an important friendship. Later in the day the Ambassador returned the visit. Teresa wrote, '. . . an irascible old gentleman I should think, but he has been very kind about helping us on our journey and made our going by the Transcaspian Railway a personal affair. I do not think if we had not been in the Caucasus the last two years we should have had the smallest chance.' She added:

> Everybody is terribly down on Dr. Lansdell. We have not heard one good thing about him. The Ambassador called him a theatrical humbug. The Ambassador told the authorities here that having made that railway they ought to let all the world see it and as for us, we had been two years in the Caucasus and they had had detectives about us the whole time and really knew more about us than we know ourselves.7

Later that day the Littledales subjected themselves to a rare interview. The interviewer was 'a Mr. Stead' of the *Pall Mall Gazette*.8 His interest in the Littledales indicates that even though they had not yet even begun to plan their greatest expeditions, they were already attracting attention.

Mr Stead described St. George as '. . . a mighty hunter before the Lord, a veritable Nimrod of the nineteenth century. In his seat at Bracknell he has accumulated a collection of trophies of sport which can probably not be equalled, much less excelled, by the collection of any other sportsman.' The article goes much further than that.

---

* The Revd Henry Lansdell had crossed Russia to Chinese Central Asia a few months earlier and was advising the Littledales.

It provides a wealth of information about the Littledales. There is a description of the couple as they are about to leave on yet another long adventure: 'Both are tall, lithe, and resolute, cheerful, and in capital spirits. They have gone a-gypsying in the mountains together for fifteen years [including Kashmir when Teresa was Mrs Scott], and they seem to rejoice at the prospect of their new excursion as much as if it had been their honeymoon.'

Mr Stead makes it clear that the Littledales were a team, and he brings out many aspects of their expedition life together: their interests, goals, methods, equipment and even their map.* During the interview St. George spread out on a table 'Mr Wyld's large map of Central Asia'.[9] At the same time he took pains to convey the impression that they were just simple people. 'I hope . . . they [the Russians] can see that we are not explorers, or geographers, or spies, or anything but a hunter and his wife, who never even wrote a book or a letter to the newspapers. . . .' On the subject of camping, the Littledales were experts: '. . . we have almost reduced it to a science. Our impediments are made as light as possible; we know exactly what we want and how it is best carried.' The writer rhapsodises:

Mrs. Littledale does not shoot. She simply travels and keeps house for her Nimrod of a husband, so that whenever he comes back exhausted from his fatiguing excursions after chamois or wapiti, he may always find the kettle singing on the hob, the table ready spread with viands, and the lady of the house doing the honours of the home just as if she were in her own dining room in England, instead of being the sole occupant of a solitary tent, perched 10,000 feet above the sea level in the Caucasus or the Rockies.[10]

It is doubtful that Teresa recognised this description.

Mr Stead asked the Littledales to write a few letters for his newspaper but they 'flatly declined'. Teresa gives their reasons in her diary, '. . .we thought the less we wrote the more chance we had of coming again if we ever wished to do so.'[11] They did not need the money and were not interested in fame. They wanted the freedom to go wherever they wished, and they wanted to be allowed to return. Later the British government would benefit from their discretion.

The next evening they took the train to Moscow and went on to Nigni Novgorod, where they caught a steamer down the Volga to the Caspian Sea. They continued south by boat to Baku, where they rehired Charles, their interpreter in 1886. After several days of shopping for more supplies, they sailed across the Caspian to Usunada, the starting

---

* Information from the interview is spread throughout this book.

point of the Transcaspian Railway. The following day they began the 900-mile train ride across hot desert through Ashkhabad and Merv. The train passed over a long wooden bridge crossing the Oxus River to Bukhara and Samarkand, where the Littledales had a room 'with a supply of fleas proportionate to the heat'.[12]

They purchased a tarantass and more supplies, and then departed for Osh, cultivating Russian connections whenever possible. In Margilan, the capital of Kokhand, they had dinner with General Korolkoff, the Governor of Fergana. Then, upon reaching Osh, they dined with Colonel Deubner, the local Naichalnik or District Governor, who commanded a wild group of officers.[13] The Littledales went on to Gulcha, a small village with the Kirghiz name for an Ovis poli ram. The caravan of twelve horses then headed south up the Taldik River and over two passes to the Alai plateau.[14] Finally they crossed the Kizil Art pass at 14,200ft and reached the Kara Julga Valley, their hunting ground.

It was desolate country with hardly a blade of grass, surrounded by lofty mountains, some over 20,000ft high. Torrents of water dashed down the cliffs from unseen glaciers above. The hunting was good. During the expedition St. George shot a total of 17 poli – 15 males and 2 females – including a record head. They moved their camp around the countryside, going as far as Kara Kul (lake). Although the main purpose of the expedition had been to obtain Ovis poli, reaching the remote Kara Kul was also a significant achievement. Few westerners had been there, and Teresa was probably the first western woman to see its waters.

By 21 September they were back in Samarkand. The next day they sent off their trophies and sold their tarantass. The person who bought it was none other than Nikolai Prejevalsky, the famous Russian explorer of Central Asia. He was embarking upon his fifth expedition. St. George wrote:

> I went to see him. He is a tall man & very fat man with deep blue eyes & pleasant manner. He did not at all seem to be the hater of Englishmen I had been led to believe. He starts tomorrow for Thibet via Tashkent & Aksu. . . . He said he hoped to be able to get to Lhassa this time. He did not know what the English & Thibetians were doing as it was a month since he left St. Petersburg. He said at first when at a great altitude the want of air bothered him but the effect wore off. He said he had been many times in the Ovis poli country & had only killed 5 or 6 [and] I the first time killed 16 or 17. I explained that I went entirely for shooting. He was a great traveller & only shot what chanced to cross his way & he had not the same opportunity. I was very favorably impressed with him.[15]

Prejevalsky left the following day. A month later he died of typhoid fever he caught by drinking from a river.[16]

On the way home the Littledales spent several days in Bukhara sightseeing and making 'heavy purchases' in the bazaar. On 2 October St. George wrote, 'An Englishman named Curzon, M.P., arrived at the Embassy. He seemed pleasant.' Littledale and Curzon struck up a friendship and went shopping together. Curzon was on a trip along the Transcaspian Railway that he would describe in his book *Russia in Central Asia*, causing a furore when it appeared the next year. Within ten days the Littledales had encountered two of the most prominent symbols of the Great Game, one at the end of his career and one at the beginning.

The Littledales went on to Merv, where St. George wrote a letter of thanks to Morier. He always took great pains to show appreciation for the efforts of others on his behalf. In this letter he added, 'As usual, nothing could possibly exceed the politeness & hospitality which we have received on all sides from the Russian Officers with whom we have come in contact.' He asked Morier to convey his gratitude to the Russian officials.[17] By early November 1888 the Littledales were back in England.

They immediately started planning their next expedition. This time they wanted to go through Russia, past Kara Kul, and all the way through the Pamir to Kashmir and India. It was an ambitious undertaking and far more than just a hunting trip. Was this a logical leap from their prior endeavours or did their meetings with Prejevalsky and Curzon help imbue them with more desire for exploration and participation in the intrigue of the Great Game?

The first hurdle was the permission. The Pamir was a sensitive arena in which Russia and Britain were jockeying for influence. In late January 1889, probably at the suggestion of Sir Robert Morier or Thomas Sanderson, St. George wrote a detailed letter to Lieutenant-General Sir Henry Brackenbury, Director of Military Intelligence, asking for help in obtaining permission to cross the Pamirs and Hindu Kush to Chitral and Gilgit. He pointed out that if the Russians allowed any British people to make the trip, it would probably be themselves. In his letter St. George even offered to spy. Among other things he said, 'On the route I would take careful notes and collect all information of the country and its inhabitants and photograph all passes and any difficult places.'[18]

St. George must have begun reporting information informally to Ambassador Morier after his 1888 trip in the Pamirs if not earlier. Almost all British and Russian travellers in Central Asia were involved with intelligence. This was not as sinister as it sounds. Geographic knowledge was useful. The audience listening to talks at the Royal Geographical Society included many people who had both personal and professional interest in the journeys described. A few travellers, usually army officers, were sent out on intelligence missions, but most intelligence activity was a casual adjunct to hunting and exploring. When a traveller returned from a trip, he might be queried about what he had seen. Perhaps even before he left he would be asked to keep his eyes open for certain activities. Undoubtedly St. George had gained the confidence of both Morier and Sanderson with his reports in prior years. By writing to General Brackenbury, he was raising his intelligence work to a more formal level. He had an ulterior motive. He needed the strongest support possible to get the travel permits he sought, which were more difficult to obtain than ever.

Brackenbury forwarded Littledale's request with an enthusiastic endorsement to Thomas Sanderson at the Foreign Office. 'It would be from our point of view useful if he could be assisted to make the journey he proposes.' He added, 'I could not ask him to go as far as this. It is quite for consideration of F.O. [Foreign Office].' A few days later, Sanderson in turn sent a private note to Morier enclosing a copy for the Russians of St. George's proposal but with the intelligence comments deleted. Sanderson stated, however, that the first step was to get approval from the Indian government. He added:

> I have a sympathy for Littledale who seems to be a good fellow, a keen naturalist, & sensible. He doesn't rub the Russians up the wrong way, or go poking about where they tell him not to, and does not get into scrapes. Brackenbury could be glad that he should make this journey as the topographical information would be of interest. I must say it is extraordinarily plucky of Mrs. Littledale. . . .[19]

In March St. George asked Dr Gunther to write a letter to Lord Salisbury supporting his application. It seemed a natural request as he would be collecting specimens for the museum, but considering the strong government support the Littledales already had, such a letter could have been intended to help reinforce the legitimate appearance of their pursuits. But their plans did not work out.[20]

Even though St. George had the support of British Military Intelligence and the Foreign Office, the Government of India opposed the trip. Colonel John Ardagh, Private Secretary to the Viceroy of India, wrote a letter to General Brackenbury objecting to the Littledales going through the Hindu Kush because India already had all the information they wanted on that side of the passes, and they did not want to give the Russians any new information (from published accounts). He added that an English lady would be very much out of place among the Afghans and the Chitralis. Ardagh suggested the Littledales cross farther to the east into Chinese territory and go to Kashmir via the Karakoram Pass. Brackenbury forwarded Ardagh's letter to the Foreign Office on 25 March. On the back of a filing envelope is the notation, 'Mr. and Mrs. Littledale. Have abandoned their tour.' With the emphasis on the word 'their', perhaps the real reason for the rejection was concern over Teresa. In any case, despite the strong support from the highest levels of the British government, St. George wisely decided to bide his time and withdrew his request.[21]

Although the Indian authorities thought that having a woman in the party was a liability, Teresa's participation may actually have been an advantage. Local people occasionally attacked foreign parties, usually out of fear or to rob them. The presence of a woman may have made the party seem vulnerable, but this perceived weakness was offset by the formidable firepower of the Littledales' modern weapons. They would not be easy victims. On the other hand, Teresa's presence made the Littledale expeditions appear more like peaceful excursions and less of a threat, eliciting a more muted response from local officials, who did not know quite what to make of them.

After his Pamir application was rejected, St. George came up with another plan. He applied for permission to go to the Altai Mountains in Siberia and Mongolia to hunt Ovis ammon (argali). He and Teresa would be joined by S. Howard Whitbread and J.D. Cobbold, who had been included in the rejected Pamir application. St. George added that they hoped to leave for St Petersburg in three weeks. The application was quickly approved by both the British and Russian governments, a measure of the confidence both countries had in St. George, even though the party would enter a remote part of Russia and cross over into China.

Permission from China came through barely in time. Sanderson forwarded the documents to the Littledales and added helpfully, 'For your information I am to enclose a copy of the Treaty concluded between Russia and China on the 12th/24th February 1881, annexed to which is a list of the Russian and Chinese Posts at which the frontier may be passed.' The enclosed documents were in Russian.[22]

Throughout the complicated diplomatic negotiations, the Littledales were preparing for the expedition. They were confident their proposal would be accepted, and for good reason. St. George and Sir Robert Morier had been exchanging private letters in which Morier was coaching St. George every step of the way. On 14 April Morier wrote a letter in which he referred to disturbances on the Chinese border. 'These things are always kept very close & I have no means of obtaining accurate information on the subject, but if there are disquietudes down there they would be certainly unwilling that the most innocent pair of English eyes should witness what was going on.'

He added that he gave a ball at which the Empress happened to sit opposite an Ovis poli head that St. George had given him and she expressed great interest in it. 'Now it has struck me that if you have another quality fine specimen which you can spare I could find out in a diplomatic manner whether were you to offer it to H.I.M. in your name & Mrs. Littledales it would be accepted. . . . There is also another bribe I have thought of. . . .' St. George agreed and Morier responded:

> The Empress has graciously accepted the offer of the head. Mind it's the Empress not Their Majesties. You should have the case addressed to me as it will come straight and not be stopped at the Custom House. . . . I cannot yet say whether I shall get you the permission you want for if it is not granted the reason will be these mysterious rumours of disquiet on the Chinese frontier, in which case they would not let St. George himself the slayer of beasts and Russian patron saint proceed thither; but I shall move heaven & earth to find out as soon as I can.

The next day he wrote that the application had been granted, and he gave detailed suggestions for the mounting of the head for the Empress. The British Ambassador to Russia was doing everything in his power to ensure that St. George knew exactly how to curry favour from the Russians.[23]

St. George was also corresponding with Thomas Moore at the Liverpool Museum, and when a 'splendid' skull of an Ovis poli arrived from St. George, Moore was delighted. At a meeting of the Literary and Philosophical Society of Liverpool he praised St. George for his many contributions to the Liverpool Museum, and both St. George and Teresa were proposed to be Corresponding Members of the Society. Teresa would be the first woman to receive this honour. Moore also wished St. George 'every success in your new & I fear most risky of all your Expeditions. . . .'[24]

The trip was not the most risky but it is one of the least known. The only information comes from several brief letters and a short article written by St. George.[25] In his request for permission, he said they intended to travel by way of Omsk and Semipolatinsk to the Altai Mountains in Siberia. Their travels were probably similar to a subsequent trip in 1897 to the Altai but not as far east. On the later trip they used a combination of river steamer and tarantass to approach their destination.

The party left London on 28 April 1889. In St Petersburg St. George finally met Nikolai de Giers personally. He wrote, 'Nothing could be more kind than the authorities here. Mons. Giers, Foreign Minister, is a charming old gentleman & has given us some letters which will be a veritable "open sesame".' St. George also borrowed a restricted map of the Altai. It would appear that he and M. de Giers had charmed each other.[26]

The next word from the party came on 22 May, when St. George wrote to both Gunther and Moore 'On the River Irtish' asking if they would like him to purchase mammoth bones. 'They occasionally can be bought here for a few shillings each. . . .' The Irtish flows out of Zaisan Nor (lake) near the Chinese border, and the party must have followed the river to the lake and gone from there into the Tabagatai Mountains on the border of Mongolia. They left the Russian frontier with a pack train of ponies, bullocks and camels, and followed an easy route through the Saiar range into the desert, 'with its familiar pests of mosquitoes and horseflies and its never-to-be-forgotten odour of sage-brush and horse-sweat'. They crossed the Chinese border without difficulty:

A passport which the natives could not read, in vermilion and yellow, secured the neutrality of those we met, but a letter of introduction to the Chinese Governor of the district procured us a typical escort of natives, excellent horsemen and good fellows, armed, however, somewhat oddly – to wit, one carrying a Russian Berdan rifle without cartridges; another provided with an old Tower musket cut off half-way down the barrel, consequently without a foresight; a third with a matchlock; and a fourth with a horn arrangement on his finger for archery. With this little army at our back we naturally threw fear to the winds, and pressed on into the strongholds of the sheep.[27]

Their quarry was found in the high ranges beyond the desert.

The Littledales returned home the same way they had come. Along the way St. George sent to Moore a large box of mammoth bones and teeth from Siberia. They stopped off in St Petersburg, returned the borrowed map, and arrived home in October. St. George donated argali and ibex to the Natural History Museum as well as forty-seven birds from the Altai.[28]

Things were going well for the Littledales. Every year the Liverpool Museum held a soiree in St George's Hall, the building after which St. George was named. In January 1890 the exhibit featured the Littledale contributions to the Museum. It must have been impressive. Fifty trophies consisting of complete stuffed animals as well as mounted heads were placed on the orchestral platform. The display included ollen stags, bear, chamois, serow (goat-like animal), ibex, and bharal, wild sheep from the Altai. The most sensational were the Ovis poli, Marco Polo sheep shot at 15,000ft in the Pamirs in 1888.[29]

Both St. George and Teresa had become favourably known. They must have been pleased but they did not have time to bask in past glories. St. George was busy renewing his efforts to obtain permission to cross the Pamirs into India. The stage was set for the first of their three great expeditions to Central Asia.

7

Across the Pamirs

> . . . it will be something to have done.
> *Teresa Littledale*

The word Pamir means a high mountain valley formed by glaciers and bordered by mountains.[1] The Pamirs of today cover a broad area that includes the highest mountains of Tajikistan, formerly part of the Soviet Union. In the Littledales' time those were called the Trans Alai Mountains. In the late nineteenth century 'the Pamirs' had a narrower meaning. They were limited to the area south of the Trans Alai Mountains and north-west of Hunza, with the Little Pamir part of what is now the Wakhan Corridor of Afghanistan. The valleys have an elevation of 12,000 to 14,000ft, with the surrounding peaks rising to 20,000ft or higher, and are buried in deep snow at least seven months of the year. There is an abundance of grazing but no cultivation of crops. The only fuel comes from a few scrubs and animal dung. The Littledales would have to go well prepared.

They planned to repeat their 1888 route to Kara Kul and continue south from there. They knew that crossing the Pamirs through the Wakhan Corridor to Chitral and India would be more than a difficult extension of their previous trip. It would involve increased risk from local people, who were hostile to all foreigners. The Littledales would also encounter political turbulence from the Great Game being played out by Britain and Russia. But there were precedents.

To the consternation of British officials in India, the Frenchman Gabriel Bonvalot and his companions, Guillaume Capus and Albert Pepin, had already traversed the Pamirs from north to south in the spring of 1887. When they appeared in Chitral, the local ruler seized them and sent them under escort to Simla, where they were interviewed by the Viceroy himself, Lord Dufferin.[2] Their expedition was proof to the Littledales that their trip was possible. Furthermore, being first is always harder. However, as the Littledales were English, they would face a different set of political problems.

Their initial challenge was to get permission at the height of the Great Game. After all, the reason they had gone to Mongolia in 1889 was because of the Pamirs rejection. That summer Colonel Ardagh, the Viceroy's Private Secretary, investigated the Indian Government's formal policy regarding travellers on its frontiers and discovered no written policy existed. As a result, he drafted a policy, whereupon Lord Lansdowne, now the Viceroy, declared himself ready to encourage explorers of 'acknowledged utility', an indirect recognition that General Brackenbury had been right regarding the usefulness of the Littledales.[3]

A close relationship that had developed between Morier and Littledale does not account fully for the success of the Littledales' Pamirs application. In the Public Record Office outside London the confirmation of what had happened appears in the Foreign Office papers for Russia under a sub-category, 'Proceedings in Central Asia'. This innocuous title disguises its contents, the confidential and secret reports and correspondence on Central Asia during the Great Game. Normally St. George's letters of application to travel in Russian Central Asia were filed with the diplomatic papers for Russia, but this time his letter was buried in the secret papers. Dated 16 January 1890, St. George had sent it to Sir Thomas Sanderson, Assistant Under Secretary in the Foreign Office. Once again he was requesting permission to travel on the Transcaspian Railway for the purpose of collecting big game in the Pamirs. He added that from what Sir Robert Morier had told him, he did not expect any difficulties from the Russians.

St. George did not know Morier had written a long letter to Lord Salisbury, the Foreign Secretary, about requests to the Russian authorities for permission to travel on the railway. Salisbury had forwarded requests for a Mr and Mrs Kennedy to go to Samarkand and for two British officers, one of whom was Lieutenant John Manners-Smith, stationed at Gilgit, to travel the railway and spend two months in Russian Central Asia. Morier was quite blunt, saying such requests were difficult for both himself and M. de Giers, the Russian Foreign Minister, and he had discussed it privately with his Russian friend. M. de Giers had told him that in Russia the person who made the decision was the Governor General of the Caucasus, and that the Russian War Ministry was adverse to giving permission to British officers. Morier did not wish to request permission for the two officers, but he would accommodate the Kennedys, '. . . having taken very great trouble to obtain for Mr. Curzon permission to go to Meshed via the Transcaspian Railway to Askabad, that gentleman's very able but outspoken letters in the "Times" have not contributed to reconcile the Russian officials to the idea of throwing open their Transcaspian provinces to the searching observation of British eyes.'[4]

Salisbury asked both the India Office and the War Office for their comments. The India Office replied that in light of Russia's attitude, applications by British subjects to travel in Russian Central Asia should not be submitted. The War Office in London was made of sterner stuff, declaring they should force the Russians to allow British officers to travel through their territory. It is hard to understand why they thought the Russians should let them go in even though the British would not allow Russian officers to do the same. The British had denied permission for Captain Gromchevsky to visit Ladakh.

The Littledales' application was looking better all the time. On 7 March they were notified by the Foreign Office that permission had been granted.[5] The last month before their departure was hectic. Besides the usual difficulties such as shipping their heavy baggage to Batum, they still needed Chinese passports 'for that part of Chinese Territory lying to the South & East of Kashgar'. The Chinese Minister, Lew Tajen, complained about Littledale. 'We are not very fond of asking for his favours.' Nonetheless he gave in and sent the passports over to the Foreign Office the day before departure. Then there were the Russian passports. They had been issued in Russian, and the Littledales were afraid that in Afghanistan, where Russians were hated, the Wakhis would think they were Russian. St. George had the Foreign Office translate the passports into Persian, a language the Wakhis would understand.[6]

Despite the last minute chaos, both St. George and Teresa were excited. For the first time this would not be primarily a hunting trip. They had more ambitious goals. Teresa was well aware of the potential significance of their journey. 'We are now off on one of our expeditions to Central Asia & hope to get across to India. It is a big trip & I do not know whether we shall accomplish it. I hope we shall for it will be something to have done.'[7]

They left London on 10 April 1890 and arrived in Odessa a week later.[8] The steamer for Batum was leaving in only 4 hours, so they spent the short time rushing frantically about, buying supplies that would not be available farther on. While St. George dashed off to make arrangements for the steamer, Teresa took the baggage to their hotel, where she met Yudin, their interpreter. He had come from St Petersburg, where Charles Eliot at the British Embassy had hired him. Yudin was wearing an immaculate shirt collar and white satin tie. When St. George saw him, his heart sank. How was this city dandy going to survive the wilds of the Pamirs? However, Yudin was efficient, and with his aid the Littledales were able to make their purchases and get their baggage aboard the SS *Tzarevna* with a little time to spare. Patrick Stevens, now British Consul in Odessa, came down to see them off. When he saw Yudin, he said, 'Why did you not ask me to find you an interpreter? I have a capital man, a Persian.' He was just what St. George needed. As the ship began to pull away, he yelled, 'Send him by next steamer – will wait.'

The *Tzarevna* slowly crawled around the Crimea with long stops at Sebastopol, Yalta, Theodosia and other ports. It was foggy and rainy and Teresa caught a bad cold. On 22 April they reached Batum, where they learned that their shipping agent's office had just burned down. Fortunately the baggage was still at the Customs House, but the keys were buried in the ashes. St. George offered some local men a liberal reward and they dug up most of the keys. This good news was offset by problems with the guns and ammunition, which had been shipped separately. As personal baggage they would have passed customs but they were not permitted as freight. It would take five days to resolve the problem.

Teresa went ahead to Tiflis with Yudin because she was still sick and the climate was healthier there. She spent her time tracking down dried ox tongues in the local shops. It took awhile since she could find only two or three at each place, but eventually she accumulated forty of them. Meanwhile, the new interpreter sent by Mr Stevens arrived in Batum and joined St. George. Joseph Abbas had travelled extensively throughout Central Asia with numerous travellers including the Reverend Henry Lansdell.

On 27 April St. George, Joseph and the baggage finally arrived in Tiflis. The reunited Littledales visited the Sunday street bazaar, and that afternoon St. George called on their friend Dr Raddé at the Natural History Museum. He also visited General Shérématieff, now the acting governor.[9] The General was impressed by St. George's reputation as a hunter. When he found out the Littledales had verbal permission to travel in Transcaspia but nothing in writing, he said that because they had been there before, he would write to General Komaroff, the Governor General of Transcaspia, and there would be no problem.

The Littledales left Tiflis on the late night train and arrived in Baku the following afternoon. The next day they boarded a steamer and crossed the Caspian. They were met at Usunada by an officer sent by Colonel Andrieff, the acting head of the Transcaspian Railway. The officer told them a special carriage would be attached to the train to take them all the way to Samarkand. Later Colonel Andrieff himself joined them for dinner on the steamer. It was a leisurely meal despite the imminent scheduled departure of the train, but the Littledales were not concerned. Colonel Andrieff was taking the same train and they knew it would not leave without him.

On the train that evening the Littledales were delighted with their accommodations. They had the entire carriage to themselves. They arranged one compartment as a bedroom with their camp mattresses on top of airbeds, and Teresa could even wear her regular nightgown to bed. There was a dining car with reasonably good food under the circumstances. The Littledales passed the time playing cards and watching people. 'We have played Piquet all day and I have won steadily. Poor Georgie cannot say it is want of shuffling.' They noticed that the Russian Consul for Kashgar was also on board. This had to be the formidable Nikolai Petrovsky, whom the Littledales would meet in Kashgar in 1893. Teresa recognised a couple from their Caspian steamer, a woman and a Russian officer. Teresa had supposed they were husband and wife, but to her surprise the officer left the train at Ashkhabad and the woman went on to Samarkand. The 2-day rail trip to Samarkand had been a restful one, thanks to Colonel Andrieff's hospitality. 'We have blessed him every hour of the journey.'

They spent four days in Samarkand, mostly making packing boxes for their supplies. A general who called on them reported that another English couple, a Mr and Mrs Kennedy, had passed through a few weeks before. Teresa must have been pleased to hear that when Mrs Kennedy told the general she was the first English woman to visit Samarkand, he informed her that Mrs Littledale had been there ahead of her.

They had to buy a tarantass for the trip to Osh but the vehicles were in short supply. Even the Chief of Police joined in the search. The only tarantass available belonged to the Governor, General Iphemavitch, who wanted 150 roubles for it. The Littledales considered the price outrageous but had to pay the full amount because it was the only tarantass for sale in the town. The local people knew the Governor wanted to sell it and they did not dare compete with him.

On 8 May the Littledales rode out of Samarkand in the tarantass under a white cover Teresa had made to keep out the sun. The baggage followed in a large cart. The water was low in the Zarafshan River and they crossed it easily. A scarcity of horses created problems. At the first station beyond Samarkand, the Littledales had to wait all night for horses before they could continue on. After trying to sleep in the tarantass, Teresa gave up and went into the station, where she read until midnight and finally fell asleep on the bench.

The road from Samarkand to Margilan crossed barren country with occasional green oases. Snow-covered mountain peaks rose to the north and south. The scenery reminded St. George of the Vale of Kashmir. They reached Margilan on 13 May. St. George tracked down Azim, their Kirghiz cook two years before, and rehired him, to their mutual delight. The next day they bought a 5-month supply of white flour as well as onions and potatoes. St. George also bought an expensive English-made revolver for Yudin, who managed to lose it a few hours later.

Teresa was unhappy. 'I wish with all my heart that I had never come on this trip.' She complained in her private diary that St. George had not brought enough money for shopping, her chief pleasure, and that having two interpreters was a waste of money, especially as both of them were ineffective at haggling in the bazaar and preparing meals. She also mentioned that St. George was sick. However, it would be a mistake to put too much emphasis on her comments. Teresa was the only woman on her expeditions and had no one to confide in. She rarely complained to St. George. It would not have been seemly at that time and she would not have wanted to be left behind. She used her diary to let off steam and then continued to soldier on in public. She could never have imagined her private writings would be read by strangers a hundred years later.

They left Margilan that evening. Yudin and Azim were to follow the next morning in the supply cart. They travelled all night with only a brief stop for tea and soup at 5 o'clock in the morning and arrived later that morning at Osh at the end of the post road, 500 miles beyond Samarkand. There they met an old friend, the former station master, who recognised them immediately – not very difficult since few foreigners had reached Osh by 1890, much less an English woman returning for the second time. The Littledales settled into a house next door to him, and he and his wife cooked for them. That afternoon St. George went to see Colonel Deubner, the local governor, whom he had met in 1888. He was busy tending to his silk worms. St. George also found his old caravan bashi, who, like Azim, was pleased to be joining the Littledales again.

They spent a week in Osh obtaining men, horses and supplies. The Littledales gave great importance to the quality and care of their gear. In selecting their equipment, they used their years of experience in camping and hunting on three continents. From their previous trip they were familiar with the rough conditions in the Pamir, especially the cold and the daily gales of wind that swept across the land, blowing out their cooking fires and dumping sand on everything.

The Littledales were prepared. They took as little weight as possible for that time and bought the best equipment available that would do the job. In the 1890s the best equipment was not light by modern standards. 'Our tent was ten feet square, American drill, with a dark-blue lining, and an outer fly with a porch. It weighed, without poles, 80 lb. Edgington made it to our own design seven years ago. We have used it every year since then, and it looks good for another seven years.' They attributed the good health they had enjoyed on their expeditions to always being warm and dry at night. They took camp beds similar to Indian charpoys but lighter. Even so, the beds weighed 20lb each. They used a ground cloth under the beds at night and slept on air mattresses, and they each had plenty of blankets and other bedding kept inside a waterproof canvas roll. They brought a folding stove, folding chair, table and stool, and a small light carpet. The stove had a chimney that 'runs together like a telescope'. St. George brought one small trunk containing such things as photographic supplies, bird-stuffing tools, aneroid barometers, boiling-point thermometers and gifts for local tribesmen. With tent, bedding, trunks, rifles, ammunition, tent poles, pegs, chair and table, they had three pony loads of gear.[10]

Teresa had 'of course' brought her side-saddle from England but St. George purchased a local Kirghiz saddle for himself. It was uncomfortable and required the rider to rely on balance, but after a few days he became accustomed to it. Based on their prior Pamir experience, they obtained a yurt for the kitchen as protection against the wind. As it turned out, the yurt was so much warmer than their own tent that they used it for sleeping and stretched the other tent over the top of the thick felt for added warmth.

More time was spent buying horses. After a few days of negotiating in the bazaar, they purchased twelve. Colonel Deubner furnished them with eight more and men to take care of them. In case of accidents he added more horses and men at no additional charge. Their old caravan bashi supplied additional horses. With the aid of Colonel Deubner, they obtained two jiguits, unofficial policemen and couriers, to serve as guards. Because of the lack of firewood in the Pamirs, the Littledales baked 2,000 biscuits and dried them in the sun until they were as hard as stone and would last indefinitely. St. George bought a sheepskin coat that reached down to his heels, and Teresa had a cape of Harris cloth lined with lambskin from Kashgar.

Departure day was 22 May. Colonel Deubner saw them off, and the caravan of eight men and about two dozen horses left Osh at 1 o'clock in the afternoon. St. George arranged for one interpreter and one jiguit to go last in the caravan line at all times, following the others so nothing could be stolen or tumble off the horses without being seen. Although he made no comment on this system, it was a clever move. One man bringing up the rear might be tempted to take something, but two men of disparate backgrounds would be keeping an eye on each other.

Two days later they reached Gulcha, where they had to stay for six days. St. George wanted to follow the Gulcha River and then cross over the Little Alai range to the Alai Plateau, but the two main passes, the Taldik (11,600ft) and the Shart (12,800ft), had been closed by snow during the winter and there was conflicting information about them. St. George sent out Joseph, a jiguit, and a local Kirghiz to reconnoitre the passes so that the entire party would not have to camp at the base for a fortnight with the horses eating precious barley.

The reconnaissance party returned four days later. They had forced their way to the summit of the Taldik but their horses sank deep into the snow. The Kirghiz had gone down the other side on foot and thought the pass would not open for ten days. Joseph added that the Terek Dawan, another pass, was impassable because melting snow had made the road too slippery. At this point St. George decided to go to Akbosaga at the foot of the Taldik Pass and wait for the pass to clear. They needed more horses to carry grain up to Akbosaga, so St. George sent the other jiguit back to Osh with a note asking Colonel Deubner to send ten to twelve horses fully loaded with barley to Kara Kul, where the Littledales would wait for them.

They left the next morning, following the Gulcha River. The trail at one point went around a rocky buttress overhanging the water, and the horses had to be led one by one. Later on the Littledales would look back nostalgically at that spot as having been relatively easy.

Along the march the Littledales bought a six-week-old puppy. It had rushed out at them aggressively from a Kirghiz yurt and barked, so Teresa suggested buying it. St. George paid 20 kopecks to the man living in the yurt. After they left, another Kirghiz rushed after St. George and claimed he was the owner, so St. George paid another 20 kopecks to him. When they reached their next campsite, the expensive puppy would not let anyone touch him. Finally St. George and some other men managed to catch him and pen him up. When the Littledales fed him, he became more friendly. They called him 'Murnok' after the name of his master, presumably the legitimate one. They tied the dog to the tent pole for the night to get him used to living by their tent, and they did not allow anyone else to feed him because they wanted him to bond with them. The next day the caravan moved on with Azim carrying Murnok on his saddle. That night the puppy barked and growled at everyone who came near the tent. It was exactly what the Littledales wanted.

They had a hot march along the river the next day. There were clumps of poplars in the riverbed and pines on the surrounding hillsides. Along the trail the Littledales met many old acquaintances among the Kirghiz, including their former hunter. He wanted to join them so St. George rehired him and promised him the same wages as before.

At 4 o'clock they reached Akbosaga at 9,300ft. In camp they met two caravans from Kashgar that had tried unsuccessfully to cross the Terek Pass and had made a seven-day detour over the Taldik because it had less snow. The Littledales spent a day resting and regrouping. The Kirghiz asked St. George to feed them and he refused. He knew he had to feed the men anyway, but he wanted it to be a gift and not an obligation so the men could not complain. He rented two yurts with two men to care for them and four horses to carry them, and he hired still more horses to carry firewood and barley. He also added five sheep to their walking larder.

On 3 June they climbed several thousand feet and crossed the Taldik Pass. Ahead of them the Alai Plateau was brown and desolate. There were no trees or bushes after Akbosaga, and except for marmots and great bustards – large ground-dwelling birds with long necks and legs – there was not a living thing in sight. The Littledales reached the campsite of Katin Art just as a thunderstorm hit.

Their yurts had preceded them and were already pitched by the time they arrived. It was cold, and to Teresa their yurt was inadequate. 'I blame St. George entirely about it. I have begged and entreated at Osh that I might have a new yurt . . . but he was determined not to spend the money for a new one. . . . Four months warmth and comfort is worth a few roubles.' She was so tired the next morning that St. George sent a jiguit back for a better yurt, and the caravan stayed in place to wait for it.

The following day the Kirghiz who were transporting the yurts went on strike. The men said they had received no money and would go no farther. They saddled their horses and tried to ride off but were stopped. St. George had paid an official at Akbosaga 15 roubles in advance for the transport of the yurts but he learned the official had kept the entire amount and the men got nothing. The Littledales considered the Kirghiz disagreeable and unreliable, but they both recognised that when it came to money, the men had been so badly cheated by their own chiefs that they trusted no one. Such swindling was a common and difficult problem. St. George negotiated with the men, and after 3 hours they agreed to work off the money he had advanced to their chief, after which they would be paid every evening.

That day the caravan crossed the desolate Alai Plain. It was very cold with frequent thunderstorms. The Trans Alai Mountains, including Peak Kauffman (Peak Communism), stretched out as far as the eye could see, with snow covering the mountains all the way down to the base. The next day the party endured hail storms and a cold river crossing, stopping several miles up a narrow valley leading to the Kizil Art in a sheltered spot where there was good grazing.

At 4 o'clock in the morning St. George and several Kirghiz went out to check the snow conditions on the Kizil Art. Upon their return, the Littledales decided to take a small party across the pass to hunt in a valley they had visited in 1888. Joseph and the main party would wait for the barley caravan Colonel Deubner was sending from Osh and then cross over the pass to Kara Kul, where the Littledales would join them.

Personal conflicts arose. The simmering discontent was brought to a head by a small packet of tea. Yudin said it was missing and he suspected that Azim, the cook, had stolen it. Both Teresa and St. George thought this was quite likely, but they told Yudin not to say anything about it to Azim as he was quick tempered and would leave, a great loss as he could not be replaced. Azim was more than a good cook. He spoke Russian, and there was no other way to communicate with the Kirghiz except through Joseph, whose English was weak. Later Azim told St. George he wished to leave because Yudin had accused him of stealing the tea. It took St. George over an hour to calm him down. Yudin had also upset Joseph. Teresa wrote, 'Yudin is so young he has no tact [and tends] to ride roughshod over them which both Joseph and Azim resent.' To solve the problem, the Littledales decided to keep everything locked up.

The next morning, 7 June, the small advance hunting party crossed the 14,200ft Kizil Art and reached the old Littledale campsite on the Markan Su (river), which flowed into the Kashgar River. The day was beautiful but cold. The jiguit who had gone back for another yurt arrived with more felt and sticks, and the Littledales erected their new yurt. Despite its warmth, Teresa was still not satisfied. 'It is very nice but rather too large.'

That afternoon St. George went out with several Kirghiz to look for Ovis poli. When he returned empty handed, the men informed him of another foreigner camped nearby, also hunting Ovis poli, and he was coming over to visit them. Soon Major Charles S. Cumberland arrived in camp, dressed in native costume.

Cumberland had spent the winter in Kashgar and was returning to England by way of the Pamirs and Russia, hunting as he went. An epidemic several years before had greatly reduced the Ovis poli herds but he had managed to shoot several of them, including one that afternoon. He heard about the foreigners and walked 2 miles to the Littledales' camp even though it was getting dark. Teresa had already gone to bed. St. George and the Major exchanged news and gossip. Cumberland had information about the capture at Samarkand of the murderer of Andrew Dalgleish, who had been killed near the Karakoram Pass in 1888. In turn, Cumberland learned that the Littledales intended to go to Kashmir by way of Chitral. He tried to dissuade them from the journey, telling them the river fords were deep and dangerous at that time of year and they stood a good chance of losing their baggage.[11] There is an intriguing entry in Teresa's diary about this meeting. Unfortunately flood damage prevents it from being deciphered completely. She wrote, 'We suppose ———— the passes —— —— as his expenses ———— paid by the Intelligence Department or rather the Indian Department to whom he has referred when he asked to be sent over here. They pay him no salary but has all his expenses ——

———— they paid ours or at least St. George's.' Even with words missing, Teresa's comments confirm that St. George was helping British military intelligence as he had proposed. At the end of their meeting, St. George gave Cumberland the books he and Teresa had finished reading and escorted him halfway back to his camp.

Azim woke the Littledales up at half past four the next morning and served them breakfast in bed. Some of the horses had wandered off in the night so they stayed in bed while waiting for them to be found. However, Major Cumberland returned unexpectedly at 6 o'clock, whereupon the Littledales jumped out of bed and offered him breakfast. He politely declined, saying he had just eaten a breakfast of cold ham and bread and jam. St. George was envious because he had been deprived of jam for some time. Cumberland gave him a good Ladakhi fur cap. St. George would have liked his saddle but did not want to say anything. Teresa thought he should have spoken up because Cumberland intended to discard everything at Margilan. Cumberland said good-bye and left for the Kizil Art.

When the missing horses had not turned up by 9 o'clock, the Littledales started off without them. For the next four days they travelled through the Kara Julga, a barren valley leading to the Kara Kul. The valley was almost devoid of vegetation. Nearby were large snow peaks, some well over 20,000ft high. A few of the side valleys were blocked by glaciers. St. George wrote:

This Central Asian scenery has a type of its own, quite different from the Swiss or Caucasian mountain scenes, where your eye when tired wanders from grand ice-fields above to a pleasant change of green pastures and then forests of pine below. Here, though the mountains are higher, the glaciers, owing to the small snowfall, are much more puny, while below there is a picture of utter desolation that would be hard to match in any other part of the world.[12]

Each day St. George rose early and went hunting. He shot several small Ovis poli but was disappointed that nothing was of trophy caliber. Furthermore he was suffering from lumbago. Several days later his back hurt so much that he remained in camp.

Friday 13 June turned out to be a lucky day. The Littledales were moving on toward the Kara Kul, and just as their route intersected the main track, they ran into Joseph and the remainder of their expedition as well as the horses from Osh loaded with the extra grain. It was perfect timing. The day was warm and the reunited party crossed the Kichkine Kizil Art at 14,200ft. Because of quicksand they were unable to drop directly down to the lake but had to make a long detour over high rough ground to reach it. Murnok, the Kirghiz puppy, ran much of the way and collapsed when the caravan stopped. They made camp in an area near a stagnant pool of alkali water and with no source of fuel, not even burtsa roots. However, they were partially compensated by the view. Snowy mountains surrounded the Kara Kul and its waters were deep blue. The Littledales had arrived at the farthest point of their first Pamir trip two years before. From now on they would be moving through territory unknown to them.

The next day the caravan marched across a flat plain for over 25 miles. Personnel difficulties erupted again, this time between Joseph and a jiguit. They had a violent argument. The jiguit was about to leave for Osh, and Joseph was so livid that he struck the other man with an axe handle. The Littledales hauled Joseph into their yurt and calmed him down so they would have an interpreter when they reached Afghanistan. Then they somehow convinced the jiguit to stay. Soon this human storm blew over and everyone got along again, at least for a few more days.

The following morning all the horses were missing. While the men went out to look for them, the Littledales moved on ahead and camped at 14,300ft below the Tuyuk Pass. They crossed the pass and reached the Murghab River on 17 June. To the east they had a fine view of snow-covered Mustagh Ata (Ice Mountain Father), 24,750ft high.

They decided to go on by way of the Alichur River and Great Pamirs to the village of Kala-i-Panj, and then up the Wakhan River to Sarhad and the Baroghil Pass. They left a supply of barley, firewood and food with the local Kirghiz headman in case they were forced to return. The weather had changed and it was hot. Teresa tied handkerchiefs around her straw hat and lined the brim with dark blue cotton. They passed a few Kirghiz yurts, where they stopped for milk. They pitched camp beside a shallow stream that became very deep by evening from the afternoon snowmelt.

The following day they crossed another high pass. At the lunch spot St. George went off hunting for Ovis poli, leaving Teresa to move on ahead and select the next campsite. She was not happy. 'The long marches are quite enough for me without having to hunt a camping ground and get the yourt pitched and everything settled. It is a horrible camping ground, so dirty and high wind which we have had in our faces all day. I am tired to death. There is no grass for the horses and I am thankful we cannot remain here.'

They made a 3-hour march down the Alichur River to look for a guide. The valley was littered with hundreds of Ovis poli horns, including some very large ones. Local Kirghiz told the Littledales that the pass they wanted to take was blocked with snow, so the party continued down the Alichur River to try another route. Close to Afghanistan territory they persuaded a Kirghiz chief to find them a guide. The man said he could take them anywhere except heaven or hell. St. George hired him. Two days later the guide got lost.

In the morning thirty horses were missing. St. George learned that all of the hired horses belonged to two men except for one belonging to the caravan bashi's brother. The other two men had bullied him into watching the horses at night alone. As he could not walk all day and watch horses all night, he fell asleep and the horses wandered. The initial hunt produced fifteen of them. Then, contrary to express orders, the caravan men rode out of camp on the Littledales' horses instead of their own to look for the rest. So St. George sent out some Kirghiz on the caravan men's horses to assist in the search. At last all of the missing animals were found, but the caravan men were furious their horses had been used. They refused to pack the horses and announced that they and their horses were leaving the expedition. St. George had to take firm action. He informed the caravan bashi that the men could leave but that the Littledales had engaged their horses for as long as they liked and they meant to keep them. Furthermore, if the men tried to take them, he would shoot every horse they had. For good measure, he reminded them that if they broke their contract and returned to Turkestan, they would be put in prison, but if they remained, they would get not only their wages but a present as well. The quarrel ended as quickly as it had begun. By evening the men were happily feasting on a sheep that St. George thought it 'politic to discover I did not want. . . . They were just like children, but firmness at first, and then conciliation, got over all our difficulties.'

The next night the Littledales assigned Iris, a jiguit from Osh, to watch over the horses for an extra 20 kopecks a night. They also picked up a hunter, an old Kirghiz with only one eye. When St. George asked him if there were Ovis poli on the other side of the passes, the hunter replied that he could not be sure because the sheep did not have houses to live in. 'A very good answer, I thought.'[13]

The following day they crossed over two high passes in one long fatiguing march. It began with a steep climb up the 15,150-ft Kundey Pass, where the view from the top revealed that their guide had taken them up the wrong valley and their climb could have been avoided had they gone farther on. They descended steeply down fine gravel and loose stones, and then climbed up the 14,550-ft Kargosh Pass, followed by a winding 7-mile descent through masses of rocks to the Pamir River. On the trail they met a lot of Kirghiz migrating from the Wakhan to the Alichur Pamir for the summer. Although camp was pitched late, the river was broad and deep with no alkali and there was grass for the animals.

The Littledales decided to make a detour to Victoria Lake for hunting. After a cold march up the Pamir River, they camped at the lake on 27 June at nearly 14,000ft. They had been in the saddle for over 9 hours. Teresa was cold despite her furs but she found the scenery magnificent, especially the mountain range to the south with its snowy peaks and glaciers and to the south-west a high triangular peak towering over the other mountains. She wrote, 'It is quite an event arriving at the "Victoria Lake." It is something to have seen what very few people have seen and no white woman.' She had every right to be pleased with her accomplishment. The lake was a major landmark in the Pamirs but it had rarely been visited by westerners.[14] She was in an exclusive group. Yet in her moment of elation, she knew that the most difficult and dangerous part of their journey lay ahead.

8

To Gilgit

Certainly one of the grandest journeys
ever performed by a lady.
Reverend Henry Lansdell[1]

The Littledales spent a day at Victoria Lake. Although it was late June,
much of the water was still covered with winter ice, and the first night
was so cold that the open water froze over. That day Ali Bey arrived in
camp. He was a guide who had been promised to them by the headman
of Murghab. He obviously knew the country well. He told the
Littledales they had come the wrong way and could not go by way of
Kala-i-panj to Sarhad in summer because the rivers were unfordable.
Instead, they would have to find a pass over to the next valley, the Little
Pamir, and follow the Wakhan River.[2] St. George was familiar with
glacier-fed rivers, which can rise from the summer snowmelt until they
become impassable. Even so, he found Ali Bey's statement
incomprehensible because Kala-i-panj was the obvious route, but Ali
Bey stuck to it so firmly that St. George changed his plans.

He sent horses back for the wood and barley they had left behind on
the Pamir River. He also sent back the rented yurts and their attendants
and the old one-eyed Kirghiz hunter. On 30 June 1890 the Littledales
left Victoria Lake. They headed east up the valley and had lunch beside
a stream full of small trout. St. George tried to shoot some. 'After
wasting numerous shot cartridges I arrived at the conclusion that if a
fish has twelve inches of water over him he is safe.'[3]

In the afternoon the party crossed a pass to the headwaters of the
Alichur Pamir and pitched camp. That night there was a tremendous
row outside their tent, and when the Littledales went to investigate,
they found it was the old guide, who was furious at the way he had
been treated by Joseph. Joseph apologised but Teresa was not appeased.
'Joseph . . . tried to make all sorts of excuses, but he is a most
passionate fellow, lazy and likes to ride rough shod over everybody. I
dislike him. We have had more quarreling in the last two expeditions
than we have ever had in all our other expeditions put together.' She
then indulged in a fantasy that many travellers have had at one time or

another about their companions. 'I would like to send Mr. Whitbread and Joseph out together.'

They made a short march to the Teter Su, where they would stay for six days. While St. George went hunting, Teresa supervised the setting up of camp. The site was at 14,800ft and exposed to wind. They drove tent pegs deep into the ground and placed rocks on them to keep the lines firm during the strong gales and heavy snowstorms. St. George kept busy. 'With an improvised needle and mesh and a ball of twine I made a net, so as to be ready for the next lot of trout we might meet.' There was also the daily crisis. This time it was the sugar. There were only four pieces left. Their four-month supply was used up in six weeks. Yudin blamed Joseph, Joseph blamed a Kirghiz hunter, but Azim had the key to the box in which it was kept. The men were given ½ piece each and were told there would be no more for the rest of the trip. Teresa took possession of the key. There was one pleasant moment. To the delight of the Littledales, Dewanna, the elder Kirghiz from the 1888 hunting trip, arrived in camp.

The next day St. George shot an Ovis poli with a head of about 50 inches. Then on the evening of 3 July he returned to camp at 11 o'clock empty handed but with a story of the sheep that got away that any fisherman would envy. He had spotted three Ovis poli rams a long way off, but before he could reach them they had disappeared during a snow flurry. When the sheep caught the hunters' wind, they bolted from behind some rocks and dashed across open ground. St. George quickly fired at the centre ram, by far the biggest sheep he had ever seen. Before he could shoot again, the sheep disappeared in a dip in the ground. When the men went to investigate, the three sheep reappeared, moving up the other side of the ravine, the huge ram lagging behind the other two. The men followed them and found a bloody track. The big sheep had been hit. St. George began to stalk the wounded animal to finish it off but it kept getting up and moving forward.

St. George marvelled at the vitality of the Ovis poli. It even climbed a thousand feet up a snow slope. Suddenly a heavy storm engulfed the hunters and covered everything in 6 inches of fresh snow. Afterwards St. George, numb and cold, tried to follow his quarry by kicking the new snow away with his feet to look for blood, but eventually he had to give up the search. He had lost his prize ram. It was terrible having to abandon a wounded animal, and he knew he would never see a greater Ovis poli.[4]

Meanwhile, Ali Bey had become ill, probably from the altitude. St. George left him in a Kirghiz yurt at the bottom of the hill and returned to camp with Dewanna. Ali Bey returned to camp the next day rather the worse for wear. St. George was not in good condition either. He had banged his knee on a rock and injured his ankle, requiring a rest of several days. However, remembering his obligations to Dr Gunther and the Natural History Museum, he offered 25 kopecks for every mouse up to 6 that anyone caught. Yudin promptly found a dead mouse on the ground.

A week later the Littledales broke camp and moved south through a storm, stopping at the base of the Andemin Pass. They had to use their last sticks of firewood to cook dinner and breakfast as no other fuel was available. During the night another storm blew in. The snow was so heavy that St. George got up at 4 o'clock in the morning and cleared it off the tent to prevent the ridgepole from breaking. Everything was soaked, but without fuel the party had to push on.

It was still snowing heavily when they started. Climbing above 15,000ft, they crossed the pass, descended the south side, and reached the Ak Su (river), which they followed until they found a campsite within a mile of the Little Pamir Lake. Fortunately there was plenty of grass and root fuel. There were also some disquieting rumours. They were now in a region claimed by Russia, China, and Afghanistan. A Kirghiz they met said he had run away from a Kunjut (Hunza) raiding party in the vicinity, and he warned the Littledales to be well prepared. St. George was sceptical of all statements from local men but he could not ignore this one. Hunza's reputation in the late nineteenth century was not that of an earthly paradise where people lived to a ripe old age, but a robber kingdom with an economy based on the raiding of trade caravans and the selling of their neighbours into slavery. The Hunzakuts' propensity for such activity had increased under the rule of Safdar Ali, who had begun his regime in 1886 by murdering his father.[5] By the summer of 1890 Safdar Ali was at the height of his intransigence. The caravan men were afraid of the Hunzakuts and asked St. George if he was going to Hunza. Although he was planning to take the men to Sarhad, he learned later that their guide had been telling the men he was taking them through Hunza to India and abandoning them.

They passed through terrain resembling a swampy Scottish moor and followed a stream teeming with trout. This time St. George had greater success. They drove dozens of trout into his newly made net and the entire party feasted on the catch. After 10 miles the valley narrowed and began to drop steeply down a gorge. At this point another stream flowed in from the south and here the party camped. Nearby was a tomb that gave the place its name, Bozai Gumbaz.[6] The location made such a slight impression on Teresa that she did not even mention its name in her diary. Within a year it would become famous as the site of one of the most dramatic encounters in the Great Game.

Beyond Bozai Gumbaz the track became a narrow slash along the steep side of a mountain. Teresa walked most of the way to avoid falling off her horse into the water. At a shallow though difficult river crossing the animals kept stumbling on large stones covering the stream bed. The men stripped down to their underwear and entered the water with ropes to help the horses across. St. George was relieved when the trunk containing his photographs and papers got across safely.

Teresa was almost disappointed in the river. 'We expected something much worse. I wished to be allowed to walk across but St. George objected. . . . He said I should have to keep my boots on if I did! There certainly was no necessity to walk so I ended in riding and got over without the least difficulty.' Her next comment reflected her Victorian background. 'I have shown a good deal of legs as I pinned my dress up around my waist to keep it dry.' During lunch they enjoyed sitting under bushes, the first shrubs they had seen since leaving Akbosaga almost two months before. The next day the gorge became narrower and steeper:

> . . . the worst road we have ever been over, frightfully steep ascents and descents. At one place the road led down to the river edge over large boulders, really no path, and no room for the packs between the water and the rocks. The horses had been unpacked and St. George and the men carried the packs on their backs along the river for a long distance and up a steep slippery rock.

At first the caravan bashi was uncooperative and refused to bring his horses along, telling St. George to carry the loads himself. St. George declared that he would. At this the bashi offered to take anything, but St. George pushed him away and picked up a load. He reproached Ali Bey for taking them the wrong way. Ali Bey replied that he had not been there for five years and that in such country an hour was sufficient to destroy a road.

The Littledales had hoped to reach Sarhad that day but it was too far so they camped on a hill with water, good grass and beautiful mountain scenery. Teresa was pleased at her effort on the expedition. She had grown stronger both physically and mentally. 'I do not know how I have the courage to ride along some of the paths along the steep sides of the mountains and the paths only about a foot or less! wide. I have surprised St. George this year. He says I am not the same woman.'

That evening Iris, one of the Kirghiz jiguits from Osh, startled the Littledales by asking them through Joseph to take him to India because he had an uncle in Peshawar and could make more money there. When St. George asked him about his wife, Joseph replied that Muslims do not mind leaving their wives for five years or so and she was living with her people. The Littledales agreed to keep him. He was hard-working and quiet, by far the best man they had, and he would be helpful later in getting them over the Baroghil and Darkot passes.

The terrain continued to be difficult. The distance from Bozai Gumbaz to Sarhad was only 42 miles but the track went over one spur after another. Teresa wrote, 'I walked up the steep places but I find it terrible hard work at such an elevation.' Some sections were too narrow for the horses with packs, and the men had to unload them and carry the loads themselves. A few years later on this track, Lord Curzon lost a Kirghiz pony that was killed when it missed its footing and fell.[7]

At the top of the last pass the Littledales stopped to let the pack horses catch up. They wanted the entire caravan to descend together into Sarhad. St. George was scouting the terrain before them with binoculars in hopes of seeing ibex, when he spotted several men and fifteen horses in the ravine below. When he switched to his more powerful telescope, he saw other men lying down, all armed. The Kirghiz guide said they were Hunzakuts on a raid. St. George wrote, 'Things promised to be interesting.' He waited until everyone was together and then unpacked an extra supply of ammunition and his two double-barrelled express rifles. He gave a rifle to one interpreter, his revolver to the other, the caravan men loaded their weapons, and the party began descending the hill. When they reached the bottom, Teresa, Joseph, two Kirghiz hunters and St. George went ahead of the caravan, and several men came forward to meet them.

After an exchange of 'salaams', the local men said they were Wakhis and were guarding the pass by order of the Afghan authorities at Sarhad. The Wakhis were polite, saying it would never do for such great people to march into Sarhad unattended, but if the Littledales waited they would send word to their chief, who would come and welcome them personally. St. George replied that while he appreciated their kindness, he preferred to move on. The men then admitted they had orders to stop the party. St. George produced his Persian language passport, saying it was an important letter that he himself had to deliver to the chief. The Wakhi leader said that since the Littledales were better armed, they could not be stopped, but the Afghans would kill him for letting them pass. St. George told him they could not stop there but if the Wakhis would take them to a camping ground they would pitch their tent and wait. The Wakhis agreed and led them a short distance to a good site. It was a fortunate compromise. As they were pitching camp, St. George noticed a line of armed men across a narrow ravine they would have entered had they not stopped for the night.

Later the headman arrived escorted by half-a-dozen dirty, villainous-looking soldiers armed with old Snider rifles. The Littledales received the chief and a second man in their tent. St. George explained that they did not want to remain in Afghanistan but wished to cross the Hindu Kush into Chitral, only 20 miles away. He again produced the passport, pointed to Lord Salisbury's signature, and said he was Queen Victoria's greatest friend. In translation Joseph enlarged on the dreadful things that might happen if the Littledales were kept waiting.

The chief replied that they could not cross the Baroghil Pass but he would send the letter off at once to the general at Faizabad 225 miles away, that the soldier carrying it would return the next day, and that he was certain that the Littledales would be allowed to continue. As this was obviously impossible, St. George tried unsuccessfully to see the headman alone.

Then the chief suggested they proceed to Sarhad, and he urged the party to go that night but the Littledales declined, whereupon he announced that he and his men would spend the night with them. The Littledales invited them to share Joseph's tent and St. George made sure Joseph gave them a good supper. Although the Littledales were not expecting trouble, they were taking no chances. They placed one man on either side of their tent, one in the rear and put Murnok at the door. St. George loaded his revolver and kept it at his side. The night was uneventful.

The next morning, 13 July, the Littledales entered Sarhad escorted by the headman and his soldiers. Sarhad was a small village with a few scattered houses and a ruined fort. The Wakhan River spread out in six or seven channels over a broad flat plain. Across the river a wide barren valley led to the low Baroghil Pass, beyond which were snow-covered mountains that appeared impassable. The elevation of Sarhad was a relatively low 11,234ft and it was hot. There were only men in the village as the women and children were on the other side of the pass with their herds. The Littledales were offered a house but politely declined, saying they preferred their tent.

The chief told them the messenger would return the following evening, and he apologised for the delay. Meanwhile, the Afghans stationed sentries around the camp to watch the Littledales, who could only wait and hope there was no trouble. Knowing how the Afghans despised the Russians, St. George instructed Yudin, the Russian interpreter, to stay out of sight in his tent whenever any Afghans appeared. Later he was horrified to find Yudin ridiculing the Afghan soldiers for their ragged appearance. He ordered Yudin back to his tent and warned him that he could get his throat cut, adding that the Afghans refused to drink their tea when they learned he had made it.

The next day there was no messenger. Instead, the captain in command at Kala-i-Panj arrived with an escort of six more men. They were dressed in a variety of uniforms, 'perfect caricatures of solders, and would have made the fortune of any pantomime. . . .' Some wore shoes with pointed toes curled up in front. Others went barefoot. The captain told the Littledales he had intercepted and destroyed the first letter to Faizabad because the headman at Sarhad was not allowed to write directly to the general. It was the start of a pattern.

At the captain's suggestion the Littledales wrote two letters, one in Persian and one in English, supposedly to be carried by messengers straight through to Faizabad. Teresa wrote, 'The captain is very civil, calls us 'brother'! but we know we cannot believe a word he says or trust any of them. I do wish we were out of the country but I do dread the road back.' They also learned why Ali Bey had told them at Victoria Lake that they could not go to Sarhad by way of Kala-i-panj. He owed money to some local citizens and wanted to avoid them.

More dignitaries arrived the following day. This time it was the Governor of Wakhan, Gholam Russul Khan, accompanied by an even larger escort of armed men. The governor was a handsome young man with flowery speech. Stamped prominently on his turban was the name 'I. Greaves and Co., Manchester'. The governor said Victoria was their queen and their country was the Littledales' country. When the Littledales asked the captain about crossing the Mastuj River beyond the Baroghil Pass he replied, 'When the order came he would make such a road that we should not know whether we were on land or water.' That night the natural order of things was upset further when the Littledales played piquet and Teresa lost.

The next day the governor told the Littledales he had intercepted the second letter because the captain should not have written to the general, so they wrote a third letter to the general. That evening the captain told them the governor was a bad man and had not sent that letter either. The Littledales then wrote a fourth letter in English and Persian that the captain promised would be sent by one of his own soldiers.

No permission came the next day but their Afghan friends did. They arrived early in the morning bringing chickens, eggs and butter, and stayed for several hours as usual. The captain returned at 4 o'clock bearing his daily bouquet of flowers for Teresa and left 2 hours later. Thinking they were free at last, the Littledales started dinner. Just as soup was being served, everyone came back with more chickens and eggs. The Littledales took six chickens and two boxes of eggs but declined the rest. They knew the food was supplied by Wakhi farmers who had been ordered to do so without compensation. Throughout their stay, the Littledales accepted as few gifts as possible and tried to determine the owners in order to compensate them. They took pictures of the governor, the captain, the soldiers and the Wakhis. Teresa joined them in one picture and the governor insisted on holding her hand. She was not pleased, but she felt better that night. She beat St. George at piquet.

The enforced stay was beginning to wear on the Littledales and they started to grasp at straws. 'A man arrived today from the right direction. . . .' The captain said the man was bringing food but he was not carrying anything. Teresa wrote, 'They are the most inveterate liars I ever came across. We cannot believe a word they say. They never tell the same story twice. The Governor never visited us at all today. We do not know why or if he does not mean to be civil.' Even their excessive politeness made the Littledales uneasy. As recipients of a multitude of lies behind a shield of courtesy, they did not know what was going on.

The following day the Littledales tried a firmer course of action. When the governor and the captain arrived in the morning, they were taken to Joseph's tent. After a long talk, the men told the Littledales they could cross the Wakhan River the next day, and that when permission came from the general the following day, they could proceed over the Baroghil Pass. St. George pointed out that if he sent all the caravan men back to Russian Turkestan, and then later the Afghans stopped the Littledales from crossing the Hindu Kush, it would be impossible for them to recross the Pamir with only Joseph and Iris and a few horses. The governor replied that they had better take everyone across the river. St. George could not understand why and suspected that perhaps the local farmers were complaining about the Littledales' animals eating their winter supply of grass. He adamantly refused so as to increase the pressure on the officials to give him an answer.

The expedition's own internal difficulties continued. Among other things, Ali Bey saddled his horse and informed the caravan bashi that he intended to take some Kirghiz and rob the caravan on its return to Osh. Then he rode out of camp. Joseph sent out two soldiers who caught him and brought him back. The problem was the money that Ali Bey owed at Kala-i-Panj. He did not expect to meet so many people from there. Back in camp the Littledales gave him 11 roubles to ease his difficulties. If he had demanded money, they would not have given it to him. They were generous with gifts and were not above bribery. However, they did not yield easily to threats.

The following morning began like all the others. The captain and the son of the vice-governor arrived. The usual strong Littledale protests were met by the usual polite lies. Then a messenger came with a letter purporting to come from the general. The Afghans withdrew to read it and did not return for a long time. When they did, they announced that the Littledales could go. St. George asked if he could have fifteen men to help them over the Hindu Kush and they replied that he could have fifteen hundred if he liked. While undoubtedly impressed with this reply, St. George also asked for six yaks to help carry baggage over the ice.

Everyone immediately went to work. They had to separate the baggage and the food, check all the horses' hoofs to make sure they were properly shod and pay the men off. They left behind everything they could spare in order to reduce their loads. They even sent back over the Pamirs a trunk of clothes Teresa had brought to wear in Kashmir.

St. George also had to deal with continuing personnel problems needing his attention. He tried to induce the caravan bashi's brother to go on with them to India, but despite generous offers, the man said he was afraid to go so far from home. He also had to soothe Azim, who was unhappy because he had wanted a different horse. Finally, St. George confronted Ali Bey about his intentions to rob the caravan on its return trip to Osh:

> I . . . explained to him that I had photographed him, and if our caravan was robbed I should write to the Governor of Kashgar, send his photograph, and say that he was the man who did it, and ask to have him crucified and disembowelled. He seemed impressed with the reasonableness of my remarks, and simply said, 'Then it was not worth the risk.'[8]

All this, as well as letter writing, kept St. George up until 2 o'clock in the morning. He and Teresa were awakened 2 hours later. It took time to pack the animals and distribute presents of money to every Afghan soldier, as well as field glasses, watches and clothes to the officials. Consequently, they did not leave until 8 o'clock. The caravan returning back across the Pamirs left at the same time. Later the Littledales would be relieved to learn that it had reached Osh safely.

It was 22 July 1890. They had been detained in Sarhad for 10 days. The main party now consisted of St. George, Teresa, Joseph, Iris, Murnok the dog, and twelve horses. They were accompanied by fifteen local men. The Littledales were uncertain about the reception they would receive in Chitral and Yasin so they took enough food to be independent. The governor came to the river to say goodbye. They crossed without incident through low water and passed through a swampy valley where the officials had suggested they camp. It was swarming with midges.

After some distance, a friend of the governor's came riding up and a great argument ensued among the Afghans. The man wanted the captain accompanying them to leave the caravan and make the Littledales find their own way. The rider also told Joseph that men were waiting to capture them in Chitral, but the Tajiks from Sarhad who were with them said they had heard nothing about it. Under a hot sun the party climbed up and over the gentle Baroghil Pass, a depression about 600yd wide at 12,460ft, 12 miles from Sarhad. Teresa thought the pass was beautiful, especially the small lake at the top. St. George stayed behind to photograph it, much to the concern of the Afghans.

On the other side they crossed the Mastuj River and pitched camp. St. George handed out farewell gifts to the Afghans. He gave the captain, 'the best of a very bad lot', a silver lady's Waterbury watch. To do this he took his gold watch off its chain and replaced it with the silver one. At the proper moment he took the silver watch out of his pocket, removed it from the chain, and gave it to the captain as if it was his own. He also gave the man Teresa's big cloak. The captain accepted them with great protestations of gratitude.

Finally, the last of the presents were distributed and the Afghans left. St. George put his hand in his pocket to put his gold watch back on its chain. 'I found, "Heigh presto," it had vanished, and the humiliating truth dawned upon me that the Afghan had got, not only the silver watch, but my gold one as well.' He was more chagrined than angry at being victimised.

The fifteen men with whom they had left Sarhad had been reduced to seven. Three more left the next morning with a yak, supposedly to get food. They never returned. The remaining men started to leave camp but St. George stopped them forcibly, whereupon they confessed that they had been ordered to desert the expedition. St. George promised them high pay if they stayed but they wanted an advance. Fortunately, one of the men had owned a sheep that the Afghan governor had given to the Littledales. The Littledales had discovered he was the true owner and had paid him well. The man now said that if the Littledales would do that, they could not be thieves and therefore the men would stay. Although St. George was pleased, he took the precaution that night of putting all the men together in one tent and placing a guard to watch them.

The following morning a minor Tajik official appeared in camp. St. George was afraid of trouble so he 'crossed his palm with silver'. The man told him the captain and the governor had left Sarhad, and he admitted he had been sent to tell the Littledales to wait one more day and to get the men to desert. He said the governor's friend was trying to stop the party.

The Littledales hurriedly packed, left camp, and tried to put as much distance between them and Sarhad as possible. Although the men wanted to stop earlier, they did not halt until they had reached the foot of the ice below the Darkot pass at 13,800ft. There was no grass for the animals but they were carrying enough barley for several days. After arranging camp, the party went to work with axes, cutting steps in the ice for the horses to use in the morning. They slept out among the rocks because they could not pitch the tents.

They arose at 3 o'clock and left at first light. The route was steep with big loose rocks. They were able to get on the glacier using the steps they had cut. Eventually they reached snow and the going became easier until the sun began to soften it. Then men and animals began to sink, the horses tumbling through the weakening crust. The loads had to be repacked constantly. St. George began to think they would not climb over the pass that day, but after skirting a few crevasses near the summit, the party finally reached the top of the Darkot Pass at 15,950ft. The views of the surrounding mountains were spectacular. However, when St. George looked down the opposite side, it appeared so difficult for horses to descend that he questioned the guide to make sure they had not come up the wrong glacier.

St. George and one of the Tajiks went ahead, using alpenstocks to probe through the snow for hidden crevasses. There were numerous crevasses and the snow over them was thin, making progress slow. Everyone was walking now. Teresa slipped and fell full length on her back. 'I felt as if every bone in my body was broken.' They came to a place where they had to leave the ice and cross a small moraine over to another glacier. It was not difficult, but when they had to leave the second glacier and go to a third one, the ice had melted away from the bordering rocks creating a separation of several feet. Moreover, the ice was undermined by rushing water underneath it. They found a place where the gap was small and filled it up with rocks.

On the third glacier the horses were forced to go down a steep ice slope covered with snow and riddled with crevasses. The lone yak descended the glacier slowly but surely with its load. All of the other animals had to be unloaded and the men carried their loads down the glacier. One of the horses at the rear of the line fell and began rolling down the slope, knocking down horses below him as he went until five of them were tumbling head over heels. The lowest one fell into a crevasse, filling it up, and the other horses slid over him onto a snow bank below. The men cut footholds in the ice above the crevasse to get a purchase, and with ropes and tent poles they managed to get the horse out of the crevasse. They picked up the scattered gear, repacked and started again.

Although the slope eased, they were now on bare ice. One horse broke loose from the string and trotted away until it was stranded on a tongue of ice between two large crevasses. There was barely enough room for it to turn around but one of the men retrieved it. The

Littledales watched with more than the usual interest. It was carrying their bedding. They got off the glacier safely but the ordeal was not over yet. They still had a long, steep descent over loose, moving rocks. The horses continued sliding and again the men had to carry their loads over the rougher spots. The back girth on Teresa's saddle broke and it slipped over her horse's head. After much wear and tear on men and animals, the party reached the bottom of the pass and pitched camp.

Just as they were leaving the next day, two men arrived who had been sent by the Mir of Chitral. He had dispatched men to Sarhad with a message for the Littledales but the Afghan officials had kept the letter from them. These men had actually seen them arrive at the Mastuj River 4 days earlier, but there were so many Afghans in the Littledale camp that they were afraid to join them. They had followed the Littledale party to the base of the Darkot Pass and then had gone over the pass in the night before finally presenting themselves, telling evidence of how much they feared the Afghans.

The Littledales were luckier than they knew. The British government had asked the Amir of Afghanistan to assist them. He replied that he had already ordered his frontier officers to send travellers back the way they had come, that he did not consider it necessary for any British people to visit Wakhan, and that if he gave permission to the British the Russians would demand similar privileges and troubles would arise.[9] The officials at Sarhad had come up with a solution: Let the Littledales leave, but for the benefit of higher authority, make a show of trying to stop them. In this way they would get rid of the problem while protecting themselves from repercussions from the Amir. It explains their inconsistent behaviour. They were more sophisticated than they appeared.

Accompanied by the two men from Chitral, the party made a short march to the village of Darkot, where they camped under some willow trees. They were near the spot where George Hayward had been murdered in 1870 with his four servants and his munshi. St. George described Darkot. 'The houses were wretched, and the whole population seemed most miserably poor. They have all jet black hair with rather an effeminate expression, but very wild-looking eyes. They wear their hair very long; it is often dressed in two plaits and fastened to the back of the hat, which is like a pork-pie with a thick roll round the bottom.' Despite their appearance, they treated the Littledales surprisingly well, plying them with butter and eggs, and the headman gave them a small lamb, no doubt the best in the village. The Littledales told them they had what they needed and did not want any presents but were pleased with the gesture. Teresa wrote, 'They have certainly had orders to look after us, but from whom we do not know.' Her hunch was correct. On 20 July the British agent at Gilgit, Colonel Algernon Durand, had heard the Littledales were being detained in Wakhan, so he had asked the ruler of Chitral to afford them every possible assistance.[10]

While the party was now reasonably safe, it did not ease the difficulty of the terrain that lay ahead. Moreover, the horses were in pitiable condition and there was not much the Littledales could do about it. They followed the Wurshigan River down the valley for 10 miles to the village of Mir Wali. 'Every village here has its stone fort, inside which are generally a number of houses, and room for their flocks, showing the insecurity of the country in the past.' And the not too distant past at that. When they reached their campsite they received their first apricots, a gift from the Mir of Yasin.

They reached Yasin the next day. The Mir came out to meet them and led St. George by the hand into his fortress home. The headman said he had received a letter from Colonel Durand with instructions to help them. The Littledales offered him various presents including St. George's sheepskin coat. The Mir responded that he was pleased with the gifts but that money would be nice too. The weather was getting warm, a welcome change from the Pamir. Yasin was surrounded by apricot trees and it was the peak of the season. Apricots were rotting on the ground by the thousands and the irrigation streams were choked with them. The sugar-laden apricots of Baltistan and Gilgit are generally considered to be the most delicious apricots in the world. Travellers gorge themselves on the fruit with predictable results. In Yasin the Littledales had a 'grand feast'.

The avariciousness of the Mir, the uncertainty of what he would demand next, a gale blowing all day, hordes of people surrounding their tent, not to mention the history of the place, encouraged the Littledales to leave as soon as possible. They tried to persuade their Tajiks from Wakhan to continue to Gilgit but the men were afraid and refused. This meant the Littledales were forced to rely on Yasin men. St. George, a connoisseur on the subject, wrote, 'a more lazy, worthless set I have never had the luck to come across. We had two men for each horse, but only two or three out of the whole lot were of any use whatever.'

They left Yasin early the next morning. It was a long, hot, difficult march. A rough, narrow track went over mountain ridges and across spur upon spur of steep rock. Frequently the horses had to be unpacked and repacked as men ferried loads on their own backs over the rougher places. They did not reach the village of Khalti until late afternoon. Teresa had already begun to dread what lay just ahead. 'The horses and ourselves are so done, we shall rest here tomorrow, so the rope bridge is postponed.'

Although they remained stationary in Khalti, it would be hard to say
that they rested. It was another 'fearfully hot' day and the flies were so
bad that Teresa remained in bed under mosquito netting. The horses
could not be permitted to graze because the grass was poisonous. Most
of the animals would not eat the straw they were carrying and went
hungry. But the apricots were the best yet, and Teresa spent the day
eating them and contemplating her next ordeal. 'The rope bridge is not
very long and not very high but . . . I wish I were over.'

The next day she wrote, 'Up at 4 o'clk and utterly disgraced myself.'
Anyone who believes her comment has never crossed a rope bridge.
Rope bridges are frightening. St. George described Teresa's ordeal:

> One night we camped by a river across which there was a jula or
> rope bridge, over which we had to go in the morning. These bridges
> are formed by three ropes made of willow twigs; you walk on one,
> and the other two you hold on by your hands; it starts high above the
> water from the rocks, and sags down in the middle. Mrs. Littledale
> had always announced that she was ready to go anywhere or do
> anything except cross a rope bridge, and how I was to get her over in
> the morning I did not know. We selected a strong man, and she got
> on his back, and they started off across the bridge. I had previously
> arranged my camera to photograph her in the act of crossing. She
> had got one-third of the way across and I climbed down to pull the
> shutter thinking all was right, but she had opened her eyes, and the
> height, the rushing water underneath, and the swaying of the bridge
> had frightened her, and she was telling them to take her back. The
> interpreter unfortunately was not there, but I shouted to them in
> Hindustani, in Russian, and in Kirghiz, to go on quickly and take no
> notice, but they did not understand me and thought I was telling
> them to return, and back they came. . . .
>
> We had to think what was to be done. The men said if I would go
> away out of hearing they would carry her across whether she liked
> it or not. Women are little thought of in those parts. I suggested a
> raft; they said at first it was too dangerous, but, since there was no
> other course, we tied inflated sheep-skins to a camp bed, and sent it
> on a trial trip with five men swimming alongside, each man having
> his own skin. It was so buoyant that Mrs. Littledale said she was
> willing to cross in it. They made her lie down, tied her fast and
> started. The river flowed over great boulders, and though the raft
> was often lost sight of in the spray, it got across safely, having been
> taken by the current a quarter of a mile down stream. We took
> some dry things over the bridge for Mrs. Littledale, who had been
> lying half under water when the raft was stationary, and when she

arrived on the other side a more draggled specimen of humanity was never seen.*[11]

The men tried to drive the horses over but they kept returning so the men had to swim them over one by one. The crossing took hours and several horses nearly drowned. The remaining march was hot. The Yasin men had packed the horses so badly that the loads kept falling off. When they reached the next village, Teresa went to bed as soon as she arrived. The night was hot and they slept with the front door of the rest hut open.

The track continued to be narrow, rocky and up-and-down. 'The packs had to be taken off perpetually and carried on the men's backs over impassible places.' The horses' unshod feet got worse. Murnok suffered in the midday heat and would lie down full length in every stream. There was no village, no grass and no trees, and they had to camp in the blazing sun.

The Mir of Gakuch, the next village, came out to meet the Littledales. He told them there was a shortcut along the river but the horses would have to take a long route over the mountain. They left before dawn to avoid the heat. St. George and Teresa walked with the Mir. Teresa wrote:

> It was a long rough walk by the lower road over the rocks. We had to creep along the steep side of the rock on narrow paths made by laying a pole from rock to rock and putting bush wood and stones on it. One place we had to creep down poles laid around a corner of a precipice. They had notches cut in them to step upon. I took off my boots. St. George went first. I could not see him when he got down. He kept calling to me that it was not as bad as it looked! which I took as a sign that it was a bad place.

One man below held Teresa's feet in the notches while another man above held her dress. 'Murnok was let down by his tail in an awful fright giving little whines. He was very pleased when we got down. He is a dear doggy.'

They sat beside the river for several hours waiting for the horses to arrive, after which they continued the tedious march over mountain spurs on a rocky trail. The heat was stifling. Teresa tried to ride a little. At one place her horse fell with her, but one of the men held so tightly

* According to Teresa's account, the men tied her too high up on the back of the porter, giving her nothing to hold on to except the man carrying her. With this top-heavy arrangement, the slightest mistake could have sent both of them tumbling into the river.

to her arm that she was unable to jump off, and for a moment she was afraid she and the horse would roll down the mountainside together. Later her arm turned black and blue. Her horse lost another front shoe.

When they reached Gakuch, they camped in a shady spot under some apricot trees. Once again there were thousands of apricots lying on the ground – and thousands of flies. A man in the village said he could make horseshoes if the Littledales had some iron. St. George gave him a few tent pins and the two iron bars they used to hang pots over the fire. The party rested in Gakuch for a day. Men and animals were exhausted, and desperate for the new horseshoes. That day the Littledales received a letter from Lieutenant John Manners-Smith, acting Political Agent in Gilgit in the absence of Colonel Durand, who had gone down to Kashmir. Manners-Smith invited them to stay with him in Gilgit at the Agency residence.

The Littledales spent most of their rest day in bed. The roof of the tent was covered with a thick layer of insects and the noise was like a distant waterfall. The ironsmith made only two new horseshoes but managed to make a few badly needed nails for horseshoes that had been shed along the way and saved.

They made a short march the next morning to Singal. A syce or groom arrived from Gilgit with a letter from Manners-Smith saying he had sent shoes for twelve horses as well as his personal attendant to put them on. The horses were so footsore that the party stayed an extra day in Singal to shoe them. It rained in the night and the day was cool. The condition of the horses remained so poor that the Littledales decided to use human porters to carry the loads. They would have to make a double march the next day because there would be no grass along the way for the horses.

They arose at 3 o'clock and left within an hour. The track continued up and down over steep rocky buttresses that dropped into the river. A fourteen-year-old porter lost his pack in the river, which rapidly swept it away. The Littledales feared it was St. George's trunk with his instruments and photographs, but the sack contained only potatoes and rice. Near a village called Cher they passed a long, high rope bridge that had broken twelve years earlier, killing fifteen men.[12]

By 7 August they were set to push all the way to Gilgit, 18 miles in one day. It was another steep, rocky track. At the bottom of each hill they waited for the porters and horses to catch up. They turned yet another corner and this time they could see Gilgit ahead of them, a green oasis in the dry desolate country. In the custom of the East, Manners-Smith rode out from town to greet them. He escorted them in through narrow lanes, past trees loaded with peaches, to the pleasant house that served as the British Agency. There were many long marches still ahead of them, but in reaching Gilgit they had achieved their objective. They had crossed the Pamirs.

9

On to India

It is a far cry from Gilgit to Srinagur, twenty-two marches along a difficult and often dangerous road.

E.F. Knight[1]

During their honeymoon, St. George and Teresa had reached Astor, near Gilgit, and although Srinagar was a month of hard marches away, to them the difficult part of their journey was over. In his article St. George dismisses the rest of the trip in three paragraphs. After all, they knew what to expect. It was a known route.

They spent several days resting at the Agency. Despite the heat, Teresa was pleased with her surroundings. 'The house and gardens are so pretty. They have furnished them with so much taste.' Manners-Smith was sick and jaundiced but he felt better the next day and offered to dispose of any unwanted horses. The Littledales kept the four best horses to ride and gave the rest to their host, who sold them at public auction. It was more difficult to part with Murnok. The Kirghiz dog had been a faithful and valuable companion but the Littledales knew he would not do well in the heat of India. When he was promised a good home in Gilgit, they reluctantly parted with him.

They left Gilgit on the afternoon of 10 August. The track was rocky and in places they had to dismount and walk. They did not get into camp until after dark. Manners-Smith had sent two sepoys ahead of them, so that when they arrived their tent was already pitched, an unaccustomed and welcome treat.

For two days they marched in the heat on a rough track that alternatively followed the river or crossed cliff faces 1,000ft up. At the village of Damot they climbed 6 miles up the Damot nullah to a grassy campsite. The nullah was famous for an abundance of markhor, and the Littledales remained there for a week while St. George went hunting.[2] This side excursion gave them a few days to enjoy more comfortable and cooler surroundings. While Teresa was resting in camp, a basket of fruit and vegetables arrived from Manners-Smith's garden. It was 12 August 1890, her fifty-first birthday.

St. George's hunting got off to a slow start. After having no success in the immediate vicinity, he left with two shikaris for another branch of the nullah and was gone for several days. Teresa remained in camp, where she baked bread and relaxed. Iris and Joseph were with her. One day a mail runner arrived from Gilgit. He had been sent by Manners-Smith. 'He has sent us another basket of fruit and vegetables, a cake. . . . It is so very kind of him. He is the kindest person I have ever met.'[3]

While the food was most welcome, the news that came with it was not. The Littledales had sent a messenger to Astor to send porters to their camp. Now Manners-Smith informed them that their porters had run away. The porters were from Baltistan. For years the Kashmir authorities had been forcing the Baltis to work on the roads. It was near Damot village two years before that Algernon Durand, the political agent at Gilgit, had met a group of Balti porters who threw themselves at his feet and prayed for help. The 53 men were the only survivors of a group of 100 who had been pressed into service 6 months before. They were suffering from dysentery caused by overwork and bad food, and more than forty of the original group had already died. It was no wonder the Littledales' porters had deserted.[4]

Furthermore, there had been an accident on the Indus. An overloaded boat with Surgeon Major George Robertson's supplies sank, losing all of his baggage and killing 2 horses and 17 men. The shikari who described the disaster was astonished when St. George commented on 'seventeen poor men'. He responded, 'There are lots more coolies, but the Sahib's baggage has gone.'

The boats used on the river were flat-bottomed vessels more suited for the quiet lakes of the Vale of Kashmir than for the turbulent Indus. Accidents were common but the Kashmiri officials in charge never made changes.[5] Manners-Smith warned the Littledales not to overload their boat.

St. George decided to go on one more overnight hunt and let Teresa, Iris, and Joseph move the camp down to Damot village, where he would join them later. The move had its crises. Teresa wrote:

A great fuss with the coolies. The loads were too heavy owing to the scarcity of coolies. Only 10 came and 4 donkeys and Joseph flew into a passion and took his whip to beat them. I flew in between and forbid him to touch one of them. I would not for the world have had a row for it to go back to Mr. Manners Smith after all they have done for us. It would be too horrid. Besides, the coolies were very civil and tried to do all they could, and coming down they took such care of me and kept putting down their loads and going back to help the donkeys. . . .

After a night at Damot, they arrived at the Indus early in the morning to cross the river to Bunji, a village with a small fort 600ft above the water.[6] The Littledales had to wait 2 hours for a raft because it was being used to ferry a Captain Tyler across from the other side. He was an Englishman on his way to inspect the roads in Chitral. The raft was a zahk, inflated cow skins tied at the legs with twine and attached to a frame of wooden poles. The zahk would take some of the Littledales' baggage over and then bring back some of the captain's. After each crossing, the raft had to be towed up river to make the return.

When it came time for the Littledales to cross, they spread their waterproof tent sheet on the centre of the zahk and put the saddles and bags on the sheet while St. George and Teresa sat on each side. Leaking air from every skin, the raft bounced across the Indus like a cork. After the baggage was ferried across, each horse was towed over separately with a man holding its head up out of the water. The river crossing took the entire day. Afterwards a storm that had been brewing over Nanga Parbat descended upon them with strong winds and heavy rain.

The next day a group of distraught Balti women approached the Littledales and asked them to intercede with the governor to allow them to return home to Baltistan from where they had been taken. The Littledales regretfully told them they could do nothing, and the women would have to apply to Manners-Smith back in Gilgit or to Colonel Durand when he returned.

The following morning the expedition would face the hardest stage of the trip from Gilgit to Srinagar. Algernon Durand described his own experience two years earlier:

> Running along the last spur between the Indus and the Astor river the path struck the watershed at the height of ten thousand feet and then dropped down the Hattu Pir six thousand feet in about five miles to Ramghat. . . . It is impossible to exaggerate the vileness of this portion of the road; it plunged down over a thousand feet of tumbled rock, in steps from six inches to two feet deep; then for a mile it ran ankle-deep in loose sand filled with sharp-edged stones; it crossed shingle slopes which gave at every step; it passed by a shelf six inches wide across the face of a precipice; in fact it concentrated into those five miles every horror which it would be possible to conceive of a road in the worst nightmare. The culminating point was that, for the whole way from top to bottom, there was not a drop of water to be found on it, not an atom of shade. . . . The road was so execrable that ponies which had made the trip once from Astor to Bunji were always considered unfit for further work without a fortnight's rest and good grazing. The Hattu Pir was a Golgotha;

the whole six thousand feet was strewn with the carcasses of expended baggage animals, and in more than one place did we find a heap of human bones.[7]

Colonel Durand had gone downhill. The Littledales would be climbing up.

They were lucky. The day was overcast without a glimpse of sun. Outside Ramghat there were two bridges across the Astor River, a rope bridge and a wooden cantilever bridge 'of great length and doubtful strength' according to Durand. The wooden bridge was 5ft wide, 50ft above the river, and without handrails. They used it anyway. It was safer than the rope bridge. They started straight up the dreaded spur of the Hattu Pir and climbed steadily for 4½ hours. There were no human bones but they saw the bodies of 8 horses. They had to walk most of the way. Teresa took off the skirt of her dress and her leather belt so as to carry as little weight as possible. At least she was spared the usual intense heat. The summit was so cold that she put on St. George's overcoat. They camped at a village on top.

Two days later they reached Astor. With its orchards and cultivated terraces, its fort and its bazaar, Astor was the metropolis of the region and a welcome relief from the surrounding countryside. It had been the seat of a Dard rajah, but for many years he was subservient to the Kashmir government.[8] In 1890 a garrison of Dogra troops was stationed there. The Littledales were pleased to meet several friends from their 1877 honeymoon, especially St. George's old shikari, who arranged for the same porters and for horses to take them to Srinagar. The Littledales received gifts of apricots and apples, and local dignitaries visited them. One Kashmiri official was surprised they had passed through Afghanistan undisguised. 'Plenty of wrong people and thief man there.'

Despite the attractiveness of Astor, the Littledales moved on to Gurikot, where the route split. In 1890 the 13,900-ft Burzil Pass was the preferred way but the Littledales decided to go over the slightly lower Kamri Pass.[9] The route took them within 10 miles of Nanga Parbat, the mountain marking the far western end of the Himalayas. At 26,660ft, it had dominated their view for many days. Teresa was happy. The road was good and she was able to ride the entire way, a great luxury.

The next day they reached the tiny hamlet of Marmai, where they were greeted by an old friend from their honeymoon, Summat Khan, who joined the travellers. Teresa noticed he had aged a great deal. The party now followed the right bank of the Kamri River past traces of deserted villages and formerly cultivated terraces. Forty years earlier, raiders from Chilas in the Indus Valley had killed the men and carried off the women and children into slavery.[10]

The Littledales camped at a grassy site below the Kamri Pass. They worried about the pass but crossed it the next day with relative ease despite a hailstorm. The following day they moved through the cultivated Gurais Valley. Plagued by insects, they marched along a river and arrived at the village of Gurais with its tumble-down fort and cluster of log huts.[11] Upon entering the village, they encountered a harbinger of approaching civilisation, an Englishman returning from a hunting trip to Skardu.

Continuing along the river through fields and villages, they encountered stretches of new road construction. That afternoon they met another English hunter and later two construction engineers, a Mr Mitchell and a Mr Blake, who asked St. George if they were Mr and Mrs Littledale. When he replied that they were, the men told them they were famous. There were stories in the British press about them, and commentators were interpreting the Littledales' experiences to support their own positions on Great Game strategy.

The following morning the Littledales descended a steep, zigzagging trail, first through forests and then over open slopes to Bandipur on the shores of Wular Lake. They boarded a boat that Mr Mitchell had arranged for them and arrived in Srinagar on 4 September 1890. It was almost six months after leaving England but not long enough for Teresa. 'I felt very sorry to think it was the last time I should ride my pony.'

The Littledales remained in Srinagar for almost two weeks. They camped at the Moonshi Bagh, an area set aside for married visitors.[12] If they were in dire need of rest after months of hard travel, their activities did not reflect it. The afternoon they arrived they went to the races. The Maharaja of Kashmir was there as well as Colonel Parry Nisbet, the British Resident, and Mr Dauvergne, a carpet merchant, who 'looked as great a snob as I remembered him'.

They spent their time sightseeing and shopping, and varied their routine by going to church for the first time in 5 months. The Littledales' clock and Teresa's watch differed by half an hour (St. George's watches were back in Wakhan with their new owner) and the church clock was fast, and so despite all the time in the world, they arrived very late. There was also time for picnicking on Dal Lake and visiting friends in the small tightly-knit British community. Some were living comfortably on houseboats on the lake because Europeans were not allowed to own property on Kashmir soil. Everything belonged to the Maharaja. Sir Robert Harvey, a hunter and good friend of St. George's, owned one of the first houseboats in Kashmir.[13] The strength of the friendship between the two men would become apparent years later.

Eventually Joseph and Iris departed, Joseph for Bombay and Iris for Peshawar with letters to traders in case he decided to return home through Afghanistan. The Littledales were not unhappy to see Joseph go but Iris had been the pleasant surprise of the trip. They paid him well and were sorry to see him leave.

On 16 September the Littledales left Srinagar for Murree, a hill station above Rawalpindi. They went down the Jhelum River in two small boats to Baramula, a small Kashmiri town at the beginning of the stage road. Until 1890 the road was a track suitable only for porters and horses. In many places there were drops of 1,000ft, and from time to time animals would go over the side. Then a road was built for carts. The construction was such dangerous work that fifty-four workers were killed, the majority by falling. The road was completed only a week before the Littledales arrived.[14]

They left Baramula in a tonga, a light two-wheeled vehicle drawn by two horses. St. George did not like having his back to the horses, so he faced forward and Teresa rode backwards. The new road was good where it was finished, but sections were badly broken and St. George walked much of the way. There were 24 stages between Srinagar and Kohala, despite a distance of only 132 miles, so they were able to change horses every 5 miles or so.[15] Two days later they arrived at Murree. They had to walk the final 2 miles up the road because the tonga could not climb the steep hill. There was only a small room at Powell's Hotel but they were promised a better one the next day.

During their stay, they received a huge packet of letters from relatives. Eliza Crutchley had enclosed news clippings about them from *The Times* and *The Globe*. Some of the stories were based on letters the Littledales had sent back to England. St. George was quoted as saying the Amir of Afghanistan had been particularly civil, when in fact the Amir had never contacted them and had even instructed his officials to turn all foreigners back. However, St. George was following his policy that favourable remarks, deserved or not, did no harm and sometimes even helped pave the way for future access. The trip received wide publicity including the following comment from an unknown Indian paper: 'It may not be generally known that Mrs. Littledale, who accompanied her husband in his adventurous journey over the Pamir Mountains recently, is a Hindoo lady of high caste.'[16]

The Littledales went on to Simla, the summer capital of the Raj. On 20 October St. George wrote a brief note from there to his friend Lord Roberts, Commander-in-Chief of the Indian Army, regarding Ovis poli.[17] The Littledale visit was not just social. Simla was the headquarters of Indian Army Intelligence and St. George provided information that was later used in an important report.[18] Duty and pleasure done, the Littledales made their way to Bombay and then back to England.

*   *   *

By the end of the year the Littledales were home, but not for long. Although they had been gone for over seven months, neither of them was capable of staying in one place. They left in January 1891 for 6 weeks of fox hunting in Cheshire. Conditions were harsh that winter: 'This frost is too annoying. We hurried home from India to get some hunting & this is the result.' In February St. George wrote, 'There was a grand gallop today, but an unfortunate contretemps!!! prevented me seeing the early portions of it!'[19]

At home St. George was active in the South Berkshire Hunt, later known as the Garth Hunt, and he went out whenever he could. Among the members of the hunt were two friends, Lord Roberts and Prince Christian, husband of Princess Helena, one of Queen Victoria's daughters.[20] An old news clipping describes one particular day:

> A very large field assembled to meet the popular Master, Mr. T.C. Garth, drew Church Wood and Mabs Copse blank, but soon found in Foxhills. One ring round the cover, and he was holloaed away by that good sportsman Mr. H. Lane, over the open for Longmoor Bog, a good few coming to grief over Barkham brook, hounds running hard, Mr. Littledale going well to the front, straight through Longmoor, by Colonel Molyneaux's house, over the fields to the left, back on to the Ridges, hounds running merrily through the heath, over the South-Eastern Railway, leaving Wellington College on the right, through Captain Rose's shrubbery (Heathlands) to the gorse. . . .[21]

Teresa continued to be embroiled in business matters, especially regarding her inheritance from Scott. She leaned heavily on her brother George, who had long since left the Harris brothers' firm but was trying to clean up the mess created by Edward. Then St. George's mother came to visit and suddenly became alarmingly ill. Mrs Turner recovered but the situation took its toll on Teresa. 'I never hope to undergo ten such weeks again.'[22]

In June 1891 the Littledales must have been happy to leave home for their third trip to the Caucasus. St. George still sought the elusive aurochs he had failed to bring home twice before. The permissions must have been readily forthcoming. By now the Littledales knew everyone and 'knew the drill'. They also had a new travelling companion. Teresa had obtained a young fox terrier that she named Tanny. Fox terriers have many characteristics that make them good expedition dogs, the most important of which is courage. They are tough, loyal, and willing to take on anything, including fights with larger dogs. They like to bark and they make fine watchdogs. Fortunately there are not many complaining neighbours in the backcountry of Asia. At the last minute the Littledales decided to take Tanny to the Caucasus.[23]

They followed the usual route across the Channel, on to Berlin, and from there to Odessa, changing trains several times along the way. Joseph Abbas, their interpreter in the Pamirs, met them in Odessa. He had brought all of their baggage from Constantinople. At Sebastopol they were met by their old friend Patrick Stevens, the British Vice-Consul. They travelled to Maikop and eventually set up camp under Mount Fiske.[24] The newest Littledale was doing well. Teresa wrote, 'Tanny is the best little traveller in the world. He has really never given us the least trouble & is so happy & such company & has grown so handsome. He takes great care of the tent. If anything comes near, he barks & growls directly. He has caught a mouse for the British Museum!'[25]

Despite the challenging terrain and terrible weather, St. George managed to shoot two auroch for the Natural History Museum, a male and a female. Afterwards an incident occurred that would greatly impress the hunting community:

> . . . I found myself face to face with a grand old bull, bigger than my first victim. We were hidden in the bush and he stood in the open wood, and grand indeed he looked. I laid my rifle down, for the temptation was great, and I would not have slain him for £1,000. I took off my cap to him out of respect for a noble representative of a nearly extinct species. I had got what I wanted, and mine should not be the hand to hurry further the extermination of a fading race for mere wanton sport. I shot the aurochsen for the express purpose of presenting them to the British Museum. . . .[26]

While it may be hard for people of today's world to understand nineteenth-century hunters, St. George Littledale showed character. He had his standards. He hunted for sport and science and there were lines he would not cross. The grand bull aurochs was one of them.

When the Littledales returned to England in October, St. George was worried about his forthcoming paper on the Pamir trip. In November he wrote to the Royal Geographical Society, 'I should much like to glance over any alterations you may have made in the paper as I particularly wish to avoid politics in it.'[27] Although he felt obligated to write the paper, it went against his better judgment. It was not just a lack of confidence in his writing ability. He was always afraid that a written record could be used against him. As he was acting against his instincts in this matter, he was extremely cautious. He would do neither himself nor his country any good by provoking the Russians.

Later that month his paper, 'A Journey across the Pamir from North to South', was read at an evening meeting of the Royal Geographical Society in the theatre of the University of London. Although St. George was present, it was Douglas Freshfield who read it. Freshfield was Honorary Secretary of the Society. A good friend of the Littledales, he was one of the world's most distinguished mountain explorers. He would later become President of both the Alpine Club and the Royal Geographical Society. Like the Littledales, he had been in the Caucasus in 1887.[28] Freshfield made a knowledgeable and diplomatic introduction to the paper before reading it. Afterwards the President of the Society, Sir M.E. Grant Duff, conducted the customary discussion period during which various eminent members made remarks. It was mentioned that despite adverse weather conditions including constant freezes and strong winds, St. George had brought home 120 species of birds. The audience included two men from the Russian Embassy, and the President concluded the meeting by thanking them for the great courtesy shown by the Russian government toward the English travellers.

The delivery of the paper could not have been better timed for maximum public impact. The Great Game was in the midst of one of its periodic crises. On 10 August Francis Younghusband had arrived at the old Littledale campsite of Bozai Gumbaz and found a detachment of Russian Cossacks there. They were guarding the supplies for a reconnaissance party across the Hindu Kush in Chitral. The main party returned, treated Younghusband most hospitably, and then expelled him from what they called Russian territory.[29]

When the Foreign Office in London received the news, their first response was, 'Where is Buzai Gambaz?' They found out. Britain became inflamed. Lord Rosebery, a past and future Foreign Minister even called it 'The Gibraltar of the Hindu Kush'. Imperial troops began assembling at Gilgit to attack Hunza. The British press volleyed and thundered. While most of their shots were aimed at the Russians, a few were aimed at each other using the Littledales as ammunition. *The Times* paraphrased General Starchy: 'Military operations could under no circumstances be conducted over such country as that traversed by Mr. Littledale.' *The Glasgow Herald* emphasised Freshfield's remarks that from the south, judging from the Littledales' experience, the way is 'anything but a military route as it leads over glaciers, passes and through well nigh impassable gorges . . .'. The advocates of a 'forward policy' seized upon Teresa's crossing the Pamir to support their opposite position. They interpreted her feat as proof that if a lady could do it, then certainly Russian regiments could do it, bringing their artillery with them. According to *The Standard*, '. . . if once a Russian force reached Sarhad the road would lie open for it – guns and all – across the Baroghil Pass into Cashmere.'[30]

However, most of the British press drew the correct conclusion that the Pamir was not especially desirable country and that it would be extremely difficult for a large modern military force to attack India through the region, a fact the British authorities already knew 5 years before the Littledales went there. This knowledge, and the courteous treatment the Russians had accorded the Littledales, which the Royal Geographical Society acknowledged openly, must have had a calming if minor influence on the crisis.

The geographical knowledge obtained by the Littledales was put to immediate use. One of Sir Robert Morier's arguments supporting British policy was based on a secret Russian-Chinese treaty of which the British had obtained a copy. The translator of the treaty from Chinese into English identified certain critical place names using the map accompanying St. George's paper.[31]

The brief Hunza campaign began in early December 1891 and ended on 22 December after John Manners-Smith (Teresa's 'kindest person') and his men stormed a ridge behind Nilt.[32] The Bozai Gumbaz crisis took longer to resolve, but after some brilliant work by Sir Robert Morier, the Russian government issued a formal apology. The Pamirs would remain quiet for a few months.[33]

Nothing could appease the Littledales' restlessness, and by the spring of 1892 they were making plans to return to the Caucasus for the fourth time. Upon writing to St Petersburg for permission, they learned of the unexpected death at sea of Victor Morier, Sir Robert Morier's son, who had withdrawn from their 1890 expedition to the Pamirs.[34] They were further saddened by the death of Thomas Moore, Curator of the Liverpool Museum. He had been a mentor to St. George. It was Moore who had first recognised the young hunter's talents, encouraged him to collect specimens for his museum, promoted his reputation through special exhibits and above all generously introduced him to the Natural History Museum. A major link to Liverpool was gone.

In preparing for the Caucasus, St. George wanted to expand the range of his collecting. He asked Gunther for a tin or two for fish specimens. Gunther sent him a container with a note:

I hope the collecting box will do. You can fill it on the outward journey with valuable articles, such as soap, quinine tablets, neckties, baro- and thermo-meters, corkscrews, whistles, powder, candles, Pear's soap, sponges and Eau de Cologne for washing your rifles, spectacles, night-caps. The last reminds me it is time for going to bed, so good-night.

St. George thanked him for the tin 'which arrived just in time. In regard to your letter, it is a fortunate thing for you that it is mislaid for I meant to have made some very damaging criticisms on the condition to which the writer must have sunk before he penned such an effusion.'[35]

The Littledales were about ready to leave for Russia when cholera broke out in the Transcaspia, and by the end of June it had reached Baku. There were articles in newspapers describing the seriousness of the epidemic, so at the last minute the Littledales cancelled their trip and spent the year at home for a change.[36]

Their expedition across the Pamirs in 1890 had resulted in new and interesting geographical information, but if they continued to travel in remote, relatively unknown regions, it would be helpful for both geographic knowledge and British Intelligence if they could produce route maps of their travels. During the year at home, St. George took lessons in map-making from John Coles, map curator at the Royal Geographical Society.[37] He also rejoined the Society, to which he had been elected a Fellow in 1876 when he was only twenty-four. He had resigned a few years later, perhaps because he was never home long enough to attend the meetings. The Society re-elected him in July 1892. His sponsors were Douglas Freshfield, Secretary, and J. Scott Keltie, Assistant Secretary and Editor of the Transactions of the Society. They were pleased to have him back.[38]

There was more than the study of map-making to occupy St. George's time in 1892. For several years he had been thinking of obtaining the Asian wild camel for the Natural History Museum. This wild Bactrian camel had been discovered by Nikolai Prejevalsky in China near Lop Nor in 1887. Besides being a worthy objective in itself, it gave the Littledales a good excuse for another challenging expedition: from west to east across Russian Central Asia and the wild desolation of Chinese Central Asia all the way to Peking. St. George immediately applied for the required permissions, and soon the Littledales had approval for the trip from both the Russian and the Chinese governments.[39]

It would be more difficult than anything they had done previously, and they would have to begin the long journey by crossing Russian Central Asia once again, only this time they would have to do it in winter.

10

Across Central Asia

We want a savage dog.
Teresa Littledale

It was not an auspicious beginning. St. George hurt his back in late December and could do nothing to prepare for the expedition except write letters. He heard from Dr Gunther at the Natural History Museum, who wanted him to collect reptiles and fish, Gunther's own areas of expertise:

> Pray Sir, can you tell me, how those Russian Barbarians whose game-preserves you intend to invade, manage to bring 100s and 1000s of reptiles and fish to St. Petersburg? . . . a highly civilised and well instructed Britisher could do likewise. . . . As you approve of my collecting boxes (the smaller kind), I have ordered four more for you, with eight keys. . . . What a glorious prospect to spend a winter at Lob Nor alt. 12,000 with O. poli, snow leopards, tartars, etc., and to have no coal bills to pay at the end of the season.[1]

With St. George laid up, Teresa had to do most of the packing, and the effort left her exhausted. On 31 January 1893 St. George left Bracknell and Teresa followed several hours later. They met in London at Charing Cross Station and caught the boat train for Paris, where they spent the night at the Grand Hotel. The next morning they took the Orient Express to Vienna. Teresa was excited. 'We are . . . on our way to explore the interior of Thibet & China & expect to return with pigtails & old manuscripts!'[2]

On 4 February they left on the express train to Constantinople. St. George covered the ordeal in less than one sentence: '. . . the intense cold was a thing to be remembered.'[3] It had been cold in Vienna and it grew steadily colder until for most of their journey it was 36°F below zero. At one stop they had to leave the train for 24 hours and could find only a tiny room in the village. Teresa wore her two fur cloaks because there was no fire. There was no food available either, but fortunately they had brought soup and cold chicken with them. The next night they arrived at a cholera quarantine station. They were taken off the train and into a shed, where they hovered next to warm stoves. During the night they were allowed to reboard the train and sleep in their compartment, which had been kept warm. The cold was so intense that the windows were coated with half an inch of frost and there was a 1in coating of ice on the bolts inside the rail carriage.

The next day the entire train was frozen hard and fast to the rails. Dozens of men with crowbars pried at the carriages to get them loose. When one was freed, they would run it back and forth, ramming the rest until another carriage moved. They broke the ice away from the two engines with picks. It took 2 hours to separate the entire train from the tracks. They reached Adrianople the next morning and were delayed for another 12 hours. They had to get dinner at a dirty hotel. There they met a Mr and Mrs Vincent Caillard. Mr Caillard had an important post in the Debt Office in Constantinople, and all the local officials were bowing and scraping to him. More significantly, he had a special sleeping carriage. He gave the Littledales a large compartment in his carriage and they finished their journey in comfort.

At their hotel in Constantinople Teresa found that the contents of two large bottles of cholera medicine had frozen solid and the bottles were cracked. It was a timely discovery. Later the medicine would have thawed and ruined everything. Even worse, the Littledales would have been without cholera protection. The next day the Littledales tried to visit the famous bazaar but it was too cold. They declined a dinner at the Caillards' because they did not have the proper clothes. However, they did accept the Caillards' invitation to go to 'Semalik' the next morning, which meant watching the Sultan go to worship in the Mosque.

The following day it had warmed up considerably and they sailed for Batum at 5 o'clock in a pouring rain. There was only one other passenger on the ship. Early the next morning they arrived at Samsun on the coast of Turkey. Just as they were finishing breakfast they learned that Lord Dunmore, a well-known hunter and traveller, was on the steamer *Mingrelia*, anchored nearby in the harbour. They promptly went to see him. Dunmore was returning to England after a year-long trip from Kashmir through the Pamirs to Kashgar and then west through Russian Central Asia to Europe. In China the Littledales would be going to Korla, the jumping-off point for Lob Nor. They had planned to go to Korla via Kuldja, but after talking with Lord Dunmore, they changed their minds and decided to go via Kashgar. His information on that route was invaluable because it was current. Even more useful was Ramzan, a Ladakhi who was accompanying him back to England. Ramzan was experienced. Not only had he been Dunmore's caravan bashi, he had also been on two trips with Francis Younghusband. Lord Dunmore offered Ramzan's services to the Littledales, who offered to pay him the same rate of 20 rupees a month. Ramzan accepted. His willingness to repeat the hardships he had just undergone was impressive. Even Lord Dunmore, who had recommended him, commented:

> It was rather odd seeing him quietly remove his luggage, which consisted only of his bedding, from one steamer to another, and return to travel all through Central Asia again, and over the Chinese Frontier with the Littledales, with as little concern as if he were only going from London to Brighton for the day, instead of on an arduous journey of nine months into China and Tibet.[4]

The Littledales were fortunate. Ramzan would prove to be indispensable before the expedition was over. Lord Dunmore gave St. George his sheepskin coat, which was warm but also full of flea powder if not fleas.

They did not leave Samsun until late the following night, and the ship crawled along the Black Sea coast, stopping at several ports along the way before eventually reaching Batum on 14 February. The Littledales were met by Patrick Stevens, who was now the British Consul there. At that time the Consulate in Batum was the key listening post in the region for the gathering of intelligence. Other consulates and independent sources funnelled their reports on Russian military strength and troop movements through Batum for transmittal back to London.[5]

Stevens and Mr de Shupfell, a Russian, shepherded the Littledales' baggage including guns and ammunition through customs unopened and without any delay, thanks to the efforts of Henry Howard, Secretary of the British Embassy in St Petersburg, who had obtained permission from the Russian government. The Littledales were travelling with the highest accreditation by the Russians. When Mr de Shupfell asked why they had not come by way of Odessa, which would have made their arrangements simpler, St. George said they had come via Constantinople because of his advice. Mr de Shupfell replied that he had not known they would be travelling as 'the Emperor's personal friends'.

At St. George's request, Howard had obtained the services of a guide named Djidyger through the offices of Petr Semenov, President of the Russian Imperial Geographic Society. Howard had instructed the guide to meet the Littledales at Kuldja, paid him in advance, and sent him off. Then St. George notified Howard about the route change and asked that the guide meet him in Osh instead. Howard was beside himself. He 'begged' his friend Semenov to do everything in his power to stop Djidyger. It would not be easy. Semenov replied that St. George could repay him by collecting beetles.

After a few days in Batum, the Littledales caught the night train to Tiflis and arrived the next morning. They spent several days in Tiflis buying ox tongues and lemons. They moved on to the Caspian seaport of Baku, and once again they sailed across the Caspian to Usunada, the start of the Transcaspian Railway. The steamer was too large to enter the port so they and 300 soldiers transferred to a large barge towed into port by a tender. It took 4 hours to get to shore and then they learned their baggage had not arrived. Fortunately the general in charge of the railroad happened to be in Usunada on an inspection tour. The Littledales persuaded him to delay the train until the following morning, but the next day their baggage arrived so late, the train could not leave until 5 o'clock in the afternoon. There were advantages to travelling as 'the Emperor's personal friends'.

They rode across the long plain from the Caspian to Merv to the Oxus and on to Samarkand, where they arrived on 25 February. They visited Tamerlane's tomb and the Blue Mosque, but it was so cold they cut their sightseeing short. Two days later they left for Margilan, using the tarantass Lord Dunmore had left behind. The carriage had no seats and could hold only one person comfortably. The Littledales rode on their baggage. Upon arriving in Margilan, they called on General Korolkof, Governor of the province of Fergana, who invited them to breakfast. He went to great effort to find their old servants, whom they wanted to rehire. They left that afternoon, arriving in Osh on 6 March. Colonel Gromchevsky, an old friend, was now the Naichalnik of Osh. He put them up at 'the Club'. Waiting there was Azim, their former cook in the Pamirs, 'the best cook and the greatest blackguard in Central Asia'.

They wanted to find Iris, the Jiguit who had crossed the Pamirs with them. Unfortunately, he had died the year before. The Littledales were stunned when they learned the manner of his death. He was stationed at a Russian military post in the Pamirs and there was an urgent message to be sent back to Margilan. Several Kirghiz tried to get the dispatch through but quit when they sank into snow up to their armpits. Then Iris volunteered. His horse died in the terrible blizzards. For days Iris struggled forward on foot. Finally his feet and legs froze and he could no longer walk. As he lay in the snow, he was attacked by wolves. He fired off all of his cartridges and defended himself with his sword until his hands became useless. Some Kirghiz found him badly bitten and severely frostbitten and carried him to Margilan, where the doctors tried to save his life by amputating his frozen legs, but it was too late. 'Thus perished one of the truest, bravest, and most faithful servants we ever had.'6

St. George was concerned about his interpreter, who was already unsatisfactory. While mentioning the problem to Gromchevsky, St. George remarked that he was probably listening. He walked briskly to the door, flung it open, and there was the man with his ear at the keyhole.

Colonel Gromchevsky invited the Littledales to dinner with several Russian officers and their wives. The Littledales wanted their opinion of Lord Dunmore and after a while they began to speak openly about him. Earlier St. George had asked Gromchevsky to sell him Lord Dunmore's tarantass but Gromchevsky had refused to have anything to do with it. At dinner he told the entire story.

Dr Karl Troll, a German geologist and explorer, had written from Kashgar asking Colonel Gromchevsky for a tarantass for Lord Dunmore. Gromchevsky located one in Margilan, but when he heard the price, he wrote to Troll that it was too expensive. He was told to get it anyway. When Lord Dunmore arrived in Osh, he complained about the price (140 roubles) and berated Gromchevsky for getting it.[7] There was more. Dunmore had been permitted to stay at the club. As he was leaving, he was presented with the bill. He asked Gromchevsky the meaning of it, saying he was Gromchevsky's guest. Colonel Gromchevsky told Dunmore to pay what he liked but that he, Gromchevsky, would have to make up the rest. These stories about Lord Dunmore's parsimoniousness are consistent with Rassul Galwan's account of how, upon reaching Kashgar, Lord Dunmore rewarded his servants by giving them his filthy, discarded old clothes.[8] St. George decided to buy the tarantass from Lord Dunmore for £7 and have Gromchevsky sell it later, giving the proceeds to Iris's widow, who was destitute.

Colonel Gromchevsky organised their caravan as far as the Chinese border. He obtained 5 riding horses and 13 baggage horses for the reasonable rate of 8 roubles apiece. He also made arrangements for sheep, firewood, and two yurts to be ready for the Littledales at every stop in Russia up to the Chinese border. They would not even have to pitch their tents. The Littledales went to the bazaar and bought everything they still needed for the journey to Kashgar. That afternoon Gromchevsky had tea with them and insisted they join him again for dinner. He sent his carriage to take them to his house, where they spent another pleasant evening.

They left the next day, 9 March, on their journey of 248 miles along the main trade route to Kashgar.[9] It took three days to reach Gulcha, where it was so cold that everything inside their yurt froze solid. During meals, a glass of water would freeze before they could drink it. Two easy marches from Gulcha took the Littledales past Sufi Kurgan, where they had separated from the main trail in 1890 to head south across the Pamirs. From here onward they would be travelling through unfamiliar country.

The weather was good and they started up the track toward the Terek Dawan carrying a two-day supply of firewood, as there would be no more fuel for several days. The Terek Dawan was used by caravans in winter in snow. However, as spring approached, the snow melted and then refroze at night, making the route impassable. During the Littledales' ascent, the snow changed to ice. There had been a partial thaw and water had come down the valley over the snow and then refrozen, making fantastic ice shapes that glistened in the bright sun. It was beautiful but hard going. One horse slid downhill sitting on its haunches. At a spot named Ravat there was a rest house with an enclosed courtyard, sheds for horses and two small rooms. The cook got the room with the fireplace and the Littledales spent a miserable night freezing in the other.

The next morning they continued up the icy path to the top of the Terek Dawan, 13,350ft in elevation. It may have been a high point for the Littledales but not for Tanny. 'At this point our poor little fox-terrier decidedly thought life was not worth living.' In fact the Littledales were suffering as well, wishing they had felt boots, as their hunting boots were not warm enough. They descended 10 miles over snow covered by frozen water, but it was less steep and St. George thought it would have made a fine toboggan run. They camped at Kok Su beside the river in 'a delightful grassy spot with glorious views, a perfect ibex country'. The yurt arranged by Colonel Gromchevsky was ready and Teresa went straight to bed.[10]

They marched a long distance the following day, crossing two steep passes, but the magnificence of the mountain scenery distracted them from their labours. Eventually they reached the Russian frontier post of Irkistan, a fort at 9,600ft on the side of a hill overlooking a rest house beside the Chuk Su. To Lord Dunmore it had resembled a lighthouse without a tower.[11] At night they kept all the domestic animals inside the compound because wolves and wild dogs roamed outside.

Shortly after leaving Irkistan they reached the Kizil Su (Kashgar River) or Red River, named after the colour of its muddy water. They followed it for several days to the Chinese frontier fort at Ulukchat, where Ramzan took their Chinese passports to the local amban (head official). A horse had kicked the amban in the ankle and it was badly swollen. The Littledales treated the patient as best they could.

They continued along the Kizil Su through arid country, climbed over a low pass, descended past a ruined fort, went through a narrow gorge between high walls, and after a 26-mile march they reached a small village. The next morning it was snowing. After it had stopped, they left and soon entered another narrow winding gorge between vertical walls of compact clay several hundred feet high. At times the walls even overhung the track, which in some places was too narrow for two pack animals to pass.[12] Teresa's horse lay down and she rolled off it. As they struggled down the rocky path, it must have been hard for the Littledales to believe this was the main trade route from Osh to Kashgar.

After several days they reached Fort Yangi Shar, where Teresa delighted in their clean room with a fire and hot water. She was not the only one. 'Tanny can hardly wait till my bed is made so that he can go to sleep. He sleeps from the time we arrive till we start next morning. He is tired out, poor little doggie.' Teresa's description of Tanny was also a fairly accurate description of herself.

Wednesday 22 March 1893. At last they were approaching Kashgar. They had been marching for 14 days straight. Ramzan went ahead with a message for George Macartney, the British agent, asking about a house for them during their stay. A note came back inviting them to stay with him at Chini Bagh, his official residence. When they reached Kashgar that afternoon, they discovered that Macartney had given them his own rooms.

Kashgar was the capital of the southern section of Chinese Turkestan, or Kashgaria as it was also known. The area consisted of the western Tarim Basin, a region of about 19,000 square miles surrounded on three sides by mountain ranges, the Tien Shan to the north, the Pamirs to the west, and the Kun Lun to the south. The Gobi Desert lay to the east. The Tarim Basin covers most of the southern portion of today's Xinjiang province and consists almost entirely of the vast Taklamakan, a sea of shifting sand and one of the most desolate deserts in the world.[13] Around the Taklamakan is a string of oases at the foot of the surrounding mountains, which provide water from melting snow and glaciers. These oases made possible the trade routes known as the Silk Road. Kashgar's location at the foot of the Pamirs made it a hub for trade in every direction for centuries. All of the Silk Road routes, north and south, east and west, met at Kashgar. It was the greatest crossroad of Central Asia.

When the Littledales arrived in 1893, Kashgar had a population of approximately 40,000 people. There were two towns, the old Muslim town and a newer Chinese town, Yangi Shar, to the south. The old town was typical of Central Asia with narrow, dark, dirty streets and identical flat-roofed houses built of mud bricks. The Muslim and Chinese towns each had moats and thick mud walls pierced by iron gates that closed at sunset. The main streets in the old town led to a market square dominated by a large mosque.[14]

Although it was difficult to reach, Kashgar was known to westerners and had become the centre of the Great Game. In 1881 the Chinese had agreed to allow a Russian consulate to be based there. The Russian

Consul was Nikolai Petrovsky, who wielded great influence over the Chinese Taotai or Lieutenant Governor. George Macartney, his British counterpart, did not arrive until November 1890. The Chinese would not allow the British to establish a consulate. Consequently Macartney was just a 'representative'. He arrived with Sir Francis Younghusband, and the Taotai gave them a one-storey house with garden called Chini Bagh (Chinese Garden) outside the walls of Old Kashgar. Younghusband left in July 1891, leaving Macartney behind to represent the British government. The son of Halliday Macartney, Secretary to the Chinese Legation in London, he was only 24 years old. He was to remain in Kashgar for twenty-eight years.[15]

The Littledales stayed at Chini Bagh for a week. Teresa wrote, 'Kashgar is such a dirty place. It is a wretched life to lead to live here alone. Mr Macartney has not a creature to speak to. The only other Europeans are the Russian Consul, his wife, and Mr Luche, the secretary to the Russian consulate and relations are decidedly strained between the two consulates. They do not visit.'

Macartney was half Chinese and had inherited his mother's Chinese appearance. Teresa thought it likely he had heard disparaging remarks from Petrovsky regarding his parentage and could not forgive him, but the situation was more complicated. Macartney was in an uncomfortable position because of Petrovsky's personality and position. A later British agent described Petrovsky:

A man of strong ambition and dominating personality, temperamental and vain, he was capable of preposterous rudeness and bitter enmity, but he could also when he wished be a charming and witty host. . . . It was a bold man who dared cross him, even in small things, for Petrovsky would pursue him with unremitting spitefulness and intrigue. Such was the man who bullied and terrified Kashgar from the Taotai downwards into submission to his will.[16]

Russian power was near; British power was far away and beyond difficult passes. No one knew this better than the Taotai, the provincial governor. Macartney's presence, despite his lack of power and even influence, did make Petrovsky's life more difficult, and the Russian was not very forgiving about it.

All of this was made worse by the situation developing in the Pamirs and coming to a climax. In 1891 there was the Bozai Gumbaz Crisis followed by the Hunza War. In 1892 the Afghans forced the Chinese out of the Alichur Pamir. In turn the Russians defeated the Afghans. The British reinforced their garrison in Gilgit and tensions increased throughout 1893. With everyone's temper rising with each new phase of the Great Game it was understandable, notwithstanding Petrovsky's personality, why relations were strained between Petrovsky and Macartney.

At Chini Bagh St. George passed on his intelligence findings to Macartney, who sent the information to the British Resident in Srinagar, Kashmir. Eventually the material was summarised and forwarded in a secret report from the Commander-in-Chief in India to the Director of Military Intelligence in London:

> Mr. and Mrs. Littledale arrived at Kashgar from Russian Turkistan on the 22nd March. Mr. Littledale found that the anti-English feeling amongst the military in Russian Turkistan had considerably increased since the Pamir incident last year. Russian military officers he said now discussed the question of an invasion of India as one worthy of a certain amount of serious consideration. Mr. Littledale noticed that the Margilan-Alai road had recently been repaired, while the road from Osh to Alai apparently had not been touched, so it is possible that Margilan and not Osh may be the base in the event of another Russian expedition to the Pamirs.

The recipient marked the sides of the paragraph to emphasise its importance.[17]

The Littledales were busy in Kashgar. They had to purchase 5,000 roubles worth of yamboos, also known as sycee silver, which were silver chunks of various sizes and weights. St. George wrote:

> In making a bargain, it was not only requisite to arrange the weight of silver to be given, but also whose scales were to be used – a very necessary stipulation, as with the pair I had there were three different arrangements by which the scales could be fraudulently altered to suit yourself, as you might happen to be a buyer or seller; and then there was the endless question as to the quality of the silver.[18]

St. George always tried to insist his own scales be used, pointing to a stamp he believed came from the Taotai of Kashgar. He usually got his way. Months later he learned that the stamp was just the price of the scales.

The Littledales also had to change translators, which was even more difficult than changing money. St. George already wanted a new interpreter, and when Petrovsky told him that Charles, their interpreter, and Azim, the cook, had been drunk in the bazaar, it was the last straw and he fired them both. Teresa wrote, 'We never dreamed that Charles drank. It accounts for his having gone so completely downhill and become so dirty. . . . I feel uneasy about our expedition. It is an adventurous one and we have not trustworthy men with us.' She was also disappointed that St. George would not buy her old pony from the caravan bashi. '[It] spoiled my day. I do so often wish I had not come on this trip and as I go on shall wish so more and more, I feel certain.' Fortunately, Macartney found them another Ladakhi, Razak Akhun, one of his mail runners. The English called him Rozahun. Akhun was to serve the Littledales well and would later go to Tibet with them. They also hired a man who spoke both Turki and Chinese. If St. George had a question for a Chinese, he had to speak elementary Hindustani to Ramzan, who translated the question into Turki, and the interpreter translated it into Chinese. By the time the answer came back, it had gone through six translations and frequently had nothing in common with the question.

Besides purchasing supplies, the Littledales bought Chinese clothes to wear. Teresa was pleased with hers, a pair of long red silk pants edged with blue and yellow, a dark blue cotton shirt that hung halfway below the knees, and over that a light blue shirt with red lining. She also purchased red and blue Chinese shoes with white socks and a black silk handkerchief to wear over her head to hide her hair. St. George acquired a Chinese outfit with grey leggings and a grey felt Chinese hat. However, he could not find a pair of Chinese boots large enough to fit him.

Although Petrovsky was at odds with Macartney, he was kind and generous toward the Littledales and gave them the benefit of his considerable knowledge of the country and its people. One evening during dinner with the Petrovskys, both the host and his wife tried to dissuade Teresa from continuing the trip, but without success. St. George wrote, 'It takes a good deal to get to Mrs. L. when she has . . . made up her mind.'[19]

The Littledales left Kashgar on 29 March. Teresa wrote, 'We do not feel in the least sure which end of the spout we will come out at or where!' Their first significant destination was Korla, a month away. 'St. George as usual felt utterly hopeless about the baggage. Was quite sure it would not be put in the carts but it all went in without any trouble.' They had three arbas, large carts without springs, with high, iron-rimmed wheels. They were pulled by four horses, one horse between the shafts and three abreast in front pulling on long ropes. The traces were long because the roads were so rough and uneven that the lead horses often had to go on one path with the wheels on another.[20] Two carts carried baggage and the Littledales rode in the third. They put their tent and bedding on the bottom and hung curtains around the sides to keep out the dust. All 220lb of silver yamboos were distributed throughout the baggage.

They travelled through good grazing land and past small villages and cultivated fields of corn until they reached Faizabad (Abode of Blessedness), the main town between Kashgar and Maralbashi. After Faizabad the road entered a level greyish-yellow barren plain as they skirted the northern edge of the Taklamakan. The Littledales were besieged by dust. They could not escape it. Sven Hedin wrote about his own experience: 'The dust penetrated everywhere, searching into our furs, into everything we had inside the cart, and collected in thick layers on the roof. . . . The dust was so thick and deep that it was like driving over a vast feather-bed, and the wheels of the arbas were almost sucked down into it.'[21]

Each day Teresa reiterated the same dusty theme in her diary. '. . . drove through a dreary desert, country all alkali and dust and arrived at the rest house about 4 o'clock.' 'A most dreary dusty day's march through desert, a few tamarisk bushes and stunted trees. . . . It is the dirtiest journey we have ever had and I do not think if we had to start again either of us would take it.' 'Another horrible dirty dusty march through alkali sand. No water fit to drink.' And the day before they reached Maralbashi: 'Without exception the most dirty dusty drive I have ever experienced. I do not know what we should have done without the curtains I made, for the front of the cart is like sand pouring in in clouds. My eyes are so sore I cannot read so that the time is terribly tedious.' This was the main route of the northern branch of the Silk Road. They could only wonder what it would be like when they left the beaten track.

The nights were spent in Chinese official rest houses or caravanserai. As seen from the road, they were large walled enclosures that could be used for defense. The traveller entered through a large gateway, often with a room over the top, into a courtyard surrounded by rooms, each with a doorway and a tiny window and sheds for animals. An inner yard had several suites of rooms for officials. These had paper windows, a fireplace, and occasionally a rickety table and some decrepit stools. The entire structure was made of mud and looked as if a heavy rain would wash it away. Everything was covered with a half inch of dust.[22] They were lively places, with traders and their donkeys crowding the outer courtyard.

Between Faizabad and Maralbashi the Littledales entered a dense poplar forest said to be inhabited by deer, antelope, foxes and wolves. Three years earlier Major Cumberland had come across the pugmarks of a large tiger. After Maralbashi it became warmer and dustier. Teresa wrote, 'The dirtiest day we have had. The dust is six or seven inches deep and like the finest flour.' They now began to travel at night, and sometimes both day and night. 'The owners of the horses seemed to think that an extra feed of corn was quite equivalent to a rest.'[23] The monotony of the trip was broken by a fight between an Afghan trader and the Littledales' caravan bashi, and St. George had to intervene. The men accused the Afghan of stealing some money. When he denied it, they pried open his mouth and found a missing piece of silver.

After several more days they crossed the Kashgar River and reached Aksu. The Littledales were carrying a letter of introduction from Petrovsky and they showed it to the Russian aksakal (local trade official), who was under his authority.[24] He gave them quiet, comfortable rooms and brought tea, bread, eggs and pears. Later he sent over a rice pilau for dinner.

Aksu was an oasis lying along the banks of the Aksu River. It was surrounded by farms with irrigated fields growing rice, wheat, corn, barley and cotton, as well as that ubiquitous cash crop, opium poppies.[25] The Littledales rested there for several days. On the second night their caravan bashi got into a fight with some Chinese and they knocked out one of his teeth. The Littledale party left town the next day. Just as they were starting up the hill out of town, they were engulfed by 'a most violent dust storm, the worst we have seen. . . . Eyes, mouth, nose, and everything were full of sand.'

The night travel was taking its toll on the men and horses. Teresa and St. George would sometimes awaken in their cart, realise they were not moving, and St. George would find the men all asleep as well. He would wake them up and start them moving again. One of their horses died along the way. After several nights of struggling though heavy sand and bouncing over large stones, the party reached the village of Bai. Here they encountered a native wearing a heavy iron collar around his neck to which was attached a thick iron bar nearly 6ft long. It was his punishment for stabbing a Chinese and he would have to wear it for the rest of his life.

During one march St. George caught two lizards and gave them to Teresa to keep, telling her they were nearly dead. Just then the cart gave a jolt and the lizards darted off. Teresa was not thrilled to have lizards in her bed so St. George caught them in his handkerchief. He tried to drown them in a stream but failed. Finally, he locked them in the spirit box, a collection box from Gunther.

Eventually the caravan arrived at Kuchar. Again the Russian aksakal found rooms for the Littledales, and he sent them apples, pears, radishes and a pilau that arrived just after they had finished lunch. They ate the pilau anyway and found it delicious.

Kuchar reached its zenith during the Tang Dynasty when trade caravans supported numerous Buddhist monasteries. In 1890 Captain Hamilton Bower was ordered to track down an Afghan who had murdered Andrew

Dalgleish near the Karakoram Pass in 1887.[26] While he was searching around Kuchar, a Turki sold him a 'book' he had found. It consisted of sheets of birch bark held together by two boards and covered with writing. At Bower's insistence, the Turki took him in the dead of night to an old stupa where he had found his treasure. He then led Bower under a cliff into some tunnels where the walls had been plastered and decorated.[27]

Bower had bought an ancient manuscript that would electrify scholars when he brought it back to India. The document was sent to the Asiatic Society of Bengal in Calcutta, where it was determined it was written in Sanskrit, probably by Indian Buddhist monks around the fifth century. It was one of the oldest written works to survive anywhere, and it started a stampede of scholars and archaeologists to Central Asia to uncover buried civilisations.[28]

When the Littledales arrived in Kuchar, they were aware of Bower's find. St. George tried to buy old manuscripts, and the locals were eager to please him. 'An illustrated book was brought, which our Chinese interpreter pronounced to be three thousand years old. On examining it, I found a picture of a frigate, and another of a man filling his wine-glass from a decanter; so, in spite of its age, I did not buy.'

St. George wanted to visit Bower's site but it was not easy to arrange. No one would take him there because the man who had guided Bower had received 200 blows for having done so. The punishment had been ordered by the amban. St. George went to see the same amban, asked for a guide, and the amban promised to provide one. St. George then arranged for men and horses to be ready at daylight so if the guide did not appear, he could go anyway.

Meanwhile, Teresa was having some excitement of a different sort. 'While St. George was at the amban's somebody tried to open my door. Luckily I had fastened it with sticks so that they could not enter. They, of course, knew St. George was gone. I wish Tanny was a better watch dog. We want a savage dog.'

When no guide had come by half past 4 in the morning, St. George and his men started out without one. They took a 'shortcut' that was hours longer than the ordinary route. When they arrived at the site 5 hours later, the promised men were waiting for them, having come the other way. St. George was impressed by what he saw:

> The caves are chambers cut out of the sandstone and clay which form the precipitous sides of a valley, through which rushes a rapid river; a great many of the caves are quite inaccessible from below without long ladders, or from above without a rope. Most of those I saw had arched roofs covered all over with endless pictures of Buddha; on one roof I counted twenty-four rows of thirty-six figures in each row. The

walls had more Buddhas, and faces of a Chinese type; opposite the doorway was usually a buttress, on which was carved a large figure of Buddha. . . . On a steep rocky promontory there was an opening, entering which we scrambled up by aid of holes for feet and hands and found ourselves in a gallery; to the right were a succession of tombs, and to the left an opening in the rock, through which we looked at the river foaming below. I should dearly like to have had a few quiet days' digging with pickaxe and shovel.[29]

It would appear that St. George was the second foreigner to view this historic site and its remarkable art. Moreover, comparing his description to Bower's, his tour was much more complete and he could see the details on the walls. Bower had been sneaking around in the dark and could barely tell the rooms were decorated. St. George was there in daylight and with the permission of the amban. It had made all the difference.

They left Kuchar that night. It was hot and the arbas moved slowly. St. George was worried about what lay ahead. 'I much fear the Chinese will be very troublesome and that we have made a definite mistake in not bringing all our camp attendants from Russia.'[30]

After a few days the sun disappeared, the temperature dropped, and Teresa had to dig out her thick cloak from her blanket roll. Heavy black clouds loomed on the horizon but it did not rain. Even so, the road was deep in water from a previous storm and St. George and Tanny had to walk a long way. At one point St. George shot a duck that fell into a swamp. Without being told, Tanny went in and retrieved it, to the compliments of everyone. Then St. George shot a beautiful pheasant he wanted to skin for their collection. Unfortunately Tanny retrieved that bird as well, tearing out its feathers and rendering it useless as a museum piece, but because of his performance with the duck, the Littledales felt they could not scold him.

St. George fell twice on the slippery road. Then the support in front of the Littledales' arba broke and knocked against the shaft, frightening the horses. They bolted and the driver up front could not reach the traces, the only method of stopping them. All he could do was hang on. Teresa was alone in the cart at the time and thought they were going to turn over, but horses and cart came to a stop with everything right side up.

They continued through desert sand and gravel and along the foot of barren hills, skirting the large cultivated fields of Korla until they came to the walled town itself.[31] It was 1 May 1893 and they had been travelling for three months to reach this isolated outpost of Central Asia. Although St. George described the 650-mile journey they had made from Kashgar as 'rather uninteresting', the Littledales knew that the route beyond Korla would become 'interesting' fast. It was time to rest and regroup.

11

To Peking

I do not know how it will all end!
Teresa Littledale

Today Korla is one of the largest cities in Xinjiang, an industrial town with over 330,000 inhabitants. However, in the late nineteenth century it was less impressive. Like Kashgar, there were two towns, Chinese and Turki. The Chinese town was fairly small, about 400yd sq inside a mud wall 35ft high. A mile away, the Turkish town was surrounded by 6 miles of crumbling walls around it and had a main street running north and south for 700yd.[1] Korla was on the bank of the Korla Daria, a river flowing south out of the Bagrash Kol, the largest lake in Turkestan, joining the Tarim River and eventually disappearing into the murky waters of Lop Nor near the hamlet of Abdal.[2] It was the last place a party heading south toward the Taklamakan or Lop Nor could pick up additional supplies.

The Littledales spent ten days in Korla, where they stayed in the house of Kul Mohammed, the Russian aksakal, who assisted them in many ways. Two years later he would help Sven Hedin on his trip to Lop Nor.[3] With the aid of their host, the Littledales purchased horses and donkeys, twenty of each, as well as packsaddles, ropes, picketing pins and other equipment. They also hired six men to look after the animals. In addition they obtained food for five months and water casks. They hired an additional thirty donkeys loaded with grain to go as far as Lop Nor. To stretch their supplies still more, they hired a few extra donkeys to carry grain for a week.

St. George practiced using a sextant and artificial horizon lent to him by the Royal Geographical Society. Initially they would follow established routes, but the lands beyond Lop Nor were new territory, and map-making would become important. Unfortunately, the jolting of the carts had damaged the glass in the artificial horizon and it no longer worked except during calm, windless conditions. There had also been accidents with other equipment. As a result, mapping became a far more time-consuming project than the Littledales had anticipated.

St. George wrote to Douglas Freshfield at the Royal Geographical Society to tell him that they planned to travel along the south side of the Altyn Tagh, the mountains in front of the Kun Lun range, and if that was not feasible, they would go along the north side, cross the Richter range, and go on to Koko Nor. 'Such is the program and how and if it will be carried out remains to be proved.' He struck a more conservative tone in a letter to his sister Nora, saying they planned to go to Peking by a new route, but if necessary they could take one of two other standard routes out of Central Asia that were safer.[4] The letters to Freshfield and his sister were classic communications from an explorer: confidence to the patron, caution to the family.

St. George also commented on their horses, '. . . it is horrid to think that in all probability the greater part of them will die on the road. They are all now so beautiful.'[5] The hired animals would be sent back along the way, but the large number of purchased horses and donkeys would continue on as far as they were able. Five years earlier in the interview for the *Pall Mall Gazette*, St. George had been asked about hiring animals versus buying them. His response at that time was, 'Always hire. If you buy, you buy the halt, the sick, and the blind at exorbitant prices, and then you have to sell for a mere song. If you hire, the owners come with their horses. You get a better lot to start with, and they take care of them all through.'[6] However, the interview took place before the Littledales had even conceived of the journeys they would undertake in just a few years, expeditions in which animals would die in the normal course of the trip. In that part of the world, all caravans lost animals.

They were not able to leave Korla until 10 May. While preparing to leave, the Littledales learned that the only men who knew how to pack the supplies on the animals were their two Ladakhis, Ramzan and Razak Akhun. Fortunately, the aksakal decided to accompany them to Lop Nor. He would be of great help in procuring additional supplies and local guides.

The route from Korla to Lop Nor followed a complex river system. Beyond the town the Korla River makes a wide arc to the west before turning again to the south-east and joining the Tarim River. Instead of following this long semicircle, travellers often took a two-day shortcut across the desert to meet the river after it turns. The Littledales' march across this bend was hot and not without incident. The aksakal had given Teresa his watchdog in Korla, but on the second day his dog and Tanny got into a fight over a crust of bread. St. George and Teresa tried to separate them. In the excitement the Korla dog bit Teresa's arm through her clothes and Tanny bit the little finger of her other hand. 'It was awfully painful. I nearly fainted three or four times and had to get off my horse and lie down on the ground. We sent the dog back to Korla. We have now a very nice sort of collie with us. We met him on the road. . . .'

Soon the party reached the Tarim River. This 'great highway', as Sven Hedin called the route, generally followed the river in a belt of forest, poplar trees and tamarisks, through scattered marshes and lakes, a green streak through the desolation of the Taklamakan.[7] Small clusters of houses with Turki names provided stopping places for weary travellers, a thin thread of life through one of the most barren regions on earth.

Some local inhabitants passed the Littledales in a dugout canoe. They were going downstream and said they would reach Abdal in four days. It would take the Littledales sixteen. They had to cross the Tarim River twice. The animals were able to swim across, and the baggage was ferried over in canoes stabilised by lashing them side by side in pairs. Farther south the weather grew 'frightfully hot'. While the caravan followed the Tarim to Abdal, St. George sent Ramzan and the Russian aksakal to Charklik for more food, animals and a guide.

One night they were hit by a Kara Buran, the Black Hurricane of the Taklamakan during which everything disappears in a dark whirl of sand. 'Their violence is almost inconceivable; they drive across the open, level plains with a force that is absolutely irresistible. Sheep grazing around the villages are sometimes swept bodily away.'[8]

The next evening they reached Abdal near Lop Nor and stayed for five days. Abdal is known in the literature of exploration because it was the end of the inhabited line. Beyond Abdal the Tarim River disappeared into a series of marshes. When the Littledales arrived, there were twenty inhabitants living in four houses made of logs tied together and covered with reeds. The reeds were also used for the roofs and floor coverings. The people were Muslims who had lived in the Lop area for centuries. They were poor and lived mainly on fish. The Littledales did not find Abdal a healthy place, and they both took quinine as a precaution. Teresa tried to take her mind off the surroundings by imagining she was elsewhere. 'I fancy it is Zurich and it is most relaxing.'

Ramzan and the Russian aksakal returned from Charklik with mixed results. They had purchased grain, but no animals were available because every camel, horse and donkey had been hired to carry supplies to miners across the Altyn Tagh. The two men had brought back a guide. The Littledales questioned him and found him useless. Instead they took two Abdal men, one of whom had been to Saitu (Dunhuang).

They left Abdal on 3 June accompanied by the local beg (chief). The animals carried heavy loads of feed. However, with the large number they had, daily consumption was high. To avoid the worst of the swamps, they backtracked up the river for a few miles and then turned south-east alongside the edge of the marsh. The sun had baked the ground until it was almost as hard as iron and so rough that it wore down the shoes of the horses. They had to camp beside the swamp. The water was brackish but the men found some that was drinkable. The beg said goodbye and returned to Abdal.

They were on the Kalmuck (Mongol) pilgrim route from Korla to Tibet, marked across the desert by bundles of reeds. With the possible exception of Marco Polo, the only other European who had been this way was Prejevalsky. He had gone about 150 miles along the north side of the Altyn Tagh before turning back.

Over the next two days there was no water except what they carried in casks so they had to push on. They covered 60 miles. On the second day the party started in the evening and marched all night. Just before reaching Kurgan Bulak at the base of the Altyn Tagh, they unexpectedly encountered a stream of cool but very muddy water from melting snow. The guides said they had never seen water there before. Thousands of sand grouse knew about it. St. George shot three of them.

They remained a day at Kurgan Bulak to rest the animals. Ramzan and Razak Akhun spent the extra day shoeing horses. Several days later they reached a ruined fort marking the point where the Kalmuck pilgrimage route turned south toward Tibet. As the expedition followed the valley, grass became more scarce. They were gaining elevation and began to cross numerous spurs and ridges running down the Altyn Tagh to the desert, separated from one another by narrow valleys so that the party found itself going up and down short steep climbs over little passes.

One day they were hit with drenching rain and sleet that turned into a heavy snowstorm. Teresa was not wearing any waterproof clothing and got soaked to the skin. The deep dust was transformed into a sea of mud, and animals were slipping and sliding. Teresa rode in front of the caravan, turned down the wrong valley, and got lost. Ramzan raced after her and they made camp in the storm. Teresa's main concern was her dog. 'Tanny was very miserable, wet and cold. When he was wiped I let him sleep in my bed to get warm. Poor little thing, he is so good and affectionate.' Four days later they arrived at Galechan Bulak, probably the farthest point reached by Prejevalsky in 1877.

As they were in uncharted country, St. George was working on his route map. He had begun it at Abdal and would continue until he reached Sining beyond Koko Nor. A time-consuming task, it was based on a compass route survey checked by astronomical observations. The speed of the caravan was measured by pacing alongside it at intervals for a fixed distance and timing it with a stopwatch. From these numbers St. George could calculate the total distance travelled. Longitude was obtained by a combination of readings from a watch that Teresa read and frequent sextant observations of the sun and stars, a long process resulting in many late nights for both Littledales. To determine latitude, St. George observed the North Star every evening whenever possible. He used the aneroid barometer to calculate elevations and took compass bearings for all prominent objects in view. Each night he painstakingly plotted the results on his map.[9]

After several more days of travel, the mountainous terrain ahead became impassable and the party had to descend to the desert to skirt the hills. It became hot, water was scarce and there was no grass. The track was stony and hard and most of the horses lost shoes. They rarely got water more than every other day and began to waste away. Each afternoon the wind would rise, engulfing the caravan in clouds of sand. 'Poor Tanny and our big dog are quite worn out. We could give them so little water not knowing what we should find at the end of the day.' The guides made the situation worse. The Littledales distrusted them and Teresa was afraid the guides would desert, leaving them stranded. One night Ramzan caught the guides sneaking off to a spring they had denied existed. The Littledales began to believe that the guides were deliberately trying to sabotage the expedition.

For some time they had been encountering tracks of the wild camel. The Littledales had not seen any but Ivela, the caravan bashi, had seen two of them following along behind the donkeys. Then on 19 June their luck changed. The Littledales usually went ahead of the caravan with a couple of men in hope of encountering game. On this day they spotted fresh tracks. Teresa and a guide stayed behind to look for water while St. George and Ivela followed the tracks up a side valley. After a short distance the tracks turned away so St. George returned, riding slowly because his horse was lame from lack of shoes.

Meanwhile, Teresa and the guide arrived at another side valley. Teresa held the horses while the guide went off to find a camel. He saw two of them and fired a shot, but he missed and the noise sent the camels running in Teresa's direction. She spotted St. George's hat behind a point of rock and started waving her handkerchief at him. He was busy taking compass bearings. He saw her but assumed she had found water, waved back, and returned to his compass. Then Teresa waved two handkerchiefs frantically and St. George rode over to her as fast as his lame horse would go. She pointed toward some rocks and he saw a camel running in his direction. He took a long shot and killed it, reloaded, saw a second camel and shot that one. He skinned both camels, keeping the skeleton of the older one. The men said it was thirty-five to forty years old. Teresa tried eating camel for lunch and did not dispute their judgment. Several days later they saw fifteen wild camels and St. George managed to shoot two more, including a female for the museum.

For several more days they travelled through desert with little or no water. One day after a long march St. George continued up a high ridge and found himself on the summit of the Altyn Tagh. Looking down the opposite side, he could see another great desert stretching away to the south. He shot a kiang, the wild ass of Tibet, and skinned it to take back to England. That night there was just enough water for the humans to drink but none for any of the animals. It was especially distressing to St. George to have to refuse water to the dogs.

After another long march they finally reached a site with good grazing and a large stream with clear water. There was also a yurt with four inhabitants, the first people they had seen since leaving Lop Nor. When the four men saw the Littledale caravan, they jumped on their horses and bolted up a hill behind them. They started to return slowly but retreated again when St. George went forward to speak with them. Then Teresa stepped in. After an hour they realised she was not a threat and came back. Two were Chinese and two were young native lamas. They were grazing sheep, horses and cows, and they offered milk to the Littledales, who hoped to hire the lamas as guides but they slipped away.

The Littledales wanted to cross over the Altyn Tagh and proceed along the south side of the range to Koko Nor. St. George offered money to the two Chinese to show him the way over the Anambarula (Anambar Mountains), but they insisted through the interpreter that they did not know of a pass.[10] At this, the guides from Lop Nor insisted on returning, so St. George hired the head Chinese to guide them to Dunhuang to get a Kalmuck guide. It would be a seven-day march out of their way to the north-east. Later St. George discovered that his interpreter was afraid of the journey and had deliberately mistranslated the information because he wanted the expedition to go to a Chinese town where he could desert them.

For the next two days they crossed a series of spurs leading down into the desert. It began raining and they hoped their water crises were over, but then they left the mountains and started marching north-east across a hard stony plain. The donkeys lost their way and the men had to go back and find them. Teresa described the second day:

29th June, Thursday. The Chinaman guide said our march was a short one today instead of which it was over 9 hours and very hard over deep sand. I am tired to death and went to bed as soon as I arrived. The weather is frightfully hot. The sun burning the sand was so hot today we could not hold it in our hands. It burnt the dogs' feet so badly that we had to take Tanny on our horses and the big dog refused to come on and did not reach camp for a long time after us. Two donkeys were ill on the road. I am sure we manage our marches this burning part rather very badly. We do not start till 7 o'clk. Therefore we travel the hottest part of the day.

There was one compensation. 'The coloring of the sand was beautiful today, the only pretty thing I have seen on this journey. It was black, red, yellow, green, pink and brown.' St. George thought it was the first attractive scenery in fifteen weeks. Teresa concluded, 'I should so like to go on at last from Saitu to Sanchowpoo and wait for St. George there and let him go by Koko Nor. I dread the journey.'

Fortunately, the worst was over. The next day their track followed an embankment about 5ft high and 10yd wide that continued to the horizon. St. George speculated it was an extension of the Great Wall.[11] On 2 July they wound their way through fields and gardens to Dunhuang and pitched camp in a meadow outside the city walls. St. George wrote that the month it had taken them from Lop Nor to Dunhuang was the exact amount of time claimed by Marco Polo.

Dunhuang was the western entrance to China. The name dates from the Han dynasty and means Blazing Beacon.[12] It was the last place caravans heading west could obtain food and supplies and the first place reached by caravans coming east from the Lop desert. It was one of the most important cities on the Silk Road.

The first thing St. George did was buy horseshoes. The second was to call on the amban to obtain a guide to Koko Nor. He had better luck with the horseshoes. As it turned out, there were three ambans in Dunhuang. The head amban was commander of the soldiers. He said there was no road, no water, no grass and no wood, and it was impossible to make the trip in summer, but if they would return in winter, he would help them. Number two amban was the town governor. According to him, the road through the mountains was impassable because they could not ford the rivers, which were in flood during that season due to melting snow. He warned St. George that the donkeys might drown, and when St. George said two or three would be an acceptable risk, the amban said, 'Suppose your wife was drowned?' That ended the subject. The first two ambans had been polite. The third one came to the Littledales' tent and made a different impression. Teresa wrote, 'I have seen no Chinaman I loathed as I do that fat beast. It was very hot and he sat opposite me. He lifted up his shirts and deliberately fanned his bare stomach and sneered at everything about the tent.' All three ambans commented that the countryside was infested with robbers, and they insisted the Littledales take the main road to Suchau. The negotiations went on for three days. At one point St. George announced he was leaving on 6 July, guides or no guides. Teresa was miserable. 'The weather is frightfully hot. I feel far from well. I feel the heat terribly. The thermometer yesterday was 101° in the tent. I do not know how it will all end!'

The Littledales' men absolutely refused to go any farther, saying they were terrified of Tangut outlaws. Only Ramzan, Razak Akhun and a man from Kuldja agreed to keep going. The other men then gave a second reason why they would not go on. They had been given water out of a cup the dogs had used. Strapped to Teresa's saddle was a rubber hot-water bottle containing water for Tanny and the Kalmuck dog. Teresa used her cup for their water dish. One day the caravan bashi had arrived utterly exhausted and had pleaded for water. The only water in the entire caravan was in Teresa's water bottle so she gave a half cup to him and to all the other men as well. Everyone was most grateful at the time, so the Littledales were not impressed by this latest excuse. St. George told Ramzan to give the men a big supper, remind them how well they were being paid, promise them presents if they stayed, and make clear how awkward it would be for them if they were left without money or clothes. These words and the threat of Chinese prison had the desired effect and they agreed to continue.

Meanwhile, St. George and Ramzan persuaded the head amban to furnish them with a guide. The next morning as they were leaving Dunhuang, the amban's wife came with her son to see Teresa, and the Littledales loaded them with gifts. The Chinese who had guided them into the town was unhappy, even though St. George deliberately paid him five times what he had been promised. Upon being questioned, the man said that when a big man gave a present, the receiver was supposed to kowtow, but if he did everyone would know he had received something and the amban would take his money. He hoped St. George would forgive him if he refrained. There were more serious matters. When the guide furnished by the amban failed to show up, St. George had to go back to the amban, who sent soldiers out to search for him. It took 3 hours to find him.

Just to the north of their next campsite was an immense number of Buddhist caves extending for nearly half a mile, three and four tiers high. Teresa commented, 'This place is very curious and well worth seeing. The rocks are a perfect honeycomb of tombs in the recesses. There are numbers of figures of Buddha. Two or three are colossal figures.* I should dearly like to dig here for manuscripts.' Her instincts

---

*   St. George estimated they were 80ft high.

were exactly on target. A modern guidebook describes the caves as 'the world's richest treasure-trove of Buddhist manuscripts, wall paintings and statuary'.[13] Teresa anticipated the most sensational archaeological discovery in Central Asia. Hidden in those caves were manuscripts first obtained by Aurel Stein in 1907.

One afternoon a wolf killed a sheep within 50yd of camp. Everyone ran out of their tents screaming and shouting to drive the wolf away. St. George grabbed his rifle and fired three or four hurried shots but sheep and the wolf were running back and forth through the boulders and he was afraid of hitting a sheep. He fired one last shot at the wolf as it ran away but by then it was too far off. To add to their problems, the Chinese guide had brought a mare. Somehow the mare got loose, St. George's stallion chased after her, and the two horses galloped away. When they had not returned 6 hours later, Ivela and another man rode out on horseback and retrieved them, but so much time had been lost that the caravan had to remain in camp for another day.

Moving on, the party climbed a 3,000-ft ridge and dropped down into a valley containing the river that flows to Dunhuang. They were now in Mongol country. After camping beside the river, they marched south-east up the valley. The snow-capped peaks of the Humboldt range rose off to their right. Mongol yurts dotted the countryside. Occasionally they passed abandoned gold mines. Since they were following a river, there was plenty of water and good grass but they had to use horse dung for fuel. They stopped occasionally to visit Mongol herders. At one yurt some lamas offered them sour milk and Teresa drank it to avoid hurting their feelings. A lama took the empty bowl from her, licked it clean with his tongue, and put it back on the shelf, washed once again. Teresa wished she had not been so polite.

The Chinese guide knew the road to Sining only by way of the Tsaidam-Gobi Desert to the south. However, the Littledales wanted to stay to the north because it was less known. They asked for a local guide but no one there knew the route. Most of the men had left to fight the Tanguts, who had been robbing them. One day St. George visited a local headman to procure a guide but the man refused to give him one. The Littledales then invited him to their tent and plied him with gifts of tea and a hunting knife. When Teresa gave him boric acid to sooth his sore eyes, he finally relented. The guide was a soldier who had been to Koko Nor. His name was Lapkee.

They continued ascending up the valley. The next two days were long marches followed by cold nights as they were above 11,000ft. The alkali soil made Tanny's paws hurt. St. George went ahead as usual and he shot two wild yaks.

After eight days, they were about to cross the Humboldt range. As Lapkee seemed to be knowledgeable and reliable, the Littledales told the Chinese guide, who had been a problem, that he could return to Dunhuang. The guide had an old servant with him who had brought his young son, a boy of about seven. The old man had arrived on foot leading a donkey carrying the child. The man's wife had died and it was apparent he was having difficulty caring for his son. He was from Hanchowfoo (Hangzhou) and was going back. They were with the party for about ten days. Teresa liked the boy. 'The little Chinese child is very good and a great pet.' Once the servant was out all night looking for a horse, and he left the boy alone about a hundred yards from camp. Everyone tried to help. The men invited him to sleep near them but he refused, saying he had to watch his father's possessions. Since the Chinese guide was returning to Dunhuang, the Littledales invited the servant and his boy to continue on with them but the man said it was too cold for his son and he was returning to Dunhuang with the guide. For some reason he no longer had the donkey, and when Ramzan asked him whether he planned to carry the boy on his back, he replied that he was going to sell him to some local Kalmucks. The old man may have been afraid he could not get another job. In her diary Teresa called him a 'brute' but he was not making sense, perhaps from a combination of fatigue, distress over the loss of his wife and possibly some dementia. Why was he selling his son to local people after saying he was leaving because it was too cold for the boy? Why did he not accept the Littledales' invitation to join them? The child would have been allowed to ride with an adult on one of the horses, and it is possible that in Hanchowfoo a family member or friend would have helped to raise him, especially as he was a boy. In any case it was a family tragedy.

Eventually the party turned south and crossed the Humboldt range by the Ping Dawan, an easy pass that St. George measured with his aneroid altimeter as 16,178ft high. Both men and animals felt the altitude. Teresa wrote, 'Ivela was sick so he ran a needle through his nostril, that being the universal cure for all ailments in horses and donkeys.'

A few days later the party descended to an area with good grass that supported large numbers of yaks, antelope and kiang. Tanny caught a baby antelope. The Littledales rescued it and Teresa fed it Swiss milk. Now they were in the country of the Tanguts, Tibetan people to whom brigandage was more than a nasty habit. It was a way of life. The Tanguts were constantly fighting their neighbours, the Mongols and the Chinese. Travellers and traders to and from Lhasa would gather in large groups for mutual protection before proceeding through Tangut territory. This helped, though not always. Sometimes the bandit gangs were even larger than the grouped caravans. Lapkee, the Mongol guide, wanted to go home but St. George would not let him. All of the men were scared except for the Ladakhis, so St. George gave them a lesson on handling the firearms.

They pitched camp a few miles from a Tangut encampment. A Tangut arrived at their tents, but even the most timid member of the Littledale party laughed when the dreaded visitor turned out to be a boy of fourteen. He told them the pass they wanted to cross to the Buhain Gol (river) that led to Koko Nor was still three days ahead, three more days than Lapkee had said. It became apparent Lapkee was not familiar with the route, and Teresa began to wonder if he knew where they were.

The following day St. George rode to the Tangut camp to visit the chief and get another guide. The chief offered St. George the customary yak butter tea. When he gently declined, the chief dipped his fingers into the rancid butter floating in his bowl of tea and smeared it over his hands and face. While it surprised St. George, in that country and climate such protection for one's skin was not a bad idea. The chief carefully examined St. George from head to foot, and after ascertaining his nationality, commented, 'The Englishman has wonderful guns but very bad clothes.' The chief undoubtedly thought St. George had his priorities right.

After St. George offered sufficient tangible inducements, the chief produced two guides to take them over the pass. However, the guides would not go farther because their relationship with their neighbours was less than cordial. Three days later the Littledales crossed the 15,000-ft Katin La and descended a long slope toward the valley of the Buhain Gol. The mountains to the south rapidly diminished in size until they became rolling grassy hills. The party started early the next morning and moved rapidly without the two Tangut guides, who had left them after pointing out the track. It was a hot day tempered by a small thunderstorm. By mid-afternoon they had pitched their next camp by the river, having covered a considerable distance. Tangut horsemen were galloping around excitedly on the opposite bank, apparently mistaking the Littledale caravan for Mongols. The Tanguts feared the Mongols as much as the Mongols feared the Tanguts.

The Littledales invited the horsemen over for a visit, and after some delay four men rode across the river. They had swords stuck through their belts and carried 14-ft lances. Several were armed with matchlock guns. At first they would not dismount, but the Littledales were very polite and eventually the Tanguts joined them for tea. Always the gracious host, St. George showed them his weapons. 'I gave them a practical explanation of the repeating-rifle, omitting to inform them, however, that after firing five shots it was necessary to reload, and they left under the impression that it went on shooting indefinitely.'

Now it rained almost every afternoon and the grazing was excellent. The horses rapidly improved in both weight and spirits. They were walking faster, and one horse gained enough energy to buck off its load.

One night 120 armed Tanguts stopped a mile from their camp. The Turki caravan men thought they were about to be attacked. After consulting with Ramzan and Razak Akhun, St. George decided it would be best for the two Ladakhis to approach the Tanguts and ask for a guide. It would demonstrate that the Littledale party knew they were there and were not afraid. The two Ladakhis carried rifles and gave the Tanguts such an effective display of their capabilities that when Akhun offered to demonstrate his revolver, the Tanguts told him he could put it away. As a precaution the Littledales had the horses and donkeys tied up close to their tent and the caravan men stood watch all night.

The next day they made a long, fast march and came within sight of Koko Nor. St. George was relieved to see the lake. He had been wondering for days whether his calculations were correct, but 'when at last we saw right ahead its blue waters dancing in the sunshine, we knew that our dead reckoning was not much wrong'.

They rode around the north side, where the shore was flat and swampy with many antelope and kiang feeding on the grass. St. George noticed four mounted Tanguts and went to meet them. When they saw him coming, they took off at a gallop. Armed with a white umbrella, he gave chase. As they fled, the Tanguts fiddled with their matchlocks but apparently could not handle them while riding horseback. It was a beautiful day but six donkeys were sick. The Ladakhis told Teresa that the donkey men were so afraid of the Tanguts that they drove the donkeys too hard to keep up with the horses. That night they pitched their tents near a large Tangut encampment with many tents and thousands of sheep and yaks grazing on the nearby hills. At the door of almost every tent a spear was stuck in the ground like a flagstaff.

The Littledales still had five sheep but when they awoke the next morning, all five were missing. Ramzan and two other men stayed behind to look for them while the rest of the caravan began a long march. When the three men arrived in camp that evening, they reported that the sheep had been stolen and they could not find them. The two Ladakhis wanted to start back at once, and if the missing sheep were not produced, they would take fifty sheep to replace them. St. George refused to allow it. He showed good judgment. The following year some Tibetans stole two horses from a French explorer. In retaliation he confiscated two horses from a local village. Despite the pleadings of his men, he refused to return them and was killed in the ensuing ruckus. St. George's restraint was prudent, but he and Teresa were saddened because one of the missing sheep was their old camp 'pet'. It had come all the way from Korla and had slept by the kitchen fire.

On 9 August they finally reached Sining. Although the adventure would continue, the exploratory part of their journey was over. It had been a geographical and scientific success. They had mapped new territory from Lop Nor to Dunhuang and onto Koko Nor. They had also obtained important natural history specimens, especially the wild camel, which had been discovered only sixteen years before. They had been among the earliest European visitors to the caves of Dunhuang, and St. George was only the second westerner to visit the site of Bower's manuscript discovery. In addition, the expedition had firmly established Teresa as the leading Victorian lady traveller in Central Asia. The trip was the stuff of hardship and accomplishment but it was not a breathtaking story. They did not run out of water in the Taklamakan like Sven Hedin or get into a gunfight with Tibetans like Nikolai Prejevalsky. They just did the job and did it right.

George Hunter, a Scottish missionary, was visiting Sining and noticed donkeys on the street. When he learned they belonged to English travellers, he followed them to the Littledales, who invited him to dinner. Hunter had arrived in China the prior year and was just beginning a distinguished missionary career. Except for one visit to England in 1900, he spent 57 years in China, becoming known for his service in Central Asia as the 'Apostle of Turkestan'.[14]

The Littledales left the next day for Lanzhou, the capital of Gansu province. Upon arriving, they did not rest. There was a relatively safe and sure cart road from Lanzhou to Peking but it would not be exciting enough for them so they immediately contacted F.A. Redfern, an English missionary stationed in Lanzhou with the China Inland Mission, and asked him about getting a raft down the Hoang-ho (Yellow River). Redfern told them that although rafts regularly made the trip, no Europeans had done it, and he added that he did not recommend that Mrs Littledale try it. This remark guaranteed Teresa would insist upon doing just that, and the next day Redfern arranged for a raft to take them down the river to Ning-hsia (now Jingjuan in the province of Ningxia). It was the last straw for the interpreter, who announced he was not going any farther and this time he meant it. St. George was unable to find another interpreter in Lanzhou, but one of the Turki caravan men said he knew a few words of Chinese and agreed to come. As it turned out, he spoke so little Chinese that he was more hindrance than help.

The Littledales were impressed with the missionaries. St. George wrote, 'It is impossible to speak otherwise than in the highest praise of the zeal and devotion of these men.' And their wives. The following year Redfern wrote to St. George for a photograph he had taken of their little boy sitting on his mother's lap. He wanted it for his wife, who was heartbroken. The child had died suddenly in an epidemic and it was the only picture ever taken of him. Redfern had gone to China in 1887 and married a fellow missionary, a Miss Ellis, in 1892. He was to die of typhus four years later and his widow would return to England. The touching story of the Redferns was typical of the missionaries. The Littledales had good reason to be impressed with the members of the China Inland Mission.

Out of twenty-one horses in the Littledale caravan, twelve had reached Lanzhou. The donkeys fared better. Thirty-four out of forty-one survived the journey. The Littledales gave their surviving horses and donkeys to their caravan men. They bade farewell to all except Ramzan, Razak Akhun and the Turki interpreter, and the men started back over the long road to Korla.

The Littledales' raft was about 50ft by 18ft with 3 sweeps at each end and a crew of 12 men. They pitched their tent over a plank floor. One of the raft men had brought baskets of peaches. The baskets got in the way but the Littledales did not object because the peaches gave the headman an additional stake in the safety of the raft. The English missionaries came to see them off, the raft was released into the rapid current, and soon Lanzhou was out of sight. They floated all day through a gorge and even went down one small rapid before tying up for the night.

The next day the gorge narrowed and the raft went dashing down between nearly vertical walls. At one place the river was little more than 20yd wide. The water was boiling and surging, and every few minutes the river made a sharp bend. At each bend the water would rise against the rocks and then dissolve in a succession of whirlpools. The raft spun around, and one especially hard bump broke some of the logs, knocking the raft askew. The Littledales' confidence was not increased by the discovery that each of the raftsmen had brought an inflated sheepskin life preserver in case of trouble. After they had bounced downstream for several hours, the gorge came to an end, the river widened out, and the pace slowed. At this point half of the raftsmen paddled ashore on their sheepskins. As it turned out, these men had been hired only for the wild ride through the gorge.

Although the river was now calm, they encountered new difficulties. The river divided into several channels and sometimes the unwieldy raft stuck fast. In channels with a strong current they usually could free the raft, but in the more shallow channels they had to dismantle it, float it piece by piece past the obstacle, and rebuild it. Earlier, the owners of some flat-bottomed boats they passed had offered to take them down to Bautu. To their later regret they declined, mistakenly thinking there would be a better choice of boats farther on. As they descended the river, the channels became more numerous and more shallow and the raft was constantly getting stuck. They would take it apart, rebuild it, push off, and then be stuck fast again.

One morning the men removed some logs from the raft to make a smaller one, telling the Littledales they would use it to tow the main raft when it got stuck again. They put the baskets of peaches onto the smaller raft 'to lighten the big one'. After climbing on the new little raft, the renegade raftsmen cut the rope and went swirling off down the river, abandoning the Littledales with three men and the remains of the big raft. Fortunately a scow loaded with wool passed by and the men agreed to take the Littledales and their baggage to Ning-hsia. Sitting on top of the wool they watched the country drift past including portions of the Great Wall of China 'twisting and turning like a great snake'. As they moved slowly down the Yellow River, St. George worked on his sketch map, taking compass bearings on prominent objects as they drifted past and sextant readings every night to determine latitude.

On 28 August they finally arrived at the landing place for Ning-hsia. Here they obtained passage to Bautu on a scow loaded with grain. The owners agreed to take them in 9 days for a fare of 22 taels. After the Littledales had paid them, some Chinese came on board and said the boat could not start until the boatmen paid them money. St. George informed them that the boat would start in 10 minutes and if they did not leave, they would be taken to the mandarin in Bautu. The intruders were ejected and the Littledales were on their way.

The desert edged the river, and there were few inhabitants along the riverbank and only an occasional village. When they had started at Lanzhou the river was red, but now it was dirty grey and shallow, with bushes and willows covering the banks. Beyond the banks there was nothing but drifting yellow sand. They rigged up a small awning to shield themselves from the sun. At night they camped on shore. Mountains to the west and north closed in and they passed a small lamasery (monastery) on each side. On 12 September, twenty-five days after leaving Lanzhou, the Littledales drifted into the small walled town of Bautu.

They hired five small carts that looked like dog kennels on wheels to take them to Kwei-hwa-cheng (Kweisui).[15] Each cart was pulled by a pair of mules harnessed in tandem, the driver sitting in front with his legs dangling over the shafts. They passed ruined towns and villages with houses still empty since the 1862 Tungan rebellion, which had devastated the province and killed 90 per cent of the population. The Littledales reached Kwei-hwa-cheng in three days and were warmly received by Dr John Steward, a medical missionary with the China Inland Mission. There was also a group of Swedish girls serving as missionaries. The Littledales became extremely concerned about the safety of the young women, who did not know the language and went around unescorted.

They continued on toward Peking, jolting along through the countryside in their carts. They spent the night in lodges when they appeared adequate or camped out in their tent. As they approached the great city, the districts became more populous and the people more accustomed to 'foreign devils'. Now they were presented with 'ludicrously extravagant' bills for their night's lodging. On 27 September they passed through the Great Wall and three days later they reached Peking, where they made a dramatic entrance. One of their carts sank up to its axles in muck and remained stuck for several hours, blocking all traffic into the city by that gateway.

After settling into a small comfortable hotel, St. George paid their Turki interpreter in rouble notes. The man sewed them into the lining of his coat and then started back alone on the long, four-month journey to Korla.

The Littledales ate all their meals at the British Legation, where they became acquainted with Nicholas O'Conor, Chargé d'Affaires.[16] Throughout his entire life St. George deliberately avoided controversy, but the Swedish missionary girls he and Teresa had noticed in Kwei-hwa-cheng were an exception. He reported the situation to O'Conor, resulting in an international uproar. We do not know what he told O'Conor, but when St. George later gave his paper at the Royal Geographical Society, he read:

In this town there were a colony of Swedish girls living alone; they had been sent out to China through the instrumentality of an American. These poor ladies had been exposed to many insults on their way up country, and to daily ribald remarks in the streets at Kwei-hwa-cheng, and one shudders to think what may be their fate. It is difficult to speak temperately of a society or individual that, in the name of religion, lightly takes the responsibility of sending these women out wholesale to a country like China, and when there, leaves them practically without supervision or protection and with the most inadequate means. . . . Though they usually go about in pairs, a girl hardly speaking a word of the language will sometimes be sent alone with a Chinaman several days' journey in a cart to visit some town where there is no European. Altogether, I don't think Mrs. Littledale or I have ever felt more sad than the day we left those kind, enthusiastic, openhearted Swedes.[17]

The seasoned Littledales had become familiar with the hazards of the countries through which they had passed. There were many unavoidable risks pertaining to missionary life, but this struck them as unacceptable and they had to speak up. Acting upon St. George's report, O'Conor sent a message to Lord Rosebery, the Foreign Secretary, who contacted the Swedish government and also wrote ' "kindly and courteously" but firmly' to Hudson Taylor, founder of the China Inland Mission.

Hudson Taylor had proposed in 1890 that 1,000 new missionaries from all denominations should go to China within 5 years. There was an especially enthusiastic response from a Reverend Fredrik Franson, an American born in Sweden. Soon numerous missionaries backed by American money were on their way to China. When they appeared on the doorstep of the China Inland Mission in Shanghai, it was not prepared to handle them. The young missionaries were courageous but inexperienced and with 'imperfect adaptation to the Chinese environment'. Many of them went to Shanxi province, where the Littledales had encountered them.

When Hudson Taylor received the message from Rosebery, he and his wife happened to be visiting China. He sent out a printed letter to the members of the Scandinavian China Alliance Mission outlining approved procedures. A number of the Swedish missionaries wanted to go into the province of Shenxi but Taylor was afraid such a rush of foreigners into an even more anti-foreign province than Shanxi might lead to riots and even murder. He had planned to stay in China only a short time. However, the situation was so serious that he cancelled speaking engagements in the United States and England and, at age 61 and in frail health, he set out with his wife in the hot summer for north China. They left Hankow in May 1894. Crossing the mountains into the province of Honan, they rode in a wheelbarrow. They returned to the coast in September with many of the problems resolved, but during their journey war broke out between Japan and China, and their visit to China was prolonged indefinitely. It was two years before the Taylors were finally able to sail from Shanghai back to England.**[18]

Meanwhile, having started this furore, the Littledales left Peking, proceeded on to Tientsin, and took a local steamer to Shanghai, where they gave a brief interview to the *North China Daily*.[19] On 14 October they returned to Europe on the French mail steamer *Oceanien*, scheduled to arrive in Marseille in a month. They took Ramzan and Razak Akhun with them on the ship as far as Hong Kong, where they put the two Ladakhis on a steamer to Calcutta, from where the men could return through Kashmir back to Ladakh. By late November the Littledales were safely home in England.

** The account of their voyage was summarised as follows: 'While still in the Huangpu River their ship came into collision with another, in which seven officers and three hundred Chinese were drowned. But an otherwise uneventful journey brought them to London on June 17.'

Toward Tibet

. . . without any material discomfort.
St. George Littledale

Upon returning to Wick Hill House, St. George sent the specimens they had collected to the Natural History Museum. He turned in 14 mammals, 10 fish, 10 lizards, 4 snakes and a toad. The spirit boxes had been put to good use. Gunther was especially delighted with the wild camels, and he wanted to exhibit them as soon as possible. St. George dreaded the next task. He had to write another paper for the Royal Geographical Society and present it. Furthermore, he had to help prepare the accompanying sketch map to be made from his field observations.

At home after their lengthy absence, the Littledales quickly caught up with news among family and friends. While they were away, Eliza Crutchley's son Percy and his wife Frederica had their first child. They named him Victor after his godmother, Queen Victoria. The Littledales were saddened to learn that Sir Robert Morier had died. It is doubtful they would have been admitted into Russian Central Asia again and again without the tremendous efforts of the Ambassador to Russia. Morier had even wanted his only son to participate in their Pamir crossing, an indication of his high regard for the Littledales, but Victor had to withdraw from the expedition and died soon after. Morier's health had been poor for some time, and he never got over the death of his son.

St. George read his paper in April 1894.[1] It was followed by the usual remarks from the floor. Later on he read a transcript of the discussion because it would be printed in the *Geographical Journal* with his article. Sir William Flower, head of the Natural History Museum, had commented on St. George shooting auroch in the Caucasus. St. George immediately wrote to J. Scott Keltie, the editor, 'It would never do to send that out to Russian officials. . . . Would it be possible . . . to print me off a dozen copies at my expense of course omitting the unfortunate 9 or 10 lines & I would send them to our friends, the Russians.' His Russian hosts had indicated they would look the other way if he got an aurochs but they could not ignore anything published. Keltie cooperated and the problem was solved.[2]

During the summer, Littledale and Gunther exchanged a flurry of letters and St. George received a formal acknowledgment from the museum thanking him for the gift of two insects taken from the nose of a wild camel. He was also invited on a hunting trip to Asia Minor. However, the Littledales had bigger things in mind.[3]

They had decided to go to Tibet. Until the nineteenth century it was relatively open, but then Tibet closed its frontiers because of pressure from China and the lamas' fear of foreigners endangering the Buddhist religion.[4] The last visitors were the French Lazarist priests, Evariste Huc and Joseph Gabet, who reached Lhasa in 1846. The mysterious Lhasa had always been an attraction and now that it had become a 'Forbidden City' it was even more of a magnet for the adventurous. Numerous explorers had attempted to reach it and all had failed, including the redoubtable Russian, Nikolai Prejevalsky. To the Littledales, Lhasa was the ultimate objective.

It would require another winter trip across the Tien Shan to Kashgar. St. George wrote to the Foreign Office in late June asking them to apply to Russia for the permissions. In early August Thomas Sanderson, now Permanent Under-Secretary at the Foreign Office, whose duties now officially included intelligence, notified St. George that permission had once again been granted to travel by the Transcaspian Railway to Samarkand and from there via Osh to Kashgar, and that he was seeking permission from the Chinese. Later that month Sir Halliday Macartney at the Chinese Legation in London forwarded their passports.[5]

The race against time began. The day after Sanderson's response, St. George asked Keltie about borrowing a 3-inch theodolite for practice. He said they planned to leave for Tibet about 1 November but the heavy baggage would have to be sent a month earlier. He also wanted an armed escort and tried to obtain Gurkha soldiers, but Lord Roberts wrote that the Government of India objected to Gurkhas being used in the vicinity of Tibet. Fortunately, Roberts and Major Hamilton Bower found some retired Pathan sepoys (soldiers) instead.[6]

In the May 1896 issue of the *Geographical Journal* St. George begins his Tibet article with a classic paragraph:

We left England on November 10, 1894, the same party as usual: – Mrs. Littledale, myself, and our dog, accompanied in addition by my nephew, Mr. W.A.L. Fletcher, of Oxford University boating renown, who proved himself to be in every respect an admirable travelling companion. My scheme was to strain every nerve to reach Tibet, and, if possible, Lhasa, with plenty of food and animals to carry it. Most of the other expeditions had failed owing to their arriving in a more or less destitute condition, and then, of course, the Tibetans could dictate their own terms. We also relied upon bribery, and went well prepared with the sinews of war for wholesale corruption.[7]

St. George had made a critical decision. Their 1893 expedition across Asia to Peking had pushed the Littledales near the limit of their collective physical resources. Although Teresa had been healthy during the Pamirs crossing, the China trip had been hard on her and she was still recovering. Tibet would be far more strenuous than anything they had done before. They would spend weeks above 17,000ft crossing the Chang Tang, the Tibetan plateau, and every illness would be magnified by the altitude. Then there was the age factor. The energetic St. George was healthy and in his early forties, but Teresa would be fifty-five years old when the trip began, and age could diminish her effectiveness and stamina. The Littledales needed another strong man in the party, someone with unquestionable loyalty and the courage and ability to cope with any and all crises that might arise. St. George invited his nephew W.A.L. Fletcher to accompany them.

William Alfred Littledale Fletcher was born in 1869, the oldest child of Alfred and Edith Fletcher, one of St. George's sisters. The Fletchers had a house for a few years at Pitlochry, Scotland, and it was there that Willie was introduced to rowing. At Eton he showed more interest in the river than in his studies. He rowed well as part of the Eton Eight at Henley, but he achieved national fame at Oxford, where he entered Christ Church College in January 1889. That year he rowed in the Christ Church Eight, which won the Ladies Plate and the Thames Cup at the Henley Regatta. In 1890 he was the stroke of the Oxford crew when it beat Cambridge after four years of defeat. Oxford proceeded to beat Cambridge for nine successive years, in the first four of which Willie was the mainstay of the Oxford crew. Although he won many other races, it was his performances in the University Boat Race that established his lifelong reputation as an oarsman.

Willie Fletcher grew to be 6ft 3in tall and weighed 190lb. Although his arms were comparatively unmuscular, his chest and back were massive. In addition to his great strength, he had tremendous stamina and determination. His friends called him 'Flea' because of his constant activity. A formidable man both on and in the water, he also played on the Oxford water polo team.

Willie lived with his parents and their large family at Allerton outside Liverpool. According to family legend, the Fletchers were sitting at dinner one evening when the butler announced, 'There's an oar at the door for Willie.' Without a pause his father replied, 'Give her a fiver and send her away.' The butler left the room and returned carrying a large wooden oar.[8]

In March 1893, the week before the University Boat Race, *Vanity Fair* ran a profile of Willie in its 'Men of the Day' series and included a caricature. Willie was described as 'a capital shot, a staunch friend, and a really good fellow, full of British pluck'.[9] At age 24 he was known throughout England.

Teresa's health remained poor. In August she wrote:

> I have been very seedy this spring & summer. Now I am suffering from abscesses in my ears. I have had three in one ear. When that was getting well the other ear began. Perpetual leeches & poultices have prevented it getting so bad as the first. I have suffered agonies for four days & nights. I cried with pain. I am <u>almost entirely</u>! deaf in both ears. . . . It is all the result of influenza which pursues me in all its forms. . . .

She continued:

> We are starting again on our travels in November. . . . St. George's nephew Willie Fletcher is going with us. I tell [his parents] he will be hopelessly bitten with a mania for travel, but . . . it is a good wholesome life, & he can save money on his expeditions when he has once got all his outfit. You cannot spend much on the Tian Shan mountains![10]

Teresa knew what it meant to be 'hopelessly bitten with a mania for travel'.

The Tibet journey began mundanely enough. The Littledales, accompanied by Tanny, left Wick Hill House after lunch, said goodbye to the Crutchleys in Ascot, and caught the 4 o'clock train to London. There they met up with Willie Fletcher, dined with the Peards, and spent the night at the Charing Cross Hotel.[11] The next morning they caught the train to Dover. After a smooth channel crossing to Ostend, they took the train to Nuremberg, where they demonstrated their mania for shopping. Although it was only the second day of a fourteen-month journey, they purchased a large copper water pot for the drawing room of Wick Hill House and a wrought iron bracket for a lamp in the upper hall. They reached Vienna the next evening. Two days later they left for Constantinople, arriving 17 November but not without a small row along the way when Turkish customs men tried to remove Tanny from the train.

In Constantinople they were reunited with their heavy baggage. They called upon Charles Eliot at the British Embassy and visited the bazaar, but a recent earthquake had almost demolished the place and all the shops were closed. According to Willie, Tanny greatly impressed the local dogs. The British Ambassador invited the Littledales and Willie to dinner on Sunday but they could not accept because they were leaving that morning. Teresa wrote that in any event they would have had to decline because none of them had brought evening clothes, formal dinners apparently being one contingency for which they had not prepared.

They left the next morning for Batum on the steamer *Medea*, but not before Turkish customs officials seized St. George's new Mannlicher rifle. Teresa had to fetch Mr Eliot, who persuaded the officials to release it, and they boarded the ship. It had been a 'narrow shave'.

On board were Captain Percy Sykes and his sister Ella. Captain Sykes was on his way to Kerman in southern Persia, where he was to be the first British Consul. The Sykes would go with the Littledales as far as Tiflis. The *Medea* was dirty and the only available cabin for the Littledales was below deck, so Ella Sykes took Teresa into her cabin and Percy took the men. Miss Sykes's maid got the Littledales' cabin down below.

The ship stopped at almost every Turkish port on the way to Batum. The Black Sea was rough, and everyone except St. George got sick. When they reached Samsun, high winds kept them rolling about at anchor far offshore for three days. However, there must have been some social life aboard the ship. In a letter to St. George from Kerman a year later, Percy Sykes, later Brigadier-General Sir Percy Sykes, KCIE, CB, CMG, added a postscript: 'Do you remember the red-haired woman on the steamer? I still blush when I think of the occurrence.'[12] As neither Teresa nor Willie mentioned a red-haired woman in their diaries, the details are lost to posterity.

The wind finally died down and the ship docked. The *Medea* then chugged on and reached Trabzon, where they stayed for another 24 hours. There was a Turkish Pasha on board with his wives. Initially he repulsed Teresa, but soon she had him sign her tablecloth and he showed her a flag given to him by the Sultan.[13] He later left the ship with his women, waving to Teresa as he went.

The Littledales reached Batum on 25 November, and thanks to an order from St Petersburg, their baggage cleared customs quickly. It filled four carts. Captain Sykes got his reward for letting St. George and Willie squeeze into his stateroom. The Russian officials had not yet received the permit for his baggage but it went ashore with the Littledales' by mistake and passed through customs as part of theirs.

They dined with their friend Patrick Stevens, and then took the night train to Tiflis. They spent two days buying lemons, figs and three dozen cooked tongues, as well as two carpets for their tents. Upon arriving at Baku the next morning they boarded the steamer for Usunada, the beginning of the Transcaspian railway. About a mile out of port, the vessel ran aground. The Russians managed to refloat it by offloading 350 soldiers onto a tug.

That night the Littledales left on the train for Samarkand. Count Rostofftsoff, Governor of Samarkand, had arranged for a special compartment for them. On 4 December they arrived in Samarkand, where they remained for several days. St. George turned forty-three on 8 December, and that afternoon they celebrated his birthday by setting off on their fourth trip to Osh. Two full carts of baggage had left ahead of them. The drivers were instructed to leave bread for the Littledales at Uratiube and then continue on and wait for them at Margilan. The Littledales and Willie loaded up a tarantass by placing their tents on the bottom of the compartment and their beds on the tents. St. George and Teresa rode inside. As there was not enough room inside for three, Willie wrapped himself in sheepskins and rode outside on the box with the driver. The carriage was so heavy they had to hitch five horses to it instead of the usual three. It was a short stage but at least they had started.

Although they had travelled the same route in winter two years before, this was more than two months earlier and would make their first experience seem almost balmy by comparison. They had no choice. They had to reach the Tibetan plateau by spring. They were able to get horses at every relay station but the extreme cold made the road treacherous. They met no other travellers. The party covered 95 versts or 61 miles in 12 hours before they stopped that evening. Teresa had been unwell at the start of the Tibet trip, and that day she developed dysentery that would plague her off and on for the rest of the expedition.

The next morning the road was slippery and the drivers kept changing the horses and beating them. It took 5 hours to finish the first stage of 32 versts or 21 miles. As there was no backrest on the box, Willie became increasingly uncomfortable and swapped seats with St. George. The sky turned black and it began snowing so heavily that the driver was unsure of the road and drove the tarantass into a drift. The men got off and pushed. Eventually they managed to free it but soon it was stuck again. When they reached Sarat, the next stage, it was snowing so hard they stopped for the night. The relay station was dilapidated, and as there was neither wood nor food, they had to eat cold rations they had brought with them.

Four inches of snow fell during the night. The stationmaster thought they could not go on but they left anyway, reaching Uratiube with their horses exhausted. They were forced to stay there overnight to wait for fresh horses coming the next afternoon. They collected the bread left by their baggage men and went to the bazaar for a melon, dried apricots and pears, all frozen hard. Later, Willie wet his hair and brushed it. When he stepped outside to clean his teeth, his hair froze stiff.

The following morning they learned that the horses would not arrive until late that night so they had to spend a second night. It was so cold that one of the drivers got frostbitten hands and feet. Other things were going wrong. The felt boots they had brought were cracking and Willie's bed was coming apart. More seriously, Teresa was feeling so ill, she stopped writing in her journal. She would not resume for almost three months.

On 13 December they got an early start. Willie sat up on the box outside in a freezing wind. At the next stage they had to stop for 5 hours because four of their five drivers were so badly frostbitten they were sent to a hospital. The only healthy driver had gone back to Uratiube and they had to wait for his return. When he arrived, they started with only three horses hitched to the heavy tarantass because there was no one to drive the other two.

That afternoon they arrived at a partly frozen river. The driver got off the box, unhitched a horse, rode it across the river, and decided the tarantass could make it. In the middle of the river the tarantass broke partway through the ice, which immediately began to freeze around it. The men beat the horses but to no avail. The tarantass was stuck. St. George and the driver mounted two of the horses and rode for help, leaving Teresa and Willie alone in the carriage trapped in the ice. Half an hour later they found three Sart horses.[14] While Teresa rode ashore on horseback behind a Sart, the three horses were hitched to the tarantass but it would not budge. One of the Sart horses fell and rolled its rider into the river. St. George hired a local arba and Willie moved the baggage into it. They reached a Sart's house that night after leaving the tarantass behind in the river.

The rooms were so smoky that the Littledales camped outside. Meanwhile, the driver wanted to leave. St. George offered the local Sarts more money and they agreed to make another effort to free the tarantass from the river. Two tarantasses arrived from down the road, but when their drivers reported there was still another river to cross, the Littledales decided to spend the night where they were. Then at 2 o'clock in the morning the stationmaster arrived in his troika so they left with him, taking half of their baggage. An hour later both their troika and a baggage cart became stuck in the next river. Once again the men unloaded them, tugged on frozen ropes for 2 hours, and freed them. The Littledales arrived at the next station at half past five in the morning. They had travelled 33 miles.

After three more days of such travel they reached Margilan, and then Osh the following day. Colonel Gromchevsky offered to put the Littledales up at the Club and they gratefully accepted. They spent three days in Osh drying out equipment, buying additional supplies, hiring a cook and repacking their baggage. Every night they had dinner with Colonel Gromchevsky.

From Osh they would be following the same route they had travelled in 1893 over the Terek Dawan to Kashgar, only now there was more snow. Gromchevsky ordered yurts, firewood and other supplies to be ready for them at every stage on their march across the Tien Shan. The party left on the morning of 22 December. They put the baggage on 18 horses. Teresa travelled in an arba but St. George and Willie rode ponies. The new cook arrived drunk so St. George made two other men escort him. It was a bright sunny day. The road was rough, especially for the carriage. They arrived at Langar late that afternoon only to learn the cook was not there. He came in with the baggage caravan 2 hours later. Everyone crowded into one room at the little station building, a small mud house.

It was another cold night. They arose early, packed the animals, and left after making sure the cook had preceded them. While crossing two small passes, Willie's horse started rolling on him. When it tried to roll while crossing the Gulcha River, he dismounted and walked the rest of the way through the snow to Gulcha. St. George and Teresa took the only room available and Willie slept in a yurt.

They remained in Gulcha for two days because Teresa was still ailing. Despite a snowfall during the night, the chief arranged for the local Kirghiz to play some games for them. In one game 150 horsemen fought over the carcass of a goat. Then they stripped to the waist and wrestled each other on horseback. Many horsemen fell onto the ice and snow but they kept going, greatly impressing Willie. The climax was a tug of war. The Littledales' caravan leader, Basil, went about striking men and horses with his whip and a good time was had by almost all. The Littledales and Willie spent the rest of the day mending harnesses, trunks and other equipment. When looking at his diary, Willie suddenly realised it was Christmas. He thought of home and wrote, 'I wonder what you are all doing. We are occupied as follows. I am writing, St. G. working at figures, TL in bed.' Teresa had been so ill on Christmas Eve that she had talked about seeing 'winding sheets in the candle', but she felt better on Christmas Day.

The following day they marched up valleys between high hills and saw many partridges and pigeons and even a large hawk. Teresa was feeling stronger. When the arba was unable to get up a hill, she got out and walked. After 18 miles, the party stopped in an open valley and stayed in two yurts under some trees. The arba driver wanted more money to continue so the following morning they sent him back and everyone rode horses instead. Icicles hung down from the animals. They started toward the Terek Dawan and camped at 8,800ft in three yurts.

The next day they crossed the Terek Dawan. A light snow was falling and the track was slippery. Tanny rode on St. George's horse and wore a fur coat Teresa had made for him. When they reached Kok Su at 10,000ft everyone was exhausted, even St. George, who lay down for a long time. They spent the night in one room of a rest house. Willie had diarrhoea he attributed to overindulging on apricots. The happiest member of the party was Tanny, who seemed quite pleased with his fur coat. St. George commented that Tanny was as warm as Lucifer.

The following day they struggled across two steep passes during a snowstorm. Willie's pony stumbled descending the second pass and fell on its side, landing on top of Willie, but the deep snow prevented any injury. At the frontier post of Irkistan, two sturdy yurts were waiting for them. The Russian soldiers at the fort welcomed them and asked for their passports. As they were leaving the next morning, some soldiers questioned them about the passports. While St. George discussed the matter, Teresa and Willie slipped away. When the soldiers went to consult with their superior, St. George sneaked away and rejoined the caravan.

It was getting even colder. Moreover, they had reached the end of Gromchevsky's hospitality. Later St. George was to write in his article, 'Thanks to his excellent arrangements, we crossed the Terek pass (12,700 feet) in midwinter without any material discomfort.' It was more than typical Littledale understatement. It was an expression of his enormous gratitude to Gromchevsky.

On 31 December they crossed the border into Chinese Turkestan. Their caravan now included two camels carrying baggage. During the night the cold became so intense, Willie's breath froze on his pillow and his moustache stuck to the bedding. They moved on toward Kashgar following the same route they had taken two years before. Teresa continued to relapse into illness. Willie was worried that if her health did not improve at Kashgar, the trip would have to be abandoned.

One day as they were pitching their tents, two Ladakhis arrived in camp. St. George had requested the services of four Ladakhis for the expedition. The men had left Leh for Kashgar months earlier because they had to cross the Karakoram Pass before winter set in. In Kashgar they had been waiting for the Littledales for four months. St. George had asked Macartney to send two of the Ladakhis out to meet their party, and now Razak Akhun and Hussin had arrived. Akhun had accompanied them in 1893 and would be their caravan bashi. He brought a horse from Macartney and an invitation for the Littledales to stay at Chini Bagh again.

During the night the cold horses kept knocking against the sides of the tent. Willie thought it was the coldest night yet. He put fur stockings over his sleeping socks but they were not enough so he put on his sheepskin. His fingers were so numb he could not button anything. The next night was warmer and everyone slept well. Even so, it was 7°F below zero. In the morning the baggage men could not wait to get to Kashgar. For the first time on the trip, they left before the Littledales.

George Macartney met the Littledales a mile out from Kashgar and escorted them to his house. They were pleased to get their mail but unhappy to learn their sepoys had not yet arrived and it would be another week to ten days before they did. They enjoyed a good dinner with Macartney and became comfortable in their quarters in Chini Bagh. It was 5 January 1895. It had taken almost two months to reach Kashgar and their journey was just beginning.

13

From Kashgar to Cherchen

> . . . travellers pile up the bones left behind
> to serve as road-marks.
>
> *Hsuen Tsiang (seventh century)*

The Littledales remained in Kashgar for two and a half weeks. Although they had to obtain animals, supplies, and especially money, the big delay was in waiting for their 'fighting men'. Their four Ladakhi servants were staying at Chini Bagh with them. The two they met in Kashgar were Kalam Rassul and Rassul Galwan.

Galwan had gone with Lord Dunmore to the Pamirs in 1892. He was gradually learning English, and in 1923 he would publish a book, *Servant of Sahibs*. Except for two articles, one by St. George and one by Willie Fletcher, Galwan's book was the only first-hand account ever published of the Littledale expedition to Tibet. It matches up well with Willie's and Teresa's diaries and provides different insights into the journey.

Several weeks after three of the Ladakhi servants had left Leh for Kashgar, a request had come for a fourth man who had travelled in Chinese Turkestan and knew some of the language. The Wazir at Leh selected Galwan. He had just married, and both his wife and his mother were vehemently opposed to his leaving. When he told the Wazir he could not go, the Wazir replied, 'You must not ask your mother and wife. They are women. You think for yourself, what is best.' Galwan thought about it all night and said, 'I will go by your order.'[1]

To get to Kashgar the Ladakhis and the Pathan sepoys who would come months later had to follow the ancient trade route from Leh to Yarkand with five passes higher than 16,000ft, including the infamous Karakoram Pass. Caravans constantly plied the route bringing goods to Yarkand, and felt, hashish, silks and carpets to Leh.[2] The track was difficult, grazing scarce, and with the altitude, rough terrain and weather, the route was littered with the skeletons of dead animals and occasionally a few humans.

When Galwan reached Kashgar he joined the other three Ladakhis at Chini Bagh. During their long wait for the Littledales, they had no work. They got expense money from Macartney and his Indian clerk, Munshi Ahmad Din, who took them under his wing. The four men were crowded into one room. When a man from Hunza arrived and was given their room, they had to move to a smaller one. They had difficulty storing their firewood but Galwan was up to the challenge. 'I tied some ropes high up under the roof, and there hung all the wood. This way we got enough sitting-place.'³

Hussin fixed their meals but the other three had nothing to do and wandered into town every afternoon. When boredom set in, they decided to study languages. Armed with Arabic and Ladakhi primers, Hussin taught the Arabic Koran to Rassul and Galwan, who in turn taught Ladakhi to the others. 'Now we read it from morning to afternoon and our small room was like a school.' Then there were the music lessons. Rassul and Galwan both learned to play the banjo.

During their stay in Kashgar, the Littledales met Mohammed Isa and Abdurahman, two Ladakhis who had just arrived from the Dutreuil de Rhins expedition with news about the disastrous trip. In the fall of 1893 Jules Leon Dutreuil de Rhins and Fernand Grenard tried to reach Lhasa by travelling south from Cherchen, an oasis east of Khotan, their base for two years while exploring the area. With great effort they found their way over the Akka Tagh by the Kara Muran Dawan (Black Water Pass) and continued south over the Chang Tang, the Tibetan plateau. They reached the large lake known as Tengri Nor or Nam Cho (Sky Lake) before they were finally stopped by the Tibetans. They had not encountered any other Tibetans for sixty days.

After a fifty-day impasse, they began their return on a north-eastern route toward the city of Sining. In a small village a Tibetan stole two of their horses. Dutreuil de Rhins ordered his men, against their advice, to take horses belonging to the villagers as hostage for the return of his animals. As they were leaving, the Tibetans attacked and Dutreuil de Rhins was mortally wounded. Grenard and the rest of the men barely escaped with their lives.⁴ It was a sobering story. However, its significance to St. George was that the Frenchmen had found an isolated route across the Tibetan plateau, enabling them to penetrate deep into Tibet with little opposition.

St. George had been planning to follow the route used by Gabriel Bonvalot in 1889–90. He too had reached Tengri Nor. The route went from Korla to Charklik near Lop Nor, then east before turning south across the Altyn Tagh into Tibet. The Littledales were familiar with much of it because it was a variation of the Kalmuck pilgrimage route they had used to the base of the Altyn Tagh in 1893. However, because it was a pilgrim route, the Bonvalot party had begun to encounter Tibetans long before they reached Tengri Nor. Even though it was midwinter, they met with increasing resistance before finally being stopped.

After talking with Mohammed Isa, St. George changed his planned route to the more isolated one used by Dutreuil de Rhins. While changing his mind, he was in the process of composing a letter to J. Scott Keltie at the Royal Geographical Society: 'We hope to start in 5 or 6 days for Lob Nor. . . .' He then crossed out Lob Nor and substituted: 'Khoten & shall go south from Kiria or Cherchand.'[5] The die was cast.

The small European community in Kashgar had expanded since the Littledales' last visit. Besides Nikolai Petrovsky, the Russian Consul-General, his wife, and George Macartney, there was now a Swedish mission.[6] Other foreigners included Adam Ignatieff, a Roman Catholic Pole, and Father Hendricks, a Dutchman by birth who had been living in Asia for twenty-five years and spoke twelve languages. The only thing the two men had in common was that they had not made any converts to Christianity. There were also the staff and escorts to Petrovsky and Macartney, which in the case of the former consisted of a secretary, two military officers, a revenue officer and fifty Cossacks.[7]

Another person in Kashgar was Sven Hedin, the Swedish explorer. He was staying with Petrovsky. Hedin was only twenty-eight years old, and although he had already made several difficult journeys, he was just beginning a forty-year career exploring Central Asia and Tibet. The Littledales and Willie spent a lot of time with Hedin and they enjoyed each other's company. It was the start of a long friendship. Hedin was not given to overpraising other explorers but he made an exception in his description of St. George in Kashgar:

> Mr. Littledale was unusually genial, manly, and unassuming in character, and I esteemed it a great privilege thus to make the acquaintance of one of the most intrepid and able of living Asiatic travellers. He himself regarded his own travels with a critical eye, was always modest, and had no pretensions. He said, that he travelled simply for pleasure, for sport, and because the active, changing life was more to his taste than the gaieties of London. But with the journey he began in the year 1895 he has written his name indelibly in the annals of Asiatic exploration, by the side of those of his distinguished countrymen, Younghusband and Bower.[8]

Hedin saw through St. George's diffidence and assessed his ability and character correctly but misjudged the permanence of his fame.

On 6 January St. George and Willie called on Petrovsky, and back at Chini Bagh they listened to Russian solders singing carols to Macartney. Father Hendricks joined them for lunch and cut their hair. Willie found it a novel experience to have his hair cut by a priest. The next day Petrovsky took Teresa and St. George back to the Russian Consulate to see Madam Petrovsky. The following day they had lunch again with the Petrovskys and Sven Hedin. And so the social life went for their entire stay in Kashgar, an endless round of reciprocal lunches, dinners, and teas.

They also met with the Chinese officials, especially the Taotai, Huang Tajen, who was the head of Kashgaria, an area including not only Kashgar but extending as far east as Cherchen. St. George and Willie paid a courtesy call on the Taotai at his yamen or official residence, a labyrinth of square courtyards with mulberry trees in the middle and wooden verandas around the sides. The Taotai met them at the first door and escorted them through several courtyards to his audience chamber, which was lined with attendants. St. George and Willie sat on a 'throne' with the Taotai, with Macartney off to one side, and had tea and bonbons.

When the Taotai returned the visit, Teresa invited him to sign her tablecloth. It took him an hour. He wrote a long message about two lotus flowers floating downstream and coming together, symbolising his meeting with the Littledales. Then Hedin arrived, and St. George had a long discussion with him about sextants.

The Taotai invited the Littledale party to an official Chinese banquet, attended also by Sven Hedin, a Russian officer, and a Chinese who spoke English. A full Chinese banquet is a remarkable experience in any setting, but in Kashgar at the far western extreme of the empire it was especially striking and it made a strong impression on Willie. The guests were seated ceremoniously and given tea followed by loaves of hot doughy bread filled with melted sugar. The servants next brought in a table covered with little dishes holding stacks of dried apricots, fruit lozenges, hard boiled eggs in jelly, cold bacon and pork, and some sort of vegetable. These were accompanied by Russian red wine in small silver cups.

The main dinner started with shark fins followed by many courses including sea slugs, duck and bamboo roots. They washed it down with tea and Chinese brandy. The Chinese played a game with their hands. Whenever one of the players shouted the correct total number of outstretched fingers, the loser had to have a drink.[9] Then the host began a game with Sven Hedin using beans. The Taotai became more and more inebriated and grew increasingly upset when his guests did not keep up with him. His servants rebuked him but he replied that his drinking did not matter because he had a bed there. When Hedin said he did not have a bed, the Taotai showed him a bedroom he could use. As Hedin had been spending months in Kashgar at the pleasure of the

Chinese officials, he did not have much choice in the matter. After three more rounds, Willie and the Littledales left. St. George commented dryly that Dr Sven Hedin added considerably to the merriment of the party.

By now the Littledales had been in Kashgar for ten days and were anxious to leave. They had obtained arbas, put covers on them, and hung curtains to hide from the Chinese. However, the non-arrival of the sepoys and other difficulties delayed their departure still further, especially money. They were having trouble getting rupees, langers and, most of all, the large chunks of silver known as yamboos. Surprisingly, it was Petrovsky's men who were successful. On 20 January, the Chinese New Year, the Littledale party finally obtained the silver, 400lb of it, and with considerable effort they moved it from the Russian Consulate to Chini Bagh.

The next problem was how to pack it. Anyone who does not appreciate the efficiency of paper currency should be the paymaster on an expedition to a region where only hard currency is accepted. Four hundred pounds of silver is hard to conceal. The Littledales were happy to follow Galwan's suggestion to hide some silver in each flour bag. It reduced the financial risk and robbers would not think to look there.

That afternoon the four Pathan sepoys arrived and saluted. The first words spoken by the havildar (sergeant) were, 'Sahibs, three sepoys have come', and he patted each of them with his stick. Their names were Badullah, Punginor and Purdil. The havildar had a red dyed beard. Willie liked him but wrote, 'Two of the others look as if they would knife one very easily & laugh at it. They are indeed fighting men.'

Their trip across the Karakoram passes in winter had taken its toll. Three of the four sepoys had frostbitten feet, especially the havildar. St. George was irate at the British native hospital assistant who accompanied them. 'This wretched man had never attempted to wash or dress their wounds, which were in consequence more serious than they need have been.' The Russian doctor examined their feet and said two men would be better in a few days but it would take at least three weeks for the havildar to recover. He treated their feet as best he could and wrapped them in cotton cloth.

The party increased. The Littledales decided to hire Abdurahman because he had been with Dutreuil de Rhins and presumably knew the route. They also hired a young Ladakhi named Galam Mahmad. Rassul Galwan knew he was a strong, hard worker and persuaded the Littledales to take him.

The expedition finally set off on 22 January 1895. Sven Hedin described their departure. 'In the middle of January our English friends left Kashgar in four large arbas draped with carpets; and an imposing sight they made as they drove out of Mr. Macartney's yard.'[10] Rassul Galwan stayed behind to care for the three frostbitten sepoys. The four men would follow in a few days. The expedition carried letters from the Taotai to the authorities in Yarkand, Khotan, Keria and Cherchen, asking for assistance. Everyone was relieved to be on their way again except possibly Tanny, who had enjoyed playing with the local Kashgar dogs and had even won a dogfight.

It was 120 'very uninteresting' miles to Yarkand over a rough road ankle-deep in dust. The carts moved slowly, swinging and shaking the occupants. They were supposed to reach their first stage at 9 o'clock in the evening but did not arrive until 4 o'clock in the morning because the carts kept getting stuck in the frozen rivers and it took hours to free them. After four days of similar travel, they reached Yarkand. Along the way the Littledales stayed in local rooms and froze, while Willie spent the nights sleeping comfortably in the cart.

With a population of approximately 60,000 people, Yarkand was the largest city in Eastern Turkestan. It was the first major town on the Chinese side of the trade route over the Karakoram Pass to India. It had a Chinese amban, a local beg or Turki official, and several aksakals or trade officials who represented the local trading communities and settled their disputes. Like Kashgar, Yarkand was a walled city. Its narrow lanes were covered with roofs of woven matting to keep off the sun, and seemed like tunnels. Strings of camels passed through streets lined with stalls.[11] The high incidence of goitre in the local population made a deep impression on visitors. Teresa wrote, 'The goiter at Yarkand is frightful, worse than any place we have seen.' Six hundred years earlier Marco Polo had observed, '. . . a large proportion of them have swollen legs, and great crops at the throat, which arises from some quality in their drinking-water.'[12] The local beg and the British aksakal met the Littledales outside the city and led them through the streets to a house that had been prepared for them. Willie thought it must be a fine residence in summer but now it was 'Cold as the grave'.

The Littledales spent an unexpected eight days in Yarkand because of the difficulty in obtaining animals and Indian rupees. They decided against using camels when they learned that camels would probably become footsore even without loads. When the British aksakal produced twenty emaciated but expensive horses, the Littledales realised they would need more time to obtain adequate animals. They had to pay in Indian currency, but the price was high because the currency was in demand by local Muslims making the pilgrimage to Mecca by way of India instead of through Russian Turkestan, their former route.

Hindu traders living in Yarkand brought gifts of food, melons, raisins and sugar that the Littledales felt obliged to keep. The traders said

Teresa was the first European woman in Yarkand. Meanwhile, Razak Akhun's brother arrived from Kashgar, having been robbed of his money along the way and some of Akhun's as well. He reported that the frostbitten sepoys were much improved.

On 3 February the Littledales decided to move on, even though Rassul Galwan and the sepoys had not yet caught up with them. It was another late start. The arbas arrived at 8 o'clock but the Chinese drivers had not brought enough horses. They went out to find the drivers and did not return until noon. Willie seized the headman by the scruff of his neck and 'ran him to Uncle who awaited him with a stick. The man cried with funk as he expected a hiding but after much threatening we promised it to him on the next occurrence.' St. George's restraint showed he had come a long way from the overreacting youth on Mount Fuji who had struck his swindling cook in the face with an alpenstock. He had learned that frequently the threat is more frightening than the reality.

The Littledales left town accompanied by the British aksakal and his munshi. After several hours they reached the Yarkand River and were ferried across in boats. They continued on for about 15 miles through irrigated paddy fields until they came to a small village, where they stayed in a Chinese serai. The next afternoon they reached Kargalik, where a relative of Rassul Galwan brought them fruit. They were following the southern branch of the old Silk Road which went from oasis to oasis, skirting the Taklamakan. After Kargalik the path became a rough, dusty route over the desert, a gravel plain on which old caravan tracks were obliterated by blowing sand. It was windy, and they were cold despite the sun. Three days later they reached the town of Guma, a large oasis with good water. The next day the horses struggled as the wheels of the carts sank into deep sand. Throughout the entire journey the Littledales were collecting plants and insects, and even on this desolate stretch they managed to catch some beetles.

That evening Rassul Galwan and the three frostbitten sepoys arrived at last, having been travelling from Kashgar for ten days. Galwan had had his hands full. Macartney had ordered the sepoys to obey Galwan in all matters and to ride in the cart. Under no circumstances were they to ride horses or walk. As a result the sepoys were angry at Galwan even as he was changing the bandages on their feet.[13]

That night the servants had a tamasha. In fact, with St. George's encouragement and at his expense, the Ladakhis had a party every night. Galwan wrote, 'Mr. Littledale always said to us: "You people must make tamasha here, and at Cherchen, everywhere are village. Why? For a long time you people will not see any human being, and no villages. Beside that, you will find much trouble in the desert." '[14]

The Littledales reshuffled the responsibilities among the Ladakhis. Razak Akhun was caravan bashi, Kalam Rassul the cook, Hussin the Littledales' table waiter, and Galwan and the others took care of the animals. Now Teresa wanted Galwan to wait on them. Razak Akhun and Kalam Rassul were not pleased but the change was made.

For the next three days they struggled through more deep sand. There were frequent sandstorms. One night Razak Akhun's poshteen (fur-lined coat) and belt were stolen out of a cart. They finally arrived at Khotan on 12 February. The Russian and Afghan aksakals rode three miles out of town to meet them.

The expedition remained in Khotan for almost two weeks to buy animals and supplies. St. George had Rassul Galwan calculate how much food they would need for six months for eleven servants. It came to about 4,000lb of rice, grain and flour. Razak Akhun made the massive purchases. At one point the Russian aksakal asked the Littledale party to leave the bazaar because their presence was raising prices. Meanwhile, Teresa made butter out of cream and put it into cans. She also made coats and hats out of Russian cloth for the men.

The three frostbitten Pathans were treated every day. Badullah and Purdil continued to improve but the havildar's big toe was in terrible condition. There was dead flesh with a half inch of bone sticking out. St. George used his bird-skinning tools to clean it. The sepoys were difficult. They considered themselves to be exclusively fighting men and felt that other work was beneath them. However, St. George and Willie told them in no uncertain terms that in such a small party everyone had to do his share.

The Littledales visited the Chinese amban to discuss the theft of Razak Akhun's poshteen and to obtain a promise from him to sign Teresa's tablecloth. The amban offered to flog anyone the Littledales wanted punished. Later he signed the tablecloth but Akhun's coat was never recovered. The amban also gave them a dinner complete with three rifle salutes upon entering and leaving his yamen.

The caravan men enjoyed themselves. There was a Central Asian custom of temporary marriages. A traveller could marry a local woman for as many days as he liked. After an agreement on an amount of money to be given to the 'bride', the mullah would conduct the ceremony. There was an old woman in Khotan who had arranged temporary marriages for the men of the Dutreuil de Rhins expedition, including one for Dutreuil de Rhins himself, and she made arrangements for all of the Littledales' servants. Galwan got married for three days but then decided he did not like the custom so he paid the woman off with gifts. The Littledales gave a big tamasha for the men in the house of 'the French sahib's short-time wife'. The room was covered

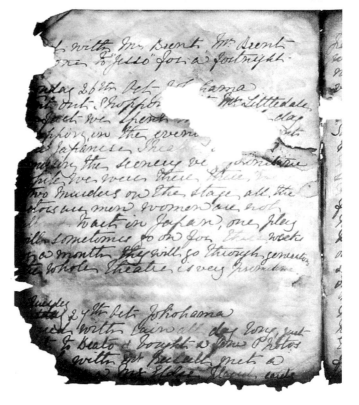

(Above) 1. Teresa Harris
Scott, probably at age 20.
(Private papers)
(Above, right) 2. William
John Scott probably at age
32. (Private papers)

3. First mention of
St. George Littledale by
Teresa Harris Scott in her
diary. (Photograph by
Elizabeth Clinch)

4. Eldon House, London, Ontario, Teresa Harris's childhood home. *(Courtesy of John and Amelia Harris Family Fonds, J.J. Talman Regional Collection, University of Western Ontario Archives, RC41003)*

5. Highfield House, West Derby, Liverpool, St. George Littledale's family home. *(Courtesy of Edith Vera Fletcher)*

6. Teresa Harris Scott, 35-year-old widow in mourning dress with veil in style made popular by Queen Victoria. *(Courtesy of John and Amelia Harris Family Fonds, J.J. Talman Regional Collection, University of Western Ontario Archives, RC80226)*

7. St. George Littledale, probably at age 24 before marriage to Teresa. *(Courtesy of John and Amelia Harris Family Fonds, J.J. Talman Regional Collection, University of Western Ontario Archives, B1458 (p. l86))*

8. Typical Tibetan valley. Photograph by St. George Littledale, 1895. *(Courtesy of Royal Geographical Society)*

9. Tibet encampment at closest point to Lhasa, Littledale tents in foreground, lama tents beyond. Photograph by St. George Littledale, 1895. *(Courtesy of Royal Geographical Society)*

10. Tibetans near Rudok who helped the Littledales. Photograph by St. George Littledale, 1895. *(Courtesy of Royal Geographical Society)*

11. Makeshift palki that carried Teresa Littledale from Goring Valley near Lhasa to Leh, Ladakh. Document in foreground orders Littledales back to Cherchen. Photograph by St. George Littledale, 1895. *(Courtesy of Royal Geographical Society)*

12. W.A.L. Fletcher and a Tibetan loading a pony during the retreat from Lhasa. Photograph by St. George Littledale, 1895. *(Courtesy of Royal Geographical Society)*

GHULAM RASSUL GALWAN

(Left) 13. Rassul Galwan, faithful servant and author of *Servant of Sahibs*. *(Servants of Sahibs, 1923, frontispiece)*

(Right) 14. Tanny's silver collar from the Royal Geographical Society. *(Courtesy of Christopher J. Inward)*

15. and 16. Patrons Medal *(front, left; back, right)* awarded to St. George Littledale by the Royal Geographical Society. *(Courtesy of Christopher J. Inward)*

17. Teresa and Tanny crossing a river with Prince Demidoff in 1897 in raft improvised from two camp beds. *(E. Demidoff, After Wild Sheep in the Altai and Mongolia, 1900, p. 206)*

18. Littledale sheep (*Ovis littledalei*) discovered by St. George Littledale in the Tien Shan. *(R. Lydekker,* Wild Oxen, Sheep, and Goats of all Lands, *1898, p. 186)*

19. W.A.I. Fletcher in the First World War. *(Wurtzburgh,* The History of the 2/6th (Rifle) Battalion "The King's (Liverpool Regiment), 1920, *frontispiece)*

20. Sir Robert Morier, British Ambassador to Russia. *(Courtesy of National Portrait Gallery, London)*

21. Prince Christian of Schleswig-Holstein. *(Courtesy of National Portrait Gallery, London)*

22. Teresa Littledale in late middle age. (Courtesy of John and Amelia Harris Family Fonds, J.J. Talman Regional Collection, University of Western Ontario Archives, RC1496)

23. St. George Littledale, probably mid-sixties upon appointment as Justice of the Peace. (Courtesy of Edith Vera Fletcher)

24. Wick Hill House as it looked when the Littledales lived there. (Courtesy of Christopher J. Inward)

with silk rugs and wall hangings and the hostess was dressed in fine silk, the result of her 'marriage'. Many kinds of fruit were served and plenty of wine and Chinese brandy. The musicians played a kind of banjo and drums, and the men danced, followed by the women, until late into the night.

By 25 February the expedition had its full complement of animals and the caravan started out. In order to conserve the strength of the Littledale horses and mules, the donkeys and some hired horses carried the loads. That evening they reached the village of Lob on the eastern end of the Khotan oasis. For the next four days the track went through sandy wastes and deep sand. Finally they arrived at the oasis of Keria (Keriya). It was impossible to take carts beyond there, even arbas, so they had to stop for several days to hire more animals to carry loads. It was important for the expedition animals to travel unburdened, conserving their strength for the push over the high Tibetan plateau.

Because of the Dutreuil de Rhins tragedy and the resulting embarrassment to the Chinese government, the Keria amban was strongly reluctant to let the expedition proceed. However, he was generous in his hospitality. St. George gave him a note absolving the Chinese government of responsibility if anything happened, and he responded by sending a sheep, rice and a good cook to the servants and they had a feast.

They left Keria on 5 March but it was another slow start. The men were tired from lack of sleep the night before and the animals were milling around. The amban sent messages to the chief begs of Nia and Cherchen ordering them to support the expedition. The grand parade now consisted of 14 horses, 10 mules and 65 donkeys, all belonging to the expedition, and an additional 66 horses and donkeys carrying loads only as far as Cherchen, where they would turn around and go home.

After two days the Littledales and Willie arrived at Nia tired out, having spent 12 hours in the saddle through sand and stone desert with no water for the horses. The baggage animals did not arrive until 8 o'clock in the evening, and when they did, Teresa and St. George learned that the horse carrying their trunks had collapsed about 5 miles out. Their personal belongings arrived late with the donkeys.

Nia was as far as the havildar went. He would not be able to walk for two months across Tibet. His frostbitten big toes were black and the bones were loose. Rassul Galwan had to amputate them, assisted by the Littledales and Willie. The havildar would return with the Keria men and the rented horses and then continue on by cart all the way back to Kashgar. There he could stay under Macartney's care until he was well enough to travel back over the Karakoram Pass to Leh. He was disappointed and he even cried for fear of losing his wages, but the

Littledales gave him his wages, medicine and money for all his expenses from Nia to his home, a journey of many weeks. Their generosity made a favourable impression on the other men.

The expedition left Nia on 9 March and went a long distance before camping. When they awoke the next morning, there were only three mules and one horse in the vicinity. All of the other animals had wandered off. While the Littledales moved on, Willie stayed behind to wait for the missing animals. After an extended search, he found them all the way back at Nia, a distance of 25 miles.

The route to Cherchen was merely a direction cross-country over rocky desert and shifting sand dunes. There were a few forests of poplars and occasional shepherds here and there where rivers crossed the track before disappearing into the Taklamakan. Stretches of chi grass marked the underground water table. The Chinese traveller Hsuen Tsiang passed over the Taklamakan in the seventh century and wrote, 'The tracks of wayfarers get effaced, and many among them lose their way. On every side there extends a vast space with nothing to go by; so travellers pile up the bones left behind to serve as road-marks. There is neither water nor grazing, and often hot winds blow. Then men and animals lose their senses and fall ill.'[15]

For ten days the Littledales marched through sandy wastes and violent sandstorms that blackened the air and obliterated their tracks. The wells along the way were choked with drifting sand and always had to be dug out. One day it would be hot and the party would stagger along in the blazing sun, the alkali in the hot soil hurting Tanny's paws. The next day it would be so cold that Teresa put on her fur-lined coat. It was sweat or freeze. The only constant was the incessant wind. The animals continued to wander at night, sometimes almost back to the previous camp. One day a chicken being transported on a donkey's back laid an egg. It was a highlight of the trip.

At last they reached Cherchen. The beg met them a mile out of town and accompanied them to the oasis, where he took them to a large house with a garden. It was Tuesday 19 March 1895. It had taken four months to reach this village. The easy part of their journey was over.

14

The Akka Tagh

The Akka Tagh is the most absolute of frontiers.
Fernand Grenard

Cherchen was a green patch in the Taklamakan Desert. All of the inhabitants were Turkis or Uighurs. There were no Chinese. Fernand Grenard spent three months there with Dutreuil de Rhins. He wrote:

> Our long stay appeared even longer in this little oasis without a town, without a market, without trade, peopled only by peasants living in scattered farms, seventy-six leagues from the nearest village, a hundred leagues from the nearest town and as isolated in the midst of the continent as is an islet never visited by ships in the midst of the sea. On every side around spreads the ocean of the sand-downs, except on the north, where, along the bank of the river, stretches a belt of forest half invaded by sand, a haunt of deer, wild boar and even tigers. The traveller rarely passes here; no caravans come to enliven the country with the tinkling of their bells, the cries of their camel-drivers, the snorting of their horses, the bustle of their arrival and departure; the news of the distant outside world does not penetrate so far, or when, sometimes, a small trader brings it with his bales of cotton and spice, it arrives distorted, vague and confused, leaving one and all indifferent.[1]

The Littledales knew they would need at least six days in Cherchen to rest animals, repair saddles, buy corn, and obtain supporting animals and drivers. They also realised they might be delayed longer if the mountains were deep in snow. In fact the expedition would not leave for twenty-four days. The local beg told them that the passes over the Akka Tagh, the main range they would have to cross to reach the Tibetan plateau, and the Tokus Dawan range in front of it were closed and would not open for three months. As the beg may have been acting on orders to stop them, St. George sent Razak Akhun and Abdurahman on a reconnaissance to see the snow conditions for themselves. Abdurahman had crossed the Akka Tagh over the Kara Muran Dawan Pass with Dutreuil de Rhins.

There was a reason for selecting Razak Akhun. St. George had asked Rassul Galwan to be sirdar but Galwan had declined because he and Akhun were both from Leh and it would permanently blacken his reputation at home if he usurped his friend. However, Akhun's supervision of the animals and food had been lax to say the least. Four horses had sore backs and four mules were cut by their girths, with some cuts two inches deep. Furthermore, the six-month supply of butter prepared in Khotan was gone and half of the sugar had already been consumed. The expedition would not get far on the Tibetan plateau if things did not change. St. George sent Akhun on the reconnaissance in order to put Galwan in charge during his absence. Galwan did such a fine job that St. George let him continue to run things afterwards, with Akhun as sirdar in name only, a face-saving solution.

Personnel problems were not confined to the Ladakhis. The sepoys required constant attention. Badullah had been made havildar over the other two sepoys, causing more problems than it solved. They still refused to work. Punginor complained to Willie that he had to fix the saddles by himself because Purdil and Badullah would not help. St. George and Willie immediately reprimanded them, resulting in Badullah and Purdil lashing out at Punginor for telling on them. The next morning the three sepoys arrived at the Littledales' tent with a loaded rifle. They claimed that Punginor had pointed it at Badullah, and Purdil had taken it away from him. St. George examined the rifle and found three cartridges in it. When he asked Punginor to explain, he replied, 'I put three cartridge [in], one for Badullah, the next for Purdil, and one for myself, but Purdil caught my hand.' He continued, 'We do not want Badullah on us havildar. If make him havildar, then I will kill him and I will die, myself.' Littledale removed the cartridges, returned the rifle to Punginor, and sent the men away. He knew the other two sepoys did not like Punginor and that Badullah went after Punginor first, so St. George and Willie appointed themselves joint havildars over all three sepoys, whereupon Badullah said he wanted to leave the expedition. St. George decided on a compromise. Badullah could be havildar but could not give any orders. Like the handling of Razak Akhun, it was unorthodox but it worked. St. George understood the importance of 'face' in the Ladakhi and Pathan cultures but it could not be allowed to keep the expedition from running properly.

Another problem was the rice for a celebration. Shortly before leaving Cherchen, the men decided to give a tamasha to thank the beg for his hospitality. Besides, everyone liked a party. Galwan collected two local coins from each man to buy a sheep, and he took rice from the expedition stores. Badullah, seizing an opportunity, reported Galwan to the Littledales. St. George could not understand him and called on Galwan to rephrase Badullah's Hindustani into simple words he could comprehend. Galwan was honest. He reported that Badullah was saying that he, Galwan, had stolen some rice from them. When Teresa asked why, he replied, 'For tamasha.' Teresa asked about meat, and Galwan said he had already collected 20 tangas for that. Teresa promptly responded that the rice was not stolen and moreover, Galwan must return the tangas to the men. As usual, the Littledales provided the tamasha.

Stealing rice was a serious charge. Diminished food supplies could jeopardise their lives. However, Teresa and St. George had the good sense to realise Galwan took the rice for the men, not for himself, and he thought his taking a small amount would not cause a problem. The Littledales knew that for their expedition to be successful, they needed the loyalty of their key men. Galwan was doing outstanding work, and by their display of confidence in him, they won his undying loyalty throughout the course of a very difficult journey.

The Littledales' main activity in Cherchen was obtaining food and the animals needed to transport it. Dutreuil de Rhins had used camels, most of which had died during his expedition. The Littledales decided to rely on horses, donkeys, and mules. Their caravan would consist of 250 animals divided into two categories, animals they bought for the trip across the Tibetan plateau and others they hired to support the first group. The hired animals would return to Cherchen as their loads were consumed, and the last were expected to go back after the expedition had crossed the Akka Tagh and reached the Tibetan plateau. The party was caught in the classic logistics pyramid of an expedition that had to be self-sufficient in food. Grazing would be scanty – in fact it turned out to be scarcer than they had anticipated – so they needed animals carrying fodder for the animals carrying loads. Then they needed animals carrying fodder for the animals carrying fodder for the animals carrying loads. Thus they had to start out with an enormous supply of corn. Besides a 6-month supply of food for the members of the expedition, the Littledales took 25,000lb of corn for the animals.

Every day they obtained more animals but only a few. The local beg proved almost useless and they began to wonder if his ineffectiveness was the result of an order by the amban. Gradually they accumulated the animals they needed. They bought corn by the charrock (16lb), and on 1 April they spent the entire day weighing 642 charrocks. Hussin made sure they got full measure. Then the men mended sacks and made cord in order to pack the corn into loads.

The long stay in Cherchen had a special benefit. It gave the animals they had brought with them a chance to recover. Willie inspected them every day and recorded their improvement in his diary. He and St. George frequently went duck hunting in their spare time. They also made an unsuccessful excursion to dig for relics in the ruins of the old city of Cherchen buried in the sand. Meanwhile, their milk supply improved. Willie wrote, 'The milk today had less water in it. Rassul [Galwan] informs me he beat the man yesterday.'

Teresa sewed constantly, repairing clothes or making new ones. She also wrote numerous letters home because she knew it would be months before she could contact her family again. On 26 March St. George took a sighting of the sun at noon to determine their longitude for his map. He also checked the pedometers he had brought. For the rest of the expedition he would concentrate on making a route map. Beginning at Cherchen, he would take observations every day. He would not keep a diary. Willie and Teresa were doing that. Willie also taught English to Galwan, who had asked for lessons. Teresa wrote to Julia Turner, 'Willie seems to enjoy the life very much, he is an excellent traveller and companion, always good tempered, he and St. George get on admirably.'[2] While it would be surprising for Teresa to say otherwise to St. George's mother, the tone of the letter indicates that she meant it.

Akhun and Abdurahman returned from their reconnaissance after ten days. They suggested waiting fifteen more days to let the snowmelt reduce, as the river was not yet fordable. Because of the delay in obtaining food and animals, this news was not as disturbing as it might otherwise have been. The weather swung between extremes. When they arrived it was cold, especially in the mornings, and there were dust storms that blew in on a cold wind. On 28 March Teresa recorded a bitterly cold night, and in the morning the thermometer in the tent registered only 1°F above freezing. Then it began to warm up, and a week later the thermometer rose to 84°F by mid-afternoon. It grew hotter and hotter. St. George wrote, 'On April 5 the apricot trees only showed faint indications of buds; two days later they were shedding their blossoms.' But the pleasures of spring were transitory on the borders of the Taklamakan. It suddenly turned cold again. Dust storms blew for two days, and St. George and Teresa sat in their tent with the door shut and worked by candlelight, Teresa in her fur jacket and St. George in his sheepskin.

The Littledales were in Cherchen during a bazaar, where they bought a little food and tent pegs. St. George was astonished at the low price of the pegs. They were made of iron that must have come all the way from Russia or India via Yarkand but the price was only 5 pence each.

Their primary concern continued to be the animals. Razak Akhun and Willie checked every horse and donkey every day and gave the horses new shoes. During the last week in Cherchen, they passed out the loads to the donkey men. They decided to load the animals relatively lightly at first, one maund (80lb) on the donkeys and two maunds on the horses. The loads would increase after the hired animals had been sent back. Some of the animals would start out unloaded because their sore backs had not yet healed.

The first ninety donkeys left Cherchen on 9 April. Akhun and Willie rode out 4 miles to see them off. Before starting, the donkey men protested that they were being underpaid. Although St. George thought it was a swindle, he decided to give in and pay to get things moving, but he announced that in the future any such demands would meet with a stern response.

The main party followed three days later. Galwan wrote that the local people came to say goodbye and many were crying. Willie's diary reflects in detail the usual confusion of the first day's start. First of all, only seventeen hired horses came instead of the promised eighteen. To the awed surprise of the crowd seeing them off, Willie ordered his men to load the beg's horse if the missing one failed to arrive. It soon came. Fifteen minutes after they left, half the loads fell off. One box burst open and had to be repacked. When St. George turned over the ground for anything missing, he found a silver yamboo buried in the sand. For the rest of the day, animals were constantly losing their packs. One horse fell in the river.

Shortly after leaving the oasis of Cherchen, they were plodding through sand and it was hard going. Fortunately for the Littledales' peace of mind, Grenard had not yet published his description of the Dutreuil de Rhins departure from Cherchen the prior year:

On the 3rd of September, the expedition started gaily in the sun. The horses, fresh and well-fed, went at a brisk pace; the long string of camels unwound itself majestically in the plain and their tinkling bells seemed to sing the end of the boredom of repose, the joy of action, the freedom of the wide horizon, the hope of fine discoveries. Alas, this music was soon to grow slower and sadder in the weariness of the endless road, the many sounds to cease, one after the other, until the final silence, when the last of those patient servants had fallen exhausted on a desert mound![3]

The Cherchen Darya, which supplies the water for Cherchen, rises in the glaciers of Ulugh Muztagh (Great Ice Mountain), the highest peak of the Akka Tagh. The party followed this river until it went through a narrow defile that was impassable for the animals. Here the expedition had to take a detour slightly south-east through the desert to the foot of the Altyn Tagh, a front range of rounded mountains. After marching for hours under a hot sun over bare gravel and sand, they reached a campsite near the base of the mountains at a riverbed that was nearly dry.

When the party left Cherchen, they were carrying twenty chickens attached to the backs of donkeys. They had a cock that was left free to roam and it rode on the donkeys, hopping from donkey to donkey several times a day. The donkey train lagged behind the horses, and camp was usually set up by the time it arrived. The moment the cock saw the tents, he would jump off and scamper into camp as fast as he could go.[4]

The routine for each day's march was similar. The expedition owned 85 donkeys and 30 mules and horses. In addition there were 135 hired donkeys and horses with 15 men from Cherchen and Keria led by Mula Shah, the donkey caravan bashi. Kalam Rassul cooked for the party and Rassul Galwan served. Five Ladakhis, Razak Akhun, Galam Mahmad, Hussin, Abdurahman and Omar Shak, and the three sepoys, Badullah, Punginor and Purdil, worked with the animals. Kalam Rassul and Rassul Galwan assisted them when their other work was done, and Willie and St. George helped with the loading and unloading of the animals.

Every morning Razak Akhun and his men collected the animals, cleaned their saddles and fed them. Afterwards Kalam Rassul made a kettle of boiling water and cooked breakfast. Rassul Galwan poured hot water in basins and filled Teresa's teapot. Then he laid out breakfast on a table, usually bread, honey and meat. After breakfast Kalam and Galwan cleaned up, packed the beds, took down the tents and packed their loads on horses. Meanwhile, the other animals were being packed with everything else.

The Littledales and Willie rode on horses, but when the going became more difficult St. George and Willie would dismount and walk for a while, letting a Ladakhi rest by riding on one of their horses. Teresa and Willie kept an eye out for badly-packed loads. St. George went ahead to find the route and the caravan followed him. When they reached camp, everyone except Teresa unloaded the animals and pitched two tents for the Littledales and Willie. Then Kalam and Galwan made their beds and laid out Teresa's clothes. The Ladakhis then pitched their own tent.

Next, Kalam started a fire while others brought wood. He would cook a meat stew with onions, and separately he cooked rice, potatoes and fruit. At dinner time Galwan set three places on the table. The Littledales and Willie would put soup mixture in their cups and add hot water. Galwan brought two hot serving plates, one with rice for Teresa and Willie and the other with potatoes for St. George. Then he set out the stew followed by the fruit in a wooden bowl.

After dinner Kalam and Galwan washed up. Then Galwan brought hot water for baths. There was never much water but the Littledales and Willie managed to wash every night. Finally Galwan filled a hot-water bottle for Teresa to help keep her warm in her bed. Teresa and Willie wrote in their diaries while St. George worked on his map calculations and sketches. As he was usually travelling on horseback, he had Badullah carry the pedometer. Meanwhile, Hussin, Omar Shak or Galam Mahmad cooked dinner for the servants. Kalam and Galwan joined them for dinner when their own work was finished. After dinner the men smoked, told stories and sang songs.

There were additional chores. Kalam Rassul cooked a three-day supply of bread and cake for the Littledales and Teresa had Rassul Galwan and Punginor do laundry twice a week. Everyone was constantly mending things, especially Teresa and Rassul Galwan. Taking care of the humans was a minor affair. It was the animals that required the most work. Over 100 animals had to be fed and cleaned, the sores on their backs treated, and their saddles fixed. At least this was supposed to happen and it usually did, but there were many variations as animals wandered, water was short, and other problems arose. The entire routine was followed every day for months.[5]

On 14 April they wound their way up a narrow valley and reached a campsite called Munar Bulak.[6] That afternoon there was another row with the sepoys. They were eating bread intended for camps where there was no firewood and therefore no cooking. When Rassul Galwan remonstrated with them, they told him they would do what they pleased. Galwan told Willie, who confronted the sepoys, but they denied having eaten the bread. Badullah and Punginor then went to St. George and threw down their rifles because they had been accused of stealing. After much talking, Punginor finally confessed. St. George reminded the sepoys that the expedition had already consumed a three-month supply of butter in two weeks. At that time food could be replaced but now it could not, and therefore he had put Galwan in charge of the food. He said that even he and his family were following Galwan's instructions and he expected everyone else to do the same.

The party climbed up through a steep, narrow, twisting ravine over a stony riverbed until they reached the summit of 9,764-ft Chokur Pass. They dropped 800ft down the southern side and pitched camp at noon at a spot with good grass and water from melting snow. It took great effort to get the animals over the pass. The donkeys straggled in later that afternoon. Willie and the men spent a long time attending to a mule that was in bad shape. The mule improved after they cut its nose, a standard treatment then for animals with altitude sickness. The expedition had crossed the Altyn Tagh.

A strong wind came up during the night and filled the tents with sand, and the wind was still blowing when they left the next morning. At first it was chilly but soon they were travelling under a hot sun. The route went over the spines of several rocky ridges. Many animals lost their loads, and the men had to scramble to repack them. By mid-morning they had reached the Cherchen Darya again. It was deep, swift and muddy, and a rock wall descended steeply into the river. The only passage was a narrow ledge leading across a point of rock 40ft above the water. They had to take the animals across one by one. They were now marching along the north side of the river up an undulating valley. Willie almost lost his mule when it went into the river for a drink, got out too far, and nearly drowned. St. George rode in and managed to retrieve it. They reached a potential ford but the water was too deep so they continued upriver towards a better ford that local people had mentioned. To avoid alkali marshes, they skirted the southern side of the hills and even climbed over a ridge descending down the Altyn Tagh. It was a long, cold, tiring march over stony ground. They stopped about a mile from the next ford.

The animals were still doing reasonably well but the arduous days were wearing on the men. Teresa wrote, 'Badullah says he is not well and has a sore throat. I do not feel quite happy about him. . . . He looks worn out. I wish he had returned with the Havildar who I am thankful has gone back. Both men are too old for such a trip and should never have been sent.' As Teresa was not feeling well, her thoughts about Badullah may have reflected thoughts about herself.

The men from Cherchen wanted to spend several days there to cut grass for the animals because they would need it farther on. St. George compromised, saying they would remain one day. The Littledales bought twenty sheep from local nomads to provide a moving larder.

The river crossing was easy. There were six branches to cross but only 2ft of water in the deepest part. Even so, St. George and Willie stayed behind to make sure all the baggage got across. Omar Shak's donkey fell into the river with him. On the south side they wandered over boggy ground to get back on a gravel plain. Razak Akhun led the caravan. They went over barren ridges of sand and rock before camping. Abdurahman had strained his back and was unable to walk so he rode a donkey.

The next day they wound around the hills and through valleys following a stream covered with 2–3ft of ice with a coating of sand and mud. It was rough going. After a cold night, the expedition travelled for many hours through ice-filled valleys between barren mountains, part of the Tokus Dawan (Musluk Tagh). They left the stream, crossed over a ridge, marched over another gravel plain, and pitched camp. For water they melted snow from a nearby hill. Abdurahman was getting worse. He was in such pain that he cried from time to time and it became apparent he would have to return. This bothered everyone, especially Willie, who wrote that Abdurahman was the best man they had for the horses. One new participant was doing well. The Littledales had obtained another dog. Teresa wrote, 'Our dog Jacob we brought from Cherchen is so happy he is fed, treated kindly and altogether thinks he is in clover and wants to play with Tanny, who cannot be induced to speak to him.'

After enduring another cold night, they crossed over the Musluk Tagh, climbing through snow over an easy pass. Abdurahman wanted to go back but he was the only man who knew the route over the Akka Tagh so St. George gave him a horse to ride. They were now at the Ulugh Su (river), which flows out of the Ulugh Muztagh glaciers and comprises the main branch of the Cherchen Darya.

It was cold the next day and they were on a marsh that was frozen solid except for the main channel of the stream, which had cut through the ice, creating embankments 4–5ft high. At the ford they had to hack an inclined path down to the water on each side of the river so the animals could cross as quickly as possible before the river rose too high from the afternoon snowmelt. St. George and Willie took off their boots, stockings and coats, and rode into the water to keep the donkeys on course and moving. It took hours to get the entire caravan across. There was no difficulty at first, but as the day grew warmer, the water began to rise and large blocks of ice started tearing downstream. They mounted a lookout to warn when the ice blocks were coming. One large block hit a man with a donkey and carried them 70yds. St. George was on horseback in mid-stream when it happened. While he was helping the man rescue the donkey, another block of ice struck his own horse in the rear and carried him and his horse 50yds before they could get clear of it. Fortunately the horse stayed on its feet. With the exception of two loads of rice and flour, all the donkey loads got across safe and dry.

Willie did not wait for the last animals to cross. He gave Razak Akhun his own horse and walked behind the donkey caravan as it shuffled on ahead. They climbed steadily uphill over a broad, sandy, gravelly plain with the snow peaks of the Akka Tagh rising before them to the south. St. George and Willie saw a large number of antelope but were unable to get a shot. They stopped after a 15-mile march and pitched camp near good grass. Teresa wrote, 'The wind is bitterly cold and it looks like snow. We are at 14,600 feet and I suppose shall not be much lower for many months. I dread the months of cold.' The Littledales were getting a good dose of the most distinguishing feature of Tibetan travel, the never-ending wind that penetrates many layers of clothing.

The expedition remained in place for one day to allow the donkeys and horses to rest and graze. The following day they marched alongside the Ulugh Su and past an old camping ground of Dutreuil de Rhins and Grenard. They saw camel droppings that looked fresh but were eighteen months old. Willie and St. George shot a kiang, a Tibetan wild ass. They continued up the riverbed and camped at noon. A deputation of animal drivers asked the Littledales for permission to go home because of the lack of grazing and the fear that donkeys would die. They had already lost two. St. George summed up the situation. 'We put them off with fair words, and plodded on some days through utter barrenness.'

The next day Abdurahman led the caravan over a difficult pass they calculated to be 17,450ft high. The altitude was bothering men and animals and their other troubles were rapidly increasing. After descending, they had to camp on a plain without grass or firewood and with little water because the stream was frozen.

Now they made the first of a series of mistakes that were to cost them dearly. They thought they would try a shortcut across the mountains and perhaps save several days over Dutreuil de Rhins's route. It did not work. Then they tried a route that Abdurahman said he knew, but after a few miles he admitted he knew nothing about it. St. George led the way up a broad nullah, where they camped beside a stream bed. Again there was no grass, no wood, and the water was frozen. St. George and Razak Akhun went ahead and finally found a route. That was the only good news. It continued to be cold with blowing snow, the Keria men wanted to return, and Willie's horse died a few minutes after arriving in camp. The Littledales and Willie dined on Silver's self-heating soup and canned tongue. Willie thought they had crossed the Akka Tagh the previous day. St. George thought they would cross it the next day. They were both wrong.

The next morning Teresa wrote, 'I was so cold I took some brandy. We melted a little ice in a cup over the candle. There was no water. We breakfasted off cold tongue. It is a privation not getting hot tea on such a cold morning.' They crossed over two passes and down another stream bed. Everyone was suffering from the altitude. Willie's new horse gave out, and after he pulled it halfway up the highest pass, he had to leave it behind. The men cut its ears and the horse continued on. St. George had the terrible thought that they had taken the wrong nullah and would have to return, but suddenly they came onto a barren gravel plain with a frozen lake in the distance to the south. Around the plain were red clay hills covered with grass, so the party camped at 16,800ft at the base of the hills. Hundreds of antelope grazed on the slopes, and St. George saw four sheep and even a wolf.

They spent four days at Camp 17, the seventeenth camp they had pitched after leaving Cherchen.[7] St. George and Willie went hunting every day and shot a few antelope for meat. It continued to be cold with frequent snowstorms. The Littledales agreed to let most of the hired donkeys and their men return to Cherchen. Abdurahman would return with them. Thirty-two donkeys and their men would continue for another week to carry corn. Teresa's chestnut pony was a hired horse, but as she liked him, St. George bought him for £2. It was important to replace Abdurahman so Mula Shah, the hired animal bashi, reluctantly took his place. Instead of returning to Cherchen as planned, he was now a permanent member of the expedition. The Littledales compensated Abdurahman generously, and as a result the other men realised that if they performed their duties properly, they would be well rewarded. Abdurahman had worked hard, even if he did not always know where he was or where he was supposed to be going.

Animal problems continued. The horses were wandering from camp to look for grass and the men had to go several miles out to catch them. Willie's new horse died. Snow fell during the last night at Camp 17. In the morning the expedition could not leave because all of the horses and most of the donkeys were missing. The men went out to get them and by early afternoon had retrieved the horses but none of the donkeys because the snow had covered their tracks. Galam Mahmad rode out to look for them but his horse died and he had to walk back. Later some donkeys were recovered. Even so, thirty-five were still missing and the party had to remain in camp for another day in order to round them up. Several men started out at dawn to find them and did not get back until noon.

The difficulties with the sepoys continued. Badullah argued constantly with Punginor, the hardest working of the three. Badullah also tried to avoid working, saying he was exhausted. However, the Ladakhis told Willie he just sat by the fire and did nothing. Purdil was not much better. Whenever St. George asked him to perform a chore, he said he would do it when he had finished smoking. Teresa had passed out dark glasses. Hussin did not receive any because Purdil had taken his. Purdil denied the charge but the next day Teresa saw him wearing them.

The altitude affected them. Willie could not get a steady aim when he was hunting because he was breathing so hard. Teresa was fighting not only the effects of altitude but also her continuing sickness. 'Remained in bed all day. It is a very miserable life that I lead. How I wish to be at home.' 'I have had dysentery now for nearly five months and it makes me feel very very seedy. . . . I feel afraid to look at the future of this trip. It is not bright for me.' Willie's diary takes note of Teresa's constant ill health but does not mention any complaints on her part. Judging from all the accounts, she kept up a strong public front. Her private diary was the only outlet for her feelings and served as her escape valve. Jacob and Tanny were the exceptions to all this misery. Jacob turned out to be an excellent and happy watchdog. Tanny felt the cold but loved lying in Teresa's coat. It was almost enough to make the humans wish they could lead a dog's life.

On 5 May the party marched in a stream bed and camped at the junction of two valleys. After two futile attempts to find a route, they broke camp and returned down the valley up which they had just come the day before. During the night their horses strayed back to their former camp. They collected the animals, packed them, and started out late. Within a few minutes half of the animals had thrown off their loads. Boxes were scattered all over the place. One had even smashed open, scattering its contents. They repacked everything and continued on. The expedition crossed a low pass onto another plain, then climbed up a nullah onto a larger plain filled with antelope. St. George tried a 450-yd shot with his Mannlicher rifle and got an antelope. He also startled the caravan animals, including Teresa's horse. Once again there was a 'tamasha'. They reloaded the animals, started off again, and Willie brought the caravan into camp. St. George stayed behind to lead Teresa's frightened horse. During this act of husbandly repentance, he was pulled off his own horse, broke his glasses, and injured his side. It hurt so much that Willie thought he might have broken some ribs.

They did not realise it immediately but they were lost. The next morning the expedition remained in place while St. George and Razak Akhun went south on another reconnaissance, with Galam Mahmad and a man from Keria heading off in another direction. St. George crossed nullahs all day and came back declaring the route to be unsuitable for donkeys. Galam Mahmad returned later. He thought he had found a way, but how far it would go he could not tell. It was decided that the expedition would wait in camp while two men went out with food for three days to try Mahmad's route. Meanwhile, St. George and Razak Akhun would try once again to find a route in the area where they had failed. At this point a Keria man with the hired animals admitted he had crossed the Akka Tagh three times and his route had branched off from the Littledale route five marches back! It must have been the route followed by Dutreuil de Rhins and Grenard. Willie and St. George were furious that he had not told them before, but the Keria man may have felt it was not his place to say anything until it became clear that they were truly lost. The two reconnaissance teams went out anyway, hoping the caravan could avoid going back five stages. Galwan wrote:

When Mrs. Littledale and Mr. Littledale separated, at that time Mrs. Littledale much sorry. I was much sorry in looking at that their love on each other, and I remember my wife. . . . I said to Mrs. Littledale . . . "Ma'am, you don't think sorry. Sahib will come soon." But she was all time sorry. Because I was room-boy, therefore I looked that all.[8]

While waiting in camp, Rassul Galwan reported to Willie that Mula Shah had stolen some flour and given it to one of the Keria men. Galwan had found a sack open, searched the Keria man's baggage, and found the flour. The man admitted that Mula Shah had given it to him. Mula Shah had received four months' wages, and Teresa and Willie thought he intended to desert, using the flour on his way back to Cherchen. Willie put him to work gathering wood and had him sleep in the big tent, where he could be watched. After that excitement, it was just a minor incident that the sheep had not been tied up, had strayed, and were not recovered until late the next afternoon.

St. George returned two days later. He had found a pass over the mountains two stages back from their camp. It was high but easy. There would be no wood or grass for two days so they would have to carry wood as well as corn for the animals. On top of the pass was a cairn presumably left by Dutreuil de Rhins and Fernand Grenard. Galam had also found a pass but it was too high and there was no grass. Meanwhile, four donkeys were missing. Teresa wrote, 'I have felt quite ill today, really unable to sit up. I do not know how I shall ever get through this terrible journey.'

The next morning nine animals were gone. The party soon found three, packed up, and started to retrace their steps, reaching their old camp area by early afternoon. One of the missing donkeys had died on the march and two were still lost.[9] Just as the Littledales arrived, it began to snow heavily. All of the men went out to gather the wood they would need for the next few days. Snow continued to fall during the night, and the following morning the ground was white. The caravan moved up a gorge and camped. Then the Keria donkey drivers went on strike because the Ladakhis, contrary to orders, had not given them meat. That was corrected but six donkeys were missing and the Littledales suspected the Keria men had stolen them.

The next day, 15 May 1895, would be a long one. Willie set his alarm for 4 o'clock in the morning. The horses and donkeys arrived an hour later but were not ready to leave. Moreover, the men did not get up when called. As a result, the party started late. They continued up the valley, crossing and recrossing a stream that became wider and deeper as the day went on. Grenard described the route. '. . . absolutely barren and desert: not a tuft of grass, not a trace of animal life, not a bird flying, nothing but a little water flowing swift and clear over the flat pebbles'.[10] A gentle but tedious ascent led them up the Kara Muran Dawan, over 18,000ft high. They reached the top, added some rocks to the Frenchmen's cairn, and gazed out upon the Tibetan plateau to the south, a brown desert with a few scattered tarns, salt lakes and low mountains. It had taken them thirty-four days from Cherchen to reach the edge of Tibet.

Throughout the day they could see the twin peaks of Ulugh Muztagh rising out of a series of glaciers and ice fields to the east. St. George worked on his map constantly. Using angles taken from several different points, he measured the height of the mountain as 25,340ft. Ninety years later a Chinese-American expedition drove to a base camp on the northeastern side of Ulugh Muztagh, climbed the mountain, and measured its height as 22,916ft (6,985m).[11] In any case, it is the highest mountain in the eastern Kun Lun range. The waters flowing from its glaciers made possible oases like Cherchen, which in turn made possible the southern branch of the Silk Road. It is indeed a 'Great Ice Mountain'.

The descent on the Tibetan side of the pass was gradual. While the donkeys lagged behind, the rest of the party continued on for about 4 hours and camped at some grass at about 17,000ft. St. George, realising it was too far for the donkeys, sent Hussin back to stop them. The food was with the donkeys but they had something else to eat. Willie had shot an antelope.

Hussin arrived in camp early the next morning with the Keria men and their donkeys. Others arrived at midday. The expedition had lost four donkeys when crossing the pass, so after much haggling, St. George bought more donkeys from the Keria men, who were returning home. They settled at 30 tangas per donkey. Once this was agreed, the Keria men departed for Cherchen. The expedition's last link with the outside world was severed.

The trip over the bleak Akka Tagh had been hard on men and animals. In this vicinity Dutreuil de Rhins had lost a camel, prompting a comment from Grenard:

One of our camels died and in the empty sky appeared black specks, which, as they came nearer, we recognised as crows of extraordinary size, hastening to the banquet. They were the forerunners of Tibet, the land of the great crows. These filthy marauders, flying from carcass to carcass, make their way everywhere, even to places where no sparrow, eagle nor kite dare venture; nevertheless, they respect the Akka Tagh, where nothing dies since nothing lives. . . . The Akka Tagh is the most absolute of frontiers, a frontier for the sky as well as for the earth, for birds as well as for men.[12]

The Littledale party was now on its own in Tibet. The hardships and the death of animals incurred in crossing that absolute frontier were a harbinger of what was to come. As harsh as the Akka Tagh had been, the desolate Chang Tang would exact an even greater toll on men and beasts. The suffering had just begun.

15

The Chang Tang

Heaven help me how shall I get through this journey.
Teresa Littledale

The Littledales and Willie were worried. The caravan had lost 25 donkeys since Cherchen. The remaining donkeys were in poor shape, most likely because they were driven too hard by Purdil and Punginor, who were cold and wanted to get to the campsite as fast as possible. St. George was especially concerned when horses died because Teresa had to ride. Galwan suggested making shorter marches, with a long halt at least once a week to let the animals rest and graze adequately. St. George thought it was a good plan but doubted that they had enough food for such an extended journey. Galwan assured him that he could still provide food for six months.[1]

They made a short march the next day across several valleys. Although the Chang Tang appears flat from a distance, in reality the ground is undulating, 'dented with little hills and hillocks, intersected by ravines, generally without water, and ploughed with a number of depressions in which lie hidden as many muddy pools'.[2] One donkey died during the night, so they put its load on Willie's horse and Willie walked. Another donkey died half a mile after leaving camp. Its load went on St. George's horse and he also walked. The altitude continued to affect everyone, and St. George's ribs were still sore from his fall. A horse carrying Willie's bedding lay down in a stream. The men were slow in reacting but Teresa jumped off her horse and quickly opened the bedding to let the water drain out. The pattern was set for crossing the Chang Tang: debilitating altitude, lack of water and grass, dying donkeys, missing animals and terrain that hid everything.

The Littledales were afraid that Mula Shah might desert so they sometimes handcuffed him at night. They did not know what else to do. They needed every man they had. Initially they were going to chain him to Rassul Galwan but Galwan objected because he worked hard all day, and sleep would be impossible with Mula Shah attached to him. As he was serving dinner, Teresa said, 'Why punish Rassul. Tie Mula Shah with a sepoy.' St. George readily agreed and Galwan's appreciation for

Teresa's wisdom grew. Despite his initial behaviour, Mula Shah became one of their best men and later he was to serve Sven Hedin with distinction.

One night the animals strayed and a heavy snowfall covered their tracks. All of the men, including St. George and Willie, had to spend the entire day on foot searching for them. That night 12 donkeys were still missing. Whether or not to tether the animals was always a dilemma. If they were not hobbled, they would wander off and it could take hours to retrieve them. On the other hand, the grazing was so poor that they needed to cover a large area to get enough to eat. Donkeys died every day. One donkey even died while they were packing the animals. Sometimes the animals were mistreated. One night St. George and Willie heard groans and found the donkeys tied neck to neck, eight of them lying on top of each other. Willie went after Razak Akhun and threatened to thrash him. This was no idle threat and it resulted in a temporary improvement.

After a week on the Chang Tang, Teresa wrote:

Marched again this morning. I am still so far from well, I do not know what will be the end of it for me. It is a terrible journey from great fatigue, intense cold and the great altitude. There is always a strong cold wind blowing which is very trying. . . . St. George does not feel at all well. I have never felt well since I left home. I would give much to be there now and it will take more than anyone has the power to accomplish to take me away again.

The hard marching continued, and Teresa wrote:

Heaven help me how shall I get through this journey. St. George now says we may reach Ladak next October, five weary weary months I feel as if I cannot bear. Why did not St. George let me return home when I begged so hard to do so and when I could have done so? We have marched today up up up another pass but have not reached the end and are camped nearly 17,000 feet up near a lake but no wood. All the men have been out trying to find fuel.

For days the caravan worked its way across the hilly terrain. One day they were caught in a heavy hailstorm followed by snow, and they had to stop where they were. 'The hail stones were enormous. It hurt so I sat for more than two hours huddled up under my waterproof cloak with Tanny. . . . I felt done. One should be a sportsman for this journey. It is not fit for a woman.' Willie wrote that the crupper on Teresa's saddle broke while her horse was drinking and the saddle flew over the horse's head. Teresa, riding sidesaddle, simply stepped off. She was so unfazed that she did not even mention it in her diary. It was just another day on the Tibetan plateau.

The 30th of May was a day that everyone remembered. When Willie awoke, all of the sheep were missing. The men had been told repeatedly to tie them up at night but had not done so. The caravan moved out anyway, leaving Razak Akhun and Purdil behind to find them. That afternoon Akhun reported that all nineteen sheep had been killed by wolves, which had bitten each one on the throat and left the carcasses uneaten. He knew that Teresa liked kidneys so he announced this disaster by presenting her with a handkerchief full of kidneys from dead sheep. She was not amused. Neither were St. George and Willie.

As the men were Muslims, they would not eat meat unless the ceremony of hallal had been performed. This meant cutting the throat of an animal while it was still alive. Unfortunately many of the kills were so far away that the animals were dead by the time someone reached them. Thus, even when there was meat for the Littledales and Willie, there often was none for the men. The loss of their sheep compounded the difficulties. It got worse. They were beset by storms. More animals strayed and died. Teresa wrote:

> 22 donkeys missing this morning. The night was very windy and in stormy weather they always stray. All were found and we started at 10 o'clock. . . . 4 donkeys were left to die on the road. Our donkeys could not be worse managed. The nights are bitterly cold and they suffer from cold and only a few of them have sacks over them. . . . Rozahun [Razak Akhun] is worse than useless. . . . We have not given the animals a rest for 13 days which is too long, for even a short march is not the same as a rest. . . . St. George thinks more of his map than anything else, and there is much else of even greater importance to be thought of. As for Lhasa, that is out of the reckoning altogether. We shall have much to be thankful for if we get through to civilisation at all.

Their predicament was common among travellers through Central Asia. The trail over the Karakoram Pass was littered from end to end with the bones of animals. Grenard lost almost all of his camels. Altitude compounds all problems. Animals, including humans, must drink a much greater amount of water at high altitude to compensate for the increased loss of water vapour through the lungs. The body also requires more calories to compensate for the added energy needed to maintain warmth, but altitude decreases appetite. Even at a much lower elevation, the Littledale animals would have been suffering from lack of water and decent grazing. At the extreme elevation of the Chang Tang, the highest plateau in the world, the effect was disastrous. It was a traumatic experience for everyone. St. George later wrote, 'Not a day passed but several animals had to be shot or abandoned. It is a gruesome subject which I will not further pursue.'[3]

In an attempt to save the remaining animals, the men cut up all the spare numdahs (felt cloths) and empty grain sacks and made coverings for the donkeys including their heads. Teresa was in despair. Because of her illness and fatigue, she identified with the struggling donkeys. During their second day at a camp with neither grass nor water she wrote, 'I am quite sure that lots of the donkeys when they have been sick and lie down, the men just leave them. Had they been brought in and been attended to they might have been saved. . . . Where shall I be left?'

Eight more donkeys died over a two-day period. Something drastic had to be done. They would have to abandon everything they did not absolutely need. They spent the afternoon sorting through their things. In what was later referred to as the 'shipwreck', they tossed out clothes, camp furniture, museum specimens, extra horseshoes, and rugs purchased by the Ladakhis for gifts. They even removed the bindings from books. The only non-essential item they kept was Rassul Galwan's banjo. Teresa insisted that he keep it. When the men asked for some of the clothes the Littledales were discarding, St. George told them they could have whatever they wanted provided they left behind something equivalent to keep the weight down. Badullah could not resist taking more clothes than he needed and he wore them all, layer upon layer. The men laughed at his appearance but the Littledales and Willie said nothing. For the next several days he staggered along leaving a trail of clothing behind him.

One day the expedition experienced what Willie called a 'Red Letter Day'. There were no deaths. Now any day in which no animals died was considered a good day. There were always new obstacles. Once they encountered a stream with quicksand on the bottom, and the animals had great difficulty crossing it. Afterwards a horse went in to drink and it took seven men to pull him out.

Two days later they had to leave another donkey behind and three others straggled in without loads. Badullah also straggled in. He did not reach camp until evening. It was obvious that he was ill but the question was how ill? He had been so lazy that for all they knew he was only trying to get a horse to ride. St. George and Willie did not trust him but they could not abandon him. They gave Badullah a choice: Walk or Die. Badullah walked.

The next day the party crossed a 19,300-ft pass, dropped down into a nullah, and camped beside a good stream. Just after pitching their tents, they were blasted by wind-driven hail and had to grab the tent ropes and hold on until they could reinforce the tent pegs with large rocks. Badullah, feeling much better, walked into camp just after the donkeys.

For the next four days the party marched up nullahs, over passes, down nullahs, and across stony plains in between, losing animals almost every day. Willie wrote, 'We can't help thinking that for the last month we have been on the top of a big ridge & that 10 miles or so either way we should have done much better. Anyway, we are here and have come to the conclusion that Tibet is one large mountain covered with lumps.'

The following day started off badly. One mule had died during the night and one horse was unable to move. A horse they had packed was unable to carry its load so Willie moved the load to his own horse and he had to walk. After 8 miles, they descended a large nullah covered with lush grass and camped. According to calculations based on their boiling-point thermometer, they were at 17,400ft. The grass was so good the party rested for five days while the animals grazed. Mula Shah went back to retrieve an ailing horse but it had died. They had lost thirty-nine donkeys since Cherchen, half of their herd, as well as four horses and a mule.

Willie reviewed the supplies once again and calculated that there was plenty of food for the men but not enough for the remaining animals. Although they had left Cherchen with 25,000lb of corn, there were only eighteen sacks left. However, they still had 320lb of suttoo (parched grain) intended for the men. As there was more than enough rice for the men, it became apparent that they would have to feed the suttoo to the horses. Following instructions from St. George, Galwan gave rice to the men morning, noon and night. This led to the 'rice crisis'. The men rebelled and Razak Akhun got into a heated argument with Galwan. When he made disparaging remarks about Galwan's wife, blows were struck and the others had to pull them apart. After they learned that Galwan was only obeying orders, everyone cooled off. Teresa wrote perceptively, 'Our Ladakis had a quarrel. They always do when we are stationary. They have nothing else to do but they soon make it up.'

It was a good rest. The stud now consisted of thirty-eight donkeys and twenty-one horses and mules. The starving animals feasted continuously from morning to night and the healthier ones quickly regained their strength. The men spotted old nomad camps and knew they would be encountering Tibetans any day. Once they were discovered they would have to move fast, and everything would depend on the condition of the animals. On the last day in camp the animals were shod.

Teresa managed to collect plants and insects for the museums despite her chronic dysentery and raging migraines. 'Caught a large bumblebee.

Hope it is of some value. . . . I have collected some plants but some of them have such gigantic roots tho very little flower or leaf shows above ground that I do not know how I shall dry them.' Later she would be praised by the Royal Botanic Gardens at Kew for the quality of her plant specimens.

'June 26, lat. 33° 12' N., and long. 88° 12' E.' St. George recorded the date and location because it delineated two memorable events, rain and humans. It rained off and on all day, sometimes heavily, their first rain since the Black Sea seven months earlier. They were now moving within range of the monsoon and would have more frequent showers in the days to come.[4]

On the march they passed two abandoned nomad camps and sheep tracks. They ascended a low pass, dropped steeply down the other side, and camped in a nullah with grass and water. St. George and Willie climbed a hill above camp to scout out the next day's route. Before them lay a large plain covered with nomad encampments and great herds of sheep and yaks. A difficult looking pass rose in the distance. They spotted seven Tibetans, the first humans in two months, and they could only speculate how many more there were. It was not unexpected but it was disappointing. They were not in any physical danger, but if they were discovered, the officials in Lhasa would find out and could prepare to stop them.

Their first thought was to do an immediate night march. Their second thought was better. The caravan animals had only just completed a march, so the party would remain hidden in the nullah for a day to rest them and move the following night. The men stood two-hour watches to keep the animals from straying and betraying their presence. St. George gave Galwan a watch to time the changing of the guard.

Willie rose at dawn and climbed a hill to look at the closest Tibetan camp. All was quiet. A few hours later he and St. George went up a different hill and saw a herd of sheep within a mile of their proposed route. The nearest encampment was by a lake, and they could see large piles of salt that the Tibetans were apparently collecting for Lhasa. St. George and Willie calculated that if the herdsmen kept their sheep close to their tents at night, the caravan would pass them about 3 miles away. Also, a favourable wind was blowing from the west, and if it continued, the expedition would be downwind and the Tibetan dogs would probably not discover them. Later Willie returned up the hill with Punginor for a last-minute check on the Tibetan position. Suddenly a man appeared. He was driving sheep, yaks and horses in their direction. For over an hour Willie watched in suspense as the animals drank from a nearby stream. Then they turned around and went back, to Willie's immense relief.

Willie and Punginor returned to camp shortly after 6 o'clock in the evening. Everyone worked fast. The men quickly loaded the animals. All of the weapons were unpacked and distributed. Those who did not have rifles carried rifle cases stuffed with theodolite legs, tripods and tent poles. Teresa wrote, 'The effect is good if not effective in a row.' They started at 8 o'clock and marched down the nullah. It was a warm starlit night with a bright early moon. At the bottom they tied the horses and mules head to tail. Tanny and Jacob were carried on the lead horses to make sure they did not bark. No one spoke. Led by the donkeys, the caravan set off across the plain in dead silence. After an hour they became mired in a swamp and floundered around, slipping and sliding in the mud before finally struggling out onto the rocky surface of the plain. Just as the last animals reached dry land, the moon disappeared behind a cloud. Now it was quite dark. St. George and Teresa led the way. Willie remained behind to make sure all of the men and animals stayed together. Even Badullah kept up. He was leading horses tied closely together. It was slow going because it was too dark to see far and the caravan had to stop whenever the weaker animals began to straggle. They halted often, or as Willie described it, 'stopping for minutes about 100 times an hour it seems'. By 2 o'clock in the morning fatigue had set in and the animals were moving slower and slower.

Day was beginning to break as they climbed up the hill on the far side of the plain. They began to fear they would not get out of sight in time. Willie dismounted and helped the men move the donkeys forward. They had hoped to cross the pass but it was too far. They managed to get the caravan over a ridge and into a nullah just as daylight came. It had been a stressful 12-mile march. Willie thought they had not been seen. Then he remembered their footprints. What would the Tibetans think? They had tried to be careful, but in the hectic crossing of the swamp, he and St. George had forgotten they were wearing European boots.

Despite their concerns, they were not discovered. They spent the next day in their camp above 17,000ft before continuing on up the pass. It was easy and marked by small cairns and prayer flags left by shepherds. Beyond the pass was another large plain. They had passed an invisible landmark. Their friend Captain Hamilton Bower of the 17th Bengal Cavalry and Dr W.G. Thorold, another army officer, had made an east to west traverse of Tibet in 1891 on a mission for British intelligence. Their objective was Lhasa but they were stopped by Tibetans south-east of the Garing Tso, a large lake.[5] Bower had made a long loop to the north and then headed east again. The Littledale party frequently referred to Bower's route as a measure of their progress. Now they had crossed it and the expedition had entered another phase. The natural difficulties would decrease; the human difficulties would increase. They were approaching the endgame.

That night they heard wolves howling around the camp but all the animals were safe. A hot march the next day was punctuated by rain and thunder. St. George and Willie went hunting for meat and shot four bharal. It was 30 June 1895. Teresa and Willie commented on the beauty of the landscape. Teresa wrote, 'The view from our camp this morning looking down the valley was lovely, a lake with mountains beyond.' Willie had additional thoughts. 'We are now anxiously looking out for men so as to avoid them if possible.'

The nervous caravan plodded on for days across rocky plains, through small streams and marshes, and over low ridges, hiding at night in nullahs with grass and water. The days continued to be hot, broken by afternoon showers. They kept the stages short to save the animals and stopped whenever they found good grazing.

Sometimes they had to travel at night to avoid detection. When they could not carry a lantern, St. George used a luminous matchbox to read the compass. One night while passing near a Tibetan camp, 'the donkey carrying our pet cock and hen chose to tumble, and there was a great cackling and fuss; then a mule trod on our Turki dog, who gave a piteous howl'.[6] Despite this experience, they continued to sneak through Tibet with a rooster.

During a reconnaissance, St. George and Willie saw a large salt marsh and a very large lake they recognised as the Garing Tso (Gagalinchin). As they carefully scanned the landscape through a haze, they could discern a large number of domestic animals. Moreover, on the near side of the marsh a horse was hobbled, which meant that men were near. They had just completed a day's march, but since the salt marsh, the lake, and the men were directly in their path, they decided to make a night march to a lake about 10 miles away. It took them an hour to go ¾ of a mile because of a difficult nullah. Moreover, a box containing candles flew off a horse, shattered into pieces, and scattered 800 candles across the landscape. The men had to pick them all up in the dark. At last they reached the lake, pitched camp, and crawled into bed at 2 o'clock in the morning. Willie rose at dawn to check for any Tibetans in the vicinity. He wrote, 'We shall not get any nearer to Gagalinchin and now make for Tengri Nor. TL very tired and no wonder after her double march yesterday.'

The next day was uneventful. Teresa was interested in the large variety of flowers but was too exhausted to collect any. They saw groups of Tibetan men and more herds. Willie wrote, 'We fear our day of discovery is near. After that there is nothing to be done but push on as hard as we can. We ought to be able to manage 50 or 60 miles in three days as our beasts are all fit and we have corn to give them.'

On 9 July the caravan reached a river it could not ford so they made a raft. They lashed the Littledales' camp beds together, turned them upside down, and covered them with waterproof floor sheets on the bottom and sides. Tent poles became gunwales. They had a man cross the river on a horse towing a rope attached to the makeshift raft, and they attached another rope to the other end so that the raft could be pulled back and forth across the river. St. George asked Teresa to climb aboard but Galwan suggested a trial run with two sacks of grain. Upon reflection, St. George agreed. The bags crossed without difficulty. Then two men went across followed by Willie and Teresa.

The remaining men stayed behind to unload the animals and ferry the loads across. Willie and the men stood in the river to pull and push the raft. It was exhausting work. When all the baggage was across, they drove the animals through the river. The donkeys were poor swimmers and one almost drowned. The caravan could be seen if they camped by the river so they had to reload the animals and move on. It was getting dark before all the animals were packed. There were subsidiary pools, and three of the horses fell into a hole. One horse nearly drowned before the men could unload it and pull it out. It was carrying tents but they had been rolled so tightly that the insides were still dry. Finally they arrived at a nullah where they camped for the night.

None of their days had been easy but this had been an especially trying one for the men. While they were working in the river, they said they wanted suttoo for dinner, and Galwan approved. One man said that even 1,000 rupees would not compensate him for this day. Galwan's reply was worthy of a Ladakhi Henry V: 'This day is among all the days of journey a courage-making day. If a man go tired in such work, that man is without bravery. Singing-time is this.'[7] Everyone agreed. Only then did they learn that one of the loads that fell into the waterhole contained their clothes and their smoking supplies.

They stayed in place for a day but it was not a rest stop. One of the mules had strayed during the night and was found close to a yak encampment. St. George went out to scout the route and was gone all day. At Teresa's insistence, Willie stayed behind. She did not want to be left alone because if the Tibetans came, she did not know how the caravan men would behave and she was afraid. Galwan was frightened as well, so much so that he sent two men out to retrieve the mule. They were instructed to tell any Tibetans they met that they were merchants going to India. If they were fired upon, they were not to return fire unless one of them was hit. At 2 o'clock the men returned with the mule. Another crisis averted. However, Teresa's health continued to decline. Bad water intensified her dysentery and she was miserable. 'My strength is completely giving out. Alas! St. George wishes to take another night march. . . . I feel that I should be at peace and if it is God's wish to take me, I shall be happier. . . .'

When St. George returned to camp, he said they could get to a pass ahead of them unseen, but beyond the hills was a plain running south with thousands of yaks and tents. When they reached the top of the pass the next day, the Tibetans and their animals were gone. For several days they moved forward, skirting the hills and camping in nullahs. They were out of meat but had to be careful hunting or the Tibetans would hear their guns. One night they ate a cold tongue they had bought in Tiflis. The horses and mules feasted on green grass and were soon in 'capital condition'.

Willie was enjoying the great adventure. On 12 July he wrote, 'We are now about 69 miles from Tengri Nor. If we can get within . . . measured distance of Lhassa, we shall leave all our things, take about 4 men, leave the rest to look after camp, and make a rush, riding as hard as we can, but that is a big IF. Of course we shall bury the silver etc.'

The next day St. George and Willie walked up a hill and saw two Tibetan camps directly on their route about 8 miles off. St. George galloped after the caravan, which had gone ahead, and had them turn into another nullah and stop. That afternoon he and Willie climbed above camp and saw Tibetans everywhere. Willie wrote, '. . . from the S to NW as far as we can see are thousands of yak. We have apparently come the only way we could without being discovered. . . . At present we don't know how soon or how far off the day is. It is most exciting slipping these people.'

The following day they left in a downpour. At noon, just as they were about to camp, Willie went ahead and suddenly found himself within half a mile of a tent and sheep. They had no choice but to go forward even though they were in full sight of the tent. The caravan moved on, found water, and camped. The donkeys arrived later followed by five Tibetans. Willie entered in his diary, 'Done. We are discovered.'

It was a false alarm. They had been seen, but so far the Tibetans had not found them suspicious. St. George and Willie went on reconnaissance and saw two tents less than a mile from camp. They would have to change their tactics. Willie wrote, 'Our decision is made. We now rush it as hard as we can go straight on our course through everything and trust to luck.' That night they gave the horses and donkeys a sack of corn to build up their strength.

Once again the men watched the animals all night. Early the next morning they noticed sheep grazing quietly near by. The plain was crowded with yaks, tents and Tibetans. By hugging the base of the hills and going in and out of nullahs, the caravan was able to keep out of sight most of the time, but eventually they had to cross over a ridge in plain view of the tents. Their nerves were on edge. They thought they saw a man ahead of them on the ridge but it was just a stone cairn.

The caravan moved into a secluded nullah and stopped. Except for the proximity of the Tibetans, it was a pleasant spot with a rushing stream, grass and a profusion of wildflowers. Teresa noticed quantities of violets and even some edelweiss. St. George went out to take a look at the next plain before them and saw many tents and thousands of yak and sheep. They had escaped detection for another day but their luck could not last. They would have to go as far and as fast as they could travel. St. George copied his map onto tracing muslin in case something happened to the original. And the men gave their now well-fed animals another precious sack of corn.

16

Confrontation

What will tomorrow bring?
W.A.L. Fletcher

The day of discovery – 16 July 1895. The party got up by candlelight and the caravan was on its way by half past 5. Dropping down the nullah, they saw two flocks of sheep above them on the hill. One of the herders thought they were merchants and called them to come to him. They ignored him, continued down onto the plain, and headed south. They could not find a nullah in which to hide, so they had to cross the plain in full view of the Tibetans and look for a secluded nullah on a more distant ridge. They passed between sheep on their right and yaks on their left, both herds about a mile away. A man from the yak camp watched the parade from a low hill but no one else paid attention. When they came within a quarter mile of a tent with a yak, the Littledales and Willie hid among the packhorses. They skirted a small swamp as more Tibetans watched from another hill.

That afternoon three men with a gun appeared on a hill before them but the party kept going, passing another flock of sheep and an old woman and a boy sitting in front of a tent. The woman wore her hair in plaits and had a sheepskin coat. Razak Akhun went over to buy a sheep or, failing that, to give her a rupee as a gift. She said her master up the valley would sell them a sheep. She insisted on giving them fresh goats milk in a yak horn, and Teresa found it very good. A short distance beyond, they bought a sheep from her master for two rupees. Now they had meat for the men. The party turned up a nullah and marched straight to the top of the pass through a large herd of yaks and sheep. The caravan stopped and pitched camp at an estimated altitude of 17,800ft. They had travelled 16 miles.

The Littledales hoped they had been taken for traders. As a precaution, they did not set up their European tents until after dark. In the morning they took down the tents before dawn and gave the animals two sacks of grain. As they were starting out, four mounted Tibetans arrived carrying guns and swords. They were the shepherds for the nearby herds. The Tibetans accompanied the caravan up the nullah and over the pass. One man rode up, stared intently into the faces of the Littledales and Willie, and then rode on. Soon more Tibetans arrived. Akhun told them they were merchants travelling to Shigatze and on to India. He showed them a passport and asked for sheep. One of the Tibetans, a local headman, said if they stopped, he would give them as many sheep as they wanted, but the caravan kept going. Descending a nullah, they came to a narrow passage jammed with boulders. It took over an hour to get the animals through. Meanwhile, the four Tibetans watched them and then went ahead by a different route.

At the bottom of the nullah the Tibetans were waiting for them. St. George had Akhun offer them five rupees to tell him the best route. The headman replied that if they were all Ladakhis, he would do whatever they wanted, but if any were foreigners he would not help them because he would lose his head if he did. It was the standard response of local Tibetan officials and it was no exaggeration. The Tibetans were loathe to use violence against foreigners but reacted severely toward any of their own people who knowingly or even unknowingly helped foreigners penetrate their country.[*][1]

After reaching the plain, the caravan proceeded south toward an opening in the hills. They were marching under a hot sun punctuated by intermittent thunder and hailstorms. One of the mules displayed an abundance of restored energy. Halfway across the plain it kicked a donkey in the head, killing it instantly.

They pitched camp in a large nullah. St. George and Willie estimated that Tengri Nor was about 21 miles away. Twelve armed Tibetans rode past. The men were filthy. They wore their hair in a pigtail with a white hat perched on top. They were armed with ancient matchlocks and each man carried a long two-pronged fork to support the gun while firing. Despite their fierce appearance, they were friendly. One man even offered to lead Teresa's horse through a stream. Nevertheless, the forces were gathering and the Littledales began to have serious doubts about reaching Lhasa.

The next morning ten Tibetans arrived in camp, including a lama. St. George and Willie were happy to show them their rifles. They learned from the lama that the Tibetans were not going to stop them that day but had sent to Lhasa for a high official. Razak Akhun overheard them say the official might not arrive for two days, so they still had a little time. Meanwhile, armed Tibetans were pouring in from all directions. Just after they started, sixty men appeared, mounted on small shabby ponies, and soon the number increased to eighty. The men wore long sheepskin coats

---

[*] Foreigners must have believed that if they reached Lhasa, the worst punishment they faced was expulsion.

tucked up at the waist, giving the appearance of kilts. Some wore coats trimmed with leopard skin or brightly coloured cloth. They slipped their coat off the right arm, leaving the arm and shoulder bare. At night they would let down the coat to cover their legs. Their boots were multi-coloured stockings that came to the knee with soles of yak hide stitched to the bottom. They were armed with a variety of weapons but they all had matchlocks and wore swords inserted diagonally through their clothes. Some carried long spears, and one man even had a bow and arrow. One imposing looking Tibetan carried a matchlock, a spear, and three swords, one stuck in his belt and two strapped to his saddle, one under each leg.

The party crossed a small pass out of the nullah and descended to another plain toward a small lake. Tibetans rode on both sides of the caravan. Everyone was in good spirits except for some local headmen who kept remarking that they would lose their heads if the party continued, but when the Littledales laughed, they laughed back. They set up camp in a nullah in the midst of sheep and yaks, pitching their tents during a heavy thunderstorm. Next to the Littledales' camp, the lama and the local headman put up a small white cotton tent with a blue border. When a local shepherd promised to sell them some sheep, their Tibetan 'escort' stopped the transaction.

Everyone was up at 4 o'clock. The lama asked them to stop packing the animals as the headman was coming. They refused, telling him they had a passport for the whole of China and no one except the amban from Lhasa had the authority to stop them. Escorted by their eighty Tibetans, they crossed the pass before them and saw Tengri Nor for the first time. Teresa wrote, 'It is a beautiful lake, the water intensely blue and surrounded by a high range of snow mountains. One peak is magnificent with snow 24,500 feet, the summit a sharp point. I am certainly the only European woman who has overlooked upon Tengri-Nor and I fancy nobody has ever been as near to Lhasa since Manning was there.' She was referring to Thomas Manning, an eccentric Englishman who drifted into Lhasa in 1811. There is no question that she was the first European woman to see Tengri Nor but she was wrong about Lhasa after Manning. Teresa undoubtedly knew that the French priests Everiste Huc and Joseph Gabet had reached Lhasa in 1846, after which Tibet had closed to foreigners. However, her long months of effort and suffering earned her the right to forget some history in her brief moment of satisfaction. Such pleasures were all too rare on this journey.

The party turned south and marched up a large valley toward Tengri Nor. As they were moving along, they met a lama who said the party should turn up a nullah on their right as it would lead to a ford across a river. The lama's advice was good but not disinterested. He wanted them to avoid a monastery directly ahead of them. They went up the nullah, crossed a pass decorated with cairns and mani stones, and went down the other side. As they descended, they saw their Tibetan escorts bowing and scraping in front of two white tents on the plain below. The Littledales assumed the high official from Lhasa had arrived and they expected trouble at any time but it was only the local tax collector, a position worthy of proper respect but not sufficiently exalted to stop the caravan.

Their hopes of reaching Lhasa rose and fell with the latest rumour. First they heard that the high official would not leave Lhasa for another three days. Perhaps they could make a dash for it. Then they heard that a high lama had arrived from Lhasa with twenty men. If so, it meant trouble tomorrow. They began to harbour hopes that they would be expelled by way of Sikkim, the shortest way out of Tibet.

The Lhasa official arrived the next morning and asked the party to stop for a day. They adamantly refused and started out. They were braced for two serious obstacles, a difficult river crossing about which they had been warned, and the increasing opposition of the Tibetans. The river crossing was surprisingly easy and they headed straight for the high snow mountains of the Ninchen Tangla, the range they had seen the day before. A large nullah ran up into the range but it was 'a most impossible looking place for a pass'. On the plain they could see the campfires of their Tibetan escort awaiting their arrival. A second river turned out to be the difficult one. While the Tibetans watched from afar, they rode up and down the riverbank looking for a ford. Two miles downriver St. George found a place where laden horses could cross. The donkey loads would have to be taken over separately. At that moment 120 Tibetans rode up and ordered them to stop. Again they refused. A rough-looking Tibetan attempted to grab the bridle of St. George's horse. St. George whipped out his revolver and the man quickly let go. They said they would lose their heads if they allowed the party to cross the river. The Littledales refused to stop and started across. While the animals were crossing, St. George and Willie fraternised with the Tibetans and showed them their rifles. The Tibetans were quite friendly despite everything.

By late afternoon the last of the donkeys had crossed. The animals were reloaded and the caravan moved on. All of the Tibetans forded the river, continued along the plain, and camped. Meanwhile, Omar Shak observed laden yaks descending a nullah so the party turned in that direction, thinking it must lead to a pass. It began to rain and soon they encountered a bog. Willie stayed back to get the donkeys across. A big bay horse collapsed and had to be left behind.

The Littledales stopped at half past 7 and pitched camp in the dark in a driving rainstorm on bumpy, swampy ground. Willie and the donkeys straggled in later. Everyone was worn out, and not just from the exertions of a hard march. It was the accumulation of a series of long, hard marches under the stress of the constant Tibetan presence and the need to press on all day and guard the animals all night. Willie wrote, 'Razak Akhun thinks we are on the right track as all the grass is eaten off. What will tomorrow bring?'

Willie was prescient in his foreboding. At midnight Razak Akhun and Omar Shak went out to locate a route, checking different nullahs for cairns or tracks for the caravan to follow in the dark. Willie told Rassul Galwan to have the watch feed the horses at quarter past 3 in the morning and to call him at 4 o'clock. He awoke at quarter past 4 to find the horses unfed, not even tied up, and Galwan starting to light the fire. Nothing was ready. Because of this delay, they were not able to leave camp until just before daylight. Akhun had found cairns so they decided to follow his route.

The next day they climbed up the nullah on a well-used track and emerged on top of a ridge. They could see only a few Tibetans below on the plain. St. George was uneasy. Either they were on the wrong trail or the Tibetans had gone ahead to confront them in some strong position. They continued winding around the side of the hill and entered another nullah. Snowcapped peaks rose above them and glaciers topped all the nullahs but the track with its marking cairns went on so they followed it. Through his telescope Willie saw men ahead. Soon they saw red flags, a lama in yellow robes, and on both sides of the narrow nullah row upon row of Tibetans behind rocks with just their heads visible. There were also men on a low ridge that ran straight across the nullah up which they were climbing. The lama rode forward to meet them, but 100yd from the caravan he turned around and went on ahead of them. As the party continued, the track entered a small basin where armed Tibetans were hiding behind the rocks on three sides of them.

St. George was afraid that if they stopped it would be fatal to their hopes, so he told the men to load their rifles. The three Pathan sepoys were carrying Colt lightning repeaters, three Ladakhis and Willie had express rifles, and St. George had his Mannlicher. The rest of the party was armed with the theodolite and camera legs stuffed inside gun covers. Teresa was ordered to stay back with the baggage animals and was upset that she was not given a rifle. When St. George checked on her, she was pointing the covered theodolite at the Tibetans as if it was a powerful weapon. As for the sepoys, 'There were the three Pathans, nursing their rifles, with murder in their eyes, impatiently awaiting the signal to begin.' This is what they had come for. The pleasure and pastime of the Pathans is war, and in the face of overwhelming odds, it was all St. George could do to restrain his three sepoys.

A lone Tibetan came near and ordered them to stop. They ignored him. Some officials and unarmed Tibetans approached, or as Willie described it, 'Then came the Big Bugs [officials], The Youthful Bug, The Yesterday Bug, and a new one of about the same standard. They were accompanied by about 8 others. . . . They told us to stop as if we went on, it would be heads off, etc. We refused flatly.'

The Tibetans threatened to shoot. It was a highly dangerous moment. Neither side wanted a fight and would rather retreat. Both parties knew that a fight would be disastrous for everyone. Even with their modern weapons, the 13 caravan members would be no match for 150 Tibetans in a strong defensive position even if the Tibetans carried only matchlocks. The Tibetan officials had reason to be afraid as well. Razak Akhun and Kalam Rassul had told them, 'If we die, the full justice of English Government . . . will take Lhasa under our government. But without your people's fault, our government cannot take the Tibet country. You people must kill us.'[2] As events would prove in 1904 when the British army marched through Tibet to Lhasa, this was plausible. No intelligent Tibetan official would want to give the British such an excuse, but both sides were bluffing to the maximum of their ability and it would take just one itchy trigger finger, Tibetan or Pathan, to set off a disaster.

As the lama approached the Littledales, he yelled back to his men not to shoot until after the parties talked. St. George told him there must have been some mistake and explained that they had come all the way from England to pay their salaams to the Deva Jung. He pulled out his Chinese passport and said it had been given to him by a greater man than any at Lhasa and no one less powerful than the head Chinese amban at Lhasa could stop them. The Tibetans were frightened by the passport, which fortunately they could not read. It specifically excluded Tibet. St. George added that if anyone interfered with his party when carrying this Chinese passport, that person would lose his head even if it were the headman at Lhasa. When the Tibetans asked who they were, St. George replied that they were English and were very great men. Later Razak Akhun embellished this, telling the Tibetans the Littledales were personal friends of the Emperor of China and dined with him when they were in Peking.

The Tibetans still refused them permission to go on. St. George then said he would go first with the Chinese passport on his chest, and if he was hit, the Ladakhis would take the bloody passport with the bullet holes in it to Lhasa and there would be the devil to pay. The slightly garbled account by Galwan, the interpreter, was, 'If you people shoot, then shoot on this passport. We have come here, by this passport order. But we have not come for a battle. If you people wanted to make war with us, does not matter. Here we have thirteen men only, but our Kingdom of India is a great place. You people must consider over this matter.'[3]

Galwan's words rattled the Tibetans a little. They would also have rattled the government of India had they known about it. They had banned travel to Tibet from India just to avoid this kind of situation. Despite what the Tibetans were told, the British were not waiting for an excuse to take over Tibet. They were controlling India by divide and rule, and by bluff. India was large and populous, and the British Indian government was heavily dependent upon just a few British regiments and the loyalty of the native soldiers of the Indian Army. As the Indian Mutiny of 1857 had shown, this was a slender reed. The last thing the Indian government wanted was an incident involving an Englishman in distant Tibet to which they would feel the need to respond in order to appear strong. To the Tibetans, however, it was a plausible threat.

The Littledale party ostentatiously loaded their rifles and the caravan started to move forward, the Tibetan officials begging them to stop. The Tibetans behind the rocks began whooping and shouting. A lama ordered them to keep their places. Galwan told the officials that now St. George was angry that the Tibetans were getting ready to fight and he was determined to go straight to Lhasa. The Tibetans replied that if the caravan would remain in place for three or four days, they would provide sheep, milk, butter, and anything else the Littledales might need.

The top-ranking Tibetan official asked for a chit acknowledging that he had done his best to stop them but that it was impossible because the Littledales had too many rifles. St. George offered to stop on the other side of the Goring La after they had reached wood and good grass, and there they would await the arrival of the amban from Lhasa. He added that if the Tibetans made trouble, his party would fight. He agreed on the chit but said that as his pen and ink were packed, he must stop the caravan, which he could not do in this bad stony place. They would have to reach grass first.

The caravan proceeded to the top of the ridge, where they found about 150 men hiding in the rocks. St. George gave them a written bond in English that his party would stay for a day waiting for the amban. Although the Tibetans wanted it written in Tibetan, St. George persuaded them to accept Ladakhi language, and Galwan wrote it in broken Ladakhi. The Tibetans laughed when they read it but they accepted it. Meanwhile, the Littledales and Willie were showing them telescopes, knives and other articles. Teresa stole the show by demonstrating how her waterproof coat repelled moisture. She poured water down the front and the Tibetans were suitably impressed. The

Littledales also showed the Tibetans pictures taken of themselves when they were younger, 'both much beautiful' according to Galwan. They started off again at noon after having become the best of friends with the Tibetan officials.

The Tibetans told the Littledales the pass was too difficult to cross so late in the day, but the party insisted on pushing on to get as close as possible to Lhasa before coming to a halt. They started south up a nullah and then the track suddenly turned up another ravine with a great glacier looming ahead of them. It was terrible going through boulders and loose rocks. The donkeys could barely move along, falling over the rocks at nearly every step, and once again the animals began losing their shoes. A steep, narrow path led around a red sandstone hill by the side of the glacier. It started to snow and the Littledales reached the summit of the Goring La, 19,587ft, at 4 o'clock in a storm. A sharp rock draped with prayer flags marked the top. Two mules collapsed including the one carrying the tents. Razak Akhun went back with two horses to bring up their loads.

For several hours the little party waited on top in the storm for the other horses and mules to arrive. Finally St. George sent a message back to the donkey party telling them to spend the night where they were. The rest of the group began to descend the far side of the pass. The first part was down a steep glacier. It was still snowing hard and all previous tracks were obliterated. Night had fallen, and St. George led the way in the dark through knee-deep snow, using an alpenstock to probe at each step for hidden crevasses. The angle lessened but the deep snow and the crevasse danger remained. St. George thought the glacier was more dangerous than the Tibetan matchlocks. He was right. The Tibetans did not want to harm him. The glacier did not care.

After a mile of ploughing through soft snow, they reached the snout of the glacier and got off. Teresa wrote, 'We camped in very rough sloping ground in heavy snow and rain after nearly 14 hours going, tired out. We had some of Silver's self-boiling soups which were excellent and most useful a tinned tongue. The donkeys had nearly all our provisions.' The men had to make do with cream biscuits that Razak Akhun happened to have brought. Willie wrote, 'We are the first to cross the pass which is the highest and the worst we have had anything to do with. . . . How TL has stood these long marches I don't know. It is hard work up at four and not getting to camp till 7.30.'

The morning was too wet for a fire, and breakfast consisted of leftover biscuits and honey. As they were starting out, eight Tibetans arrived including a headman who told them his group had passed the donkeys on the glacier and one had died. The gorge remained rocky for another mile. It continued to rain and everyone was wet and cold. Their sheepskin coats were back with the donkeys. They halted briefly even though there was no firewood and the yak dung fuel was soaked. Galwan built a fire for tea by tearing apart an old abandoned donkey saddle and burning the grass from which it was made. The Tibetans wanted them to camp but there was not enough grass. At noon they stopped in a drenching rain. The eight Tibetans camped near them. They were still in a gorge between high snowcapped mountains. St. George asked for sheep but the Tibetans told him they were too far away. St. George said they could not wait without meat and if sheep were not forthcoming that day, they would have to march farther the next day. The sheep were promised for that night. The donkeys finally straggled in, having lost most of their shoes. They were in bad shape but at least the party had its food supply again and the warm coats.

It snowed all night and at dawn the snow turned to steady rain. Everything was sopping wet. The mule carrying the tents was left behind below the pass and Purdil went after it while the rest of the men did their best to shoe the animals. It was difficult to nail the shoes on because their hooves were worn so thin. Teresa rested in bed trying to regain her strength. The Tibetans visited them and brought ghi, butter and milk of dubious quality. They promised sheep for the next day as well as the high official from Lhasa. Purdil returned that afternoon with the tent mule. It had been such a gruelling week for the men that St. George told them he would pay them an extra week's wages for their efforts. He added that if they reached Lhasa, he would pay everyone an additional month's wages.

The next day Teresa wrote, 'Got off at 6.45, the Tibetans entreating us not to go, saying their heads would be cut off by the Lhasa people. We all like these Tibetans better than any natives we have ever seen. They told us the big man would arrive in two hours. . . .' He came just as they were leaving. 'Such a funny little round-about creature, very good-natured. He is in command of this district and said we must not go on.'

The Tibetan official was a jovial man with a round cheery face and he wore a broad-brimmed straw hat covered with silk. Despite his efforts to stop them, St. George liked him, but he told the man he was dissatisfied with his rank, they would not discuss their plans with such a lowly official, and they would not stop for anyone less than the Chinese amban. He also said they needed a better campsite with grass and firewood. As the party started, the Tibetans went out ahead of them.

St. George and Willie stopped to speak with a Ladakhi lama. He told them Lhasa was a ten-day march away. Then he reduced the number to two but added that with a fast horse, a rider could get there in one day.

The lama described the route ahead as a one-day march through a narrow gorge with no grass, then a large river with a bridge over it, and many tents and men beyond that. This was believable. They said goodbye and rode off to catch up with the expedition.

Just then Teresa began waving frantically. They raced over and saw that about 100 Tibetans had stopped the caravan. St. George gave the order to march. When the Tibetans tried to stop them, he and Willie whipped out their revolvers and the Tibetans stepped back. The headman kept begging them to stop, saying he would be executed if he let them continue. As they neared a narrow place in the gorge, the headman said he might as well be killed by their bullets as have his head cut off. St. George realised the Tibetans would fight if he went on and they could stop him. He decided to halt. He then made a great show of explaining that only because they did not want heads cut off or fines levied, they would camp where they were. By doing this, he took credit for the inevitable. Relations between the Tibetans and the Littledales improved instantly. It was Wednesday 24 July 1895, the seventy-sixth camp since Cherchen, at latitude 30 degrees 12' 12", about 48 or 49 miles from Lhasa according to St. George's calculations, closer than any other foreigners since Huc and Gabet in 1846.

They were at 16,600ft in a large nullah with glacier-covered mountains on both sides. Despite the scenery, it was 'a miserable place to camp and wait indefinitely. Very high, cold and wet.' The relieved Tibetans brought them firewood and two sheep they bought for two rupees each. The friendly headman came by their tent, presented them with another sheep, and gave them information. A message had been sent to Lhasa, where five high ranking officials were consulting about the Littledales. One of them would arrive in two days. The Goring La, over which they had just come, was open only two to three months in the year and even then it was frequently closed by storms. It had closed since the Littledales had crossed and might remain closed indefinitely if the weather did not improve. The Tibetan said no other foreigner had been over the pass. He also volunteered the information that a road to Shigatze lay before them and Darjeeling was seventeen to twenty-five days away. He added that the nullah where they were setting up camp would be full of snow in a month.

All they could do was wait for the Lhasa officials. Willie inspected the animals. This time the mules were in the worst shape. Their backs were in horrendous condition as a result of going down hill with inadequate, dilapidated saddles made at Cherchen with the wrong kind of grass. Willie put the men to work repairing them.

The Tibetans brought them milk, ghi, and pima, a sort of curdled milk or soured clotted cream. The headman tasted each item in front of the Littledales, a local custom because of the Tibetans' fear of poisoning. The pima had hair and dirt in it. Teresa could not bring herself to eat it but Willie did. They gave a tea party for the local headman. It was not a success from the Littledales' point of view. They had hoped he would come alone so they could pump him privately for information. Instead he brought three friends. The headman had little information though many questions. Was the great heat of Calcutta caused by a big tree that sent heat out of all its branches? Could the Littledales see through mountains with their telescope?

The next day St. George and Willie prepared to meet the officials from Lhasa. They cut each other's hair 'in the latest style so as not to appear like beggars' and donned their best suits. Soon three Tibetan lamas arrived at the Littledales' tent. The head lama, about thirty-five years old, was dressed in a yellow silk gown with a sage-green lining and a scarlet sash. Number two lama, a much older man, and number three each wore a plain yellow gown and a brown silk shirt. All three wore Chinese hats and boots. Number two lama had a bad chest cold and was so hoarse he could hardly speak. The lamas began the conversation by asking who the Littledales were, where they had come from, and what they wanted. St. George replied that they had come to pay their salaams to the Dalai Lama, who they had heard was a very good man, and then the party was going on to India and Darjeeling by way of the Sikkim road. The lamas said that because the Littledales' religion was different, they were not allowed in Lhasa, that no one of a different religion ever went to Lhasa, and that the Littledales must do what all the others had done, turn back. Teresa wrote, 'We utterly refuse to go back an inch. They said their heads would be cut off if they did not send us back. I at once told St. George to say that if it was a question of my dying going over the pass or their heads being cut off, I preferred the latter.'

St. George emphatically passed on Teresa's message to the Tibetans. He asked why the Chinese amban had not come to see them as the Littledales were carrying a Chinese passport. The lamas replied that he never came out, and moreover, the Tibetans had nothing to do with the Chinese or their passport. At that time the Chinese wanted everyone to believe they controlled Tibet. The Tibetans went along with it when it suited their convenience, but in reality they were making the decisions, and the regent for the under-aged Dalai Lama was the ultimate authority.

The Tibetans said they were sent by the Deva Jung or governing council and repeated their problem with the Littledales' religion. St. George replied that his party had come on a nine-month journey to pay its respects to the Dalai Lama and was not going back. He asked them what they thought would happen if news reached India that the Littledales, bearing Chinese and English passports, had been shot while passing peaceably through their country. The Tibetans quickly replied that there would be no fighting. The discussion lasted for hours but went nowhere.

The Tibetans presented 50lb of flour to the Littledales, who decided to accept this most welcome gift but told the Tibetans they had months of provisions and were not dependent upon the Tibetans for supplies. They added that it would please them to buy sheep, pima and ghi. The Tibetans said they would provide everything the Littledales wanted as well as two sheep every three days. The Littledales tried to help the sick lama but he was so fearful that he hesitated to take any medicine. However, he accepted a linseed leaf from Teresa and throat lozenges from St. George. After hours of mutual indignation, the Tibetans departed as friends and returned to their camp, now a village of 14 tents, 150 people and 200 horses. Some young Tibetans who were servants to the officials joined the Ladakhis at their tent. They would not accept any food but they participated in the communal singing.

The pattern had been set. The lamas were not going to agree to anything except for the Littledales to turn back. St. George and Willie adopted the strategy of holding out for Lhasa until the lamas recommended another road. They had to be cautious. St. George was afraid to suggest a specific return road because the Tibetans might insist on a different route that was unacceptable. The first move had to come from the Tibetans.

The safest and quickest way home was by way of Darjeeling, but the lamas' opposition to that route was almost as strong as their opposition to the Littledales entering Lhasa. At the very least, the Littledales had to be allowed to return by way of Ladakh. St. George said they would rather die fighting than try to return over the Chang Tang and the Akka Tagh to Cherchen. He was not exaggerating. It would mean certain death for Teresa, if not for all of them. A road to China through northeastern Tibet and Amdo was also out of the question because of danger from winter storms and bandits, and in addition, China was on the verge of another revolution.

The Littledales hoped for an opportunity to use the 'Golden Key' as they referred to bribery. The difficulty was in getting a private conversation with a high enough official. Perhaps it was for this reason that the Tibetans came in groups. Bribery was a standard practice. According to Rassul Galwan, there was an earlier encounter near Tengri Nor during which a local lama offered a bribe of 3,000 rupees to the Ladakhi servants to stop the Littledales. Most were tempted to accept, and when Galwan hesitated, the lama offered even more.

Galwan somehow persuaded the other Ladakhis not to take the money. He made the right choice. His own career was to prosper because of his reputation for honesty.

It was four days before they met again with the Lhasa officials. During that time there was no news from the capital. While they were waiting, they collected specimens for the museums. Willie chased butterflies. There were hundreds and he wished he had brought a net, but he did the best he could with his hat. He also inspected the animals. One lame mule had hooves so worn down that when its shoes came off, blood oozed from the nail holes. Many of the animals had sores on their backs, and despite a rest, they were not improving. Willie began to suspect the local grass was bad.

Teresa's health continued to decline. On 30 July she wrote, '[St. George] got a lot of plants which I have pressed. Very seedy all night – a fine day.' It was the last entry in her diary. Her dysentery worsened and there was no medicine for it. The altitude was affecting her as well as the constant dampness and cold. She was not eating and could not sleep at night. She started taking Chlorodyne to help her sleep but showed no improvement in the morning. Her morale grew weaker as her strength seeped away.

The one ray of light in all this was the local headman. He had a backhanded way of passing on information such as 'Suppose Lhasa was close he would lose his head if he said so.' He also had an extraordinary range of facial grimaces and gestures while talking. Willie thought he would have made a first-rate comic actor. Everyone was fond of him.

The three lamas finally returned bringing an interpreter, a Muslim trader named Wohabjew who spoke Hindustani. He had spent several years in Ladakh and knew the fathers of the Ladakhis, who invited him to dinner. The discussion was like a broken record with the same themes being played over and over again. After a while the Tibetans said that if the Littledales crossed back over the pass and kept to the north of the mountains, they could go anywhere they wanted. St. George responded that since Teresa was ill they would give up Lhasa. They wanted only to go through Shigatze to Darjeeling to get her to a doctor as soon as possible. The lamas kept insisting the expedition had to leave the Lhasa district and go back. St. George offered to travel at night if the lamas did not want them to see any more of the country, and he added they would not go back and would rather die fighting their way out instead. The arguments continued. He concluded the meeting by saying that if they had nothing else to offer, his party would have to start a fight.

The Tibetans returned with two new high officials from Lhasa, resplendent in their yellow silk gowns. St. George heard that one was the

Governor of Lhasa and the other one head of the army. Everyone crowded into Willie's small tent because Teresa was ill in the Littledales' larger one. The debate went on for 2 hours. It was futile. St. George and Willie were becoming more and more afraid they would have to take the long road to Ladakh and trust to luck. Afterwards, still hoping to change the Tibetans' minds, they decided that the next day they would prepare to leave looking as if they intended to fight their way out.

Early the next morning they saddled the animals. After breakfast Teresa announced that she wanted to see the head Tibetan personally and if possible alone. The head of the three original Lhasa officials came to her tent but she refused to speak with him and turned him away. He came back with the two high officials. Teresa was sitting in bed propped up with pillows. A group of Tibetan onlookers stood outside the tent peering in at them. Teresa told the Tibetan chiefs she wanted only to get quickly to medical help and she would die if she went back. She then asked the local headman to agree with her that she was getting worse daily. The headman replied that he would be killed if they went on.

Suddenly Teresa asked Willie to give her the Mannlicher. The number two Tibetan lama tried to dash out of the tent but St. George collared him and hauled him back. Teresa handed the rifle to the Tibetan chief, and with tears streaming down her face she ordered him to shoot her, saying she would rather die than go back the way they had come. Again the second lama tried to bolt. Again St. George hauled him back. The stunned chief lama repeated that they would be killed if the Littledales went on.

St. George replied that if the Tibetans did not care for the Chinese passport, they would have to account for his English one, and he pulled it out. He said they were big people and such a passport was given only to big people and if Teresa died or any of them were hurt, 3,000 sepoys would take Lhasa in 3 months. The Tibetans reiterated that they would lose their heads. St. George suggested they be allowed to go two marches down the Lhasa road where the ground was much lower, and camp there because Teresa could not stay where she was. He asked the Tibetans to write to the Deva Jung that the Littledales were big people, Teresa was dying, and if they were not allowed to go on the Sikkim road to get to a doctor quickly, the Littledale party would fight. He then sent the Tibetans away to think it over. Meanwhile, the sepoys were growing impatient. They asked Willie for more cartridges, saying that if there was any fighting, they wanted to be sure they were included.

Wohabjew, the merchant-interpreter, brought a message from the lamas to St. George, and while he was there, he imparted a wealth of information on Tibet, its people and customs, which St. George dutifully recorded. He described the process of selecting a Dalai Lama and mentioned that the current one would come of age in November, the two previous Dalai Lamas had died between the ages of 18 and 20, and the current regent had held office for forty years. St. George could not help noticing that one's twenty-first birthday was a peculiarly fatal period in the life of a Dalai Lama.

The following day the lamas sent word that they would send the letter to the Deva Jung in Lhasa if the Littledales would stay in place, and that they would have to wait at least four days for a reply. St. George replied that they would leave immediately but Teresa was too ill to move without a palki (sedan chair). The Tibetans promised to ask for one. Teresa felt a little better the next morning. She had slept through the night and even drank some milk. Although she had taken a little Chlorodyne in the evening, Willie thought it was her dramatic performance that had made the difference. It had exhausted her, enabling her to sleep. At lunch she talked about the future and what they should do on the way to Ladakh.

St. George and Willie went with a local Tibetan to look at a sick mule. The man told them the animals were being poisoned by a grass that grows under a shrub. He showed them a plant about 18in high with fingery leaves and a purple flower. It was an added incentive to move to another location.

A week went by with no word from Lhasa. Later St. George learned that the letter had to be circulated to all the Lamaseries and each one had to hold a meeting of its lamas. Meanwhile, the Tibetan community around them continued to grow. There were now forty tents surrounding them and more up the valley. Willie counted ten campfires above them. Every day yaks coming down from the Goring La were passing them on their way to Lhasa.

The twelfth of August was Teresa's fifty-sixth birthday but it was not an occasion to celebrate. She was feeling worse again. Furthermore, the negotiations were not working. By 15 August the expedition had been stationary for three weeks. St. George asked the Tibetans to send another letter to the Deva Jung but they refused and said they would seize any messenger the Littledales sent. They meant it. Razak Akhun was sent off with a letter and was promptly stopped. St. George threatened the Tibetans with the full wrath of the Indian government but still they did not budge. Meanwhile, Teresa had stopped drinking milk and the daily rain showers were turning to snow.

It was becoming more and more apparent they would have to return to India by way of Ladakh and Kashmir, 1,200 miles away. It would take two-and-a-half months just to get to Leh. Moreover, the need for supplies would delay their start. They calculated that 10 November was the earliest they could get over the Zoji La, the pass between Ladakh and Srinagar, Kashmir, but the pass could close before then and they would have to spend the winter in Ladakh.

That night it snowed heavily. Willie was awakened by a sharp crack he thought was a rifle shot and found himself pinned to his bed. His first thought was that the Tibetans had attacked, but after a few heart-stopping moments he realised the heavy snowfall had collapsed his tent and snapped the tent pole. The jagged end had cut through the bedding by his head. He took refuge with the Ladakhis for the rest of the night.

The next day the Tibetans gave Lhasa's answer. The expedition would have to go back to Cherchen. St. George and Willie refused. After more arguing, the Tibetans told the Littledales they could go to Ladakh but only by a route far to the north. This was impossible as there would be no grass and a critical pass would be closed in about ten days. Both sides agreed it was a difficult situation for all of them.

It was more than difficult for the Littledales. It was desperate. They could not make it back to Cherchen alive and they could not stay much longer in their camp. Animals were dying and Teresa's health was rapidly sinking. Early the next morning St. George and Willie went to see the Tibetans. After a long discussion it was agreed that they would go back over the Goring La and then go south of the Garing Tso (lake) and head west for Ladakh. They needed a palki for Teresa. There were two in Lhasa, one belonging to the Dalai Lama and the other to the Chinese amban. St. George sent polite messages to both men asking to buy one of the palkis but neither would sell. The Tibetans told him a palki could be made at the camp and they were bringing men with wood, leather, iron and other materials to make it. St. George gave them 400 rupees as an installment on food and supplies to be bought in Lhasa.

Later Wohabjew brought a letter saying they were not to go in Lhasa territory. As the Ladakh road was in Lhasa territory, this was unacceptable. St. George then dictated a letter to Wohabjew stating their understanding, but Wohabjew did not write what he was told and inserted a statement about not entering Lhasa territory. St. George and Willie learned of his treachery only because Rassul Galwan was able to read Tibetan.

They stormed into the Tibetans' tent the next morning to make them keep their original promise. The Tibetans now insisted that the party go back beyond Tengri Nor and around the north side of the Garing Tso. They also said the Littledales must stay outside of Lhasa territory, which meant they could not use the main road to Ladakh. The two parties argued over the route for hours. Finally St. George agreed to go around the north side of the Garing Tso in exchange for an order to the local Tibetans along the route to supply the caravan with horses and grain at regular prices. The officials refused to give such an order to St. George but said they would give it to Razak Akhun and Rassul Galwan. With that understanding an agreement was reached. The Tibetans said they would furnish yaks to help cross the pass and the materials for the palki would arrive the next day.

The Littledales had not reached Lhasa. They had not even been able to get out by way of the Darjeeling road, but they had made an extraordinary march and had come closer to that Forbidden City than many more famous explorers. But fame was the last thing on their minds. Two more animals died, a horse and a donkey. All of their attention was now focused on getting out alive. They knew it was going to be close, especially for Teresa. It was going to be so close that by the end of the day neither St. George nor Willie had summoned up the courage to tell Teresa they would have to go north of the Garing Tso.

17

Return

We have had a ripping time. . . .
W.A.L. Fletcher

On 19 August the horses were sent over the Goring La to get them away from the poisonous grass. The Littledales and Willie remained in camp to wait for the palki, which was nearly finished, and to buy more animals and supplies. After two days of haggling, they bought sixteen more ponies at 43 rupees per head, 'an awful swindle'. St. George began to worry about how to pay their men at the end of the trip.

Teresa's health slowly kept declining. They had spent a full month at the unhealthy campsite, and Willie thought that the conditions were killing her. St. George's normally positive attitude deserted him and he became very depressed, confiding to Willie his doubts that Teresa would reach Ladakh alive. Although the road would be lower, it would not be low enough. They would still be travelling above 14,000ft and it would be cold.

The Littledales and most of the men started for the Goring La on 23 August, leaving Willie and three others behind to obtain the rest of the supplies. Twenty Tibetans took turns carrying Teresa in her palki to the foot of the glacier but she had to ride a yak over the ice and across the pass. The men carried her in the palki down the rocks on the other side. It was hard work with the downhill men carrying most of the weight and the uphill men having to hunch over to keep the palki level. St. George encouraged them by promising to pay each man an extra two rupees a day if they brought her down safely. He kept his promise but noticed to his disgust that the lamas took the money and the men received nothing. They descended the nullah and pitched their tents. The next day they crossed the river, camped, and waited for Willie and the others.

Willie was having his difficulties. He managed to get 2 tons of food including 900lb of tsampa (parched barley flour). However, he wanted more tsampa because it was easy to prepare, but the Tibetans said they did not have any and they kept offering him the more expensive rice instead. Willie knew they were lying because tsampa is the basic staple of the Tibetan diet and everyone ate it.

Willie and his men repacked everything into 80lb loads. They needed fifty yaks to carry it all. That evening the remaining supplies arrived except for potatoes and rope. Rope was critical for strapping on the loads, and the Tibetan officials were collecting all they could from the locals. Willie was also out of tobacco. The Tibetans gave him Wills' Bristol Bird's Eye, making Willie wonder how it had found its way from England to Tibet.

The yaks arrived early the next morning and left before noon with their attendants and two sepoys. (Things always seemed to run well when they facilitated the departure of foreigners.) Soon the head lama arrived, and he haggled with Willie for 4 hours over the final accounting. Amazingly, after all the days of constant friction, Willie and the lama parted as friends. They discussed Willie's next visit to Lhasa territory and Willie gave the lama a pair of opera glasses.

Willie and Razak Akhun left that afternoon. They had stayed longer at the camp than any of them could have imagined. It was a lovely day with a hot sun, and the surroundings were magnificent. The prior month Willie had crossed the pass in storm and darkness. Now he soaked in the scenery with the sun. In every gap in the snow-crowned mountains were glaciers glistening in the bright sunlight. He arrived at the foot of the pass, pitched his tent, and sent a message to St. George saying he was on his way.

The small party started up the Goring La early the next morning. The snow on the glacier sparkled. Everywhere Willie looked he saw mountains with sharp peaks. By mid-morning he had reached the top of the pass and begun descending the rocky nullah up which he had so laboriously climbed. It would be fifty-one years before the Goring La was crossed by any other foreigners, Peter Aufschnaiter and Heinrich Harrer in 1946 on their famous journey to Lhasa.[1]

When Willie arrived at the Littledales' camp, he was shocked at his aunt's condition even though St. George told him she was better than when they had arrived. 'Her eyes are staring and looking ghastly. Can't sleep without Chlorodyn which is a terrible thought as our stock of it can't go on forever. The only thing she looks forward to is that. . . . She was terribly shaken in the Palki and had great pains after her arrival here.'

They paid off the hired yaks that had come over the pass and put loads on the horses, but they needed more animals and had to hire local yaks. St. George and Teresa left while Willie was still loading the animals. It was a struggle. The horses had eaten well on the good grass, and with energy restored, they kept running away and kicking their packs off. At one point most of their horseshoes and nails were strewn over the ground. It was a fine day, and even better, the river was down and the donkeys could cross carrying their loads. The Tibetans showed them the best route and they saved 7 miles.

The next day the Tibetans showed them an even more direct route and they made 14 miles. The party camped in a nullah full of sheep. They had to keep changing yaks whenever they went beyond the boundary of the owners. Some days they changed yaks three times. Despite the cold and even hailstorms, Teresa grew more animated. She talked about what to do in Ladakh instead of when she would die.

They marched 22 miles during the next two days before finally joining their familiar old road. St. George bought more horses from the local Tibetans, and they followed the road across a plain and pitched camp by a spring near some nomad tents. Despite the urgency in getting to Ladakh, St. George decided to spend a day there to buy still more horses as it might be their last opportunity. They bought some for their men to ride and others to carry loads. They also purchased fifteen sheep and had no intention of feeding them to the wolves. Their stud now totalled fifty-four horses and mules and twenty-eight donkeys.

The next morning horses were galloping all over the place throwing their packs again. The 'tamasha' was especially bad the following day. Several of the boxes were smashed to pieces. Once the caravan had started, however, they made good time, covering 15 miles in about 6 hours. Teresa was doing much better, sleeping at night using less and less Chlorodyne. One night she even dozed a little without any medicine, earning a comment in Willie's diary.

Two days later they recrossed the Sachu Chu, the river they had previously crossed with a makeshift raft. This time the water was lower and they were able to ride across. The Tibetan escort and the hired yaks turned back. That night a large group of men came into view and two of them entered their camp. They were from the Senja Jung, the governing council of the province, and they had orders from the Deva Jung in Lhasa to see the caravan through their territory. The Littledales were to go directly west where grass and water were good, and the officials would furnish whatever supplies they needed.

The next day the party was hit by a severe thunderstorm. As lightning flashed all around them, they were pelted with hail. The wind was so strong that they were unable to face it and had to turn their backs to the storm and wait it out. When it finally cleared, they made camp. Just after the tents were pitched, sheets of rain fell on them. They could not build a fire as all the dung was wet. St. George, Teresa and Willie dined on canned tongue and Silver's self-heating soup. The men ate cold tsampa. Teresa was angry with Galwan for the lack of fuel and asked him why he did not carry a pony load of dung. For the rest of the trip, there was always a load of dried dung. It was such a good idea that Galwan was to carry it on many of his future expeditions.[2]

On 10 September they passed the Garing Tso and turned west toward Ladakh. Now they were in country new to them. At least they were going parallel to the ridges and not across them. They went up one valley after another with gentle passes between them. In two days they covered 25 miles. They were 600 miles from Ladakh.

Riding in the palki was a terrible ordeal for Teresa but there was no alternative. The chair was suspended from shafts attached to a mule in the front and a mule in the rear. It took two men to accompany it to make sure nothing happened. Late one night Teresa awoke with a great pain in her side. She was crying out in agony. St. George thought an abscess on her liver might have burst. Willie did not see how she could ride in the palki, but if they delayed too long, the supply of Chlorodyne would run out.

St. George realised they could make longer marches if they obtained more yaks to lighten the loads on the horses. Even Teresa was amenable when it was explained to her that 6½ hours of travel instead of 5 would get them to Ladakh 14 days sooner. The two men from the Senja Jung made the arrangements. St. George paid them for hiring the yaks but the money stayed in their pockets. They never paid the yak owners.

They were making long marches every day – 13 miles, 17 miles, 15 miles – through rolling plains with snow-covered hills to the north and south. The nights were cold but the days were warm with occasional rainstorms. For the time being, Teresa was drinking milk again and her dysentery was nearly gone. One day the palki shafts slipped off the lead mule, and the palki fell to the ground. Fortunately Teresa was not hurt. The animals were taking a beating. Ten horses had bad withers and the donkeys were getting footsore because there were no replacement shoes for them. Even so, by 19 September they were 464 miles from Ladakh and moving well.

After two more long stages, they had to stop for a day. The yaks they were using had to be returned and their replacements had not yet arrived. Willie passed the time by trying to hunt bharal, which were becoming quite numerous. The following morning the horse that Willie had been riding for months was missing and they found it dead in a bog. Willie would have to ride a little Tibetan pony. Teresa had a bad night so they did only a short march.

Her dysentery returned with a vengeance. It was especially discouraging to her as she had been free of it for some days. Her condition seemed to go up and down as much as the Tibetan landscape, keeping everyone, especially St. George, in a constant state of tension. This time she was in such great pain that the party remained in camp for two days.

They moved on over rolling plains. Now they were encountering small herds of Ovis ammon, which Willie chased with more enthusiasm than success. The days and nights were getting colder. In the morning their bread was frozen solid so they started taking it to bed with them at night. Furthermore, their clothes were falling apart. Willie wrote, 'Patched my knickerbockers with leather. They are getting quite artistic but they are chilly.'

On 27 September they crossed the route followed by the pundit Nain Singh in 1874 on his journey from Leh to Lhasa. They were proceeding due west, south of the pundit's route, in country unexplored by foreigners. Two days later they reached the end of the territory of their two Tibetan companions. The men had been helpful and Willie was sorry to see them go. The headman from the next district had not arrived. Worse yet, neither had his yaks. The party remained in place for a day while Razak Akhun went out to find them. It was midnight before Akhun, yaks and men finally arrived. In the morning they resumed their journey and covered another 16 miles. The casualty list was increasing. That night St. George did not feel well and had to be put to bed. Meanwhile, Teresa was 'completely helpless'.

The fresh yaks came without expense to the Littledales. Willie and St. George thought it was due to an order by the Deva Jung but Rassul Galwan had a more interesting explanation. Galwan had become good friends with the two Senja Jung men and had asked them to tell the local people that the order to give yaks to the Littledales came from the Deva Jung. They were happy to do so. Why not? The yaks did not come from their district. However, there was a problem with the constant changing of yaks every few miles. How could they persuade the later nomad encampments to give them animals? Razak Akhun and Kalam Rassul pretended to be lamas and Rassul Galwan passed as a lama servant to the Littledales. They told the local Tibetans that Teresa was a sister of Queen Victoria and was sent to see the Dalai Lama to convey friendship from Britain to Tibet. Galwan said they had brought many mule-loads of presents to the Dalai Lama, they had been his guests for a month, and he had given them animals and food. He had even sent a high official as far as the Sachu Chu to help them. Galwan added that although one official had returned, another lama (Razak Akhun) was going with them as far as Ladakh to make sure everything went well. Then Razak Akhun told them the Dalai Lama ordered everyone to give them yaks, help watch the ponies, and have firewood at every camp. Galwan applied the finishing touch by giving the Tibetans what he said were the sacred pills of the Dalai Lama. When it came time to give dinner to the Tibetans who were looking after the horses, Galwan was extremely liberal in passing out the tsampa, giving the Tibetans a full stomach and a favourable impression of Littledale generosity. The scam worked for days until they entered the district of Rudok.

The party was travelling between high hills. The wind, always cold, was becoming increasingly bitter but they were making progress. On 4 October Willie estimated they were 340 miles from Leh. They covered 15 miles, but the hard, fast pace was taking its toll on the animals. Two donkeys had been left behind the day before. Several days later a horse would die on the road. Ravens were driving the animals mad by sitting on their sore backs and pecking at the raw flesh. One day they had to cross a pass almost 17,000ft high. The descent was steep, too steep in places for the palki, so Teresa had to ride a horse. It was intensely cold again. This time five donkeys had to be left behind on the road. St. George decided to let the best mules and horses travel unloaded in hopes that they could be sold in Leh, still a month off. Finances as well as animals were getting depleted.

During these daily marches Willie made constant hunting forays, usually after bharal and ravine deer, and occasionally Ovis ammon. It was not easy getting within range of the animals, but one day he got three bharal with three shots and made the wry comment in his diary, 'The rifle is going up in price.'

The animals grew worse. The yaks furnished by the Tibetans to carry supplies kept the situation from becoming critical, but the riding horses were footsore and had to be reshod. They were down to ten donkeys. On the other hand, they were still making good progress and Teresa's health was improving again. Her dysentery was in remission, she was able to eat a little solid food, and slowly she was getting stronger.[3] Even so, she would need all of her strength for the difficult days that lay ahead.

They spent a day reshoeing the horses and then pressed on. They carried ice to melt because there would be no water for the next two days. The party crossed over a low but steep pass, again too steep for the palki so Teresa climbed out and rode. Beyond the pass they travelled through a stony valley, increasing the hardship on the animals. Three more horses were left behind. Willie's hands were sore and the skin on his thumbs was cracked. At first he had been disgusted by the filthiness of the Tibetans. Later he realised it was water in the cold, rarefied air that caused the skin to crack until it hurt to touch anything. Following the Tibetan example, he stopped washing his hands.

One morning six horses and two of the palki mules were missing. Their tracks headed toward the next camp. Using St. George's horse on the palki, the party set out. Along the way they collected their animals one by one until they had retrieved all of them. It was another cold day with a biting west wind. Two more donkeys were left behind.

On 19 October some Tibetans arrived, closely followed by the munshi to the headman at Rudok, the main town of western Tibet. The munshi gave the usual greeting to foreigners: 'Go back the way you came.' More precisely, they were told to retrace their route all the way back to Cherchen, a distance of about 1,500 miles. The munshi added that there was no use talking as he had a letter from the Deva Jung. St. George had Rassul Galwan read the letter. It said the Littledales were to be turned back no matter where they were, they were not to put one foot inside Tibetan territory, and no one was to help them. It was signed by the same head lama who had given the Littledales the letter permitting them to go west to Ladakh. Both letters were dated the same day.

St. George showed the munshi his own letter from the lama, and to add emphasis to his position he ordered the sepoys to take out their rifles. The munshi demanded that the party stay where they were. St. George refused and ordered the donkeys to leave. Some Tibetans moved to stop them but the munshi took one look at the sepoys, who were spoiling for a fight, and called back his men. The caravan moved out. Despite the munshi's opposition, St. George had sympathy for him. 'I never saw anybody so crestfallen; I really felt sorry for the fellow; he had come up a very big man indeed.' St. George understood what a tremendous loss of face the munshi had suffered.

Meanwhile, one of the Tibetans offered Galwan a bribe if he would lead the party away from Rudok. Galwan turned down the money but said that as he was a neighbour he would be glad to assist them. He confidentially told the munshi that St. George planned to go to the temple in Rudok to wait for two days before going on to Ladakh. It would be his last chance to carry out his real mission, which was to start a war with the Tibetans. He and Mrs Littledale had come all the way to Tibet to die in order to give the British an excuse to take over the country, but unfortunately they had been unsuccessful as the Tibetans had not yet killed them. Rudok would be their last chance to achieve their objective. Galwan was a master of artful lying. This was his greatest lie.

The Tibetans may not have believed this nonsense but as they were close to British Ladakh, it was bound to make an impression. Moreover, the munshi knew the Littledales were trying to get out of Tibet, not into it, and they would not see anything that had not already been observed and recorded by agents of the British Raj. Rudok was only three days from the border, and it would not be wise to stand between a wounded animal and the exit.

The munshi sent to his superior at Rudok a copy of the lama's letter to the Littledales, and he kept pleading for the caravan to wait for the reply. St. George kept refusing and said he expected to be furnished with yaks, and if they were not forthcoming, the party was prepared to fight. They marched 9 miles before camping. Willie stayed behind the main group to make sure the hired yaks came. After the excitement with the Tibetans, the temporary disappearance of twelve horses seemed a minor matter. Another donkey was left behind. That night the temperature was 4°F below zero. St. George later wrote:

> If we . . . forgot to take the bread to bed, we found a frozen loaf made a poor breakfast. The difficulty of dressing in the morning, with the thermometer 6°, 8°, and 10°, below zero in the tent, was overcome by not undressing overnight. Wherever our breath touched the sheet was ice in the morning; and on one occasion Mr. Fletcher found that before he could lift his head he had to loosen his hair from the pillow, to which it was frozen fast.[4]

The munshi came the next morning and asked them to go by way of the Indus, a much longer route. St. George refused but said if there was a road close to Rudok, he would take it without entering the town. Galwan told St. George that the munshi's predecessor in office had been put in jail in Leh by the Wazir for having defrauded some Ladakhis who had been trading in Tibet. He added that this munshi was going to Leh in a month and was afraid of the same fate. Galwan had warned the munshi that jail for life was the best he could expect if the party lost one rupee's worth of property. Two days later they met the munshi again at a junction in the road. His superior at Rudok had said they had to go back. If they refused, they would have to take a longer southern way. St. George refused both alternatives. The stalemate continued.

St. George had repeatedly asked for yaks. He asked for them once again and produced the letter authorising the party to hire them. His request was denied. He then said they would take as much of their baggage as they could, leave the rest behind for the Tibetans to bring, and if it did not come, the munshi would be held responsible, and when he reached Ladakh he would be jailed. At this point the party broke off the talks and began to sort and pack the baggage, taking enough food to last fifteen days. The Tibetans came by every few minutes, begging them to stop. Just as they started off, the munshi relented. The yaks would bring the supplies after all.

They left the junction, crossed the river, and followed the Rudok road down another valley, stopping after 14 miles. Willie summarised the ordeal: 'Four horses gave out today. 3 degrees below Zero. Washed my hands first time for 9 days. Two donkeys left behind.' They were now 6 miles from Rudok.

St. George and Willie expressed sympathy to the munshi for his difficult position caught between conflicting letters, but they kept reminding him of his Ladakh predicament. As a result, he gave them men to look after all their animals and even two additional men to watch their horses at night. It was not over yet. The munshi showed up early the next morning with fifty men, saying he had come to stop them. St. George offered to skirt Rudok if the yaks were furnished but otherwise the expedition would enter the town. The munshi agreed to produce the yaks if the Littledale party gave him a letter stating he had tried to stop them. The letter was promptly forthcoming.

The Littledales left camp, marched down the valley for 2 hours, and finally came within sight of Rudok. There were about 200 houses built up the side of a rocky hill jutting out into the north side of the plain. On the top of the hill were a stone fort and three monasteries painted red. The party kept to the south and passed about 2 miles from town. Three friends of the Ladakhis arrived from Rudok and gave Rassul Galwan and the other servants news of family and friends. They were happy to learn that a good friend had become the Wazir of Ladakh. After crossing the plain, the caravan ascended a nullah between hills and stopped at a small village where they found the first trees and cultivated fields they had seen since leaving Cherchen six months before. That night Rassul Galwan wrote a letter to his friend the Wazir of Ladakh, giving him news of the expedition. He also notified the headmen of all the Ladakhi villages on their route, giving their expected dates of arrival and asking that everything be ready for the Littledales. The weather continued to be cold. The horses were in pitiable condition, bony and covered with sores. Fortunately the munshi furnished yaks. Although he had been forced to follow orders from above, he himself had been hospitable to the Littledales and they liked him. St. George rewarded him with a load of rice as a parting gift and he returned to Rudok. The party made a fast march down the valley, passed a freshwater lake, and camped by a stream after having come 18 miles. They were at 15,100ft. As they approached the border, the Ladakhis put on their best clothes, making an impressive sight.

That day they had to leave another donkey behind. While always a sad occurrence, this time it was especially poignant. Back at Khotan someone had palmed off on them a two-year-old donkey. They had tried to exchange it several times but were unsuccessful so they let it carry a load as best it could. To everyone's astonishment, it proved to be the best donkey they had. It was always fat and never sick. As they neared the end of the trip, it was one of only three survivors, but now the intense cold was too much for it and they were forced to abandon it.

The following day they followed a stony track along a lake for 14 miles. The terrain was the same as before but with one significant invisible difference. They had entered Ladakh, British territory. There would be no further political problems with the Tibetans. Unfortunately, the border had no effect on the weather and it was getting colder all the time. For several days in a row the temperature plummeted well below zero, once reaching minus 17°F.

On 27 October the party reached the Ladakhi village of Shusall, a few houses and trees at the foot of a hill with a small monastery perched on top. As they were in well-known country, St. George finally put away his mapping instruments. He had surveyed 1,700 miles of land. The Tibetans left and the Littledales were sorry to see them go. They had provided free yak transport and now the Littledales would have to pay for it. This inspired them to cut back once again and get rid of all excess baggage. They travelled along Pangong Lake to its west end and turned down a narrow nullah with high mountains on both sides. Along the way, they passed several hundred sheep carrying loads of grain to Rudok. Two or three men could handle as many as 100 sheep, each carrying 20–30lb.

The Littledale party was below 14,000ft for the first time in almost six months. The route descended a narrow, steep trail so rough that Teresa's palki had to be carried by men. The next day they reached the village of Durga, a scattering of houses and cultivated fields strung along 2 miles of trail at the foot of the Chang La (pass). Everything was ready for an early start over the pass the next day. The Ladakhis decided to celebrate with a tamasha. The Littledale men and the locals had a grand time playing banjos, dancing and singing. They had earned a good time but they were so distracted that they forgot to check the horses. They had put out grass for the animals but during the party someone stole the fodder, and unknown to everyone, the horses went unfed. The results were disastrous.

In the morning the party started out with the yaks and unfed horses. They climbed slowly up a narrow nullah through rocky terrain. Several times the track went around narrow corners and Teresa had to ride because they could not carry her in the palki. By noon they had reached snow. They continued upwards for another several hours. After a climb of over 4,000ft, they reached the 18,400-ft summit of the Chang La and looked out on the Indus River and the snow-covered mountains behind it. They descended on a narrow trail and camped at the first grass they encountered. The small group sat around a fire and waited for the yaks and horses to arrive. It was evening before some of the weakened animals straggled in. Several made it into camp only because they were fed grain during the march, but ten horses had to be left behind.

An old man brought a message from the Wazir promising them more men and animals, and when they reached the next village the extra horses were waiting for them. Reinforced by the fresh animals, the party reached the Indus and travelled through cultivated land alongside the river. They passed under trees and through fields of grain in a large valley with high mountains on both sides. After 17 miles they pitched camp.

Leh at last! The Ladakhis were so excited to be nearing home that they could not sleep. In the morning they again put on their best clothes and the caravan continued down the Indus valley. Several hours later the Littledales turned up a nullah and reached their destination. Ramzan Ali met them 4 miles out of town and escorted them in. He had been sirdar of their expedition across China in 1893. They went to the dak bungalow (resthouse) and waited for the caravan to arrive. The Wazir called on them and sent potatoes and cabbages, as well as cigarettes from the bazaar for Willie.

While the Littledales and Willie slept, the Ladakhis and their families celebrated. The men had been gone for over a year, and during their absence no one could be certain they would return alive. Moreover, in that time and place the men could not be certain their families would be alive. When Rassul Galwan had returned from a previous expedition, he had learned that his first wife had died while he was gone. This time the Ladakhis had received news of their families when they were approaching Rudok, so the suspense was gone but not the pleasure. In Galwan's family the joy was dampened by the news that Galwan would have to leave in a few days to accompany the Littledales over the Zoji La to Srinagar. His wife was unhappy about this. They had been married just before he left for Kashgar to join the expedition, he had been gone for over a year, and now, after only a couple of days, he would be gone again over the Zoji La with winter moving in and a safe return doubtful. The pass might close for the winter before he could get back. Galwan quoted his wife as saying, 'Why do you go Kashmir now, if you are love me? We don't need so much money. You did enough long journey.'[5] Galwan, however, felt responsible for helping Teresa reach Kashmir safely, and he promised his wife he would somehow return to Leh no matter what.

The next day was a Sunday but not a day of rest. It was imperative to leave for Kashmir as quickly as possible. Everyone spent the day sorting supplies, arranging for animals, and getting a dandy made. It was similar to the palki but shorter and lighter. The weight was critical as it would be carried by men the entire way. There was a telegraph running out to Srinagar so St. George sent a short telegram home. That afternoon the Littledales called upon Dr Ernest Shawe and his wife, who were Moravian missionaries from Germany. Since the Littledales' visit during their honeymoon, the Moravian Church had established a hospital and school in Leh. It was considered an extreme hardship post. The missionaries rarely took leave, and several of Dr Shawe's predecessors had died there in the prime of life. Foreign visitors were a welcome relief to their harsh existence.[6]

Rassul Galwan, his wife, his mother, and the wives of the other Ladakhis came to call on Teresa. They were wearing their best finery including the perag, a spectacular Ladakhi headdress sewn with rows of turquoise and coral. Willie was especially impressed by Ramzan Ali's wife with her headdress, necklace and rings. Teresa made appropriate pleasant remarks, with St. George and Rassul Galwan serving as interpreters. She gave small gifts to the women and told Galwan's wife she was young and beautiful, assuring her that after going to Kashmir, Galwan would live with her for a long time.

Later the Wazir visited them again. The Littledales presented him with Badullah's rifle. The Wazir asked them to attend a big tamasha for the men for which the Littledales were paying. The entertainment began in the evening and was held out of doors. The Littledales, Willie and the Wazir sat under a large tent. Dancing girls turned slowly around and around to the beat of drums and what sounded to Willie like bagpipes. Then the men took over, followed by vigorous sword dances by Razak Akhun, Galam Mahmad and Ramzan Ali. The flickering of a fire burning on a pedestal cast a weird glow over the dancers. The festivities continued long after the Littledales went to bed.

They arose early the next morning but did not leave until noon because they had to pack the animals and pay off the men. The previous day they had given the men two horses each. The animals were hopelessly weak and one of Galwan's ponies died the same day. St. George sent candles and other supplies to the Moravian mission and then had the men draw lots for the remaining items.

At last the caravan got off. Besides the Littledales and Willie, it consisted of Galwan, Hussin, the three sepoys, and the porters for Teresa's dandy, as well as eight mules they hoped to sell in Srinagar. Their Ladakhi servants escorted them a short distance out of town before turning back. The Littledales had travelled from Leh to Srinagar back in 1877. Then the rugged, bare country must have seemed strange but romantic. Now, with the lateness of the season and Teresa's failing health, it was familiar yet ominous as they raced the oncoming winter weather by doing double stages in order to cross the Zoji La before it closed. The Wazir accompanied them. Teresa's dandy was comfortable but moved slowly carried by the men. Even so, they covered 18 miles. They followed the north side of the Indus and spent the first night at

Nimu, a resthouse. The Wazir took the best rooms so the Littledales and Willie ended up on the drafty top floor.

They did two stages again the next day, the dandy men moving at a rapid pace, chanting all the way. The next resthouse bungalow was ready for them. The schedule was hard on Hussin and Rassul Galwan. At each stop they had to cook dinner and clean up, and then rise in the dark to prepare breakfast and get everything packed so the party could leave. There was little time for sleeping. As usual the sepoys were not much help, but they knew the reason for the rush so for once they did not complain.

The next morning they reached the village of Khalatse and a bridge over the Indus, which they crossed to the south bank. Leaving the Indus, they followed a nullah on a winding path up the face of cliffs overhanging a stream. St. George's and Willie's horses gave out so they walked. Then a sepoy's horse died. Willie wrote that they had lost a total of fifty-eight horses. After 18 miles they reached a village. There was no bungalow, just a chilly serai. Teresa refused to stay there so they pitched her tent in the yard. The town hovered above them on the hill, with houses resting on logs driven into the side of the mountain. The following day they crossed the border from Ladakh into Kashmir. Again there was only a serai, so Teresa and St. George slept in their tent while Willie stayed in a dirty but well ventilated room. There was no door or window but it had two open holes in the roof.

The party ascended a valley, went over the Namika La at 12,200ft, and continued on a track along the side of steep hills. The pony Willie rode was small and the saddle girth was too long. On one descent it came loose and Willie flew over the horse's neck, hit the ground, and slammed his knee hard against a rock. By the end of the day it was stiff and swollen. Light snow fell during the afternoon, increasing their worries about crossing the Zoji La. Their anxiety was increased further by a man who had crossed the pass and reported 8ft of snow at the top.

It snowed again during the night. They dropped down the valley, then climbed some hills and descended to the small town of Kargil on the Suru River. An important junction, it had a telegraph office. The Wazir was already there and had wired ahead to inquire about conditions on the Zoji La but there had been no answer.

On Sunday 10 November the Littledales left Kargil. It was exactly one year since they had left Charing Cross station in London. This time, instead of saying goodbye to friends and relatives, they said farewell to the Wazir of Ladakh, who had been so helpful to them. The following day they finally arrived at Dras, the main village on the north side of the Zoji La. They reached the resthouse and collapsed in exhaustion.

The next day they climbed steadily for 5½ hours and camped at a small hamlet.

It was cold when they arose in the morning to go over the Zoji La. This was the critical day. Crossing this dangerous pass had been their goal ever since they had started back over the Goring La nearly three months before. Although the Zoji La is relatively low, 11,500ft, about the elevation of Leh, the steepness of the Kashmir side and the condition of the trail in unfavourable weather made it a formidable obstacle, especially for laden animals. The baggage yaks started before breakfast and the party left soon after. They climbed steadily through the snow over a track coated in ice and melting snow. Along the way they passed a man who was struggling under a heavy load of baggage. He told them his horse had fallen off the edge after reaching the top.

The party was blessed with good weather but the treacherous surface of the narrow trail zigzagging among snow-laden trees made the steep descent into Kashmir hazardous. Willie's horse fell and was killed. Fortunately Willie had dismounted and was leading it, and he managed to get out of the way. There were more animal casualties. The tent mule and another horse went over the side. Purdil's horse also slipped, but Purdil grabbed it by the tail and held it for a few moments until other men were able to help him. Three weeks earlier, seven horses and three men had been killed on the pass.

The Littledales were grateful to reach the resthouse at the little hamlet of Baltal. They were in the Sind Valley. Pine trees covered the surrounding hills and snow-covered peaks loomed beyond. On the road the next day, they received a letter from Captain G.F. Chenevix Trench, the British Resident in Kashmir, inviting them to stay with him in Srinagar.

On 16 November they finally reached Srinagar. It was raining heavily. Captain Trench met the bedraggled group a short distance from his house and led them to a guest bungalow, where they stacked the wet baggage. They paid off Rassul Galwan, Hussin, and the three sepoys and presented them with gifts. They also gave money to Rassul Galwan and Hussin to cover their expenses for the return trip to Leh. The two men left immediately and were able to make it home safely. Teresa saw a doctor. Her health was so poor that he forbade her to have any visitors, a great disappointment to Galwan, who had wanted to say goodbye. Later he was pleased to receive a letter from Teresa telling him he was like a son to her.

The Littledales and Willie parted. Teresa and St. George left in a tonga for Murree, the hill station above Rawalpindi. Willie stayed behind to go hunting in the Kashmir hills. He wrote in his diary, 'We have had a ripping time and not a single row. . . .'

It had been an incredible journey. They had been on the road for over a year, had overcome almost insurmountable obstacles through vast little-known regions, and had come closer to Lhasa than any other westerners for nearly fifty years. Out of their original 170 animals, only 2 horses and 6 mules reached Srinagar. Later would come recognition and honours, but as the Littledales lay in their room in Captain Trench's bungalow, they knew their real accomplishment from the expedition. They were alive.

18

Russians and Royalty

... my greatest traveller and sportsman
Edward VII

Somehow they arrived back in England in December 1895, and with the last ounce of her strength Teresa got as far as a hotel in London but no farther. Her sister Mary Peard described her condition:

On Tuesday the 22 at 6 o'clock we got a telegram from St. George from Dover to say they would be at the Metropole that evening & come to see them in the morning. It was a bitter cold day. Brough [Teresa's maid] . . . arrived at the Metropole at 12 o'clk Saturday night. . . . We sent George [Peard] to meet them at Charing X. . . . He found Teresa very weak and had to assist her with the cab. He said he felt her bones. Tanny, her dog, was with her. George went with her to the Metropole. When Brough came into her bedroom she kissed her & burst into tears & they soon got her into bed. . . . The next morning, Shuldham, Helen & I went down to see her. Of course one was shocked to see how thin & all she looked. . . . She told us what a terrible journey they had. The cold was intense. I asked her very little about her journey for when talking of it, she had such a frightened look. She said it was a journey quite unfit for a woman to take. It might do for a strong man. I asked her when she first got ill. She said the end of November [1894] she got dysentery. . . . She said sometimes she screamed all night with pain & being up so high, 19,000 odd ft. high, she could not sleep without taking Chlorodyne. . . . They got within 44 miles, two days marching of Lhasa where they were discovered by the lamas & ordered back. . . . They were within ten days of India. They tried all they could to go that way & had to go by some lake. It took them 2 months before they got to Srinagar. She was carried in a litter. . . .

'We have told Eliza [Crutchley] about her by degrees. . . . The Dr. has been here this morning & says nothing . . . but he has given impressive orders for nourishment every two hours. Dr. Sims asked for meat jelly made from beef, chicken, and calf's foot. . . . The Dr.

says she must have port wine, brandy, fish, eggs, meat, in fact anything that is nourishing. She is so extremely weak. He says every day is of importance. . . . You never saw her or can have any idea how very thin she is. I saw her arm & it was like a long stick. . . .[1]

Dr Sims also specified no visitors. Teresa needed complete quiet. He did not allow her to go home for over two months.[2]

St. George stayed at the hotel with Teresa and conducted his affairs from there. He corresponded with Albert Gunther, who had lost his position at the Natural History Museum, and he also wrote to the Royal Botanic Gardens regarding the plant specimens from Tibet. 'During the month that we were stationary . . . I pressed & dried every plant I could find. Possibly in my ignorance I may have stumbled across something new. . . . Botany is so completely out of my line that I am quite at sea.'[3] One of the grasses from the Goring Valley proved to be a new species, and it was named after St. George.

Teresa was still bedridden at the hotel on 24 February when St. George read his Tibet paper at the Royal Geographical Society. The talk was well received. Afterwards there were comments by William Thiselton-Dyer, Director of the Royal Botanic Gardens, Colonel R.G. Woodthorpe, former head of Military Intelligence in India, Sir Henry Howorth, historian on Tibet, and Delmar Morgan, who had also explored Central Asia. Morgan commented, 'From the geographical point of view, Mr. Littledale's paper is of great importance. His route – or hardly a route; it is more a track, made for himself across the most inaccessible part of Northern Tibet – lies a little to the west of the route of M. Bonvalot and Prince Henri of Orleans. . . .' Clements Markham, the president, concluded the meeting:

We now only have to thank Mr. Littledale for his most interesting paper, giving us an account of a journey which has seldom been equalled for its extraordinary hardships and the resolution with which they have been overcome. We have heard from Mr. Thiselton-Dyer that very important botanical results have come from Mr. Littledale's collection of plants, and I must express my own admiration for the splendid scientific work he has done for geography – for the way in which he got up every morning, without, I believe, missing a single one, to take observations regularly, from the time he started until he reached Leh, and his dead reckoning shows that he did his work with most remarkable accuracy.[4]

Markham's praise was deserved. Yet despite the reception his talk received, St. George was concerned about the impending publication of his paper. He wrote to J.S. Keltie, 'Will you kindly look over it & put it into <u>English</u>.'[5] He should not have worried. The paper was a classic.

The Tibet trip cemented the Littledales' reputations as explorers. They had accomplished three difficult expeditions in five years, made fine route surveys, and brought back a wide range of specimens for the museums including insects and fish. Their efforts, or at least St. George's, were recognised on 15 June 1896 at the Royal Geographical Society when Clements Markham presented the Patron's Medal to St. George. Markham said:

> In 1893, your memorable journey from Kokhan to Peking included the examination of a considerable area of previously unknown country. Last year I consider that you surpassed all your previous efforts by crossing the Kuenlun and traversing the whole of the great plateau of Tibet from north to south under difficulties of no ordinary character. It was not only as an intrepid traveller that the grant was made to you, but it was for having so diligently fixed your positions under great difficulties day by day, and for having mapped your routes with great care, that the Council was so unanimous when your name came before them for recognition.[6]

St. George responded with his usual modesty, giving credit to others.

He began getting requests for lectures, and Edward Arnold, a well-known publisher, prodded him to write a book. 'I feel sure you greatly underrate the value that would be attached to a record of your journey. Why the exciting situations and personal adventures you mention are the very things people most enjoy reading about.' When St. George refused, he wrote, 'It would surely be possible to narrate your adventures of sport and travel without going much into Central Asian politics. . . .'[7] He offered an advance of £300 but St. George turned him down. A paper in the *Geographical Journal* was one thing. A book was another. The Littledales did not need the money, they did not crave the publicity, and what St. George did not say or write would never come back to haunt them.

Letters came from friends and strangers. Lord Curzon congratulated St. George on receiving the medal. Lord Roberts wrote, 'I am glad you found the native soldiers useful. They are grand fellows.'[8] St. George must have considered the three sepoys to be first in war and last in peace.

One letter from a stranger was significant. It came from Prince Demidoff, a young man who was attached to the Russian Embassy in London. He admired St. George as a big game hunter. Demidoff wrote that he had just returned from a hunting trip to the Caucasus with the

Grand Duke Sergius Mikhailovitch in the same area where St. George had hunted. In June he planned to hunt near Mount Ararat and in November he hoped to go to the Pamirs and Tibet. He asked how the Littledales liked Joseph Abbas, their interpreter. The letter ended, 'Please excuse this note from an unknown person, but I have heard so much of you everywhere I went, that this will be my best excuse.'[9]

Elim Demidoff was descended from a family of mine owners in the Urals. Nikita Demidoff, the founder of the family fortune, built the first iron foundry in Siberia in 1701. A few years later he discovered copper in the Urals. Successive generations of Demidoffs greatly expanded the family's mines, foundries and financial assets. By the mid-nineteenth century they were possibly the richest family in Europe. Elim was married to Countess Sofia ('Sofka') Vorontzov-Dachkov, who was connected with the Russian royal family.[10] Like St. George, Demidoff had a passion for big game hunting. At the turn of the century he would write three books about his adventures.

Demidoff changed his plan to travel to the Pamirs and invited St. George to join him in the Caucasus instead. The Prince's unexpected appearance was especially timely because Nikolai de Giers, the Russian Foreign Minister, had died while the Littledales were in Tibet, and with the passing of both Sir Robert Morier in 1893 and de Giers in 1895, they had lost their most powerful patrons. The arrival of a young man who went hunting with the uncle of the Tzar and whose own family ruled large parts of Russia more than adequately filled the gap.

Although Teresa was recovering well, she did not feel strong enough to accompany St. George to the Caucasus so he went without her. He left in late August and returned in October. It was a highly successful trip. His trophy bag was decent if not spectacular, but more importantly he and the well-connected Demidoffs became lifelong friends. Prince Demidoff wrote a book describing the expedition and dedicated it to St. George.[11]

On Christmas Day 1896 Teresa received from the Royal Geographical Society a silver-gilt dog collar for Tanny for his 'pluck and fidelity'. The inscription read, 'From the Royal Geographical Society to Tanny, Who accompanied Mr. and Mrs. Littledale across Asia in 1893 and across Tibet in 1894–1895'. Teresa wrote to Dr Keltie, 'Mr. Littledale & I join "Tanny" in thanking you for the beautiful collar. We are all three very proud of the Decoration! He has so many friends that the collar is always on view & much admired. I am writing to Sir Clements Markham to thank him also.'[12] Teresa's letters were usually neat but not this one. Words are scratched out and others overrun the edge of the folded page. One can picture Teresa sitting at her desk and dashing off the note with Tanny wriggling on her lap. Her large, bold handwriting was even bigger and bolder than usual, and she signed it in letters ¾in high. As she did not bother to recopy it, she clearly was not in awe of the Royal Geographical Society.

The collar was a touching gesture but there is more to the story. Earlier St. George had written to Keltie, 'I send you by post "Tanny's" collar. The little fellow besides the Tibetan expedition went with us on the Lob Nor – Peking trip. I should like to concoct something short & pithy. Mrs. Littledale is hugely delighted that her dog is really to be decorated.'[13] While Teresa knew an award was coming, she was unaware that St. George had arranged it. The willingness of the Society to go along with the scheme is more remarkable than if the officers had done it on their own initiative. It puts a human face on the institution at the height of its pomp and glory.

During this period St. George was at the peak of his shooting prowess. In 1897 he fired a five-shot group at 100yd that was so tight it was reproduced in exact size in several publications. After his death it was reproduced again in *The Field* with the comment, 'This wonderful group of a clip of shots all touching one another will never, I should think, be excelled.'[14]

By the end of 1896 Teresa had fully recovered, and it was not long before the Littledales began thinking about their next expedition together. After her ordeal in Tibet, Teresa's willingness, if not eagerness, to participate in another expedition demonstrates how misleading her private diaries are. She wrote like a hypochondriac but behaved like an intrepid explorer.

The Littledales and Demidoffs joined forces for a trip to the Altai and Mongolia to hunt Ovis ammon, the rival of the more famous Ovis poli in bulk, weight, and mass of its horns. The horns of the poli are greater in length but the ammon is a larger animal and its horns are more massive.[15] This would be a different experience for Teresa. On all of her prior expeditions, she had been the only woman in a party of men. Now for the first time she would have a female companion.

They left in May and travelled by boat, train and river steamer to Barnaul, capital of the Altai district, then by cart and horseback to Kosh Agatch, the last village before the Siberian-Mongolian frontier. The cart ride was not without excitement. At one station the horses were replaced by five Mongol horses that had never been in harness. The headman started them out but then jumped off the moving cart, leaving 'quite a boy' as driver. Five minutes later the horses bolted off the road toward a riverbank with a 30ft drop straight down. St. George shouted to Teresa to jump out, which she did, and he followed her a few moments later after a suspense-filled delay. He asked Teresa how Tanny got out. 'I told him he had him clasped tightly in his arms when he bundled out.' After great effort, the boy managed to stop the horses only 2ft from the edge, 'a very narrow shave'.[16]

Constantly moving camp and hunting, they crossed the border into Mongolia. One day they encountered a difficult river crossing. Relying on their experience in Tibet, the Littledales improvised a raft out of camp beds and waterproof sheets. By evening everything and everyone was on the far side of the river and the Kalmucks had a new respect for their employers. The Littledales arrived home in October after another successful hunt. The party had shot 32 sheep, 2 ibex and 5 antelope. St. George bagged the largest Ovis ammon on record. The Littledales had also amassed a sizeable collection of botanical specimens.

Teresa had enjoyed the trip, but despite a comfortable camping experience, the rigors of expedition travel had again taken its toll on her health. Her sister Mary Peard came to visit. 'Teresa having a bad attack of asthma. She had had it for two months. . . . She looked <u>very</u> thin and older. . . . She is too old to go exploring.'[17] The plants were delivered to the Royal Botanic Gardens at Kew, where they were greatly appreciated. Although St. George had contributed to the effort, the primary plant collector had been Teresa.

Mrs. Littledale made an excellent collection of dried plants. . . . It comprises between two and three hundred species. Although there are probably few, if any new species, the specimens are specially valuable on account of the admirable care with which Mrs. Littledale has prepared them. In all cases where it was possible the entire plant, including root, was procured. Few professional collectors take as much pains as Mrs. Littledale has done.[18]

The year 1898 was not a good one for the Littledales. It began with the death of Mary Peard on New Year's Day of complications from pneumonia. Teresa was as stunned as everyone else but she stepped in and took charge of the funeral. St. George was not able to help. He was confined to his bed because of a riding accident. After a fall, his horse had stepped on his chest, breaking three ribs. He recovered from his broken ribs, went hunting again, and added to his score by breaking another one.[19] He passed it off lightly in a letter to Prince Christian:

I got away with the hounds & they took us very fast up to the corner of South Hill Park & then turned back left handed. Just as we met some of the field my animal, whether it was for joy at the rencontre or merely that he thought it a suitable occasion, stood on his head. I did precisely the same, irreparably damaging a new hat & breaking a fresh rib. It is a very slight affair & I intend soon to be riding again, but in the mean time 'am of all men most miserable'.[20]

Then Teresa's sister Eliza lost her husband, General Crutchley. Teresa was deeply affected because throughout most of her life Charles Crutchley had been a pillar of the family. In a way she also lost her sister, for immediately after the General's funeral Eliza began packing the contents of Sunninghill and moved to Bad Homburg, Germany, with her daughters.[21]

Meanwhile, St. George remained unwell. He may have brought some of his troubles upon himself by refusing to slow down.[22] His friends and associates bolstered his morale. He must have especially appreciated a letter from Sven Hedin, who was well known for his strong dislike of the English:

> You say there is no use for you to write the old story about my book as the papers have been full of favorable reviews but I must protest – as nothing could make me more happy than your opinion. Nobody could judge the book better than you and I put much more value in your opinion than in all the reviews taken together – as there is no other geographer living who has seen and experienced more of Asia than you have.[23]

During this time, St. George became more involved with the Royal Geographical Society. He was elected to the governing council in May 1898, but his attendance was irregular and he served for only one year. There were the inevitable controversies, two of which illustrate fundamental differences in leadership between the Littledales and other travellers in Tibet.

The most acerbic one involved Henry Savage Landor. In 1897 Landor had entered Tibet over the Himalayas from India. Early in the trip, Landor had an altercation with a Tibetan servant and punished him by making him lick his boots.[24] All of his men deserted him except for two servants, but he managed to reach Mansarowar Lake near the holy mountain of Kailas. The three men started toward Lhasa but were captured by the Tibetans, who brutally mistreated them and then expelled them back into India. Previously the Tibetans, while harsh with their own people, had shown restraint in dealing with foreigners. When Landor returned to England, he wrote newspaper articles and a two-volume book that were short on geographic detail and long on descriptions of various tortures inflicted by the Tibetans. Certainly his behaviour must have encouraged the Tibetans to mistreat him. Even so, St. George expressed to Dr Keltie his doubts about Landor's account.[25]

The other controversy involved Captain M.S. Wellby. In 1896 he and another British officer traversed the northern Chang Tang from Ladakh to Xining along the 35th parallel. They started with ten Ladakhis, including Rassul Galwan. During an altercation between two men, a Ladakhi standing nearby was gravely injured when a gun went off, blowing away the lower part of his face. Another Ladakhi became seriously ill and could barely keep up. Wellby put the injured man in the care of the sick one, gave them two animals and food, and left the two invalids behind. They were never seen again. Under the leadership of Rassul Galwan, most of the remaining Ladakhis deserted Wellby and headed for Lhasa. With great effort, Wellby, his British companion, and four other men finished the journey, eventually reaching Xining. At a meeting of the Royal Geographical Society in June 1898, Wellby read a paper about the expedition in which he described the Ladakhis abandoning him. St. George confided to Keltie that Galwan had stood by the Littledales. 'I do feel rather sore about "Gholam" [Rassul Galwan] for . . . he was one of the few Ladakhis of our party who really meant fighting when the Tibetans tried to stop us near the Tengri Nor.'[26]

The experiences of Landor and Wellby in Tibet stand in stark contrast to those of the Littledales. While there is not necessarily a direct correlation between how things are done and the results that ensue, Landor and Wellby were asking for trouble. Their overbearing manner towards their own men and the Tibetans was counterproductive to say the least.

Wellby was not Landor. He was much more experienced and competent, but like many British officers of his time, he relied upon intimidation to control his men. Moreover, he advised taking men with no experience. Experienced men 'become inflated with their own importance and vainly think that no expedition can manage without them'.[27] Rassul Galwan and the other Ladakhis had stood loyally beside the Littledales when danger threatened. A year later they abandoned Wellby in the middle of the Tibetan plateau. What was different? It was not the Ladakhis. The Littledales' manner worked in their favour. If they thought it necessary they could be forceful with their men, but the Littledales 'took care of the troops'. They gave respect and loyalty and they received respect and loyalty in return. They did more than command. They led.

Julia Turner, St. George's mother, kept a family 'Fact Book'. For the year 1899 she wrote, 'St. George and Teresa to the North Cape and Iceland.' Under 'Deaths' is the stark entry, ' "Tanny" St. G's dog'. Tanny died in July of 1899, probably from natural causes. He was buried on the grounds of Wick Hill House. Losing a beloved pet can be like losing a member of the family, especially for a childless couple. Tanny certainly was loved, and he was a source of comfort under many trying circumstances. That he accompanied the Littledales on their journeys was not unusual. Like the local people, most Central Asian explorers had dogs. Dogs were their alarm system. They provided night-time security as well as companionship. When dogs were present, it was more difficult for an intruder to approach a camp without being detected. Other explorers had fox terriers. A terrier named Ruby accompanied Wellby across Tibet. Even so, Tanny was special, as recognised by the officers of the Royal Geographical Society when they agreed to give him the silver collar. Tanny had participated in two lengthy, gruelling expeditions across Central Asia and Tibet as well as trips to the Caucasus and the Altai. His presence made the extraordinary look ordinary. The image of a fox terrier trotting across the wastes of Central Asia where explorers had crawled through the sand reinforced the impression deliberately given by the Littledales of just an English couple wandering through some of the harshest country on earth. Tanny was a symbol of ordinariness created by the Littledales, whose competence and toughness made the difficult appear easy. More than a pet was lost when Tanny died. Tanny had earned his place in the family 'Fact Book'.

By the spring of 1900, St. George was eager for another major trip. He and Demidoff discussed several destinations, ultimately deciding on Kamchatka. Demidoff had by now written two books on big game hunting in two areas of the Russian Empire, the Caucasus and the Altai, and he wanted to complete a trilogy with an account of hunting in the Far East. Kamchatka had large bears as well as Ovis nivicola, otherwise known as the Kamchatkan snow sheep. The land was little known and in 1900 it was still difficult of access. Kamchatka would provide the interesting challenge they sought.

Although Sofia Demidoff was going, Teresa decided not to participate. St. George was still in his prime but she had turned sixty and was not in robust health. Although she had not gone to the Caucasus in 1896, Kamchatka was the first major expedition she would miss.

On 19 May 1900 the Demidoffs met up with St. George in Moscow.[28] They would have to reach Vladivostok in time to catch an annual supply ship to Kamchatka. They raced for weeks by rail and riverboat across Russia and Siberia, and made it to the ship, the SS *Baikal*, with less than three hours to spare. On 23 June they finally reached Petropavlovsk, the metropolis of Kamchatka. They moved inland to Ganal, a village with eighty inhabitants and log huts, fish sheds, and a small church that was visited by a priest two or three times a year. It also had mosquitoes. '. . . their numbers were so great that the walls of almost every hut were covered and concealed by them to the depth of half an inch'.[29] The next morning they came onto an open marshy waste known as the Ganal tundra, and the mosquitoes increased further. Demidoff wrote:

> Many a tale had we heard of that interminable swamp, such as dogs and even men having been devoured there by overwhelming swarms of mosquitoes; that day's experiences were sufficient to make one believe the most incredible statements. For hardly had we ploughed our way a few yards through the tundra when clouds of these merciless insects instantly surrounded us, blinding the ponies and men. It was almost impossible to advance. . . . I kept every moment brushing off the insects from my clothes, killing thousands of them in one sweep of my gloved hand, and at one place Littledale simply fled at my approach to avoid the lumps of mosquitoes on my net. The horses streamed with blood, and it was no easy job for the men to prevent a stampede.[30]

Several days later they arrived at their hunting ground near the headwaters of the Kamchatka River. The men went out early the next morning to hunt. Demidoff tried to use his binoculars to spot sheep but mosquitoes attacked his bare hands and unprotected face. One day while he was returning to camp, he saw eight large bears wandering about on a snowfield. He guessed they were there to escape from the mosquitoes.[31]

St. George was disappointed with the hunting but he shot one ewe for the British Museum. When the party returned to Petropavlovsk, they learned that the Boxer Rebellion had broken out in China. The SS *Baikal* was expected any day, but as it would spend a month going to Vladivostok, they decided to go by way of the Amur River instead. Although Russian troops controlled both banks of the river, nearly all navigation had been closed by marauding Chinese firing on riverboats. Complete closure would have meant a long return home via Vladivostok, Japan and America. Fortunately, a riverboat got through the blockade, having run the gauntlet of Chinese fire. Several bullets had gone through the second class cabins. It took a week to go 600 miles up the Amur from Khabarovsk to Blagovestchensk. Now and then Chinese bodies floated past. The party arrived at its destination on 28 August. Across the river was the smouldering ruin of what had once been a flourishing Chinese town. Eventually they reached Moscow, where St. George parted from the Demidoffs. Although it had been a long hard trip for relatively little hunting, the three of them considered the expedition to be a success. However, it would appear that in declining to participate, Teresa had made the right choice.

St. George arrived home in late September 1900 after a four-month absence. That October he sold Oak Hill, the Liverpool estate he had inherited when he turned twenty-one. Perhaps he wanted to simplify his life at home. He was not planning to reduce his travels. Already he was preparing for another major journey. He could never sit still.

*   *   *

On 22 January 1901 Queen Victoria died. She had reigned for nearly sixty-four years and most of her subjects could not remember a time when she had not been queen. The subsequent Edwardian era was not an extension of the Victorian age. Britain was beginning to lose some of the complacency it had at the height of its empire. There were rumblings for change. The wealthy would have a large house with six or seven servants. Help was inexpensive. Their cooks received only about £30 a year and maids considerably less. The wealthy hosted each other in their homes, sometimes for weeks. Those with the most money were 'madly busy, half crazy with snobbery, trying to get themselves into the accepted upper class, to mingle at ease with the nobility and "real gentry" belonging to old landed families', or as Trollope described it, 'Growing upwards towards the light'.[32]

For many years the Littledales fit this pattern, especially Teresa. They had a large house with servants, and they constantly entertained at home when they were not visiting others. St. George was comfortable with his position in this stratified society. He may not have been nobility, but with his family background and long-time wealth, he moved easily through the ruling class. He felt as one of them. Teresa was always insecure. Throughout her married life to Scott and then to Littledale she was obsessed with money and position, even more than the general custom. This was the product of her upbringing by her mother. The Harrises may have been prominent in Canada but Canada was not England. Moreover, after John Harris died, the family had relatively little income. Although Teresa married money, in the class society that was Britain, money was not enough. Scott did not care but Teresa did. Even when she eventually moved in the highest circles, she never felt totally at ease.

A significant contribution towards the loss of complacency in Britain was the Boer War. After a long period of friction between the British and Dutch in South Africa, war broke out in October of 1899. Like many families in England, the Littledales had a personal interest in the war, especially with the participation of Willie Fletcher. After the Tibet expedition Willie had remained heavily involved with rowing, coaching the Oxford and Cambridge crews in successive years. Whichever crew he coached won the race against the other. In February 1900 he volunteered for the South African War and joined the Lancashire Hussars as a lieutenant. He was sent to South Africa and soon found himself in the thick of the fighting.

That December Fletcher demonstrated the toughness he had shown in Tibet. He was in command of a force of thirty-one men protecting a supply depot in an isolated house outside Hamelfontein near Colesberg. One day he sent out an early morning patrol that never came back. At half past 10 while he was half a mile from camp, the Boers attacked in force. Fletcher ran back to the house, rushed the men to their posts, and sent reinforcements to an outlying picket. Then he mounted his horse and galloped off toward the post. His horse was shot out from under him, which was fortunate because just as he reached the top of a hill, he saw the enemy overrun the picket.

He now had only 23 men. Slowly he and his soldiers were driven back from their outlying positions to the house. They were down to 16 riflemen. Meanwhile, the Boers increased their numbers to 250. Their commander sent a note that read, 'Sir, –You are hereby requested to surrender unconditionally, by refusal we will continue firing on your men. As you must know you are altogether surrounded.' Fletcher replied, 'I beg to acknowledge the receipt of your note. I have been put in charge here and will remain in charge until I receive orders to give up the house', an impossibility under the circumstances. He then ignored a second demand in which the Boer commander said he had sent for two cannons. The enemy came within 15yd of the house and the troopers inside braced for a final rush. The men took separate rooms, barricaded all the doors, and waited at the windows with fixed bayonets. The assault never came. The fighting went on for nearly twelve hours. In the evening the Boers asked the British to take in a couple of their wounded. Fletcher agreed but the men died from their wounds during the night. The next morning the enemy had disappeared, carrying off the rest of their wounded and leaving two dead men on the field. Willie wrote, 'They could not last the course.'

In another engagement there was a hot fight, and all the British wounded were on the wrong side of a river. Fletcher found an old boat, patched it up, and single-handedly rowed the wounded across the river through a swift current, earning him the title, 'Admiral of the Orange River'. He won the D.S.O. for his action at Hamelfontein, and in September 1901 King Edward presented it to him personally.[33]

The beginning of the Edwardian era represented a change for the Littledales, especially for Teresa. In the future she and St. George would continue to travel extensively together but her expedition years were over. In 1901 St. George was planning another expedition. Teresa would stay home. In March he wrote to Thiselton-Dyer, Director of the Royal Botanic Gardens, to obtain a lightweight flower press. He wondered if Kew had any interest in plants from the Yulduz Valley in the Chinese Tien Shan as he was thinking about going there in the autumn.[34]

Two months later he wrote to Sir Thomas Sanderson about his proposed plans to visit Kuldja and the Yulduz 'for the purpose of making zoological & other collections'. He asked Sanderson to obtain permission from the Russians once again to travel along the Transcaspian Railway, and he also requested an introduction to the Governor General at Tashkent for assistance in travelling beyond there.[35] Sanderson, in his position at the Foreign Office, was still in charge of intelligence. St. George's letter to Thiselton-Dyer would indicate he was just out to gather plants and animals, but Sanderson must have asked him to keep his eyes open regarding the Russians in that remote part of the world.

He left England alone in early July 1901 and was gone for four months. There is little information about his long trip. He took the Transcaspian Railway to Tashkent and then travelled overland across the Chinese border to Kuldja. After obtaining supplies and hiring local guides, he went south into the Kok Su Valley in the Tien Shan. It was another productive trip. The list of plants St. George collected for Kew filled three typed pages and the hunting was extremely successful. He obtained lynx, bear, sheep, Siberian roe deer and the Asiatic ibex. The zoologists at the Natural History Museum decided his specimens included a new variety of sheep and they named it after him, calling it Ovis littledalei. The ibex included three heads of record dimensions but the largest would not remain in his possession for long.[36]

The trip had its exciting moments. In a letter to Thiselton-Dyer, St. George wrote, 'I am sorry to say that the flower press you kindly lent me came to an untimely end. Its horse fell down a place and was killed and the press was damaged beyond repair.' Thiselton-Dyer praised him for the quality of his specimens. 'You are really a master in the art of botanical collections. The loss of the press is not of the slightest consequence.'[37] Teresa's meticulous plant-collecting abilities had rubbed off on her husband.

St. George had a long friendship with Prince Christian, husband of Princess Helena, the third daughter of Queen Victoria. For several decades the two men carried on an extensive correspondence, and their letters record the growth of their friendship over the years. They shared a basic modesty as well as common interests in shooting and fox hunting. In December St. George wrote to the prince:

We had some people staying over Sunday & they came out to see me start this morning. It was hard to say whether horse or rider came in for the most admiration!! 5 minutes afterwards the horse with head and tail well up returned pursued in another 5 minutes by its owner on foot with a dirty back. So galling to ones pride. To keep the affair a dead secret a complete change was necessary.[38]

The prince was responsible for one of the Littledales' most memorable events. On 22 January 1902 the Court Circular in *The Times* reported, 'The King, attended by Lord Churchill and Major-General Sir Stanley Clarke, left Windsor Castle before luncheon on Saturday and went for a drive in his motor-car. The weather was fine and seasonable. His Majesty and suite returned to the Palace about 20 minutes to 5 o'clock. The King gave a dinner party at the Castle on Saturday evening.' What the account did not mention was that King Edward had visited the Littledales.

On the preceding Thursday they had received a telegram from Windsor Castle stating that the King wanted to come for lunch on Saturday, only two days away. It caught them by surprise and threw them into a flurry of activity.[39] Teresa described the occasion in a letter to her sister Amelia:

The King notices everything, nothing escapes him. He had not been in the house ten minutes, when he took me in to luncheon and said as we passed down the room 'you have some very beautiful brocades and embroideries in your house.'. . .

When the King arrived St. George met him on the door step and knelt on one knee and kissed his hand so gracefully. . . . I stood a little farther in and made my deepest curtsey and kissed his hand. . . . He examined everything in the house and when he was looking at a piece of iron work in the drawing room he said to St. George, 'I see Mr. Littledale you are not only my greatest traveller and sportsman, but you are also a connoisseur.'. . .

We had thirty people to luncheon that day. Luckily my cook never lost her head and did it well. The King arrived at 1.45 and did not leave until after 4 o'clock. All seem to be of the opinion that had he not enjoyed himself he would not have stayed so long.

Prince Christian wrote today to tell St. George that he must attend the Levee on 11th February and expressed his wish to present him. I also have been told that I must attend 'A Court'. I have asked Lady Emily Van de Weyer if she will present me. . . . How pleased Mamma would have been for it is an honour to entertain the King.

He expressed the pleasure it would be to him to accept one of St. George's horns, so, of course, the largest has to go to Windsor Castle. . . . It is rather a wrench to part with the biggest, but I tell St. George Windsor Castle will be there long after Wick Hill House has disappeared. . . .

Lord Churchill told me we must write our names in the Kings and Queens books at Windsor Castle so of course I went over on Monday and did so, and when they move to London I am told to do so at Marlborough House. . . . Fancy their caring whether we wrote our names.[40]

Teresa had finally reached the light.

The King had selected his host's prize trophy, which he had just brought back from the Tien Shan. St. George had it remounted on a new shield, appropriately re-inscribed, and sent it off. Although St. George felt honoured, he was more forthright in a letter to Baron Speck von Sternburg: 'Edward VII came over to lunch & walked off with my best Ibex. . . .'[41] Nevertheless, the Littledales' connection with the royal family was to continue for many years with numerous invitations to events at Windsor.

St. George maintained his interest in collecting both flora and fauna. In July 1902 he went to the border area of the Kopet Dagh (mountains) in Northern Persia, an area he had visited in 1888. Both he and Prince Demidoff obtained significant heads of both ibex and sheep from 'Russian Turkestan'. As St. George in his private correspondence referred to the area as Northern Persia, his reference to Russia may have been for diplomatic reasons. He returned to England before the end of August.[42]

Because of a severe drought, his plant collecting was less successful than before. However, one aspect of the trip was an unqualified success. Like Teresa, he enjoyed acquiring art objects for Wick Hill House. While passing through Warsaw on his way home, he fell in love with a sixteenth-century Flemish tapestry 60ft long, depicting the months with planets and moons. St. George was stunned when he heard the price. He returned to England, described his find to Teresa, and the two of them, now equally excited, went back to Warsaw for another look, bringing a tapestry expert from the British Museum. When they arrived, both seller and tapestry had vanished. It took a month to locate the owner. After prolonged haggling, the Littledales purchased the tapestry for an unknown amount and installed it at Wick Hill House. As the tapestry was in two sections, they wrapped it around their two drawing rooms. St. George wrote, 'The stitch is unusually fine and the preservation is extraordinary. There is such an amount of detail in it that each time one looks one discovers something fresh.'[43] It became the Littledales' favourite possession.

The Littledales' lives were more than just one adventure after another. They had progressed from big game hunting for sport to the collection of zoological specimens of all kinds for the Natural History Museum and plants for the Royal Botanic Gardens. Their priorities had then shifted to map-making and intelligence. Now they were about to enter a new phase. St. George wanted to hunt red deer that had been exported from England to New Zealand in the 1850s and had thrived there. In early February 1903 the Littledales sailed from Liverpool for New York. Upon their arrival, they caught the first train to San Francisco and immediately boarded the *Sierra* for New Zealand.

In New Zealand the hunting was successful but the trip held greater significance than just the collection of more trophies. It occurred to St. George that the landscape and climate were appropriate for many types of game animals, especially certain deer and goats. He would now deal with the collection of live animals. He suggested that New Zealand import moose, Caucasian deer, Carpathian deer, Asiatic wapiti and ibex. The New Zealand government liked the idea. T.E. Donne, Superintendent of the New Zealand Department of Tourism, shared St. George's enthusiasm and asked him to do his best to obtain the animals.[44]

The Littledales travelled on to Java and Japan. On their way home they crossed the United States again and visited President Theodore Roosevelt at the White House. It is likely the two men were brought together by Baron Speck von Sternburg, now German Ambassador to the United States and a friend of the president. St. George presented his idea of exporting game animals to New Zealand, and the president offered to contribute American wapiti (elk).[45] The efforts of the two world travellers and hunters to procure game for New Zealand became the basis of a long friendship.

In England St. George persuaded the Duke of Bedford to send six Himalayan tahr from his wild animal collection at Woburn. Five of the animals reached New Zealand safely and were released near the Hermitage in the Southern Alps.[46] The American wapiti were a more complex undertaking, but after some complicated international negotiations, twenty elk were put in special crates designed by Donne and sent by rail from Washington DC to San Francisco, where they were eventually loaded onto a ship. Finally the elk began their 6,000-mile odyssey across the Pacific. All was going well until they approached New Zealand, when the ship encountered a violent storm. It was tossed about by huge waves, and two of the elk fell and died of broken spines. In March 1905 the eighteen survivors were released at the head of George Sound on the South Island. The efforts of Littledale, Donne and Roosevelt were successful. The herd thrived and spread over Fiordland.[47]

During these years St. George and Prince Christian continued to correspond. As they became more comfortable with each other, their bantering increased, just as it had earlier between St. George and Albert Gunther at the Natural History Museum. The prince accepted an invitation to Wick Hill House to compare recent hunting trophies. St. George wrote, 'But what I am specially looking forward to with great joy is making you break and flagrantly break a certain commandment when you see our 16th century tapestry.'[48]

By the spring of 1904 St. George was once again getting restless. Two friends had returned from a trip to Alaska with two fine moose, and he longed to do the same. He left for Alaska in July 1904, visiting President Roosevelt along the way. Teresa stayed home.[49] His destination was the mountains above Turnagain Arm off Cook Inlet on the Kenai Peninsula. The hunting was disappointing and as in Kamchatka, the few sheep were too tame to provide good sport. However, one day he happened upon a fine specimen:

> He came feeding so close to the rock behind which I was hiding, that a vision appeared of a sudden spring, a rough & tumble, & an Ovis Dali in the Zoological at Washington. I unbuckled my gloves & belt in preparation but at the very last moment he sauntered away. He had given me an intensely interesting half hour so I took off my cap to him & we parted friends.[50]

It was a scene reminiscent of his 1891 encounter with the great aurochs in the Caucasus.

St. George was concerned about the rampant killing of moose and sheep to feed men and dogs at the mining camps. 'The position in Alaska rather resembles Russia where the law breaking peasants have a saying "The heavens are high & the Czar is far off", & there is no doubt that the only game wardens who will be popular in Alaska are those who don't enforce the law.'[51]

While St. George was in Alaska, his mother died in Liverpool. Julia Turner was buried at St John's Church, Knotty Ash, Liverpool, next to her two husbands. Although her death could not have been totally unexpected, it must have affected Teresa as well as St. George. Both of them had been close to her. It appears that unlike members of the Harris family, Mrs Turner had never criticised Teresa and seemed to understand her. Teresa, in turn, was more open with Mrs Turner than with her own family.

In March 1905 the Littledales left England for Japan and China and were gone for six months. Afterwards St. George resumed his long trips without Teresa. A journey to Newfoundland in September 1907 was to be his last significant hunting trip.[52] On the way home he described his experience in a letter to Baron Speck von Sternburg from the *Lusitania*. As in Kamchatka and Alaska, he did not find the hunting challenging enough for good sport. The caribou were too tame and simply ignored him. Nonetheless, he considered his efforts a success. 'A very fine stag was silly enough to let me have a shot at him. As far as Ward's book of head measurements goes, it is longer & wider & as thick as anything mentioned there unless my memory is at fault.' The trip had its adventures:

We had two or three days when life was strenuous enough to suit even the President. We had only a canvas sheet (2 Micmacs & myself) with a fire in front. Theoretically it is a perfect arrangement provided you camp in thick woods & the wind does not change, but the 22nd October we had a blizzard right round the compass & we had to shift fire & camp 5 times during the night. On one occasion the Indian carried the red hot ashes in his hands. On my remonstrating he said, 'My fingers are too cold to burn.'[53]

In December 1907 St. George turned 56. Although it was not a milestone birthday for him, it reminds one that Teresa had turned 56 in August 1895 during their attempt to reach Lhasa. Most people would have given up expedition travel after surviving such a harrowing experience but not Teresa. Two years later she had joined the Demidoffs on the long journey to the Altai. Yet by the time St. George reached her age, he was no longer undertaking major expeditions. Despite Teresa's seeming frailty all her life as well as the comments in her private diaries, her adventurous spirit did not flag, and the comparison to her husband at the same age is a measure of her toughness.

In June 1908 St. George arranged a hunting trip to a shooting ground in the Caucasus that he and Prince Demidoff had purchased a few years earlier. The territory was still wild. One day he was stalked by bandits as he was stalking game, but 'after a somewhat exciting morning had the satisfaction of seeing the enemy decamp'. He obtained a number of trophies, some of which ended up in his study at Wick Hill House, and he donated an East Caucasian tur and a chamois to the Natural History Museum. He also collected plants for Kew.[54]

The following summer Teresa turned 70. Although St. George was only 57, both of them were showing signs of slowing down. However, their adventurous lives would never grow dull. There was more excitement to come.

The Clock Years

. . . a hundred lectures in his mind.
E. Rosslyn Mitchell, MP

Now that the Littledales were no longer making expeditions to distant lands, they found a new challenge, especially St. George. They had a grandfather clock, a year clock that could run for thirteen months without rewinding. In March 1913 when it was time for the clock to be rewound, St. George asked Prince Christian do the honours.[1] The event marked the beginning of a tradition. Each year a prominent person wound the clock, and beginning with the second year, the winder signed a special book. That year it was Lord Roberts. Initially winders were friends, but as the years went by, getting the clock wound would grow into an ever grander project. The pattern of the clock winding mirrored the Littledales' expeditions, the challenge increasing as St. George stalked more and more difficult prey. The willingness of the leading men of the day to wind the clock indicates that the Littledales were known in the highest circles.

At first the designated winders came to Wick Hill House, but during this period the Littledales acquired a car and hired a chauffeur, Leonard Solesbury. When the winder could not come to the clock, the clock went to the winder, and Solesbury would drive the Littledales and the 7-ft clock to London or elsewhere in England. Later they would put the car on a ferry to the Continent and have Solesbury drive the clock through Europe.

In February 1914 Albert Gunther died. By the time he left the Natural History Museum in 1895, he and St. George had become such good friends that they must have stayed in frequent contact. Gunther's humorous bantering with Littledale belied his status as a distinguished scholar, and his reputation continued to flourish in his later years.

A few months later, outside events began to intrude into the Littledales' insular world. The war that would shatter Europe caught its citizens unawares, including St. George and Teresa, who left in the middle of July with Solesbury to go on a motoring trip through northern Germany. They sailed to Hamburg and drove to Danzig. Although war had been declared between Austria and Serbia, the Littledales did not know it was about to break out between Germany and Russia. However, they sensed trouble and decided to return to England immediately. On 31 July they drove to Berlin, where they obtained a passport and a full tank of petrol. They were advised to leave through Holland but the road was blocked at Brandenburg and they were arrested, then released and allowed to return to Berlin. By now they needed cash but could not change even a £5 note. Afraid they would run short of money, the Littledales moved from their hotel to a cheap boarding house, where their kindly German landlady treated them as guests and told them not to worry about paying her until the war was over. 'She gets a silver salver with an inscription from us directly peace is signed.'[2]

Early the next morning St. George and Solesbury went to the British Consulate to get a separate passport for Solesbury. When they arrived, they learned that Germany and Britain were at war. Solesbury was arrested, but at the police station an official reviewed St. George's passport, gave German documents to both men, and let them go.

Then Baroness Speck came to their aid. Baron Speck von Sternburg had died in 1908. Now the widow of their old friend informed them that a special train would be leaving the next morning to evacuate the staff of the British Embassy, and they could take the same train if they got a special pass from the German Foreign Office. At 1 o'clock in the morning none other than Dr Arthur Zimmermann, the Under Secretary of State for Germany, arrived at their bedroom in the little boarding house with the pass they needed. He told them he could not trust a messenger with the task. Then he left to attend to more important duties.[3] The Littledales and Leonard Solesbury caught the special train and made it back to England safely.

In 1915 Lord Curzon wound the clock at Wick Hill House. That December St. George invited Theodore Roosevelt to wind the clock the following year and Roosevelt accepted. Later St. George even made out the shipping label but reason prevailed. 'The fear of submarines has prevented my risking the clock on the Atlantic this year but hope to trespass on your good nature in 1917.'[4]

Roosevelt never did wind the clock. St. George's friend Rudyard Kipling stepped in as substitute winder. Kipling wrote into the clock book:

> Also time running into years,
> a hundred places left behind,
> and men from both hemispheres,
> discussing things of every kind.

Thus began the custom of having the winder add a few appropriate words or a quotation for which he was famous.

The war on the Western Front became a bloody stalemate, and although supplies were still getting across the Atlantic, the German submarine campaign was tightening the noose on Britain. Teresa had relatives fighting in the war including Eliza Crutchley's grandson Victor, a lieutenant in the navy, and Willie Fletcher returned to the army, this time to the 2/6th Rifle Battalion, The King's Liverpool Regiment.[5] Some of the early training took place at Allerton, his family home. In 1915 the 2/6th Liverpool Rifles moved to Canterbury and then to Margate. Willie was promoted to Lieutenant-Colonel and given command of the unit. The battalion was sent to France in February 1917, and within a few days the men were in the trenches near Armentières. Willie was everywhere:

> One of the special delights of the Commanding Officer was crawling about exposed parts of the sector by day. It was not only his anxiety to acquire an accurate knowledge of his sector . . . he wanted to find out where every derelict trench led to, what secrets lay hidden in those areas of abandoned chaos in which the sector abounded, and no one could ever have known his sector better than did Colonel Fletcher. . . . Major Geddes more than once accompanied him on these excursions, as he crawled and wriggled on his stomach from place to place. . . . Home the pair would come at last, with the perspiration streaming down their faces. 'Well, that is the best afternoon I have had since the war started!' the Commanding Officer would exclaim, as he sat mopping his face and drinking large cups of tea.[6]

The intensity of the fighting increased. On the night of 29 July at the beginning of the Battle of Passchendaele, the battalion began its regular relief rotation out of the front line. It had reached Armentières when it was struck by a heavy bombardment. Mixed with the high explosives were hundreds of shells containing a new gas that filled the streets and the ruined houses. It was mustard gas. Breathing it was like inhaling red-hot air and it choked the soldiers immediately. Even after an area appeared clear and there was little odour of gas, it affected the eyes. Exhausted men fell asleep, and when they woke up they were blind. Willie was tireless in his efforts to find his men. Nearly everyone was gassed, including Willie Fletcher. He was hospitalised for over a month and then returned to the front in a greatly weakened condition.

Meanwhile, St. George developed serious eye troubles and both he and Teresa feared he was going blind in his left eye. Teresa wrote to Prince Christian, who was comforting and supportive:

. . . you can very well be able to get on through life with one eye, as I know from experience. I lost my eye on Boxing Day, 1891. I have written and read a great deal since then. I have shot a great many pheasants and rabbits, have hunted a great deal. . . . From the beginning I made up my mind not to think of the loss of my eye but to go on if possible as formerly. . . . I hope you don't mind my writing all this but I thought the account of my experience might give Mr. Littledale some confidence.[7]

In the autumn of 1917 St. George had eye surgery. Teresa was so distraught that she wrote to Prince Christian again. He replied with a consoling note. It was his last letter to the Littledales. He died three weeks later on 28 October.[8]

The death of Prince Christian was a blow to the Littledales, especially to St. George. Their common interests had continued to bring them closer as the years went by. Twenty years older than St. George, the Prince was more than a friend and a connection to the royal family. He had served as a mentor to St. George. Despite poor health at the end of his life, he was more concerned about his friend's well-being than his own. Like his wife, he was loyal to family and friends. He was a decent man.

The war was coming to a climax. Victor Crutchley had been assigned to the battleship *Centurion* and had fought in the Battle of Jutland. Later he volunteered for the raids on the German U-boat ports of Zeebrugge and Ostend. He was assigned to the *Vindictive*, a block ship to be sunk in the Ostend Canal. Both the captain and the second-in-command were killed on board and Crutchley had to take over, scuttling the ship under a hail of fire. For his leadership and valour Victor Crutchley, Queen Victoria's godson and namesake, won the Victoria Cross.

Teresa and St. George were thrilled by the exploits of Eliza's grandson but they worried about Willie Fletcher, who kept alternating between the front lines and hospitalisation. He never fully recovered his health, and in July 1918, on his own volition, he stepped down as Battalion Commander because he was afraid of suffering another breakdown during action, endangering his men. 'His whole heart and soul were wrapped up in the 2/6th, and leaving it must have been painful to him indeed.'[9] Willie's war had ended.

On 11 November the armistice was signed and the fighting stopped. The killing was over but the dying continued. After Fletcher returned from France, he was elected Chairman of the Committee of Management of the Henley Regatta for 1919. His lungs never healed from the gas attacks of 1917 and on 14 February 1919 he died at

Allerton of bronchial pneumonia. He was buried in the family plot at St Nicholas Church, a little chapel at Halewood, near Liverpool.

The obituaries and stories that appeared after Fletcher's death mentioned the D.S.O. he had won in the Boer War and his service in the First World War, but the heaviest emphasis was on his extraordinary rowing career. It was summarised on a bronze plaque with a relief of his profile and placed in the Oxford University boathouse by the oarsmen of both Oxford and Cambridge.[10] However, Fletcher was far more than a champion oarsman. His strength, toughness and courage had been critical factors on the Tibet expedition. The qualities he had displayed appeared in the Boer War and again during the First World War. Captain C.E. Wurtzburg, the battalion adjutant, summed it up:

> As a Commanding Officer many found him hard and exacting, but he was even more exacting and hard on himself. . . . Wonderfully strong himself, he impressed others with his own strength; lofty in ideals, he led others to a higher plane. Nothing that was mean or selfish, that was not strictly true and honest, would he tolerate for a moment; and never was a man more outspoken in his condemnation of anything that was not right in the highest sense. . . . Colonel Fletcher represented the highest type of British gentleman. . . .[11]

St. George had chosen well.

There is a mystery regarding the relationship between Willie Fletcher and the Littledales. Willie wrote near the end of his Tibet diary that they never had an argument, but after they separated there was very little communication between them, at least not in surviving records. Despite numerous opportunities, it appears that St. George never asked his nephew to join him on any more trips. Willie would probably have been available for hunting trips in the Caucasus after the Boer War, but there is no evidence he was ever invited. Even more telling is Teresa's silence. Her letters tend to be chatty and full of gossip, but for the rest of her life, in her many letters to relatives in England and Canada, she never mentions Willie again. What could have happened? After the Tibet expedition, the return to England would take many weeks, and St. George could have used Willie's help to get Teresa home. It is unlikely that he would have turned his uncle down. However, it is possible that for some reason St. George, or more likely Teresa, did not want him to accompany them. We will never know the answer.

Teresa, the youngest in a large family, began losing her siblings in increasing numbers. In 1910 Eliza Crutchley died, and by the end of 1916 Teresa was the only surviving Harris sister. In June 1919 she was feeling her age:

This is a very busy week here 'Ascot Race Week' not that it affects me, for I positively refused to go. St. George has gone alone. . . . He has promised to describe accurately how <u>un</u>dressed all the ladies are! My 80th birthday on the 12th of next August does not make me so keen about amusement & I get tired. . . . They all say I do not look as old as I am. If so! I think it is because I am so thin & slight & active, but the years are there all right.[12]

The stalking of clock winders was one activity that continued to enliven the Littledales' lives. Now St. George and Leonard Solesbury would deliver the clock to the winder. In June 1919 the Rt. Hon. David Beatty, Admiral of the Fleet, responded to an intermediary whom St. George had used to approach him. 'I, of course, will be glad to wind up the clock and write "The German Flag shall be, etc".' He wound the clock on 7 July.*[13]

In 1921 St. George pursued Lord Douglas Haig, Commander-in-Chief of the British Army in the First World War. Lord Osborne Beauclerk, a friend of St. George's, served as intermediary. Back came the reply, 'My Dear Obbey, I am always delighted to get a letter from you but please tell your old friend that my many engagements prevent me from visiting Bucks to wind up clocks!' Lord Beauclerk forwarded the reply to St. George with the comment, 'My dear old friend Littledale, Enclosed from Ld. Haig is not encouraging. I wrote <u>Berks</u> distinctly not Bucks. . . . I don't want enclosed back. Gum it on the clock if you like!'[14] Sometimes the wind shifts and the game gets away.

The following year St. George fell back on an acquaintance he had known since at least 1914, Sir William Edward Goschen, British Ambassador to Germany when the war broke out and on whose train the Littledales had escaped. What he wrote in the clock book had more than the usual significance: ' "Just for a word neutrality – just for a scrap of paper – England was going to make war against a sister nation who desired nothing more than to remain on good terms with her." German Chancellor, August 4, 1914. W.E.G.' Later, when it was questioned whether 'scrap of paper' was actually uttered by the German Chancellor, Goschen's entry in the clock book was used as evidence.[15]

In 1919 St. George became that epitome of the establishment, a Justice of the Peace. Percy Crutchley, Eliza's son, had been a JP since he was 24, eventually becoming Chief Magistrate in Reading, and it was he who brought St. George into the system. For centuries Justices of the Peace met four times a year in 'Quarter Sessions', and originally had police and governmental as well as judicial functions. They came from

---

* 'The German flag is to be hauled down at sunset and is not to be again hoisted without permission.'

the gentry and were the leaders of their counties. By 1919 they had only a judicial role and served as the lowest court, handling petty criminal and civil matters. The justices were not lawyers but they obtained legal advice from their clerk, who was versed in the law and was also the court administrator. The JPs largely determined questions of fact that required common sense along with knowledge and experience of the world at large. St. George's expeditions were valuable training for a judge. He was constantly settling disputes among the men, and he must have brought to his new position a highly refined ability to read body language, a skill developed through years of dealing with people with whom he could not directly communicate. As a magistrate he established a reputation for being thoughtful, kind and judicious.[16]

At home St. George continued to lead a life best described as that of an English country gentleman even though his income did not come from land, and the size of the Wick Hill House estate was relatively limited compared to estates of the landed gentry. Relatives remembered him from the 1920s as being fairly tall with a moustache, and he always dressed in tweed suits or plus fours. He did not drink alcohol, somewhat surprising for his place and time, but he offered it to his guests. Dorothea Fletcher, who was married to his nephew Harold Fletcher, remembered him well. 'Uncle Georgie took great trouble in being charming. Goes down terribly well. Always enchanting to me.' Mrs Fletcher described Teresa as 'indomitable'. She remembered her as a moderately tall woman who always dressed in black. She was nice but 'not a cosy sort of person'. Although Teresa got along with people, she had a cool relationship with her sister-in-law, Edith Fletcher, and St. George had often visited his favourite sister without her.

Wick Hill House was a three-storey structure on the top of a hill with a few outbuildings, stables and fields. Henry Rix, the butler, supervised the staff, which included housekeeper Eleanor Ablitt, some maids and several gardeners. The furnishings could charitably be described as eclectic. There were hunting trophies everywhere, and the house was crammed with treasures gathered in a lifetime of wandering through foreign bazaars. One family member commented that staying there was like living inside the Arabian Nights.[17] An enormous carved Buddha sat on a 3-ft pedestal under an arch. (Somewhere in the house were twenty small statues of Hindu gods and goddesses that the British Museum would subsequently reject as obscene.) All of these objects held meaning for the Littledales, especially as they grew older. Teresa wrote, 'They are a journal when one gets them home and a great pleasure.' St. George was nervous about burglars and had the entire house wired with alarms. He also kept a loaded revolver at his bedside.[18]

Central Asia continued to be of significant interest to the Littledales. St. George was an early member of the Central Asian Society, of which Sir Francis Younghusband was a founder. In addition, various old Central Asia hands would drop by Wick Hill House from time to time. Among the most surprising visitors were Robert and Katherine Lee Barrett, two Americans who showed up unexpectedly in the early 1920s carrying a large manuscript.

The Barretts were a wealthy couple from Chicago. Before the First World War Robert Barrett had travelled through Central Asia for two years with Rassul Galwan as his sirdar. He had taught English to Galwan, listened to his stories, and encouraged him to write a book about his experiences. The result was the manuscript the Barretts presented to St. George. He did not bother to read it because he doubted his Ladakhi friend could write English. Later he wrote, 'I have nothing whatever to do with the book. . . . I implored the Yankee who apparently godfathered the work not to publish it, thinking it would only appeal to people who had travelled with caravans in Central Asia. . . .'[19] However, St. George did write to Rassul Galwan and enclosed pictures of Teresa, Tanny and himself.

Galwan responded in July 1923 from Kashmir. He was about to set off with the Barretts on a long trip to Baltistan and Ladakh. He brought St. George up to date on his life since their Tibet adventure. His wife, whom the Littledales had met, had died. They had had four children but a son and daughter died young. His oldest daughter was married and had a son. In 1914, when he returned to Leh after a trip with Dr De Filippi, his mother and his younger daughter had died, and a year later his older daughter and grandchild died, leaving him alone. He remarried, had two more sons, and was rejoicing in his new family. He added, 'I was very sorry to heard [sic] that Mr. Fletcher died. He was a brave man in our journey he was a great help with the bad mules.' He reminded them that Teresa and Willie had given him English lessons at Cherchen, and he said Barrett had taught him English for the book. 'I hope you and Mrs. Littledall like this my style may be understand. I was very glad to see the catur [picture] of Tanny. I hope he be well and old. . . . Now I am getting an old man and my bear[d] is white. . . . I hope now you and Mrs Littledall will read my full story very soon. Please give my many many Sallam to Mrs Littledall and to Sir Francis Younghusband.'[20]

A few weeks later the Littledales heard from Katherine Lee Barrett from Gund, a small village on the Kashmir side of the Zoji La. 'I am wondering if you made camp here on your way to Srinagar when Mrs. Littledale was so ill? [They did.] Rassul was made very happy by a letter from you with pictures of medal and necklace, the giving of which he heartily approved, "to wise dog Tanny, who go in dangers place".'[21]

Servant of Sahibs, Galwan's book, came out later that year. Sir Francis Younghusband wrote the introduction. To St. George's astonishment, it sold well. The publishers asked him to correct any mis-statements he noticed as they were going to publish a second edition. 'There is a large demand in U.S.A! & I was wrong as usual.' He finally read the book and was impressed with the accuracy of Galwan's account. Borrowing one of Galwan's phrases, he wrote in the flyleaf of a family copy, 'There is very little "lie matter" in the book concerning our party.' He also sent a copy to Lord Curzon, who thanked him with the comment, '. . . it will add a new terror to travel in Asia. Caravan bashis or attendants in general are all the while taking notes about ourselves.'[22]

During the 1920s St. George became active in the affairs of the Wokingham Lecture Society. Founded in 1918 by Ernest Seward Whaley, it was a great local success. St. George became an enthusiastic member and made himself useful in any way he could. In addition he sometimes hosted the out-of-town speakers at Wick Hill House. He kept a low profile, but in January 1924 he was persuaded to take the chair for a lecture by Francis Kingdon-Ward entitled 'Travel and Plant Hunting in Eastern Tibet'.[23]

In 1926 St. George arranged for Sir Charles Bell to give a lecture at Wokingham. Bell, the political agent in Sikkim for many years, was a friend and advisor to the Thirteenth Dalai Lama. He went on a mission to Lhasa in 1921 and was an eminent Tibetan scholar. Littledale invited George Macartney to Wick Hill for the occasion. The former British representative in Kashgar was living in Jersey. He declined the invitation but added, 'The sight of your handwriting brings back pleasant memories of old Kashgar days. And what wouldn't I give to go back again to those early times when you & Mrs. Littledale, by your fleeting passages through Kashgar, lent a temporary brightness to old Chini Bagh. All that seems now as if it belonged to a previous existence.'[24]

Many Wokingham speakers experienced the hospitality of the Littledales and they never failed to be impressed. In December 1926 E. Rosslyn Mitchell, a Scottish MP, wrote to Teresa:

. . . it is not the lecture that I think of now. It is the atmosphere of an English country house, shored with trophies of many a hunter land, the treasures of craftsmanship of so many races but above all the gentleness and warmth of heart of its owners and <u>their friends</u>! Altogether it was a remarkable series of new experiences for me, even to the fox-hunt in that quaint village, the beautiful horses, the eager hounds and the keen riders in the exhilaration of the runs through those fields. Your husband fascinates me. I would gladly have listened to him talk of the world that is unknown to us, for hours. Indeed I feel how foolish it seemed for me to be giving the lecture when he was about with a hundred lectures in his mind.[25]

As the years went by, St. George had to cut back on his fox hunting, but as he had always enjoyed salmon fishing, it became his main recreational pastime. Almost every year he went fishing on the Spey in Scotland, and in 1923 he went to Iceland. 'I had a very amusing trip . . . & we caught tons of salmon, 752 I believe to be accurate. The fish were lively & fought very hard. . . . I took a Scotch gillie with me & he opened his mouth wide at the number of salmon caught but said if the fish had as much room to play about in as in the Spey, it like be the man who would be tired first.'[26]

Teresa turned 84 in August. The difference in age between her and her husband was becoming more apparent, leading to town gossip involving one of their friends. Cecily Arkwright was a descendant of Richard Arkwright, whose spinning machine had helped usher in the Industrial Revolution. Miss Arkwright was in her fifties and was renowned locally as a gardener. She would ride around town on a bicycle with a sack in the front basket. She wore an old Panama hat in summer and winter along with a well used Burberry. Once a week she went to Wick Hill House for lunch and to play tennis, and was always so well dressed during those visits that the striking difference from her customary appearance caused the town tongues to wag.[27] St. George gave her a copy of *Servant of Sahibs* with the inscription, 'C. Arkwright from S'George Littledale, Xmas 1923'. That does not prove much. Miss Arkwright would hardly be expected to show up at Wick Hill House in her gardening clothes. Moreover, she was also a family friend of the Crutchleys. Besides, further events would show that St. George was as devoted to Teresa as his wife was to him. On the other hand, in his will, written after Teresa died, he left to Cecily Arkwright the considerable sum of £500.

Throughout this period the Littledales continued to entertain friends and distinguished visitors, even including Neville Chamberlain.[28] And there was always the clock. In 1924 St. George managed to persuade King George and Queen Mary to have lunch at Wick Hill House and wind the clock. The arrival of the royal couple was witnessed by a young woman who described it sixty years later. At that time 'there was little crime in Bracknell, only occasional drunks on a Saturday night'. The town had two policemen, brothers named Bailey. Nora Pond was riding her bicycle past Wick Hill House when she noticed one of the Bailey brothers standing outside the entrance to the property. 'He said, "Would you like to see the King and Queen?" I said, "Yes, are they coming here?" "Yes, it's all very secret but they are going to the

Littledales to lunch and to wind the clock. . . ." So I waited. Rather a long time. Something had gone wrong.' For security reasons, the Windsor authorities had the police bring them up the back drive. 'Of course they couldn't do it with a Rolls. . . .' The limousine was too long to make the sharp turn and got stuck. The chauffeur and footman climbed out. The King graciously raised his bowler to Nora but Queen Mary, 'dressed in cream', was sputtering. Eventually the car made the turn and the royal couple entered Wick Hill House. The King wound the clock and signed the book, putting under his signature, 'Wake up England!'[29] The following year the Littledales drove the clock to Rome, where it was wound by Benito Mussolini. He did not put any words of wisdom under his signature.[30]

In 1925 Edward Harris died in Canada. His brother George had predeceased him by two years. Teresa recognised that George had devoted much of his life to straightening out the difficulties created by his brother. It is somewhat ironic that Edward, having made so much trouble for his entire family, outlived all of his brothers and sisters except for the youngest. He had caused Teresa much distress with his gross mishandling, if not outright taking of her money. It was Edward who had said their mother would be lucky to marry off Teresa, the plainest of the Harris sisters. Later he had developed a higher opinion of her, commenting with a tone of surprise on what a smart woman she had become, the only Harris to marry well twice and travel the world with both husbands. Now Teresa was the last of her Harris generation.

The 27th of February 1927 marked the Littledales' golden wedding anniversary. There is no record of how or even whether they celebrated the occasion, but with so many of their relatives having predicted disaster if they got married, Teresa and St. George must have considered their long and happy marriage to be one of their finest achievements.

20

The Last Expedition

Pass and be forgotten with the rest.*

On 12 August 1927 Teresa Littledale turned eighty-eight. Throughout her life, despite the fears of those who knew her and considered her frail, despite the illnesses that constantly afflicted her, her iron constitution carried her through. For over fifty years she had been and still was the mistress of Wick Hill House, hospitable to all comers. Now, like Tennyson's Ulysses, she was 'made weak by time and fate'.

Teresa continued to be the gracious hostess throughout 1927, but towards the end of the year when William Augustus Scott came for a visit, she had changed. Scott was a trustee with Percy Crutchley of her first husband's marriage settlement, and he visited Teresa from time to time. Usually he found her in good health and spirits. Now she seemed feeble and ill.[1]

In January 1928 Sir Francis Younghusband gave a talk to the Wokingham Lecture Society, and Wick Hill House filled up with an exotic gathering of old Tibet travellers for the occasion. St. George described the occasion:

> We had a most interesting Tibetan evening on Wed. Frank Younghusband, Sir C. Bell (a year in Lhasa), Col Trench all staying in the house & two Tibetans, one in the Lhasa Government when we so rudely knocked on the door. He knew all about us. He said that he thought the risk was too great for any of them to have taken a bribe. It meant forfeiture of land & banishment if discovered. How Willy would have enjoyed it hearing the other side.[2]

It must have been an extraordinary evening, the Littledales who had 'rudely knocked' on the door of Lhasa, two Tibetans who had stood behind the door, Younghusband who had knocked the door down, Sir

---

* From 'The Whiffenpoof Song', based on the poem *Gentlemen-Rankers* by Rudyard Kipling.

Charles Bell who had helped to rebuild the door, and Colonel G.F. Chenevix Trench, the British Resident in Kashmir when the Littledales arrived there in 1895 who had watched all of this happen. It was a reunion of Tibetan expedition legends in the twilight of their years, and St. George wished his nephew was there so he would understand that the Tibetan officials were not bluffing in 1895 when they said they faced dire consequences if they permitted the Littledales to continue on to Lhasa. If the Littledale party had been as aggressive as Willie probably wanted them to be, there would have been a disastrous fight.

When Teresa turned 89 on 12 August, it was to be her last birthday. On 1 November she died suddenly and unexpectedly at Wick Hill House. The cause of death was listed as bronchitis and influenza. The funeral took place two days later at Easthampstead Parish Church. It was a choral service presided over by the rector, the Reverend Wilford T. Stubbs. Teresa had outlived all of her siblings, and so it was the next generation of Harris relatives who attended the service. Sir Lionel Fletcher, Willie Fletcher's brother, attended as well, giving his uncle support. Numerous friends of the Littledales were present including Cecily Arkwright and St. George's good friend Sir Robert Harvey.[3] Teresa was buried in the church cemetery. St. George erected a large gravestone with the simple inscription, 'Teresa, wife of St. George Littledale. Born 12 August 1839. Died 1 November 1928'. He left room on the stone for his own inscription.

The death of Teresa must have thrown St. George into a deep depression. They had gone everywhere and done everything together as a team. Now his companion was gone and he was reminded that his own life was winding down but, unlike the clock, it could not be wound up again. Only six days after her death he began giving away some of their most cherished possessions. In early January he contacted the Victoria & Albert Museum to say he was drawing up a new will, and to offer to the museum the Littledales' favourite treasure, the Flemish tapestry. The offer was accepted.[4] He arranged to bequeath his entire collection of hunting trophies to the Natural History Museum on condition that any specimens not accepted should go to his nephew, Sir Lionel Fletcher.[5]

St. George's friends went out of their way to cheer him up, especially Prince Demidoff. He wrote:

> I just got a letter from Charles Hambro who writes amongst other things that 'St. G. Littledale is one of the nicest men I know & when you consider that for two months in the wilds of Iceland he consorted amicably with three of my young men (in fact he was quite old enough to be their grandfather) it is very good proof of what a charming character he is. . . .' I just wrote this to say that I also recognize the companion of old days.[6]

Somehow St. George retained his sense of humour. A young hunter recalled sitting next to him at a formal dinner, and after listening to some of his stories, asked where he was going on his next expedition. With a twinkle in his eye he replied, 'To the cemetery, I expect'.[7]

He did not forget the clock. In 1929 the winder was Fridtjof Nansen, the famous Norwegian explorer and statesman. Nansen had received the Nobel Peace Prize in 1922 for his work as League of Nations High Commissioner for refugees. What he wrote could be applied to the Littledales. 'Rooted deep in the nature of every one of us is the spirit of adventure, the call of the wild – vibrating under all our actions, making life deeper and higher and nobler.'

Late that year St. George visited the French Pyrenees. He also thought about going to the Balearic Islands and mentioned it in a letter to Lord Baden-Powell about winding the clock. Baden-Powell had founded the Boy Scouts, and the patron saint he had chosen for the scouting movement was St George. Baden-Powell's wife responded, 'It is MOST kind of you to invite us to come over and to stay with you for the "clock winding ceremony"!'[8] Lord Baden-Powell wound the clock and signed the book on New Years Day 1930. Under his signature he wrote, 'It is not what you get out of life but what you put into it – that counts.'

The Demidoffs continued to boost the morale of their old friend. 'Dearest Littledale, . . . Why not come with us & have a last trip in our old age! How enjoyable it would be. Do think it over & bring that old Mannlicher of yours out again. We could start all together from Athens. Best love from both. Yours affly, Elim.'[9]

On 8 December St. George turned 79. His health was deteriorating and he was suffering from gout. In January Demidoff wrote, 'I hope your gout is better or rather that you feel better. It is indeed most undeserved. When I come to think you used to take an occasional glass of port as medicine, something like children being given castor oil. . . . I do hope you won't have to stop your only pleasure – salmon fishing.'[10]

St. George was fishing for more than salmon. He needed his next clock winder, and this time he pursued Albert Einstein. He tried to enlist the assistance of Sir Frederic George Kenyon, Director and Principal Librarian of the British Museum but Sir Frederic turned him down. 'I'm sorry but I fear I don't know Einstein. I live in a world of three dimensions, and have no acquaintances in the fourth. I don't know if he so far recognizes time as to wind up a clock.'[11]

In March St. George was again fishing on the Spey, and his friend Sir Robert Harvey was there at the same time. It is highly probable that the two old friends were fishing together. The men were much alike and their friendship went back many years. Like St. George, Sir Robert hunted big game in Central Asia. He was a pioneer of houseboating in Kashmir and was mentioned as one of 'two rich sahibs' in Rassul Galwan's book, *Servant of Sahibs*. Sir Robert lived in Slough, owned about 11,000 acres in Buckinghamshire, and was a former High Sheriff of the county. He had a reputation for friendliness, kindness and modesty.[12]

Both men spent six weeks salmon fishing in Scotland and both returned home in early April in poor health and went to bed. Sir Robert looked especially ill. The next day he appeared much brighter though still weak. On 4 April he remained in bed but refused to see a doctor. That afternoon his wife Emily, Lady Harvey, went to Wick Hill House to visit St. George. While she was sitting at his bedside, her husband back at home took a revolver out of its case and shot himself in the head. When the butler brought tea, he found the baronet lying in a pool of blood. The funeral was held a few days later, and St. George managed to pull himself together enough to attend the service.[13]

The next day St. George had a severe attack of angina. He was in such pain that he could speak only in short sentences. It was difficult to understand him and he got annoyed when the doctor did not catch the meaning of his words. They had to give him occasional doses of morphine. He ordered his servants to remove the loaded revolver he kept beside his bed. On the morning of 16 April he said, 'Miss Peard arrives in London in a day or two and she must come down & stay when Miss Julia [Crutchley] is here.' That evening he was in his sitting room talking with Harold, his nephew, when he suddenly keeled over dead. The death certificate listed the cause of death as angina pectoris.[14]

St. George's death had been anticipated but its suddenness caught everyone by surprise. The distress felt by those who knew him was expressed in a note that Eleanor Ablitt, his housekeeper, wrote to Helen Peard, Teresa's niece. 'I am sorry you were just too late to see Mr. L. again, but for Sir Robert Harvey's horrible death you <u>would</u> have seen him many more times. That alone is responsible for our gentleman's death.'[15]

The funeral took place on 20 April at Easthampstead Parish Church. Alfred Littledale, St. George's older brother, led the mourners. A large number of other relatives attended as well as the staff from Wick Hill House. In the understatement of the *Wokingham Times*, 'The church was crowded and some of those present were visibly affected.' More than fifty people sent wreaths.

The service began with the hymn 'Abide With Me' followed by Psalm 90, 'Lord, thou has been our refuge'. After the service St. George was buried beside Teresa in the churchyard next door with a solemn recitation of the *Nunc Dimittis*. Later another simple inscription would be added to Teresa's headstone: 'C. St. George R. Littledale. Born 8 December 1851. Died 16 April 1931'.

The day after the funeral the County Magistrates met at Wokingham. The chairman opened the meeting by announcing St. George's death:

> They had lost a colleague – a very charming gentleman, in the person of the late Mr. Littledale. He was known not only in this country but practically throughout the whole world where geography and travel were concerned. . . . Mr. Littledale had not been a member of the Bench for very many years – some ten or eleven – but during that time he had proved a very able colleague, and they all wished to express their regret that they had lost him (hear, hear).[16]

St. George left the bulk of his estate to his nephew Harold, son of his younger brother. Harold must have been short of money. Within days of the funeral he brought in the appraisers. Eleanor Ablitt was upset. '. . . apparently he thinks of turning into money as much as possible. Rather heartbreaking isn't it when one knows how Mr. & Mrs. L. loved all in this beautiful house.' She added, 'Did you know Mr. L. left me £100. It will greatly help towards the cottage I hope to have one day.'[17]

During his peak expedition years, St. George donated 122 mammals to the Natural History Museum from the Caucasus, Central Asia and Kamchatka.[18] He gave many others to the Liverpool Museum. He had already sent numerous mammals to both museums in other years as well as quantities of birds. The museums were not just dumping grounds for sportsmen. They needed and even requested the specimens in order to study them. Now the Natural History Museum selected ninety-four additional trophies out of approximately one hundred and fifty that filled the house.[19] By June the museum had received the trophies and the Victoria & Albert Museum had the Flemish tapestry and other items agreed upon earlier.

An obituary appeared in *The Times* describing St. George Littledale as 'one of the most distinguished of the band of travellers who in the last quarter of the nineteenth century did much to make known to the world the hitherto mysterious regions of Inner Asia'. It gave a brief account of his ability as a hunter and of his three most outstanding expeditions in Central Asia. A few days later an article appeared in *The Field* entitled, 'Big Game Trophies for the Nation. St. George Littledale: Traveller, Hunter and Explorer'. It was signed 'Cheviot', the name used by Theodore A. Cook, the editor. Cook, a former Oxford oarsman, had visited Wick Hill in 1925 for a story on Willie Fletcher. The article about St. George gives a slightly garbled account of his expeditions but there is no mistaking what the author thought of him:

His name has been familiar for years to students of Rowland Ward's *Records of Big Game*, and some of us last month, perhaps, hardly realised that he was still with us. Yet there at his house, Wick Hill, at Bracknell, there was living one of the greatest of English explorers – a capital example of a holder of records that cannot be broken. He had one of the finest collections in existence of big game heads, and the walls of our museums will be greatly enriched by what he has bequeathed to them. No big game hunter can ever again have all his chances.[20]

In *Big Game Shooting Records*, published the following year, Edgar Barclay wrote:

As a hunter of big game in the Northern Hemisphere, the name of Littledale must surely stand alone. His success in this sphere has never I think been equalled, most certainly never surpassed. During the course of his long and adventurous life he penetrated into many of the most inaccessible regions, and obtained some of the rarest trophies that have ever fallen to the rifle of a hunter.[21]

The irony of such praise was that St. George's achievements as an explorer and traveller tended to be downplayed compared to his hunting. Also downplayed was Teresa, who had been with him almost every step of the way.

When Teresa died, the obituaries and memorials were brief and her first name was never mentioned. The *Geographical Journal* was typical. 'Mrs. Littledale was a courageous traveller, accompanying her husband upon many of his journeys.' And, 'Mr. Littledale has testified frequently to his wife's qualities as a traveller, and assistance she rendered him in his survey work.' In Teresa's time a woman's identity merged into her husband's so completely that in her case she never received the recognition she deserved. It is St. George who is listed in a modern biographical dictionary of botanists, even though by his own description he was 'quite at sea' on the subject. Most of the plants were collected by Teresa.[22] Upon St. George's death, she came to public attention in some of his obituaries, but only because the accounts of his trips had to mention that she was with him.

Teresa would have led an adventurous life even if she had never met St. George Littledale. Bored with the life of a Victorian lady with its rounds of visits and social activities, she emerged from the Middle East in 1873 'hopelessly bitten with a mania for travel'. A new world had opened before her and she was determined to pursue it. St. George was not necessary to free Teresa from the monotony of her existence, but with him she was able to reach heights of accomplishments she otherwise would not have found possible. In turn, she was invaluable in encouraging St. George to ever greater efforts. Together they made a formidable team.

A memorial regarding St. George and, in passing, Teresa, appeared in the *Geographical Journal*. It was written by Sir Francis Younghusband, symbol of British exploration in Central Asia and of the Great Game. He summarised their achievements and explained why they were not better known:

> Mr. Littledale was an explorer of an unusual type. He was endowed with a sufficiency of this world's goods, and he was by nature a sportsman, given to hunting, fishing, and shooting. When he travelled he travelled for the sheer love of travelling and of shooting new animals. He conscientiously had himself trained in surveying and, once he was at it, took a keen interest in his map making; but he never had the 'there's-a-blank-space-on-the-map-I-must-go-and-fill-it-up' kind of feeling. He remained essentially the sportsman and naturalist; and when he returned to England he resumed his life as a country gentleman.
>
> Consequently, his name has never been so well known as his achievements entitled it to be. And perhaps the fact that he took his wife with him on all his three great journeys predisposed people to think they could not have been very adventurous or arduous. 'If a woman could go there it cannot have been so difficult a journey' people would then be inclined to say. But Mrs. Littledale was no ordinary woman. She was of the toughest fibre – as the fact that she lived to her ninetieth year shows. And as a fact, every one of their journeys would nowadays be considered an accomplishment of note.
>
> The field of Littledale's journey was the highlands of Central Asia and Tibet. The ordinary way of approach to these regions for an Englishman would be by India. But Littledale was gifted with the happy knack of getting on with all kinds and sorts of people, and of carrying them along with him. And possessed of this grace he was able to induce the Russians to let him use Russian Turkistan as his jumping-off ground and thus saved himself the necessity of crossing the Himalaya at the start.

Younghusband then went on to summarise the Littledales' three greatest expeditions, crossing the Pamirs from north to south, crossing Central Asia from west to east over unknown territory, and their year-long attempt to reach Lhasa.[23]

Teresa and St. George Littledale had discovered a formula for success – and obscurity. Do it quietly, respect the local people, and minimise trouble. By making friends and by deliberately moving under the radar of public attention, they could go almost anywhere they pleased. They built upon their experiences, and as their competence grew, so did their goals. For many years they pushed the boundaries until they were crossing the Tibetan plateau almost to the Forbidden City of Lhasa.

Vilhjalmur Stefansson, the great Arctic explorer, used to say, 'Adventure is a sign of incompetence.' Stefansson was not decrying adventure. He knew that risk is an unavoidable element of exploration. His remark was meant to counter a common recipe for immortality: Foul it up and go down bravely. Stefansson would have approved of the Littledales. They chose to sacrifice fame for performance. They never wrote a book and so vanished into the footnotes of history. They appeared to be just a husband and wife travelling with a little dog, but inside them was a hard core of skill and will. They pushed to their limits but could judge the line they should not cross. They barely made it out of Tibet, but they made it. Throughout their many expeditions, they contributed to science, geography, and to their country. The Littledales did it right.

The Clock Winders

1913 Prince Christian of Schleswig-Holstein
1914 Earl Roberts of Kandahar, Commander-in-Chief, Indian Army 1885–93
1915 Earl Curzon of Kedleston, Viceroy of India 1899–1904, Foreign Secretary 1919–24
1916 Rudyard Kipling
1917 James W. Lowther, Speaker of House of Commons 1905–21
1918 David Lloyd George, Prime Minister 1916–22
1919 Admiral David Beatty, Admiral of the Fleet 1916–19, First Lord of the Navy 1919–27
1920 A. James Balfour, Prime Minister 1901–5, Foreign Secretary 1916–19
1921 Herbert Henry Asquith, Prime Minister 1908–16
1922 William Edward Goschen, British Ambassador to Germany 1908–14
1923 Venizelos Eleftherios, Premier of Greece 1910–15, 1917–20, 1924, 1928–32, 1933
1924 King George V
1925 Benito Mussolini
1926 Viscount Grey of Fallodon, Foreign Secretary 1905–16
1927 Stanley Baldwin, Prime Minister 1923–4, 1924–9, 1936–7
1928 Adolphe Max, 'Burgomaster Max', Mayor of Brussels 1909–39
1929 Fridtjof Nansen, Norwegian explorer and statesman
1930 Lord Baden-Powell, founder of Boy Scouts [St George, patron saint]

Glossary

aksakal	local trade official
amban	Chinese chief
arba	Chinese cart with high wooden wheels rimmed with iron for going through sand
argali	*see* Ovis ammon
art	pass (Kizil Art)
aurochs	European bison
barasingh	Kashmir red deer
bashi	headman or leader such as a caravan bashi
beg	native governor of a district or minor province
bharal	wild or blue sheep of Himalayas
(burrell)	
caravanserai	inn surrounding a courtyard where caravans rest at night
dagh	mountain
dandy	light two-wheeled cart
darya	river
(daria)	
Dard	person from Hunza (formerly Dardistan)
dawan	pass (Terek Dawan)
gol	river
havildar	native Indian non-commissioned officer
ibex	wild goat with large horns transversely ridged in front and curved backwards
jiguit	unofficial policeman and courier
kul	lake (Kara Kul)
(kol)	
la	pass (Goring La)
lambardar	village headman
markhor	large mountain goat with long spiral horns

munshi	secretary or clerk
naichalnik	Russian chief
nor	lake (Tengri Nor)
Nilgiri tahr	mountain goat with wrinkled backward-curving horns
nullah	large steep-sided gully
ollen	Russian for red deer
Ovis	sheep
Ovis ammon (argali)	large sheep with thick massive horns
Ovis poli (Marco Polo sheep)	large sheep with long wide-spreading spiral horns
palki (palanquin)	enclosed sedan chair carried on men's shoulders or on animals by means of projecting poles
poshteen	long fur-lined sheepskin overcoat
rajah	chief
sepoy	Indian private soldier
serai	short for caravanserai
shikari	professional hunter
sirdar	headman or head porter
su	river
tagh	mountain
tamasha	party, spectacle, commotion, chaotic situation (such as animal loads falling off)
tanga	Central Asian coin worth about 3 pence
tarantass	low-slung four-wheeled Russian carriage resting on two long springy poles, usually pulled by three horses (can be mounted on sledge runners for travel in snow)
tonga	light two-wheeled carriage
troika	Russian cart pulled by three horses abreast
tur	wild Caucasian goat
yamen	residence and headquarters of Chinese amban
yurt	circular domed tent of felt or skins used by Mongolian nomads
zahk	raft of inflated skins

Notes

Key

EVF	Edith Vera Fletcher papers
IP	Christopher J. Inward papers
LM	Liverpool Museum, Archives
LP	Littledale papers held by authors
NHM	Natural History Museum, London, Archives
PP	Private papers, anonymous
PRO	Public Record Office (National Archives), Kew
RBG	Royal Botanic Gardens, Archives
RGS	Royal Geographical Society, Archives
TRP	Theodore Roosevelt papers, Library of Congress, Manuscript Division
UWO	University of Western Ontario Archives, J.J. Talman Regional Collection, John and Amelia Harris Family Fonds

Introduction: On the Trail of the Littledales

1. Two French explorers passed the mountain during an attempt to reach Lhasa, but the book about the expedition lacks details. F. Grenard, *Tibet, The Country and its Inhabitants* (London, Hutchinson, 1904).

Chapter 1: Central Asia, Land of Extremes

1. S. Legg, *The Heartland* (New York, Farrar, Straus & Giroux, 1971), p. 75.
2. Fitzgerald, 'Chinese Expansion in Central Asia', *Royal Central Asian Journal*, Vol. L, Parts III & IV (July/October 1963), 290.
3. J. Keay, *The Gilgit Game* (London, John Murray, 1979), pp. 56–77.
4. F. Drew, *The Jummoo and Kashmir Territories* (London, Edward Stanford, 1875), p. 455.
5. D. Sinor, *Inner Asia* (Bloomington, Indiana University, 1971), p. 11.
6. R. Grousset, *The Empire of the Steppes: A History of Central Asia* (New Brunswick, Rutgers University Press, 1970), p. xxii.
7. Sinor, *Inner Asia*, pp. 8–9.
8. Until the Russians moved into Siberia and Central Asia with firearms, only the Indo-Europeans in about 1,500BC and Alexander the Great marched from west to east.

9. The compound bow was made of wood, horn and sinew. A mounted archer could shoot it with accuracy and power in any direction, even behind him, at a range of 80yd. E. Hildinger, *Warriors of the Steppe: A Military History of Central Asia, 500 B.C. to 1700 A.D.* (New York, Sarpedon, 1997), pp. 21–7.

10. W.H. McNeill, *The Rise of the West* (Chicago, University of Chicago Press, 1963), p. 245.

11. Hildinger, *Warriors*, pp. 9–10.

12. K. Hopkirk, *A Traveller's Companion to Central Asia* (London, John Murray, 1994), p. 186.

13. W.H. McNeill, *A World History* (New York, Oxford University Press, 1967), pp. 204–8.

14. J. King, J. Noble and A. Humphreys, *Central Asia: A Lonely Planet Travel Survival Kit* (Victoria, Australia, Lonely Planet, 1996), p. 16.

15. D.A. Christian, *A History of Russia, Central Asia and Mongolia* (2 vols, Oxford, Blackwell, 1998), Vol. I, *Inner Eurasia from Prehistory to the Mongol Empire*, p. 426.

16. Grousset, *Empire*, pp. 304–9; H. Yule, ed. and tr., *The Book of Ser Marco Polo*, (2 vols, London, John Murray, 1929), Vol. 1.

17. Legg, *Heartland*, pp. 313–14; S.E. Morison, *Admiral of the Ocean Sea: A Life of Christopher Columbus* (Boston, Little, Brown, 1942), p. 71.

18. Legg, *Heartland*, p. 327.

19. J.K. Fairbank, *China: A New History* (Cambridge, Harvard University Press, 1992), pp. 122–7.

20. Grousset, *Empire*, pp. 531–42.

21. Legg, *Heartland*, pp. 324–7; J.M. Roberts, *History of the World* (New York, Oxford University Press, 1993), p. 422; Hildinger, Warriors, p. 203.

22. M. Edwardes, *A History of India from the Earliest Times to the Present Day* (New York, Farrar, Straus and Cudahy, 1961), p. 237.

23. G. Morgan, *Anglo-Russian Rivalry in Central Asia, 1810–1895* (London, Frank Cass, 1981), pp. xv–xvi, 19; Edwardes, *History of India*, p. 241.

24. T.G.P. Spear, *India, a Modern History* (Ann Arbor, University of Michigan Press, 1972), p. 246; P. Hopkirk, *The Great Game* (London, John Murray, 1990), p. 116; G.J. Alder, *British India's Northern Frontier, 1865–1895: A Study in Imperial Policy* (London, Longmans, 1963), p. 2 .

25. Hopkirk, *Great Game*, pp. 123, 140–8.

26. Hopkirk, *Great Game*, pp. 188–209, 257–69; Morgan, *Anglo-Russian Rivalry*, pp. 28–31; Edwardes, *History of India*, pp. 244–5; Spear, *India*, pp. 245–7 .

27. Hopkirk, *Great Game*, pp. 270–9.

28. F.S. Roberts, 'What are Russia's vulnerable points? And how have recent events affected our Frontier policy in India?', *Notes on the Central Asian Question and the Coast and Frontier Defences of India, 1877–1893* (London, War Office, 1902), p. 43.

29. Hopkirk, *Great Game*, pp. 289–92; Spear, *India*, pp. 268–78; P. Mason, *A Matter of Honour: An Account of the Indian Army, Its Officers and Men* (London, Jonathan Cape, 1975), pp. 317–19.

30. G. Hambly, *Central Asia* (New York, Delacorte Press, 1969), p. 210.

31. Spear, *India*, pp. 331–2; Hopkirk, *Great Game*, pp. 379–86, 389–401; Morgan, *Anglo-Russian Rivalry*, pp. 178–82.

32. Hopkirk, *Great Game*, pp. 388–9, 402–7.
33. H.E. Richardson, *Tibet and its History* (London, Oxford University Press, 1962), pp. 50–60, 68–71; W.D. Shakabpa, *Tibet, A Political History* (New Haven, Yale University Press, 1967), pp. 153–69, 173; D. Waller, *The Pundits* (Lexington, University Press of Kentucky, 1990), p. 10.
34. Waller, *Pundits*, p. 14; J. Keay, *When Men and Mountains Meet* (London, John Murray, 1977), pp. 150–9.
35. B.S. Singh, *The Jammu Fox: A Biography of Maharaja Gulab Singh of Kashmir, 1792–1857* (Carbondale, Southern Illinois University Press, 1974) pp. 3, 9, 23–37, 191; Keay, *Men and Mountains*, p. 172.
36. Keay, *Men and Mountains*, pp. 179–88.
37. For a fine account of these courageous men, *see* Derek Waller's book, *The Pundits*.
38. Hambly, *Central Asia*, pp. 298–300; Fairbank, *China*, pp. 197–8; F.M. Hassnain and T.D. Sumi, *Kashgar – Central Asia* (New Delhi, Reliance Publishing House, 1995), pp. 64–75.
39. Morgan, *Anglo-Russian Rivalry*, pp. 159–65.
40. Morgan, *Anglo-Russian Rivalry*, pp. 192–3; Hopkirk, *Great Game*, p. 416; Alder, *British India's Northern Frontier*, pp. 152, 198–9; Keay, *Gilgit Game*, p. 158.
41. A party led by Colonel William Lockhart explored the country in 1885–6 and concluded there was no danger of invasion by the Russian army. Alder, *British India's Northern Frontier*, pp. 154–6.
42. Hopkirk, *Great Game*, p. 450.

Chapter 2: Teresa Harris

1. F.H. Armstrong, *The Forest City: An Illustrated History of London, Canada* (London, Windsor Publications, 1986), p. 46.
2. R.S. Harris and T.G. Harris, eds., *The Eldon House Diaries: Five Women's Views of the 19th Century* (Toronto, Champlain Society, 1994), pp. xxxi–ii; PP, Copy of Admiralty record; Armstrong, *Forest City*, p. 82; S.E. Morison, *The Oxford History of the American People* (New York, Oxford University Press, 1965), p. 390.
3. Harris, *Diaries*, pp. xxxi, xxxiii.
4. *Dictionary of Canadian Biography*, ed. W.S. Wallace (Toronto, Macmillan, 1963); Communication from Robert Mutrie, 20 January 2000.
5. *Dictionary of Canadian Biography*, 1982 edn, Vol. 11, p. 782; University of Western Ontario Archives, J.J. Talman Regional Collection, John and Amelia Harris Family Fonds, Box 7, George Harris paper (untitled and unpublished), p. 7; Harris, *Diaries*, p. xxxvi; Foster Learning Inc., *John Brownlee's Norfolk County Years*, p. 1, www.fosterlearning.com/norfolkbrownlee.htm (18 January 2000).
6. Armstrong, *Forest City*, pp. 22–3; Harris, *Diaries*, p. xxxix.
7. Morison, *Oxford History*, pp. 462–6; D. Creighton, *A History of Canada: Dominion of the North* (Boston, Houghton Mifflin, 1958), pp. 233–45; J.B. Brebner, *Canada, A Modern History* (Ann Arbor, University of Michigan Press, 1970), pp. 235–41.

8. Armstrong, *Forest City*, p. 82; Harris, Diaries, p. xliv; Morison, *Oxford History*, p. 465; UWO, Box 8, *Narrative of John Harris re the Caroline Incident in December 1837*.

9. Armstrong, *Forest City*, pp. 58–61; John Mombourquette, 'The Harris Family', London and Middlesex Historical Society, posted 1 November 1999 at www.Londonhistory.org/harris.htm.

10. UWO, Box 3, Inscription in Harris Family Bible; Letter from Robin Harris to authors, 11 January 1988; UWO, Julius Airey to Miss Harris, 8 November [1839?].

11. UWO, *The Eldon House Property*; Harris, *Diaries*, p. 41; Conversation with Peter H. Smith, Education Co-ordinator, London Regional Art & Historical Museums, 3 June 2000.

12. Harris, *Diaries*, pp. lxv–i; Armstrong, *Forest City*, 37.

13. Harris, *Diaries*, pp. xlv–iii.

14. Portman Square in London, England, was named after the family. P. Thorold, *The London Rich: The Creation of a Great City, from 1666 to the Present* (London, Viking, 1999) p. 138.

15. Harris, *Diaries*, pp. xlviii–ix.

16. UWO, Address by Robin Harris, 19 May 1964 (unpublished); W. Webster to Amelia Harris, 1845; Teresa Harris to Charles Crutchley, 13 January 1854; Harris, *Diaries*, p. 85; Conversation with Peter H. Smith, 3 June 2000.

17. Harris, *Diaries*, pp. xlix, l; UWO, Amelia Harris to John Fitzjohn Harris, 18 August 1854, 3 May and 16 August 1857.

18. Harris, *The Eldon House Diaries*, pp. lxxii, 64–6; UWO, Amelia Harris to John Fitzjohn Harris, 11 July 1857.

19. Sources for Scott's birth date vary. 1827 date was deduced by authors from inscription on his tombstone.

20. Harris, *Diaries*, pp. 93–8.

21. Harris, *Diaries*, pp. 100–3.

22. Harris, *Diaries*, p. 109.

23. Harris, *Diaries*, p. 120; UWO, Box 8, Series 3, File 216a, Marriage Settlement, 17 August 1859.

24. Harris, *Diaries*, p. 121–2.

25. UWO, Teresa and William Scott to Amelia Harris, 2 October 1859.

26. UWO, Teresa and William Scott to Amelia Harris, 1 November 1859.

27. UWO, Eliza Crutchley to Amelia Harris, 8 November 1859; Harris, *Diaries*, p. 133.

28. UWO, Teresa Scott to Amelia Harris, 2 December 1859. Letter begins, 'I do not want you to show this letter – it is only for you.'

29. A.H. Curtis, *Obstetrics and Gynecology* (New York, W.B. Saunders, 1933), p. 192; H. Graham, *Eternal Eve: The Mysteries of Birth and the Customs That Surround It* (London, Hutchinson, 1960), p. 255.

30. UWO, Teresa Scott to Sophia Ryerson, 18 January 1860; Teresa Scott to Amelia Harris, 19 March 1860.

31. Harris, *Diaries*, pp. 181, 185.

32. Harris, *Diaries*, p. 196; UWO, Amelia Harris to George Harris, 3 September 1862.

33. Harris, *Diaries*, p. 209; UWO, Teresa Scott to Amelia Harris, 8 September 1862.

34. UWO, Teresa Scott to Amelia Harris, 17 and 25 September 1862; William Scott to Edward Harris, 23 October 1862.

35. UWO, William Scott to Edward Harris, 16 October 1862, 11 and 16 December 1862.
36. UWO, William Scott to Edward Harris, 1 June and 4 July 1865, and Scott to George Harris, 1 June 1865.
37. UWO, Shuldham Peard to Edward Harris, 6 January 1863.
38. UWO, Mary Peard to Amelia Harris, 29 October 1862.
39. UWO, Teresa Scott to Amelia Harris, 24 April 1863.
40. UWO, Teresa Scott to Amelia Harris, 24 April 1863, and Eliza Crutchley to Amelia Harris, 27 June 1863.
41. UWO, Teresa Scott to Amelia Harris, 19 June 1863.
42. UWO, the Scotts to Amelia Harris, 27 July and 11 August 1863.
43. UWO, Teresa Scott to Amelia Harris and William Scott to Amelia Harris, 22 September 1863.
44. UWO, William Scott to Edward Harris, 22 October and 17 December 1863, and Teresa Scott to Amelia Harris, 22 October 1863.
45. UWO, Amelia Griffin to Eliza Crutchley, 3 November 1864.
46. UWO, Teresa Scott to Amelia Harris, 24 November 1964.
47. Harris, *Diaries*, p. 269.
48. UWO, George Harris to Amelia Harris, 27 November 1867; William Scott to Edward Harris, 1 May 1868.
49. UWO, William Scott to Edward Harris, 3 June and 1 July 1868.
50. UWO, William Scott to Edward Harris, undated [1868]; Teresa Scott to Lucy Harris, 18 July 1868.
51. UWO, William Scott to Edward Harris, 22 August, 2 October, and 22 October 1868.
52. UWO, Teresa Scott to Amelia Harris, 23 May and 23 September 1870; Shuldham Peard to Amelia Harris, 14 July 1870.
53. UWO, Teresa Scott to Amelia Harris, 4 August 1872.
54. UWO, William Scott to Edward Harris, 7 November 1872; Teresa Scott to Amelia Harris, 7 November 1872.
55. UWO, Teresa Scott to Eliza Crutchley, 24 November 1872.
56. B.M. Fagan, *The Rape of the Nile* (New York, Charles Scribner's Sons, 1975), pp. 305–6; UWO, Teresa Scott to Carrie Crutchley, 30 November 1872, and to Amelia Harris, 1 December 1872.
57. UWO, Teresa Scott to Carrie Crutchley, 30 November 1872, to Amelia Harris, 1 December 1872, and to Eliza Crutchley, 6 December 1872.
58. A year later Amelia B. Edwards made the identical journey and described it in her classic book, *A Thousand Miles up the Nile* (London, George Routledge and Sons, 1888).
59. UWO, Teresa Scott to Julia Crutchley, 18 December 1872.
60. UWO, Teresa Scott to Julia Crutchley, 2 February 1873.
61. UWO, Teresa Scott to Amelia Harris, 23 March 1873.
62. UWO, Teresa Scott to Amelia Harris, 23 March 1873; Teresa Scott to Mary Peard, 30 March 1873.
63. UWO, Teresa Scott to Mary Peard, 30 March 1873.
64. UWO, Teresa Scott to Amelia Harris, 6 June 1873.
65. UWO, Teresa Scott to Amelia Harris, 6 June 1873; William Scott to Edward Harris, 3 June 1873.
66. UWO, Teresa Scott to Amelia Harris, 13 July 1873.

67. UWO, Eliza Crutchley to Amelia Harris, 21 August 1873.
68. UWO, Teresa Scott to Amelia Harris, 8 October and 28 November 1873.
69. UWO, Teresa Scott to Amelia Harris, 28 November 1873.
70. Harris, *Diaries*, pp. 331, 333.
71. Littledale Papers, Teresa Scott's Japan diary.
72. LP, Teresa Scott's Japan diary.
73. LP, Teresa Scott's Japan diary; UWO, Teresa Scott to Amelia Harris, 6 April 1876.
74. LP, Teresa Scott's Japan diary.

Chapter 3: St. George Littledale

1. J.A. Picton, *Memorials of Liverpool, Historical & Topographical* (2 vols, Liverpool, Edward Howell, 1907), Vol. 2, *Topographical*, pp. 200–1.
2. Chandler, *Liverpool* (London, B.T. Batsford, 1957), pp. 435–6; Picton, *Memorials*, Vol. 1, *Historical*, pp. 600–3.
3. Picton, *Memorials*, Vol. 1, p. 603; *Liverpool Mercury*, June 1856.
4. T. Ellison, *The Cotton Trade of Great Britain, including a history of the Liverpool Cotton Market and of the Liverpool Cotton Brokers Association* (London, Effingham Wilson, Royal Exchange, 1886), pp. 213–14.
5. Ellison, *Cotton Trade*, p. 214; Ellison, *Gleanings and Reminiscences* (Liverpool, Henry Young & Sons, 1905), pp. 108–9, 169.
6. Gawsworth Hall, Macclesfield, Cheshire, has pastels by George Richmond of the Littledale children, including St. George at age three.
7. J.D. Hayward, *A Short History of the Royal Mersey Yacht Club, 1844–1907* (Liverpool, 1911), p. 19.
8. 'An Authentic Account of the Destruction of the Ocean Monarch, by Fire, off the Port of Liverpool. . .', *The Illustrated London News*, 2 September 1848, pp. 137–9; A.A. Hoehling, *They Sailed into Oblivion* (New York, Ace Books, 1959), pp. 11–20; A.S. Davidson, *Samuel Walters, Marine Artist* (Coventry, Jones-Sanas Publishing, 1992), pp. 142–6; A. Clyne, 'Centenary of the Burning of the "Ocean Monarch" ', *The Nautical Magazine*, Vol. 160 (1948), 348–50; *Liverpool Echo*, 27 August 1948, 28 August 1954, 30 August 1963, 22 April 1989.
9. Davidson, *Samuel Walters*, pp. 142–3.
10. R. Muir, *A History of Liverpool* (London, Williams & Norgate, 1907), pp. 176– 83.
11. Railways had existed before 1830 but used horses, and later, stationary engines. R.K. Webb, *Modern England* (New York, Dodd, Mead & Company, 1958), p. 263; Muir, *History of Liverpool*, p. 259.
12. Muir, *History of Liverpool*, p. 259; T. Lane, *Liverpool: Gateway of Empire* (London, Lawrence & Wishart, 1987), p. 23; C. Petrie, *The Victorians* (London, Eyre & Spottiswoode, 1960), pp. 73–9.
13. *Liverpool Mercury*, June 1857, reprinted in *Pen-and-Ink Sketches of Liverpool Town Councillors* (Liverpool, Edward Howell, 1866), p. 91.
14. *The Illustrated London News*, 3 December 1853, p. 473.
15. *Liverpool Mercury*, October 1853.
16. *Liverpool Mercury*, June 1857, reprinted in Pen-and-Ink Sketches, pp. 92–3.

17. His date of death is given as 3 April in a newspaper account but 25 March on the death certificate.
18. *Rugby School Register*, ed. A.T. Michell, rev. edn (3 vols, Rugby, A.J. Lawrence, 1901–4), Vol. 2, p. 263; Communication to authors from R. Maclean, Rugby School, 28 April 2000.
19. *The Liverpool Courier*, 5 September 1884; Ellison, *Cotton Trade*, p. 227.
20. J.B. Oldham, *A History of Shrewsbury School, 1552–1952* (Oxford, Blackwell, 1952).
21. Shrewsbury School, Reverend H.W. Moss, *Register*, 1866.
22. Oldham, *Headmasters of Shrewsbury School, 1552–1908* (Shrewsbury, Wilding, 1937), pp. 74–5; Oldham, *History*, pp. 154–5.
23. In 1844 a previous headmaster, Dr. Benjamin Kennedy, was unhappy to learn that the boys were tearing up copies of his book, the Latin Grammar, for paper to mark the trail.
24. J.M. West, *Shrewsbury* (London, Blackie & Co., 1937), pp. 128–35; G.W. Fisher, *Annals of Shrewsbury School* (London, Methuen, 1899), pp. 393–6.
25. Shrewsbury School, Fisher to Reverend J.E. Auden, 25 November 1897.
26. Fisher, *Annals*, p. 396; Letter to authors from James Lawson, 10 July 1997; Shrewsbury School, *Royal Shrewsbury School Hunt Hound Book, 1859–1867*.
27. R. Millington, *The House in the Park* (Liverpool, Corporation of the City of Liverpool, 1957), pp. 9–10.
28. PP, Julia Turner's 'Fact Book'.
29. LP, Littledale to Julia Turner, 11 and 14 February 1874.
30. LP, Littledale to Julia Turner, 28 April 1874.
31. A.E. Pease, *Edmund Loder, Naturalist, Horticulturist, Traveller and Sportsman: A Memoir* (London, John Murray, 1923), p. 174.
32. LP, Littledale to Nora Littledale, 4 August 1874.
33. LP, Littledale to Nora Littledale, 4 August 1874.
34. LP, Littledale's Yesso diary; Littledale to Julia Turner, 8 November 1874.

Chapter 4: Together

1. L. Pemba, *Tibetan Proverbs* (Dharamsala, Library of Tibetan Works and Archives, 1996), p. 68.
2. LP, Littledale to Julia Turner, 8 November 1874.
3. LP, Teresa Scott's Japan diary.
4. LP, Teresa Scott's Japan diary.
5. W. Durant, *Our Oriental Heritage* (New York, Simon and Schuster, 1954), p. 778; Fairbank, *China*, pp. 89, 124–5.
6. LP, Teresa Scott's Japan diary.
7. LP, Teresa Scott's Japan diary.
8. LP, Littledale to Julia Turner, 1 March 1875.
9. UWO, William Scott to Edward Harris, 13 January 1875.
10. LP, Teresa Scott's Japan diary.
11. UWO, William Scott to Edward Harris, 10 February 1875; LP, Teresa Scott's Japan diary.

12. LP, Teresa Scott's Japan diary; Littledale to Julia Turner, 10 March 1875; Pease, *Edmund Loder*, p. 174; UWO, William Scott to Edward Harris, 10 March 1875.
13. LP, Teresa Scott's Japan diary.
14. LP, Littledale to Julia Turner, 15 May 1875.
15. UWO, William Scott to Edward Harris, 12 May 1875.
16. LP, Littledale to Julia Turner, 15 May 1875; UWO, Scott to Edward Harris, 12 May 1875.
17. LP, Littledale to Julia Turner, 29 May 1875.
18. UWO, Scott to Edward Harris, 12 May 1875.
19. UWO, Littledale to Edward Harris, 18 June 1875; LP, Littledale to Julia Turner, 18 June 1875.
20. UWO, Littledale to Eliza Crutchley, 16 June 1875.
21. LP, Littledale to Julia Turner, 18 June 1875.
22. LP, Littledale to Julia Turner, 18 June 1875; UWO, Littledale to Edward Harris, 18 June 1875; General Register Office, London, Marine Register of Deaths, *Reports of Deaths at Sea . . . during the Month of July 1875*.
23. UWO, Sophia Harris to Amelia Harris, 11 July 1875.
24. UWO, Sophia Harris to Amelia Harris, 11 July 1875.
25. UWO, Eliza Crutchley to Sophia Harris, July 25, 1875.
26. PP, Charles Crutchley to Scott, Moncrieff & Wood, 15 July 1875.
27. UWO, Sarah Dalzell to Amelia Harris, 12 September 1875.
28. UWO, Teresa Scott to Amelia Harris, 9 December 1875; Eliza Crutchley to Amelia Harris, 4 January 1876.
29. UWO, Teresa Scott to Edward Harris, February 12, 1876.
30. UWO, Teresa Scott to Amelia Harris, 6 April 1876.
31. UWO, Teresa Scott to Amelia Harris, 26 April 1876; Sophia Harris to Edward Harris, 3 May 1876.
32. 'Sir Edward Coley Burne-Jones', Microsoft Encarta.
33. UWO, Sophia Harris to Edward Harris, 16 May 1876, and to Amelia Harris, 23 May 1876.
34. Passenger manifest, Newfoundland-Grand Banks newspaper, *Harbour Grace Standard*, Ship news, 28 October 1876, at http://ngb.chebucto.org/Newspaper-Obits/hrgrace-standard-1876.shtml.
35. UWO, Mary Peard to Amelia Harris, 12 December 1876.
36. UWO, Teresa Scott to Amelia Harris, 20 December 1876.
37. UWO, Teresa Scott to Charles Crutchley, 30 December 1876, and to Amelia Harris, 22 January 1877; Charles Crutchley to Alfred Fletcher, 6 January 1877.
38. UWO, Mary Peard to Amelia Harris, 16 January 1877.
39. UWO, Sarah Dalzell to Amelia Harris, 26 January 1877.
40. UWO, Teresa Scott to Amelia Harris, 29 January and 12 February 1877; Littledale to Amelia Harris, 14 February 1877.
41. UWO, Teresa Scott to Amelia Harris, 29 January and 12 February 1877.
42. UWO, Teresa Scott to Amelia Harris, 12 and 23 February 1877; Mary Peard to Amelia Harris, 28 February 1877.
43. UWO, Eliza Crutchley to Amelia Harris, 14 March 1877; Sarah Dalzell to Amelia Harris, 27 February 1877.
44. UWO, Teresa Littledale to Eliza Crutchley, 17 and 29 March 1877.

45. UWO, Teresa Littledale to Amelia Harris, 25 April 1877; J. Ince, *The Kashmir Hand-book: A Guide for Visitors* (Calcutta, Wyman and Col, 1876), p. 52 [definition of Kuhars].
46. UWO, Mary Peard to Amelia Harris, 25 April 1877; Shuldham Peard to Charles Crutchley, 10 May 1877.
47. LP, Teresa Littledale to Julia Turner, 11 May 1877; St. George Littledale to Nora Littledale, 11 May 1877.
48. LP, Teresa to Julia Turner, 21 June 1877
49. LP, Teresa to Julia Turner, 21 June 21 1877.
50. LP, Teresa to Julia Turner, 21 June 1877.
51. LP, St. George to Julia Turner, 13 July 1877.
52. LP, Teresa to Julia Turner, 13 July 1877; St. George to Nora Royds, 5 August 1877.
53. LP, Teresa to Julia Turner, 31 July 1877; St. George to Nora Royds, 5 August 1877.
54. LP, Teresa to Julia Turner, 28 August 1877.
55. LP, Teresa to Julia Turner, 18 September 1877.
56. Not to be confused with Bandipur in southern India where St. George went bison hunting.
57. LP, St. George to Julia Turner, 11 November 1877; Teresa to Julia Turner, 26 November 1877.
58. LP, Teresa to Julia Turner, 22 December 1877.
59. LP, Teresa to Julia Turner, 26 November 1877.

Chapter 5: From the Rockies to the Caucasus

1. G.M. Trevelyan, *English Social History, A Survey of Six Centuries: Chaucer to Queen Victoria* (London, Longmans Green, 1942), p. 506.
2. UWO, Julia Crutchley to unknown aunt, 21 July 1878.
3. W.T. Stead, 'Nimrod, His Wife and Marco Polo's Sheep', *Pall Mall Gazette*, 14 June 1888.
4. R. Ward, *Records of Big Game*, 5th edn (London, Rowland Ward, 1907), p. 357.
5. *Church Guide, Parish Church of St Michael and St Mary Magdalene, Easthampstead, Berkshire* (1983).
6. UWO, unpublished entry in Amelia Harris diary, Robin Harris work papers; Natural History Museum, London, *Zoological Accessions Register, Mammalia, 1930–1936*; Harris, *Diaries*, p. 356.
7. UWO, Mary Peard to Amelia Harris, 9 June 1880.
8. UWO, Mary Peard to Amelia Harris, 9 June 1880.
9. LP, Teresa Littledale's 1881 diary; Harris, *Diaries*, p. 365.
10. *Webster's Revised Unabridged Dictionary of the English Language*, ed. Noah Porter (Springfield, Massachusetts, 1913), p. 250; S. Blanchard & M.J. Atha MSc, 'Indian Hemp and the Dope Fiends of Old England', http://www.idmu.co.uk/indian.htm; R. Moodie and C. Borthwick, *Internet Journal of Health Promotion* (1998), http://www.monash.edu.au/health/IJHP/1998/11.
11. UWO, Teresa Littledale to Amelia Harris, 3 August 1881; P.J. Vesilind, 'Chasing Tornadoes', *National Geographic*, April 2004, p. 14. Hail can be apple-sized in this type of super storm.

12. UWO, Teresa Littledale to Amelia Harris, 9 August 1881.
13. Stead, 'Nimrod', *Pall Mall Gazette*.
14. Stead, 'Nimrod', *Pall Mall Gazette*; LP, Teresa Littledale's 1881 diary.
15. PP, Harris Magee Co. to Percy Crutchley, 11 November 1881.
16. Harris, *Diaries*, p. 367.
17. UWO, Teresa Littledale to Lucy Harris, 3 and 18 April 1882.
18. LP, Teresa Littledale's 1882 diary.
19. LP, T. Moore and S.G. Littledale, 'On the Rocky Mountain Goat', *Literary and Philosophical Society of Liverpool*, 27 April 1885; LM, Littledale to Moore, 25 November 1884; S.G. Littledale, 'After the White Goats of Alaska', *Pall Mall Budget*, 15 December 1892.
20. LP, Ward, *Records*, p. 352; Moore and Littledale, 'On the Rocky Mountain Goat'.
21. LM, Littledale to Moore, 27 April 1886.
22. LM, Littledale to Moore, 17 May 1886.
23. LM, Littledale to Moore, received 15 June 1886.
24. LM, Littledale to Moore, 10 July 1886.
25. The account of this trip is based on a diary kept by St. George Littledale.
26. LP, St. George Littledale's 1886 Caucasus diary; Teresa Littledale to Julia Turner, 12 August 1886; F. Maclean, *To Caucasus: The End of all the Earth* (Boston, Little, Brown and Company, 1976), p. 30.
27. LP, Littledale's 1886 Caucasus diary; F.C. Grove, *The Frosty Caucasus* (London, Longman, 1875), p. 200.
28. LP, Littledale's 1886 Caucasus diary.
29. Stead, 'Nimrod', *Pall Mall Gazette*.
30. According to Ward, *Records of Big Game*, p. 433, 'The name aurochs, so commonly misapplied to the bison, belongs to the extinct wild ox of Europe.' For purposes of clarity we will continue to misapply it here.
31. LP, Littledale's 1886 Caucasus diary; D. Carruthers et al, *The Gun at Home and Abroad* (4 vols, London, London & Counties Press Association Ltd, 1912–15), Vol. 4, *The Big Game of Asia and North America*, pp. 42–3.
32. LP, Littledale's 1886 Caucasus diary.
33. UWO, Shuldham Peard to George Harris, 13 November and 20 December 1886.
34. *Proceedings of the Literary and Philosophical Society of Liverpool*, 1886, p. 4; Ward, *Records*, p. 382.
35. UWO, Mary Peard to Lucy Harris, December 7, 1886.
36. NHM, Moore to Gunther, 30 April 1887, Zoological Dept. Letters, 1887, Vol. 1, #267; Zoological Accessions Register, 5 May 1887, 'Presented and collected by St. Geo. Litt. (Through T.J. Moore, Esq. Liverpool Museum)', *Zoological Accessions Register – Vertebrates*, 1876–1890, p. 389.
37. NHM, Littledale to Gunther, 20 June 1887; LM, Littledale to Moore, 24 June 1887.
38. LP, Teresa Littledale to Julia Turner, 3 July 1887.
39. Littledale's 1887 Caucasus diary is severely damaged and only partly legible but there are published accounts: S.G. Littledale, 'Caucasian Aurochs', *Big Game Shooting, Badminton Library* (2 vols, London, Longmans, Green, 1894), Vol. 2, pp. 65–72, and C. Phillipps-Wolley, 'Mountain Game of the Caucasus', pp. 59–63.

40. LP, Littledale's 1887 Caucasus diary; LM, Littledale to Thomas Moore, 22 November and 11 December 1887.

Chapter 6: *The Alai and the Altai*

1. LM, Littledale to Thomas Moore, 11 December 1887.
2. NHM, Flower to Salisbury, 15 March 1888.
3. Public Record Office, FO 65/1330, Morier to Salisbury, 19 April 1888.
4. PRO, FO 65/1330, Nikolai de Giers to Robert Morier, 26 April 1888; Morier to Salisbury, 26 April 1888; FO 65/1334, Telegram from Morier, 27 April 1888.
5. PRO, FO 65/1343, Littledale to Sanderson, 15 May 1888; NHM, Littledale to Albert Gunther, 24 and 29 May 1888; H. Lansdell, *Chinese Central Asia* (2 vols, Scribner, 1894), Vol. 1, p. 95.
6. G.N. Curzon, *Russia in Central Asia in 1889 and the Anglo-Russian Question* (London, Longmans, Green, and Co., 1889), p. 1; LP, St. George Littledale's 1888 Pamir diary.
7. LP, Teresa Littledale's 1888 Pamir diary. Both St. George and Teresa kept diaries. Most of St. George's is illegible but it is more helpful than Teresa's, which ends abruptly on 14 June. The Littledales repeated their route to Kara Kul in 1890 on their journey across the Pamir. The description of the country along the route is covered in the next chapter because the surviving records of the second trip are more detailed.
8. Stead, 'Nimrod', *Pall Mall Gazette*. This was the Editor, William Thomas Stead, a prominent and controversial crusading journalist who later went down in the *Titanic*.
9. J. Wyld, *Wyld's Military Staff Map of Central Asia and Afghanistan* (London, James Wyld, 1880).
10. Stead, 'Nimrod', *Pall Mall Gazette*, 14 June 1888.
11. LP, Teresa's 1888 Pamir diary.
12. LP, St. George's 1888 Pamir diary.
13. PRO, FO 65/1436, Eliot to Morier, 29 February 1892, p. 17. The nature of the Russian officers in Central Asia was demonstrated by the game of 'Cuckoo', as described by Gromchevsky to Charles Eliot when he visited Osh in 1891. Popular with young officers, it was a form of Russian roulette played at night. First the players would deposit their money. Then one man would go outside and hide in the dark. The rest would follow, guns drawn. The man in hiding would yell 'Cuckoo' and run. The others fired at where they guessed he would be. If he escaped, he won the pot, but if not, the others confiscated his stake.
14. LP, St. George's 1888 Pamir diary.
15. LP, St. George's 1888 Pamir diary.
16. The River Chu near Pishpek. D. Rayfield, *The Dream of Lhasa* (Athens, Ohio University Press, 1976), pp. 197–201.
17. Balliol College Library, Oxford, Morier Papers, Box 22.2.
18. PRO, FO 65/1373, Littledale to Brackenbury, 30 January 1889. The letter was written on War Office stationery, indicating that St. George wrote it in General Brackenbury's office after discussing the matter with him.
19. PRO, FO 65/1373, Mr. St. G. Littledales's Proposed trip from Ferghana (Turkestan) through the Pamirs, Chitral, etc to India, 30 January 1889;

Brackenbury to Sanderson, 2 February 1889; Balliol College Library, Oxford, Morier Papers, Box 22.2, Sanderson to Morier, 13 February 1889.

20. NHM, Littledale to Dr Gunther, 12 March 1889; Flower to Salisbury, 19 March 1889; Foreign Office letter to Flower, 30 March 1889.

21. LP, Ardagh to Brackenbury, 4 March 1889; PRO, FO 65/1373, Brackenbury to Philip Currie, 25 March 1889; Currie to Flower, 30 March 1889.

22. PRO, FO 65/1373, Littledale to Salisbury, 5 April 1889; FO 605/178 & 145, Russia – Diplomatic Telegrams, 9 April 1889 & 1 May 1889; FO 17/1092, T.H. Sanderson to Littledale, 11 April 1889; Littledale to Sanderson, 21 April 1889; LP, Sir Halliday Macartney to Littledale, 23 April 1889; Sanderson to Littledale, 25 April 1889.

23. Christopher J. Inward Papers, Morier to Littledale, 14, 25 and 26 April 1889. The Ambassador's private coaching left nothing to chance: 'If I may venture to give you a hint it would be to make your mounting of the head very plain and to put at the foot of it [drawing of head on shield] or on the frame if room enough a little gilt board (like those under pictures in galleries) with in black letters on it "Head of Ovis Poli. Shot – Sat. 1888 on the Pamirs by St. George Littledale Esq." '

24. LM, Littledale to Moore, 12 April 1889; Moore to Littledale, 12 and 30 April 1889.

25. St. George Littledale, 'Ovis Argali of Mongolia', *Big Game Shooting*, Vol. 2, pp. 73–6.

26. IP, Morier to Littledale, 5 May 1889; NHM, Littledale to Albert Gunther, n.d. [early May 1889]; Balliol College Library, Oxford, Morier Papers, Box 22.2, Draft of letter from Morier to Nikolai de Giers, 7 May 1889.

27. Littledale, 'Ovis Argali', *Big Game Shooting*, Vol. 2, p. 74.

28. LM, Littledale to Moore, 8 October 1889; LP, Morier to Littledale, 17 October 1889; NHM, Littledale to Gunther, 25 November 1889.

29. J. Hoult, *West Derby, Old Swan and Wavertree, Historical & Topographical* (Liverpool, C. Tinling and Co., 1913), p. 33.

Chapter 7: Across the Pamirs

1. A common name for the Pamir is 'Roof of the World' from the local name for the region, 'Bam-i-Dunya'. G.N. Curzon, *The Pamirs and the Source of the Oxus* (London, Royal Geographical Society, 1899), pp. 15–16.

2. *Proceedings of the Royal Geographical Society*, Vol. 10 (1888), 171; Hopkirk, *Great Game*, p. 449.

3. PRO 30/40, Ardagh papers; Alder, *British India's Northern Frontier*, p. 5.

4. PRO, FO 65/1392, Morier to Lord Salisbury, 8 January 1890; FO 65/1389, Littledale to Sanderson, 16 January 1890.

5. PRO, FO 65/1392, India Office to Under Secretary of State, Foreign Office, 29 January 1890; War Office to Foreign Office, 8 February 1890; Philip Currie to Littledale, 7 March 1890.

6. PRO, FO 17/1105, Littledale to Philip Currie, 4 April 1890; Memorandum, Mr. Littledale 5 April 1890 Journey to China; FO 17/1104, Lew Tajen to Salisbury, 9 April 1890.

7. UWO, Teresa Littledale to George Harris, 13 April 1890.

8. The Littledales provide the main sources for the Pamirs expedition, a diary kept by Teresa and an article by St. George, 'A Journey Across the Pamir from North to South', *Proceedings of the Royal Geographical Society*, Vol. 14, no. 1 (January 1892), 1–35.
9. Curzon, *Russia in Central Asia*, p. 29.
10. Littledale, 'Journey Across the Pamir', p. 5; Stead, 'Nimrod', *Pall Mall Gazette*.
11. C.S. Cumberland, *Sport on the Pamirs and Turkistan Steppes* (Edinburgh and London, William Blackwood and Sons, 1895), pp. 229, 261–2.
12. Littledale, 'Journey Across the Pamir', p. 11.
13. Littledale, 'Journey Across the Pamir', pp. 14–15.
14. The first known westerner to reach the lake was Lieutenant John Wood of the Royal Navy in February 1838 while searching for the source of the Oxus. Three members of Douglas Forsyth's second mission to Kashgar got there in 1874, followed by several members of a Russian scientific expedition in 1883. These men were the Littledales' only western predecessors. Curzon, *The Pamirs*, pp. 71–83.

Chapter 8: To Gilgit

1. Lansdell, *Chinese Central Asia*, Vol. 2, p. 19.
2. In winter the frozen rivers become the roads, making the country more accessible. Roland and Sabrina Michaud accompanied a winter camel caravan on the Wakhan River that they described in *Caravans to Tartary* (New York, Viking Press, 1977).
3. Littledale, 'Journey Across the Pamir', p. 16. This article and Teresa's diary continue to be the main sources for the Pamir expedition.
4. Littledale, 'The Ovis Poli of the Pamir', *Big Game Hunting, Badminton Library*, Vol. 2, pp. 374–6; LP, Teresa Littledale's 1890 Pamir diary.
5. Keay, *Gilgit Game*, p. 93; Alder, *British India's Northern Frontier*, p. 159.
6. Curzon, *The Pamirs*, pp. 40–2.
7. Curzon, *The Pamirs*, pp. 58–9.
8. Littledale, 'Journey Across the Pamir', p. 22.
9. India Office Library, L/PS/7/60/letter 122.
10. India Office Library, L/PS/7/60/No. 107.
11. Littledale, 'Journey Across the Pamir', pp. 26–7.
12. Or so St. George was told, but the number may have increased over the years. It is hard to imagine fifteen men on a rope bridge simultaneously.

Chapter 9: On to India

1. E.F. Knight, *Where Three Empires Meet* (London, Longman, Green & Co., 1893), p. 282.
2. A. Durand, *The Making of a Frontier* (London, John Murray, 1899), p. 31.
3. Lieutenant John Manners-Smith would make a different impression on others a year later. In December 1891 during the brief Hunza war, he led an attack up a 1,200-ft precipice and took the Hunzakut stronghold at Nilt Ridge, for which he won the Victoria Cross. Hopkirk, *Great Game*, pp. 476–9; Knight, *Where Three Empires Meet*, pp. 440–53.

4. Durand, *Making of a Frontier*, pp. 31–2.
5. Durand, *Making of a Frontier*, pp. 30–1.
6. Durand, *Making of a Frontier*, p. 29.
7. More accurate measurements today read 4,000ft. Even so, it is a long, hard climb, especially in hot weather. Durand, *Making of a Frontier*, pp. 24–5.
8. Drew, *Jummoo and Kashmir Territories*, p. 403; Durand, *Making of a Frontier*, p. 19.
9. Drew, *Jummoo and Kashmir Territories*, pp. 528–9; Major-General Le Marquis De Bourbel, *Routes in Jammu and Kashmir* (Calcutta, Thacker, Spink and Co., 1897), pp. 159–66.
10. J. Duke, *Kashmir and Jammu, a Guide for Visitors*, 2nd edn (Calcutta, Thacker, Spink, 1910), pp. 309–10; Durand, *Making of a Frontier*, p. 19.
11. W.M. Conway, *Climbing and Exploration in the Karakoram-Himalayas* (2 vols, London, T. Fisher Unwin, 1894), Vol. 1, p. 76.
12. Ince, *Kashmir Handbook*, p. 123.
13. Knight, *Where Three Empires Meet*, p. 37; Duke, *Kashmir and Jammu*, p. 26.
14. Ince, *Kashmir Handbook*, p. 97; Duke, *Kashmir and Jammu*, pp. 9–10; Alder, *British India's Northern Frontier*, pp. 145–6.
15. Duke, *Kashmir and Jammu*, pp. 16, 8.
16. LP, Littledale scrapbook.
17. Littledale to Lord Roberts, October 20, 1890. General Sir Frederick Sleigh Roberts was Commander-in-Chief of the Indian Army 1885–93. He had won the Victoria Cross in the Indian Mutiny of 1857 and was the hero of the Afghan war of 1879–80, especially for his relief of Kandahar. He became the 1st Earl Roberts of Kandahar and became known to the public as 'Roberts of Kandahar'.
18. In 1893 when a Great Game crisis flared in the Pamirs, the Intelligence Branch of the Quarter Master General's Department rushed out ten copies of a secret report. Scattered throughout this report was information obtained from St. George Littledale. W.R. Robertson and E. Peach, *Routes from Russian Territory in Central Asia towards Afghanistan and India* (2 vols, Simla, Central Printing Office, 1893–94), Section 1, Robertson, *The Pamir Line of Advance*.
19. NIIM, Littledale to Gunther, 14 January 1891; PP, Littledale to Percy Crutchley, 3 and 24 February 1891.
20. P.H. Ditchfield, 'The Garth Hunt', *British Hunts and Huntsmen* (4 vols, London, Biographical Press, 1908), Vol. 1, *The South-West of England*, pp. 239–50; J.F.R. Hope, *A History of Hunting in Hampshire* (Winchester, Warren and Son, 1950), pp 205–24.
21. LP, unidentified newspaper clipping, Littledale scrapbook.
22. NHM, St. George Littledale to Gunther, received 9 April 1891; UWO, Teresa Littledale to George Harris, 11 August 1891.
23. LP, Teresa Littledale's 1891 Caucasus diary.
24. LP, Teresa's 1891 Caucasus diary; St. George Littledale to Julia Turner, 20 July 1891.
25. LP, Teresa Littledale to Julia Turner, 12 August 1891.
26. Phillipps-Wolley, *Big Game Shooting*, Vol. 2, 69–72.
27. RGS, St. George Littledale to unknown recipient at Royal Geographical Society, 6 November 1891.

28. E.J. Garwood, 'Douglas William Freshfield (1845–1934)', *Alpine Journal*, 46 (1934), 166–76.
29. Alder, *British India's Northern Frontier*, pp. 225, 242–7. Hopkirk, *Great Game*, pp. 470–1.
30. *The Times, The Glasgow Herald, The Standard*, 24 November 1891.
31. Alder, *British India's Northern Frontier*, p. 243; PRO, FO 65/1434, FO 65/1440.
32. Knight, *Where Three Empires Meet*, pp. 387–468.
33. Alder, *British India's Northern Frontier*, pp. 243–7.
34. UWO, Helen Peard to Lucy Harris, 14 April 1892; LP, Charles Eliot to St. George Littledale, 10 June 1892.
35. NHM, Littledale to Gunther, undated; Littledale to Gunther, 13 June 1892; LP, Gunther to Littledale, 9 and 14 June 1892.
36. *The Times*, 28 June 1892, p. 5.
37. John Coles was appointed Map Curator in 1877 and taught map-making to travellers for twenty-two years. He was also travel editor of *The Field* from 1884 until just before his death in 1910.
38. *Geographical Journal*, August 1910, 227–9; *Proceedings of the Royal Geographical Society*, June 1892.
39. PRO, FO 65/1460, FO 65/1421, FO 17/1166, FO 17/1167.

Chapter 10: Across Central Asia

1. LP, Gunther to Littledale, 2 November 1892.
2. UWO, Teresa Littledale to George Harris, 3 February 1893.
3. St. George Littledale, 'A Journey Across Central Asia', *Geographical Journal*, Vol. 8, no. 6 (June 1894), 445. This article and a diary kept by Teresa Littledale are the main sources for the expedition.
4. Earl of Dunmore, *The Pamirs*, 2nd edn (2 vols, London, John Murray, 1893), Vol. 2, p. 340.
5. L. Atherton, *Top Secret, An Interim Guide to Recent Releases of Intelligence Records at the Public Record Office* (London, PRO Publications, 1993), p. 8.
6. Littledale, 'Journey Across Central Asia', p. 451.
7. Dunmore, *Pamirs*, Vol. 2, p. 279.
8. G.R. Galwan, *Servant of Sahibs* (Cambridge, Heffer & Sons, 1923), p. 75.
9. A.N. Kuropatkin, *Kashgaria: Eastern or Chinese Turkistan*, tr. Walter E. Gowan (Calcutta, Thacker, Spink and Co, 1882), p. 30.
10. Littledale, 'Journey Across Central Asia', p. 447.
11. Dunmore, *Pamirs*, Vol. 2, p. 255.
12. Lansdell, *Chinese Central Asia*, p. 6.
13. Kuropatkin, *Kashgaria*, p. 21; I.M. Franck, *The Silk Road, A History* (New York, Facts on File Publications, 1986), p. 13.
14. S. Hedin, *My Life as an Explorer* (Garden City, NY, Garden City Publishing Company, 1925), p. 99; Dunmore, *The Pamirs*, Vol. 2, p. 220; C.P. Skrine, *Macartney at Kashgar* (London, Methuen, 1973), p. 19.
15. Alder, *British India's Northern Frontier*, p. 79; Skrine, *Macartney at Kashgar*, p. 16.
16. Skrine, *Macartney at Kashgar*, pp. 24–5.

17. Alder, *British India's Northern Frontier*, p. 250; PRO, FO 65/1465, George Macartney to The Resident in Kashmir, 23 March 1893; FO 65/1467, Afghanistan, Baluchistan, Kashmir, Chitral, Gilgit, Pamirs and North-West Frontier, Summary of Diary for June 1893.
18. Littledale, 'Journey Across Central Asia', p. 448.
19. LP, Littledale to Douglas Freshfield, 6 May 1893.
20. Lansdell, *Chinese Central Asia*, p. 146; S. Hedin, *Through Asia* (2 vols, London, Methuen, 1898), Vol. 1, p. 251; Cumberland, *Sport on the Pamirs*, pp. 139–40.
21. Lansdell, *Chinese Central Asia*, p. 430; Hedin, *Through Asia*, pp. 442–4.
22. Littledale, 'Journey Across Central Asia', p. 450.
23. Hedin, *Through Asia*, p. 447; Cumberland, *Sport on the Pamirs*, p. 157; Littledale, 'Journey Across Central Asia', p. 448.
24. Aksakals were like consular agents to the merchants of their nationality and acted upon their disputes. Both British and Russian aksakals were scattered throughout Chinese Turkestan. Hedin, *Through Asia*, p. 654.
25. Hedin, *Through Asia*, p. 649.
26. Eventually Bower's agents found the murderer in Samarkand. P. Hopkirk, *Foreign Devils on the Silk Road* (London, John Murray, 1980), p. 45.
27. J. Bonavia, *The Silk Road* (London, Harrap Limited, 1988), pp. 251–2; H. Bower, 'A Trip to Turkistan', *Geographical Journal*, 5, no. 3 (March 1895), 254–6.
28. For a good account of the ensuing scholastic scramble see Hopkirk, *Foreign Devils on the Silk Road*.
29. Littledale, 'Journey Across Central Asia', p. 451.
30. NHM, Littledale to Gunther, 23 April 1893.
31. M.S. Bell, 'The Great Central Asian Trade Route from Peking to Kashgaria', *Proceedings of the Royal Geographical Society*, 12 (1890), 84; F.E. Younghusband, *The Heart of a Continent* (London, John Murray, 1896), p. 148.

Chapter 11: To Peking

1. Younghusband, *Heart of a Continent*, p. 14; Cumberland, *Sport on the Pamirs*, p. 185.
2. The location of Lop Nor varies because the path of the Tarim River changes. Sven Hedin, *Through Asia*, 864–84. The Lop Nor mentioned here was explored by Nikolai Prejevalsky. N.M. Prejevalsky, *From Kulja, Across the Tian Shan to Lob-Nor* (London, Sampson Low, Marston, Searle, & Rivington, 1879), pp. 55–7. Lob is a spelling variant of Lop.
3. Hedin, *Through Asia*, p. 855.
4. LP, Littledale to Douglas Freshfield and to Nora Royds, 6 May 1893.
5. LP, Littledale to Douglas Freshfield, 6 May 1893.
6. Stead, 'Nimrod', *Pall Mall Gazette*.
7. Hedin, *Through Asia*, p. 867.
8. Hedin, *Through Asia*, p. 867.
9. Littledale, 'Journey Across Central Asia', p. 475.
10. A pass did exist. In 1901 Sven Hedin would go through those mountains.
11. In 1907 Aurel Stein visited the same place and concluded that the gravel embankment was intended as a roadmark during dust storms and as

protection from the wind. M.A. Stein, *Ruins of Desert Cathay* (2 vols, London, Macmillan, 1912), Vol. 2, pp. 74, 79.

12. M. Cable, *The Gobi Desert* (London, Hodder & Stoughton, 1942), pp. 42–3.
13. Bonavia, *The Silk Road*, p. 148.
14. M. Cable, *George Hunter, Apostle of Turkestan* (London, China Inland Mission, 1948).
15. H. Taylor, *Hudson Taylor and the China Inland Mission* (London, Morgan & Scott, 1919). Folded map in Taylor book shows Kweihwating, possibly Liangchen on modern maps; Younghusband, *Heart of a Continent*, p. 62.
16. A. Lamb, *Britain and Chinese Central Asia: The Road to Lhasa 1767 to 1905* (London, Routledge and Kegan Paul, 1960), p. 159.
17. Littledale, 'Journey Across Central Asia', pp. 470–1.
18. M. Broomhall, *Hudson Taylor and China's Open Century* (London, Hodder & Stoughton and the Overseas Missionary Fellowship, 1989), Vol. 7, *It is not Death to Die!*, pp. 125, 155–60, 198–203, 246–7; Taylor, *Hudson Taylor and the China Inland Mission*, pp. 520–33.
19. *North China Daily News*, 1 October 1893; LP, Littledale to Julia Turner, 1 October 1893.

Chapter 12: Toward Tibet

1. Littledale, 'Journey Across Central Asia'.
2. RGS, Littledale to J. S. Keltie, received 7 June 1894.
3. NHM, Littledale to Gunther, 3 July 1894.
4. Richardson, *Tibet and its History*, p. 71. Shakabpa, *Tibet, A Political History*, p. 173.
5. PRO, FO 65/1482, Sanderson to Littledale, 2 August 1894; FO 17/1210, Sir Halliday Macartney to Francis L. Bertie, 31 August 1894.
6. RGS, Littledale to J.S. Keltie, 3 August 1894; LP, Lord Roberts to Littledale, 11 and 14 August 1894.
7. St. George R. Littledale, 'A Journey across Tibet, from North to South, and West to Ladak', *Geographical Journal*, Vol. 7, no. 5 (May 1896), 453–82.
8. It was Fletcher's custom to have oars from each of his major winning races inscribed with the details of the event.
9. 'Men of the Day. No. 559. Mr. William Alfred Littledale Fletcher', *Vanity Fair*, 18 March 1893, n.p.
10. UWO, Teresa Littledale to Lucy Harris, 26 August 1894.
11. The account of this expedition is based primarily on diaries kept by Willie Fletcher and Teresa Littledale, and on St. George Littledale's article in the *Geographical Journal*.
12. LP, P. Sykes to Littledale, 22 December 1895.
13. Teresa took white tablecloths on this and many other expeditions and had various dignitaries sign them. She later embroidered their signatures into the cloth with white thread.
14. Sart was a commonly used name for an urban or settled inhabitant in contrast to a nomad. It has no ethnological significance. E. Schuyler, *Turkistan, Notes of a Journey in Russian Turkistan, Khokand, Bukhara, and Kuldja* (2 vols, London, Sampson Low, Marston, Searle, & Rivington, 1876), Vol. 1, p. 104.

Chapter 13: From Kashgar to Cherchen

1. Galwan, *Servant of Sahibs*, pp. 127–8.
2. Skrine, *Chinese Central Asia*, pp. 4–5.
3. Galwan, *Servant of Sahibs*, p. 134.
4. Grenard, *Tibet, the Country and its Inhabitants*, p. 105.
5. RGS, *Littledale to Keltie*, 10 January 1895.
6. G. Jarring, *Prints from Kashgar* (Istanbul, Swedish Research Institute in Istanbul, 1991), p. 8.
7. Hedin, *Through Asia*, pp. 235–6.
8. Hedin, *Through Asia*, p. 436.
9. Skrine, *Chinese Central Asia*, p. 84.
10. Hedin, *Through Asia*, pp. 436–7.
11. Hedin, *Through Asia*, p. 724.
12. Yule, *The Book of Ser Marco Polo*, p. 187.
13. Galwan, *Servant of Sahibs*, pp. 146–7.
14. Galwan, *Servants of Sahibs*, p. 149.
15. Stein, *Ruins of Desert Cathay*, p. 317.

Chapter 14: The Akka Tagh

1. Grenard, *Tibet, The Country and its Inhabitants*, pp. 31–2.
2. LP, Teresa Littledale to Julia Turner, 7 March 1895.
3. Grenard, *Tibet, The Country and its Inhabitants*, p. 33.
4. W.A.L. Fletcher, 'A Journey toward Lhassa', *Transactions of the Liverpool Geographical Society*, 5 (1896), 8.
5. Galwan, *Servant of Sahibs*, pp. 180–2.
6. Forty years later the famous travellers Peter Fleming and Ella Maillart would pass Munar Bulak on their trip across Central Asia. P. Fleming, *News from Tartary* (London, Jonathan Cape, 1936), p. 228; E.K. Maillart, *Forbidden Journey* (London, Heinemann, 1937), p. 174.
7. The camps are clearly numbered and circled on Littledale's map.
8. Galwan, *Servant of Sahibs*, p. 173.
9. A year later Sven Hedin found the body of the dead donkey shrivelled up like a mummy, completely preserved, and untouched by wolf or vulture. Hedin, *Through Asia*, p. 999.
10. Grenard, Tibet, *The Country and its Inhabitants*, p. 38.
11. Molnar, 'Ulugh Muztagh: The Highest Peak on the Northern Tibetan Plateau', *Alpine Journal*, 92 (1987), 110–11. This figure is as close as one can get. The expedition used a global positioning system, a microwave ranging system and a theodolite.
12. Grenard, *Tibet, The Country and its Inhabitants*, p. 39.

Chapter 15: The Chang Tang

1. Galwan, *Servant of Sahibs*, pp. 174–5.
2. Grenard, *Tibet, The Country and its Inhabitants*, p. 39.

3. Littledale, 'Journey across Tibet', p. 464.
4. Littledale, 'Journey across Tibet', p. 465.
5. P. Hopkirk, *Trespassers on the Roof of the World* (London, John Murray, 1982), pp. 83–91; H. Bower, *Diary of a Journey Across Tibet* (London, Rivington, Percival, 1894), pp. 83–7.
6. Littledale, 'Journey across Tibet', p. 461.
7. Galwan, *Servant of Sahibs*, p. 194.

Chapter 16: Confrontation

1. The government executed some Tibetans who had helped the pundit Sarat Chandra Das reach Lhasa in 1882. L.A. Waddell, *Lhasa and Its Mysteries* (London, Methuen, 1906), pp. 7–9.
2. Galwan, *Servant of Sahibs*, p. 208.
3. Galwan, *Servant of Sahibs*, p. 208.

Chapter 17: Return

1. H. Harrer, *Seven Years in Tibet* (New York, E.P. Dutton, 1954), p. 123.
2. Galwan, *Servant of Sahibs*, p. 227.
3. This is not quite what the distinguished historian Thomas Holdich had in mind when he wrote, 'He [St. George] took his wife with him on his journeyings, and his wife was more or less of an invalid. The pure, fresh air of the Tibetan highlands restored her to health.' *Tibet, The Mysterious* (London, Alston Rivers, 1904), p. 281.
4. Littledale, 'Journey Across Tibet', p. 477.
5. Galwan, *Servant of Sahibs*, pp. 240–1.
6. A. Schulze, *World-wide Moravian Missions in Picture and Story* (Bethlehem, Comenius Press, 1926), p. 130.

Chapter 18: Russians and Royalty

1. UWO, Mary Peard to Lucy Harris, 27 December 1895.
2. UWO, Mary Peard to Lucy Harris, 6 March 1896.
3. RBG, Director's Correspondence, 154–121; Littledale to Joseph Hooker, 11 January 1896.
4. Littledale, 'Journey Across Tibet', p. 482.
5. RGS, Littledale to J.S. Keltie, n.d.
6. *Geographical Journal*, July 1896, 88.
7. LP, Edward Arnold to Littledale, 5 January and 5 March 1896.
8. LP, Lord Curzon to Littledale, 28 April 1896; Lord Roberts to Littledale, 9 January 1896.
9. PRO, *Foreign Lists*, 1896; LP, E. Demidoff to Littledale, 7 January 1896.
10. *The Times Saturday Review*, 19 April 1969; *The Modern Encyclopedia of Russian and Soviet History*, ed. J.L. Wieczynski et al (59 vols, Gulf Breeze, Academic International Press), vol. 9 (1978), pp. 51–4.

11. Dr H.D. Levick, 'Third Hunting Expedition in the Kouban District of the Caucasus', in E. Demidoff, *Hunting Trips in The Caucasus* (London, Rowland Ward, 1898), pp. 235–319.
12. J. Scott Keltie, 'Thirty Years' Work of the Royal Geographical Society', *Geographical Journal*, Vol. 49, no. 5 (May 1917), 371; RGS, Teresa Littledale to J.S. Keltie, 25 December 1896.
13. RGS, Littledale to J.S. Keltie, n.d.
14. *The Field*, 23 May 1931, p. 747.
15. Carruthers, *The Big Game of Asia and North America*, p. 180.
16. LP, Teresa Littledale to Nora Royds, 6 June 1897.
17. UWO, Mary Peard to Lucy Harris, n.d. [autumn 1897].
18. *Kew Bulletin*, 1898, p. 26; Demidoff's book, *Hunting Trips in the Caucasus*, contains a long list of botanical specimens that the Littledales donated to Kew.
19. UWO, Amelia Griffin to Lucy Harris, 19 January 1898.
20. IP, Littledale to Prince Christian, 15 February 1898.
21. UWO, Eliza Crutchley to George Harris, 1 April 1898; PP, Eliza Crutchley's 1898 diary. Eliza's rush to leave her house and even England remains a family mystery.
22. UWO, Eliza Crutchley to Lucy Harris, 2 June 1899.
23. LP, Hedin to Littledale, 6 November 1898.
24. A.H.S. Landor, *In the Forbidden Land* (2 vols, New York, Harper & Brothers, 1899), Vol. 1, pp. 102–3.
25. Landor, *In the Forbidden Land*; RGS, Littledale to Keltie, 6 April 1898.
26. RGS, Littledale to Keltie, 11 May 1898.
27. Wellby, *Through Unknown Tibet*, p. 8. Galwan omits any mention of the Wellby expedition in *Servant of Sahibs*.
28. E. Demidoff, *A Shooting Trip to Kamchatka* (London, Rowland Ward, 1904), p. 26. This book is the main source for the account of the Kamchatka expedition.
29. Demidoff, *Shooting Trip*, p. 171.
30. Demidoff, *Shooting Trip*, pp. 174–5.
31. Demidoff, *Shooting Trip*, pp. 210–11.
32. J.B. Priestley, *The Edwardians* (London, Heinemann, 1972), p. 103; A. Trollope, *Can You Forgive Her?* (2 vols, London, Oxford University Press, 1942), Vol. 1, p. 217.
33. Julia Turner's 'Fact Book'; An Old Blue, 'Fletcher of Christ Church', *The Field*, Christmas 1925, pp. 22–3; T.A. Cook, *The Sunlit Hours: A Record of Sport and Life* (London, Nisbet & Co. Ltd., 1925), pp. 71–82.
34. RBG, Director's Correspondence, 152–171, Littledale to William Thiselton-Dyer, 16 March 1901.
35. PRO, FO 65/1621, no. 149, Littledale to Sanderson, 5 May 1901.
36. RBG, Director's Correspondence, Littledale to Thiselton-Dyer, 6 April 1902; Ward, *Records of Big Game*, p. 400; NHM, Zoological Accession Register.
37. RBG, Director's Correspondence, Littledale to Thiselton-Dyer, 25 November 1901; LP, Thiselton-Dyer to Littledale, 28 November 1901.
38. IP, Littledale to Prince Christian, 30 December 1901.
39. IP, Littledale to Prince Christian, 24 January 1902.
40. UWO, typed transcription of letter from Teresa Littledale to Amelia Griffin, 27 January 1902.

41. IP, Littledale to Prince Christian, 28 and 29 January 1902; LP, Sandringham to Littledale, 17 April 1902; Library of Congress, Manuscript Division, Theodore Roosevelt papers, Littledale to Baron Speck von Sternburg, 1 February 1903.

42. TRP, Littledale to Baron Speck von Sternburg, 1 February 1903; NHM, Zoological Accession Register, 172, 187; Ward, *Records of Big Game*, pp. 379, 409; RBG, Director's Correspondence, 164–237, Littledale to Thiselton-Dyer, 12 September 1902.

43. TRP, Littledale to Baron Speck von Sternburg, 1 February 1903.

44. LP, T.E. Donne to Littledale, 29 June 1903; T.E. Donne, *Game Animals of New Zealand* (London, John Murray, 1924), pp. 165–6.

45. TRP, Littledale to Roosevelt, 13 December 1903.

46. LP, Carl Hagenbeck to Littledale, 14 and 24 October, and 24 November 1903; Duke of Bedford to Littledale, 7 December 1903; draft of Littledale reply to Duke of Bedford, n.d.

47. D.B. Banwell, *Wapiti in New Zealand: The Story of the Fiordland Herd* (Wellington, AH and AW Reed, 1996), pp. 29–30.

48. IP, Prince Christian to Littledale, 22 October 1903; Littledale to Prince Christian, 24 October 1903; Prince Christian to Littledale, October 25, 1903; Littledale to Prince Christian, 5 and 25 December 1903.

49. TRP, Littledale to Roosevelt, 7 February, 15 May, 5 October 1904; T. Roosevelt, *Theodore Roosevelt, An Autobiography* (New York, Charles Scribner & Sons, 1920), Vol. 5, *The Vigor of Life*, p. 3.

50. TRP, Littledale to Roosevelt, 5 October 1904.

51. TRP, Littledale to Roosevelt, 5 October 1904.

52. RBG, Director's Correspondence, 116–1061, Littledale to Director of Botanic Gardens, 28 August 1907.

53. TRP, Littledale to Baron Speck von Sternburg, 16 November 1907; NHM, Zoological Accession Register, Mammalia, 1908–1910, p. 140.

54. PRO, FO 371/517, Littledale to Mr Norman, 23 June 1908; Frank Wallace, 'Mr. St. George Littledale's Trophies', *Country Life*, 11 February 1911, pp. 196-7; NHM, Zoological Accession Register, Mammalia, 1908-1910, 189; RBG, Director's Correspondence, 138–256, Littledale to W. Botting Hemsley, 20 October 1908.

Chapter 19: The Clock Years

1. IP, Prince Christian to Littledale, 29 June 1914.

2. *The Westminster Gazette*, 10 August 1914; TRP, Littledale to Roosevelt, 11 July 1915.

3. Dr Zimmermann became Foreign Secretary in November 1916 and sent the famous 'Zimmermann telegram' that helped push the United States into the First World War. *The Westminster Gazette*, 10 August 1914; TRP, Littledale to Roosevelt, 11 July 1915; R. Thoumin, *The First World War* (New York, G.P. Putnam's Sons, 1964), p. 350.

4. TRP, Littledale to Roosevelt, 11 July 1915; IP, Roosevelt to Littledale, 7 August and 7 December 1915; TRP, Littledale to Roosevelt, 12 March 1916.

5. C.E. Wurtzburg, *The History of the 2/6th (Rifle) Battalion "The King's" (Liverpool Regiment) 1914–1919* (Aldershot, Gale & Polden, 1920),

pp. 90–1. This is the main source for the account of W.A.L. Fletcher in the First World War.

6. Wurtzburg, *The History of the 2/6th (Rifle) Battalion*, pp. 90–1.
7. IP, Prince Christian to Teresa Littledale, 11 February 1916.
8. IP, Prince Christian to Teresa Littledale, 7 October 1917.
9. Wurtzburg, The History of the 2/6 (Rifle) Battalion, p. 199.
10. *The Field*, 19 March 1921, 354. The boathouse burned to the ground in September 1999.
11. Wurtzburg, *The History of the 2/6th (Rifle) Battalion*, p. 263.
12. UWO, Teresa Littledale to George Harris, 17 June 1919.
13. IP, David Beatty to 'Henri', 1 June 1919.
14. IP, Lord Haig to Osborne Beauclerk, 5 December 1920; Beauclerk to Littledale, 10 December 1920.
15. IP, undated clipping from *The Times*.
16. T. Skyrme, *The Changing Image of the Magistracy* (London, Macmillan, 1979), pp. 1–9, 173–7; Conversation with Sir Matthew Farrer GCVO, 31 August 2001; *Wokingham Times and Weekly News*, 24 April 1931.
17. Interview with Dorothea Fletcher, 30 June 1987; Interview with Audrey Littledale Fletcher & Alfred William Fletcher, 22 July 1987; UWO, Teresa Littledale to Lucy Harris, 4 January 1899.
18. Interview with Audrey and William Fletcher, 22 July 1987; UWO, Helen Peard to unknown person, 2 May 1931.
19. EVF, Littledale to a Mr Hunter, n.d. [1924].
20. EVF, Rassul Galwan to Littledale, 12 July 1923.
21. EVF, Katherine Lee Barrett to the Littledales, August 1923.
22. EVF, Littledale to a Mr Hunter, n.d. [1924]; Inscription in *Servant of Sahibs*; IP, Lord Curzon to Littledale, 4 January 1924.
23. *The Berkshire Chronicle*, 7 October 1921; PP, E.S. Whaley to Cecily Arkwright, 19 November 1931.
24. IP, George Macartney to St. George Littledale, 20 November 1926.
25. IP, E. Rosslyn Mitchell to Teresa Littledale, 12 December 1926.
26. UWO, St. George Littledale to Helen Peard, 12 September 1923.
27. Interview with Nora K. Pond, 3 March 1987.
28. IP, Neville Chamberlain to Littledale, 7 February 1927.
29. Interview with Nora K. Pond, 3 March 1987
30. UWO, Julia Crutchley to unknown relative in Canada, March 1925.

Chapter 20: The Last Expedition

1. PP, William Augustus Scott to Percy Crutchley, 16 December 1927.
2. IP, Younghusband to Littledale, 12 January 1928; EVF, Littledale to Lionel Fletcher, n.d. [January 1928].
3. *Reading Mercury, Oxford Gazette, Newbury Herald, and Berk. County Papers*, 10 November 1928, p. 10.
4. Victoria & Albert Museum, Tapestry Archives, 14 and 26 January 1929.
5. NHM, Littledale to Colonel Dollman, 22 January 1929.
6. LP, Demidoff to Littledale, 25 January 1929.

7. H.F. Wallace, *Big Game: Wanderings in Many Lands* (London, Eyre and Spottiswoode, 1934), p. 30.
8. M. Collins, 'St. George', 16 April 2002, www.britannia.com./history/stgeorge.html; IP, Lady Baden-Powell to Littledale, 6 December 1929.
9. LP, Demidoff to Littledale, 4 November or December 1929.
10. IP, Elim Demidoff to Littledale, 13 June 1930; LP, Sofka Demidoff to Littledale, 8 November 1930; Elim Demidoff to Littledale, 8 January 1931.
11. IP, F.G. Kenyon to Littledale, 5 February 1931.
12. *The Times*, 9 April 1931.
13. *The Times* and *The Daily Telegraph*, 6 April 1931; *The Times*, 8 and 9 April 1931; UWO, Helen Peard to Milly Harris, 2 May 1931.
14. Farrer & Co., Dr Ernest Ward to Farrer & Co., 3 June 1931; Eleanor Ablitt to Sir Lionel Fletcher, 18 May 1931; UWO, Milly Harris diary; Helen Peard to Milly Harris, 2 May 1931.
15. UWO, Ablitt to Helen Peard as quoted by Peard to Milly Harris, 2 May 1931.
16. *Wokingham Times and Weekly News*, 24 April 1931, p. 1.
17. UWO, E. Ablitt to Helen Peard to Milly Harris, 2 May 1931.
18. NHM, *The History of the Collections Contained in the Natural History Departments of the British Museum*, Vol. 2 (1906), p. 44.
19. Farrer & Co., G.F. Herbert Smith to Farrer & Co., 4 May 1931; NHM, J.G. Dollman to Dr W.T. Calman, 24 April 1931, Collection of skulls and horns of the late C. St. George Littledale, of Wick Hill House, Bracknell.
20. *The Times*, 6 May 1931; Cheviot [T.A. Cook], 'Big Game Trophies for the Nation', *The Field*, 9 May 1931, 659-60; LP, Theodore A. Cook to Littledale, 1 June 1925.
21. Edgar N. Barclay, *Big Game Shooting Records* (London, H.F. and G. Witherby, 1932), pp. 206–7.
22. *Geographical Journal*, February 1929, 192; NHM, Littledale to Natural History Museum, n.d. [1908 or 1909]; R. Desmond and C. Ellwood, *Dictionary of British & Irish Botanists and Horticulturists* (London, Natural History Museum, 1994)
23. *Geographical Journal*, July 1931, 95–6.

Select Bibliography

ORIGINAL SOURCES

Family papers privately held*
Balliol College Library, Oxford, Morier Papers
Berkshire County Record Office
British Library, India Office Records, Letters Political & Secret
British Library, Newspapers, Colindale
Eldon House Musuem, London, Ontario
Farrer & Co., Littledale legal papers
Library of Congress, Manuscript Division, Theodore Roosevelt Papers
Liverpool Museum, Archives
Natural History Musuem, London, Archives
Parish Church of St Michael and St Mary Magdalene (formerly Easthampstead Parish Church), Bracknell, Berkshire
Principal Registry, Family Division, Somerset House, Wills
Public Record Office (National Archives), Kew, Foreign Office papers
Royal Botanic Gardens, Kew, Archives
Royal Geographical Society, Archives
St Catherine's House, births, marriages, deaths
Shrewsbury School, Archives
University of Western Ontario Archives, J.J. Talman Regional Collection, John and Amelia Harris Family Fonds
Victoria & Albert Museum, Archives

* Papers include Littledale, Fletcher, and other family papers held by the authors and by Christopher J. Inward, by various members of the Fletcher family, and by others who wish to remain anonymous.

SECONDARY SOURCES

Adshead, Samuel Adrian Miles. *Central Asia in World History*, New York, St. Martin's Press, 1993

Alder, Garry J. *Beyond Bokhara: The Life of William Moorcroft, Asian Explorer and Pioneer Veterinary Surgeon, 1767–1825*, London, Century Publishing, 1985

——. *British India's Northern Frontier 1865–95: A Study in Imperial Policy*, London, Longman, 1963

Armstrong, Frederick H. *The Forest City: An Illustrated History of London, Canada*, London, Windsor Publications, 1986

Atherton, Louise. *Top Secret: An Interim Guide to Recent Releases of Intelligence Records at the Public Record Office*, London, PRO Publications, 1993

Baillie-Grohman, William Adolphus. *Fifteen Years' Sport and Life in the Hunting Grounds of Western America and British Columbia*, London, Horace Cox, 1900

Baines, Thomas. *History of the Commerce and Town of Liverpool and of the Rise of Manufacturing Industry in the Adjoining Counties*, London, Longman, Brown, Green and Longman, 1852

Banwell, David Bruce. *Wapiti in New Zealand: The Story of the Fiordland Herd*, Wellington, A.H. & A.W. Reed, 1996

Barclay, Edgar N. *Big Game Shooting Records*, London, H.F. and G. Witherby, 1932

Baumer, Christoph. *Southern Silk Road: In the Footsteps of Sir Aurel Stein and Sven Hedin*, Bangkok, Orchid Press, 2000

Beal, Merrill D. *The Story of Man in Yellowstone*, Caldwell, Idaho, Caxton Printers, 1949

Beckwith, Christopher I. *The Tibetan Empire in Central Asia*, Princeton, NJ, Princeton University Press, 1987

Bell, Sir Charles Alfred. *Tibet, Past & Present*, Oxford, Clarendon Press, 1924

Bellew, Henry Walter. *Kashmir and Kashgar*, London, Trubner & Co., 1875

Blackmore, Charles. *The Worst Desert on Earth*, London, John Murray, 1996

Bonavia, David. *Tibet*, Hong Kong, Shangri-La Press, 1981

Bonavia, Judy. *The Silk Road*, London, Harrap Limited, 1988

Bonney, Orrin H. *Battledrums and Geysers*, Chicago, Sage Books, 1970

Bonvalot, Gabriel. *Across Thibet*, 2 vols, London, Cassell & Company, 1891

——. *Through the Heart of Asia: Over the Pamir to India*, 2 vols, London, Chapman and Hall, Ltd., 1889

Boulger, Demetrius Charles. *England and Russia in Central Asia*, 2 vols, London, W.H. Allen & Co., 1879

Boulnois, Lucette. *The Silk Road*, New York, E. P. Dutton & Co., 1966

Bourbel, Marquis de. *Routes in Jammu and Kashmir*, Calcutta, Thacker, Spink and Co., 1897

Bower, Hamilton. *Diary of a Journey across Tibet*, London, Rivington, Percival, 1894

Brebner, John Bartlet. *Canada, A Modern History*, Ann Arbor, University of Michigan Press, 1970

Briggs, Asa. *Victorian People*, revd edn, Chicago, University of Chicago Press, 1972

Broomhall, Marshall. *Hudson Taylor and China's Open Century*, Book 7, *It is Not Death to Die!* London, Hodder & Stoughton and the Overseas Missionary Fellowship, 1989

Bryce, James. *Transcaucasia and Ararat*, London, MacMillan, 1877

Burke, Sir Bernard. *A Genealogical and Heraldic History of the Landed Gentry of Great Britain*, 12th edn, London, Harrison & Sons, 1914

——. *A Genealogical and Heraldic History of the Peerage and Baronetage, The Privy Council, Knightage and Companionage*, 79th edn, London, Harrison & Sons, 1917

Burrard, Gerald. *Big Game Hunting in the Himalayas & Tibet*, London, Herbert Jenkins, 1925

Cable, Mildred. *George Hunter, Apostle of Turkestan*, London, China Inland Mission, 1948

——. *The Gobi Desert*, London, Hodder & Stoughton, 1942

Carpenter, Captain A.F.B. *The Blocking of Zeebrugge*, Boston and New York, Houghton Mifflin Company, 1922

Carruthers, Douglas, et al. *The Big Game of Asia and North America*, Vol. 4 of *The Gun at Home and Abroad*, 4 vols, London, The London & Counties Press Association, 1915

Chandler, George. *Liverpool*, London, B.T. Batsford, 1957

——. *Liverpool Shipping: A Short History*, London, Phoenix House, 1960

Chapman, Stanley David. *The Cotton Industry in the Industrial Revolution*, London, Macmillan, 1972

Chohan, Amar Singh. *The Gilgit Agency*, New Delhi, Atlantic Publishers & Distributors, 1986

Christian, David A. *A History of Russia, Central Asia and Mongolia*, 2 vols, Oxford, Blackwell, 1998, Vol. 1, *Inner Eurasia from Prehistory to the Mongol Empire*

Church, Percy W. *Chinese Turkestan with Caravan and Rifle*, London, Rivingtons, 1901

Clayton, Peter A. *The Rediscovery of Ancient Egypt*, London, Thames and Hudson, 1982

Cobbold, Ralph P. *Innermost Asia: Travel & Sport in the Pamirs*, London, William Heinemann, 1900

Conway, William Martin. *Climbing and Exploration in the Karakoram-Himalayas*, 2 vols, London, T. Fisher Unwin, 1894

Cook, Theodore Andrea. *The Sunlit Hours: A Record of Sport and Life*, London, Nisbet & Co., Ltd., 1925

——. 'Big Game Trophies for the Nation', *The Field, The Country Gentleman's Newspaper*, 9 May 1931, pp. 659–60

——. 'Fletcher of Christ Church', *The Field, The Country Gentleman's Newspaper*, Christmas 1925, pp. 22–3

——. 'The Late Colonel W.A.L. Fletcher, D.S.O.', *The Field, The Country Gentleman's Newspaper*, 22 February 1919, p. 219

Creighton, Donald. *A History of Canada, Dominion of the North*, Boston, Houghton Mifflin, 1958

Cumberland, Charles Sparling. *Sport on the Pamirs and Turkistan Steppes*, Edinburgh and London, William Blackwood and Sons, 1895

Curzon, George Nathaniel. *Leaves from a Viceroy's Note-Book*, London, Macmillan and Co., 1926

——. *The Pamirs and the Source of the Oxus*, London, Royal Geographical Society, 1899

——. *Russia in Central Asia in 1889 and the Anglo-Russian Question*, London, Longmans, Green, and Co., 1889

Darrah, Henry Zouch. *Sport in the Highlands of Kashmir*, London, Rowland Ward, 1898

Davidson, A.S. *Samuel Walters, Marine Artist*, Coventry, Jones-Sanas Publishing, 1992

Debrett's Peerage, Baronetage, Knightage and Companionage, London, Dean & Son, 1902

Demidoff, Elim. *After Wild Sheep in the Altai & Mongolia*, London, Rowland Ward, 1900

——. *Hunting Trips in the Caucasus*, London, Rowland Ward, 1898

——. *A Shooting Trip to Kamchatka*, London, Rowland Ward, 1904

Dictionary of Canadian Biography, ed. W. Stewart Wallace, Toronto, University of Toronto Press, 1963 and 1982

Donne, T.E. *Game Animals of New Zealand*, London, John Murray, 1924

Drew, Frederic. *The Jummoo and Kashmir Territories*, London, Edward Stanford, 1875

Duke, Joshua. *Kashmir and Jammu, A Guide for Visitors*, 2nd edn, Calcutta, Thacker, Spink, 1910

Dunmore, Earl of. *The Pamirs*, 2 vols, London, John Murray, 1893

Durand, Algernon. *The Making of a Frontier*, London, John Murray, 1899

Durant, Will. *Our Oriental Heritage*, New York, Simon and Schuster, 1954

Dutreuil de Rhins, Jules Leon. *Mission Scientifique dans la Haute Asie*, 3 vols, Paris, E. Leroux, 1897–8

Edwardes, Michael. *A History of India From the Earliest Times to the Present Day*, New York, Farrar, Straus and Cudahy, 1961

——. *Playing the Great Game*, London, Hamish Hamilton, 1975

Edwards, Amelia B. *A Thousand Miles Up the Nile*, London, George Routledge and Sons, 1888

Ellison, Thomas. *The Cotton Trade of Great Britain: including a history of the Liverpool Cotton Market and of the Liverpool Cotton Brokers Association*, London, Effingham Wilson, Royal Exchange, 1886

——. *Gleanings and Reminiscences*, Liverpool, Henry Young & Sons, 1905

Elwes, Henry John. *Memoirs of Travel, Sport, and Natural History*, London, Ernest Benn Ltd., 1930

Fagan, Brian M. *The Rape of the Nile*, New York, Charles Scribner's Sons, 1975

Fa-hsien. *The Travels of Fa-hsien, (399–414 A.D.) or Record of the Buddhistic Kingdom*, tr. H.A. Giles, Cambridge, Cambridge University Press, 1923

Fairbank, John King. *China, A New History*, Cambridge, Harvard University Press, 1992

Fisher, George William. *Annals of Shrewsbury School*, London, Methuen, 1899

Fleming, Peter. *News from Tartary*, London, Jonathan Cape, 1936

Fletcher, W.A.L. 'A Journey toward Lhassa', *Transactions of the Liverpool Geographical Society*, no. 5 (1896), 74–92

Forsyth, Thomas Douglas. *Report of a Mission to Yarkund in 1873*, Calcutta, Foreign Department Press, 1875

Franck, Irene M. *The Silk Road, A History*, New York, Facts on File Publications, 1986

French, Patrick. *Younghusband*, London, HarperCollins, 1994

Freshfield, Douglas William. *Travels in the Central Caucasus and Bashan*, London, Longmans, Green, 1869

Galwan, Ghulam Rassul. *Servant of Sahibs*, Cambridge, Heffer & Sons, 1923

Gates, Elgin T. *Trophy Hunter in Asia*, New York, Winchester Press, 1982

Gilmour, David. *Curzon*, London, John Murray, 1994

Gordon, Thomas Edward. *The Roof of the World*, Edinburgh, Edmonston & Douglas, 1876

Gougaud, Henri. *Egypt Observed*, New York, Oxford University Press, 1979

Green, William. *Tourist's New Guide containing a Description of the Lakes, Mountains, and Scenery, in Cumberland, Westmorland, and Lancashire*, 2 vols, Kendal, R. Lough and Co., 1819

Grenard, Fernand. *Tibet, the Country and Its Inhabitants*, London, Hutchinson, 1904

Grousset, René. *The Empire of the Steppes: A History of Central Asia*, New Brunswick, Rutgers University Press, 1970

Grove, Florence Crawford. *The Frosty Caucasus*, London, Longmans, 1875

Gunther, Albert E. *A Century of Zoology at the British Museum: The British Museum Through the Lives of Two Keepers, 1815–1914*, London, Dawsons of Pall Mall, 1975

Hambly, Gavin. *Central Asia*, New York, Delacorte Press, 1969

Harrer, Heinrich. *Seven Years in Tibet*, New York, E.P. Dutton and Company, Inc., 1954

Harris, J.R. *Liverpool and Merseyside*, London, Frank Cass and Company, 1969

Harris, Robin S. and Terry G. Harris (eds). *The Eldon House Diaries: Five Women's Views of the 19th Century*, Toronto, Champlain Society, 1994

Hassnain, F.M. and Token D. Sumi. *Kashgar – Central Asia*, New Delhi, Reliance Publishing House, 1995

Haupt, Herman Jr. *The Yellowstone National Park*, New York, J.M. Stoddart, 1883

Hayward, John D. *A Short History of the Royal Mersey Yacht Club, 1844–1907*, Liverpool, 1911

Hedin, Sven. *Central Asia and Tibet*, New York, Scribners, 1903

——. *My Life as an Explorer*, Garden City, NY, Garden City Publishing Company, 1925

——. *Southern Tibet*, 9 vols, Stockholm, Lithographic Institute of the General Staff of the Swedish Army, 1916–1922

——. *Through Asia*, 2 vols, London, Methuen, 1898

Hellwald, Friedrich von. *The Russians in Central Asia*, London, Henry S. King & Co., 1874

Hildinger, Erik. *Warriors of the Steppe: A Military History of Central Asia, 500 B.C. to 1700 A.D.*, New York, Sarpedon, 1997

Holdich, Thomas Hungerford. *The Gates of India*, London, Macmillan, 1910

——. *Tibet, The Mysterious*, London, Alston Rivers, 1904

Holdsworth, Mary. *Turkestan in the Nineteenth Century*, Oxford, Central Asian Research Centre, 1959

Holgate, William. *Arka Tagh*, Gwynedd, The Ernest Press, 1994

Hope, J.F.R. *A History of Hunting in Hampshire*, Winchester, Warren and Son, 1950

Hopkirk, Kathleen. *A Traveller's Companion to Central Asia*, London, John Murray, 1994

Hopkirk, Peter. *Foreign Devils on the Silk Road*, London, John Murray, 1980

——. *The Great Game*, London, John Murray, 1990

——. *Quest for Kim*, London, John Murray, 1996

——. *Trespassers on the Roof of the World*, London, John Murray, 1982

Hoult, James. *West Derby, Old Swan and Wavertree, Historical & Topographical*, Liverpool, C. Tinling and Co., 1913

Hoyos-Sprinzenstein, Ernst. *With a Rifle in Mongolia in the Altai and the Tian Shan*, Long Beach, CA, Safari Press, 1986

Hsu, Immanuel C.Y. *The Ili Crisis*, Oxford, Clarendon Press, 1965

Hutton, James. *Central Asia: From the Aryan to the Cossack*, London, Tinsley Brothers, 1875

Hyde, Francis E. *Liverpool and the Mersey*, Newton Abbot, David & Charles, 1971

Ince, John. *The Kashmir Hand-book, A Guide for Visitors*, Calcutta, Wyman and Co., 1876

Jarring, Gunnar. *Prints from Kashgar*, Istanbul, Swedish Research Institute in Istanbul, 1991

Jina, Prem Singh. *Famous Western Explorers to Ladakh*, New Delhi, Indus Publishing Company, 1995

Keay, John. *Eccentric Travellers*, London, John Murray, 1982

——. *The Gilgit Game*, London, John Murray, 1979

——. *When Men & Mountains Meet*, London, John Murray, 1977

Keegan, John. *The First World War*, London, Hutchinson, 1998

Keyes, Admiral Sir Roger. *The Naval Memoirs of Admiral of the Fleet Sir Roger Keyes*, New York, E.P. Dutton, 1935

King, John, Noble, John and Humphries, Andrew. *Central Asia: A Lonely Planet Travel Survival Kit*, Victoria, Australia, Lonely Planet, 1996

Kipling, Rudyard. *Kim*, Pleasantville, NY, Reader's Digest, 1990

Kish, George. *To the Heart of Asia: The Life of Sven Hedin*, Ann Arbor, University of Michigan Press, 1984

Knight, Edward Frederick. *Where Three Empires Meet*, London, Longman, Green & Co., 1893

Kuropatkin, A.N. *Kashgaria: (Eastern or Chinese Turkistan)*, tr. Walter E. Gowan, Calcutta, Thacker, Spink and Co., 1882

Kwanten, Luc. *Imperial Nomads: A History of Central Asia*, Philadelphia, University of Pennsylvania Press, 1979

Lamb, Alastair. *Britain and Chinese Central Asia: The Road to Lhasa 1767 to 1905*, London, Routledge and Kegan Paul, 1960

Landor, A. Henry Savage. *In the Forbidden Land*, 2 vols, New York, Harper & Brothers, 1899

Lane, Tony. *Liverpool: Gateway of Empire*, London, Lawrence & Wishart, 1987

Lansdell, Henry. *Chinese Central Asia*, 2 vols, New York, Scribner, 1894

——. *Russian Central Asia*, 2 vols, London, Sampson Low, Marston, Searle and Rivington, 1885

Larner, John. *Marco Polo and the Discovery of the World*, New Haven, Yale University Press, 1999

Lawrence, Walter Roper. *The Valley of Kashmir*, London, Henry Frowde, 1895

Legg, Stuart. *The Heartland*, New York, Farrar, Straus & Giroux, 1971

Littledale, St. George R. 'After the Wild Goats of Alaska', *Pall Mall Budget*, 15 December 1892, pp. 1845–6

——. 'A Journey Across Central Asia', *Geographical Journal*, Vol. 3, no. 6 (June 1894), pp. 445–75

——. 'A Journey Across the Pamir from North to South', *Proceedings of the Royal Geographical Society*, Vol. 14, no. 1 (January 1892), pp. 1–35

——. 'A Journey Across Tibet from North to South and West to Ladak', *Geographical Journal*, Vol. 7, no. 5 (May 1896), pp. 453–83

Lydekker, Richard. *The Game Animals of India, Burma, Malaya, and Tibet*, London, Rowland Ward, 1907

——. *Wild Oxen, Sheep, & Goats of All Lands, Living and Extinct*, London, Rowland Ward, 1898

Macartney, Catherine. *An English Lady in Chinese Turkestan*, London, Ernest Benn, Ltd., 1931

MacLean, Fitzroy. *Eastern Approaches*, London, Jonathan Cape, 1950

——. *To Caucasus: The End of all the Earth*, Boston, Little, Brown and Company, 1976

Maillart, Ella K. *Forbidden Journey*, London, Heinemann, 1937

Marks, Steven G. *Road to Power: The Trans-Siberian Railroad and the Colonization of Asian Russia 1850–1917*, Ithaca, Cornell University Press, 1991

Mason, Philip. *A Matter of Honour: An Account of the Indian Army, Its Officers and Men*, London, Jonathan Cape, 1975

Maurois, Andre. *The Edwardian Era*, New York, D. Appleton/Century Company, 1933

McCusker, John J. *How Much is That in Real Money?*, Worcester, American Antiquarian Society, 1992

McNeill, William H. *The Rise of the West*, Chicago, University of Chicago Press, 1963

——. *A World History*, New York, Oxford University Press, 1967

Meyer, Karl E. *Tournament of Shadows*, Washington DC, Counterpoint, 1999

Michaud, Roland. *Caravans to Tartary*, New York, Viking Press, 1978

Millington, R. *The House in the Park*, Liverpool, Corporation of the City of Liverpool, 1957

Morgan, Gerald. *Anglo-Russian Rivalry in Central Asia, 1810–1895*, London, Frank Cass, 1981

Morgan, Gerald. *Ney Elias*, London, George Allen & Unwin, 1971

Morison, Samuel Eliot. *Admiral of the Ocean Sea*, Boston, Little, Brown and Company, 1942

——. *The Oxford History of the American People*, New York, Oxford University Press, 1965

Mountfield, Stuart. *Western Gateway: A History of the Mersey Docks and Harbour Board*, Liverpool, Liverpool University Press, 1965

Muir, Ramsay. *A History of Liverpool*, London, Williams & Norgate, 1907

Neve, Arthur. *The Tourist's Guide to Kashmir, Ladakh, Skardo etc*, Lahore, Civil and Military Gazette Press, 1913

Oldham, J. Basil. *Headmasters of Shrewsbury School, 1552–1908*, Shrewsbury, Wilding, 1937

——. *A History of Shrewsbury School, 1552–1952*, Oxford, Blackwell, 1952

Packard, Jerrold M. *Victoria's Daughters*, New York, St. Martin's Press, 1998

Pease, Alfred E. *Edmund Loder, Naturalist, Horticulturist, Traveller and Sportsman, a Memoir*, London, John Murray, 1923

Pemba, Lhamo. *Tibetan Proverbs*, Dharamsala, Library of Tibetan Works and Archives, 1996

Petrie, Sir Charles. *The Victorians*, London, Eyre & Spottiswoode, 1960

Phillipps-Wooley, Clive. *The Badminton Library: Big Game Shooting*, 2 vols, London, Longmans, Green and Co., 1894

——. *Sport in the Crimea and Caucasus*, London, Richard Bentley & Son, 1881

Picton, James A. *Memorials of Liverpool, Historical & Topographical*, 2 vols, Liverpool, Edward Howell, 1907

Prejevalsky, Nikolai Mikhallovich. *From Kulja, Across the Tian Shan to Lob-Nor*, London, Sampson Low, Marston, Searle & Rivington, 1879

Priestley, J.B. *The Edwardians*, London, Heinemann, 1972

Rayfield, Donald. *The Dream of Lhasa*, Athens, Ohio University Press, 1976

Richardson, Hugh E. *Tibet and its History*, London, Oxford University Press, 1962

Roberts, Frederick Sleigh. *Notes on the Central Asian Question and the Coast and Frontier Defences of India, 1877–1893*, London, Printed at the War Office by Harrison and Sons, 1902

Roberts, J.M. *History of the World*, New York, Oxford University Press, 1993

Robertson, W.R. *Routes from Russian Territory in Central Asia towards Afghanistan and India, Section 1. The Pamir Line of Advance*, Simla, Government Central Printing Office, 1893

Robertson, William. *History of Rochdale Past and Present: A History & Guide*, 2nd edn, Rochdale, Schofield & Hoblyn, 1876

Roosevelt, Theodore. *Theodore Roosevelt, An Autobiography*, Vol. V, *The Vigor of Life*, New York, Charles Scribner & Sons, 1920

Royal Geographical Society. *Hints to Travellers, Scientific and General*, 2 vols, London, Royal Geographical Society, 1901

Rugby School Register, ed. A.T. Michell, rev. edn, 3 vols, Rugby, A.J. Lawrence, 1901–4

Ryerse, Phyllis A. *The Ryerse-Ryerson Family*, Ontario, Ryerse-Ryerson Association, 1994

Sandberg, Graham. *The Exploration of Tibet*, Calcutta, Thacker, Spink & Co., 1904

Schaller, George B. *Tibet's Hidden Wilderness*, New York, Harry N. Abrams, 1997

——. *Wildlife of the Tibetan Steppe*, Chicago, University of Chicago Press, 1998

Schulze, Adolf. *World-Wide Moravian Missions in Picture and Story*, Bethlehem, PA, Comenius Press, 1926

Schuyler, Eugene. *Turkistan: Notes of a Journey in Russian Turkistan, Khokand, Bukhara, and Kuldja*, 2 vols, London, Sampson Low, Marston, Searle, & Rivington, 1876

Seaver, George. *Francis Younghusband*, London, John Murray, 1952

Sedgefield, W.J. *The Place-Names of Cumberland and Westmorland*, Manchester, University of Manchester, 1915

Shakabpa, W.D. *Tibet: a Political History*, New Haven, Yale University Press, 1967

Shaw, Robert Barkley. *High Tartary, Yarkand, and Kashgar*, London, John Murray, 1871

Singh, Bawa Satinder. *The Jammu Fox*, Carbondale, Southern Illinois University Press, 1974

Sinor, Denis. *The Cambridge History of Early Inner Asia*, Cambridge, Cambridge University Press, 1990

——. *Inner Asia*, Bloomington, Indiana University, 1971

Sissons, C.B. *My Dearest Sophie: Letters from Egerton Ryerson to his Daughter*, Toronto, Ryerson Press, 1955

Skrine, C.P. *Chinese Central Asia*, London, Methuen, 1926

—— and Nightingale, Pamela. *Macartney at Kashgar*, London, Methuen, 1973

Skyrme, Thomas. *The Changing Image of the Magistracy*, London, Macmillan, 1979

Spear, Thomas George Percival. *India, A Modern History*, Ann Arbor, University of Michigan Press, 1972

Stead, William Thomas. 'Nimrod, His Wife and Marco Polo's Sheep', *Pall Mall Gazette*, 14 June 1888

Steele, Peter. *Eric Shipton: Everest And Beyond*, London, Constable, 1998

Stein, Marc Aurel. *Ruins of Desert Cathay*, 2 vols, London, MacMillan, 1912

——. *Sand-Buried Ruins of Khotan*, London, Hurst and Blackett, 1904

Sykes, Ella. *Through Deserts and Oases of Central Asia*, London, Macmillan & Co., 1920

Taylor, Howard. *Hudson Taylor and the China Inland Mission*, London, Morgan & Scott, 1919

Thompson, F.M.L. *The Rise of Respectable Society*, London, Fontana Press, 1988

Thorold, Peter. *The London Rich, The Creation of a Great City, from 1066 to the Present*, London, Viking, 1999

Thoumin, General Richard. *The First World War*, New York, G.P. Putnam's Sons, 1964

Trevelyan, George Macaulay. *English Social History, A Survey of Six Centuries: Chaucer to Queen Victoria*, London, Longmans, Green, 1942

Trollope, Anthony. *Can You Forgive Her?*, 2 vols, London, Oxford University Press, 1942

Tuchman, Barbara W. *The Guns of August*, New York, MacMillan, 1962

Valdez, Raul. *Lords of the Pinnacles*, Mesilla, NM, Wild Sheep and Goat International, 1985

——. *Wild Sheep and Wild Sheep Hunters of the Old World*, Mesilla, NM, Wild Sheep and Goat International, 1983

——. *The Wild Sheep of the World*, Mesilla, NM, Wild Sheep and Goat International, 1982

Waddell, L. Austine. *Lhasa and Its Mysteries*, London, Methuen, 1906

Wallace, H. Frank. *Big Game: Wanderings in Many Lands*, London, Eyre & Spottiswoode, 1934

——. 'Mr. St. George Littledale's Trophies', *Country Life*, 11 February 1911, pp. 196–7

Waller, Derek. *The Pundits*, Lexington, University Press of Kentucky, 1990

Walton, John K. *Lancashire: A Social History, 1558–1939*, Manchester, Manchester University Press, 1987

Ward, A.E. *The Tourist's and Sportsman's Guide to Kashmir & Ladak, etc*, Calcutta, Thacker, Spink, 1896

Ward, Rowland. *Records of Big Game*, 5th edn, London, Rowland Ward, 1907

Watson, Francis. *A Concise History of India*, New York, Charles Scribner's Sons, 1975

Webb, R.K. *Modern England*, New York, Dodd, Mead & Company, 1968

Wellby, M.S. *Through Unknown Tibet*, London, T. Fisher Unwin, 1898

West, J.M. *Shrewsbury*, London, Blackie & Co., 1937

Whittell, Giles. *Central Asia*, London, Cadogan Books, 1993

Wieczynski, Joseph L. *et al*. (eds). *The Modern Encyclopedia of Russian and Soviet History*, Gulf Breeze, FL, Academic International Press, Vol. 9, 1978, and Vol. 43, 1986

Wood, Frances. *Did Marco Polo go to China?*, London, Secker & Warburg, 1995

Wurtzburg, C.E. *History of the 2/6th (Rifle) Battalion "The King's" (Liverpool Regiment), 1914–1919*, Aldershot, Gale & Polden, 1920

Wyld, James. *Wyld's Military Staff Map of Central Asia and Afghanistan*, London, James Wyld, 1880

Younghusband, Francis Edward. *The Heart of the Continent*, London, John Murray, 1896

Yule, Henry. ed. and tr., *The Book of Ser Marco Polo*, 2 vols, London, John Murray, 1929

Acknowledgements

After pursuing the Littledale story over many long years, we find it difficult to acknowledge everyone who helped make the book possible. From its inception we were both surprised and gratified by the level of enthusiasm we encountered everywhere we went. The response touches us to this day.

Members of the Fletcher, Harris and Littledale families provided a wealth of information. We are so deeply indebted to William Fletcher, his wife Olive and his sister Audrey Littledale Fletcher, all now deceased, that we had to dedicate the book to them. Guy Fletcher has continued the generosity shown by his parents. The late Dorothea Fletcher described the Littledales and Wick Hill House as she remembered it. Edith Fletcher loaned documents from a family trunk under her sideboard. We are grateful to many other Fletchers including the late John Fletcher, the late Daphne Don-Fox, Sue Matthews, Peter and Frances Wise, J.F. Peto and others. Evelyn Beres Fairclough, Olive Fletcher's sister, was supportive throughout.

Profuse thanks go to the late Robin Harris, who was responsible for the Harris family archives and led us to them. He and his wife Terry also provided much additional information. We thank other Harris family members in Canada including the late Lucy Little, her son Anthony Little, her daughter Frances Kumar, A.G.S. Griffin and William Griffin. In England we are especially indebted to the late William Crutchley and his wife Annie.

On the Littledale side, John and Joan Hunter provided genealogy information at the start. Anne DeBuck and her son Robin D. Almond kindly showed us the 'Fact Book' and other Littledale family papers. Special thanks go to Christopher J. Inward, who generously loaned wonderful old letters and helped in countless other ways. His sister Valerie A.G. Macduff described life at Wick Hill House and his daughter Louise produced other information. Helen Littledale, though not directly related, gave us valuable insights and research tips.

We thank Ellen Enzler-Herring of Trophy Room Books for leading us to Elgin T. Gates and for reading the big game hunting portions of the manuscript. Mr Gates, in turn, inspired us with his enthusiasm for St. George Littledale as a hunter and, most importantly, he gave us all of the Littledale documents in his possession, an unexpected gift. To our awe, Linda K. Ogden's magical restoration turned the coal of burned papers into diamonds of information.

Sir Matthew Farrer GCVO retrieved the Littledale legal papers from the archives of Farrer & Co. and then let us use his desk to go through them. We are indebted to the late Canon Alan Campbell of St Michael's Church, Easthampstead, for leading us to Nora K. Pond, who entertained us with colourful stories about the Littledales. Philip Solesbury, nephew of Leonard Solesbury, the Littledales' chauffeur, provided a vivid description of life with the Littledales and their clock-winding adventures.

We thank his daughter Jean Hole and her husband Ron for arranging our meeting. Bruce Giddy sent us a history of the Garth Hunt, Kenneth Goatley unearthed past events at the Wokingham Lecture Society, and Bruce D. Banwell provided information on the New Zealand wapiti.

We certainly gained a new respect for libraries and archives and the dedicated people who staff them. At the University of Western Ontario Archives John H. Lutman and Theresa Regnier did everything they could for us. The late Peter M. Smith of London, Ontario, was a gold mine of information on Eldon House, the Harris family and early Canada.

The Royal Geographical Society helped us throughout. Nigel Winser, former executive director, was a pillar of encouragement and support. Joanna Wright, curator of photographs, turned up pictures from the Tibet expedition, and Justin Hobson helped us obtain them. David Wileman, the librarian in 1986, started us on the trail of the Littledales by referring us to the Natural History Museum, where there are too many people to thank by name. However, we must mention former librarian Rex Banks, who unearthed Littledale and Fletcher bequest letters on our first visit and then advised us on tracking down leads. The late John Thackray, archivist, produced volumes of documents, and when we kept asking for more, he led us across a back alley into a separate building, down into the basement archives, and turned us loose.

We received excellent service from David McGrath at the British Newspaper Library at Colindale, Tony Parker at the Liverpool Museum, and David Stoker at the Liverpool Record Office and Local Studies Library. James Lawson, librarian and archivist at Shrewbury School, located the material on St. George Littledale's school days. The helpful staff at the Balliol College Library, Oxford, produced Sir Robert Morier's correspondence. At the Royal Botanic Gardens at Kew, archivist Lesley Price turned up so many documents that our expected short visit turned into an exciting full day. By coincidence we encountered her later in the archives of the China Inland Mission at the School of Oriental and African Studies, University of London. We thank Margaret G. Dainton of the Overseas Missionary Fellowship for granting us access and for providing additional information. John Falconer of the India Office Library found pertinent photographs and showed us how to find more. Judith Curthoys, archivist of Christ Church, Oxford, sent material on W.A.L. Fletcher. Terence Pepper, curator of photography at the National Portrait Gallery, offered his help and then lugged a huge volume of old newspapers up from the basement. We thank Rosamond Brown, librarian at the Scottish Borders Archive and Local History Centre, for information on the Scotts of Teviot Bank. Robert Hale, archivist at the Berkshire Record Office, suggested good sources for background on the Littledales' life in England.

The Huntington Library in San Marino, California, was a fine source of information on nineteenth-century England and on English public schools in particular. Special thanks go to Virginia J. Renner, Jill Cogen and Susi Krasnoo. Closer to home, at Stanford University, the staff of Green Library located the microfilms of Theodore Roosevelt's correspondence at the Library of Congress, and the staff of the Hoover Library led us to information on the Demidoff family. The Palo Alto Main Library was a constant source for basic reference materials.

The Public Record Office (National Archives) at Kew set a high standard for material and service. We received friendly and effective assistance from everyone at every level at that treasure trove of information and it was a pleasure to work there.

The British public should be proud of their institution. Sarah Tyacke CB, Keeper, expressed great interest in the Littledales, and years later it was through her efforts that we acquired a publisher. We could never have asked her for this.

In addition we should mention the General Register Office at St Catherine's House, the Kensington Central Library, Linnean Society, National Army Museum, Reading Central Library, Rochdale Local Studies Library, Royal Archives, Royal Commission on Historical Manuscripts, Rugby School, Somerset House (wills) and the Victoria and Albert Museum.

Many additional individuals played an important, even crucial, role. Roger and Ann Chorley stand out among them. Roger was President of the Royal Geographical Society when we began our research, and both he and Ann backed us from the very first day, providing unstinting encouragement for over twenty years. Peter Hopkirk was also with us from the start. He had briefly described the Littledales' Tibet expedition in *Trespassers on the Roof of the World*. We met over a breakfast of scrambled eggs, and from then on he gave useful advice on Central Asia, writing, publishing, genealogy, tips on organising material and much more. His wife Kathleen was also a strong supporter and advised us on maps. John Randall and David Chilton, antiquarian book dealers and experts on Central Asia, provided advice and assistance throughout the long effort. Derek Waller, an authority on Tibet and the Pundits, was a fount of wisdom and information. In 1990 William Holgate mounted a lightweight expedition that followed the trail of the Littledales up to the Dawa Muran Davan on the border of Tibet. Later he offered some of his photographs, one of which was selected for the book jacket. We are grateful to Gill Pattinson for a memorable afternoon rummaging through the attic of the museum at Sandringham House in search of the ibex head that St. George Littledale gave to Edward VII. Maree Vanderlaan kindly gave us access to Wick Hill House. For years Felicity Brown and John Mallet provided assistance and advice. We must also mention George and Susan Band for their long and strong support.

David Roberts, mountaineer and author, jump-started us into the publishing world, indirectly leading us to Gerald Gross, a New York editor who made invaluable suggestions for the manuscript. We thank our readers, Gwen Allmon, George Band, Tom Hornbein and John Rawlings, who did their collective best to correct the error of our ways. Bennett Ashley provided important legal assistance.

We are grateful to Chris Bonington for agreeing to write the foreword. We thank Dee Molenaar for his hard work on the maps, and Robert and Susan Christiansen for finalising them. We must also recognise the Champlain Society for granting permission to quote from *The Eldon House Diaries*, Stuart Leggett of Sotheran's for furnishing the picture of the Littledale sheep, and Elizabeth Fischbach of Stanford University Libraries for scanning numerous photographs. Helen Peters provided the fine index.

We also appreciate the support from Sutton Publishing, especially Jaqueline Mitchell, Jane Entrican, Sarah Flight, Catherine Watson and Yvette Cowles.

Finally, we thank our long-suffering family and friends, who had to listen to the Littledale project for too many years. A special thanks goes to the staff of the old Ebury Court Hotel for their good care when it was our 'home away from home'. Most of all, we want to thank the many kind people throughout Great Britain who were so nice to us. We have joined the chorus singing, 'There'll always be an England'.

Index